The Emergence of Conservative Judaism:

The Historical School in 19th Century America

The Emergence of Conservative Judaism
The Historical School in 19th Century America

Moshe Davis

GREENWOOD PRESS, PUBLISHERS
WESTPORT, CONNECTICUT

Library of Congress Cataloging in Publication Data

Davis, Moshe.
   The emergence of Conservative Judaism.

   Reprint of the 1st ed. (1963), published by the
Jewish Publication Society of America, Philadelphia,
which was issued as no. 15 of the Jacob R. Schiff library
of Jewish contributions to American democracy.
   Bibliography: p.
   Includes index.
   1. Conservative Judaism—History. 2. Judaism—
United States—History. I. Title. II. Series: Jacob
R. Schiff library of Jewish contributions to American
democracy ; no. 15.
[BM197.5.D3 1977]   296.8'34   77-22180
ISBN 0-8371-9792-9

Originally published in 1963 by The Jewish Publication Society
of America, Philadelphia

Reprinted with the permission of The Jewish Publication Society
of America

Reprinted in 1977 by Greenwood Press, Inc.

Library of Congress Catalog Card Number 7722180

ISBN 0-8371-9792-9

Printed in the United States of America

*Dedicated
to
the Faculties
and Board of
Directors
of the
Jewish
Theological
Seminary
of America—
Present
and Past*

When it was first proposed that I prepare a volume on the beginnings of the Conservative Movement, I intended to adapt my earlier study, *Yahadut Amerika Be-hitpatchutah,* which had appeared in Hebrew in 1950. But as I returned to my subject it became clear that nothing other than a new book would do. Recent years have brought a remarkable advance in American Jewish historiography. Several centers of documentation and research have come into being and a number of scholarly publications have appeared, which necessitated further examination of basic source material and the re-examination of previous conclusions. Furthermore, the differences in cultural and religious backgrounds between Hebrew and English readers called for an entirely different approach to the organization of the material and the writing of the book.

The greatest obstacle to my proper evaluation of the rise and development of the Conservative Movement, I feared, was my own deep involvement in the goals of the Movement and my identification with its institutions—primarily, the Jewish Theological Seminary. Ideological commitment and past experience within the Movement, though helpful in themselves to comprehend its inner motivations, might have impeded the objective assessment of its sources. To some degree, I believe, this imbalance has been corrected by my residence in Jerusalem during the writing of this volume The environment of the Hebrew University, and the stimulation of colleagues and students who, for the most part, approach this subject from without, helped me to achieve greater perspective than I might otherwise have hoped for. In Jerusalem, too, I have been able to benefit from a measure of distance from my subject, indispensable to any scientific inquiry.

It is good to be able to express gratitude to those whose help has been unfailing. I have learned about the origins of the Conservative Movement, not only at the study table in libraries, but also from the insights of teachers, associates and students at the Seminary, colleagues in the Rabbinical Assembly, and from working with laymen in many of the congregations throughout the United States and Canada which constitute the United Synagogue of America.

I am indebted to teachers, colleagues and friends: most particularly to my masters and teachers at the Seminary, Professors Louis Finkelstein, Mordecai M. Kaplan and Saul Lieberman for their continuing counsel; to Professors Ben Zion Dinur of the Hebrew University and Salo W. Baron of Columbia University, who first guided me into my chosen field of research and then received me as their colleague; to Professor Jacob R. Marcus of the Hebrew Union College, who taught me through his own writings and his critical analyses of the manuscripts I submitted to him; to Professor Allan Nevins, of Columbia University and the Huntington Library, whose learning and friendship are an inspiring influence; to Dr. Solomon Grayzel, editor of the Jewish Publication Society, who encouraged me to undertake this new work and gave freely of his time and effort much beyond the requirements of editorial responsibility; to Dr. Jacob J. Neusner, younger colleague and friend, from whose invaluable comments on style and content I have benefited greatly.

I wish especially to acknowledge the generous help of Dr. Michael Wyschogrod of Hunter College. Miss Francine Schnitzer proved to be an able and assiduous research assistant. Checking of references was a complex overseas assignment, involving requests from Jerusalem to New York, and the assistance of Drs. Gladys Rosen and Lloyd Gartner

of the American Jewish History Center is gratefully acknowledged. Dr. Maxwell Whiteman made many excellent suggestions which were incorporated into the text. Thanks are
due also to Priscilla Fishman of New York for preparing the
index to the revised edition.

The libraries and the staffs of the Jewish Theological
Seminary, the American Jewish Archives, the American Jewish Historical Society, the Dropsie College, the New York
Public Library (Jewish Division) and the Hebrew University
graciously made available their facilities.

The last, to speak in Hebraic idiom, is the dearest. Without the loving presence and concern of my wife Lottie,
neither this work, nor any other I have undertaken, would
have been completed. For myself, and our children, Zev and
Tamar, she has endowed our life in Jerusalem with the quality of a mitzvah.

When I finished my first book in Jerusalem, I prayed that
I might be granted the privilege of completing other writings
in the Holy City. This remains my abiding prayer.

Moshe Davis

Jerusalem
Elul, 5722
September, 1962

Contents

List of Illustrations

The Emergence of Conservative Judaism

The Historical School in Nineteenth-Century America

Throughout its long history, Judaism has come in contact with a variety of traditions and cultures. It has been affected by them and has, in turn, contributed to many of them. Confrontation with the American environment has proved to be especially strong and pervasive. Conscious and unconscious forms of identification and adaptation were introduced by the Jews into their Tradition as they established themselves in America and were acclimatized there. Elements of the Jewish spirit, latent in other ages and experiences, were vitalized as they met American thought, life and expression. The historic idea of Judaism, which was congenial to the American temper, was introduced in Colonial times by the earliest Jewish settlers. It has undergone widely diverse changes. It is still undergoing complex changes, for the Jewish settlement in America is comparatively young and reflects constant mobility in a land and in an age which are characterized by continuous change and growth.

Any attempt to describe the authentic spirit of Judaism in America has to be based, in large measure, on religious group life and institutions. In the history of Judaism, the religious institutions had been the chief bearers and interpreters of the Tradition. Without in any way underestimating the vital place of all other forms of communal expression, it was primarily through religious institutions that the Tradition also expressed itself in America. To grasp the essential nature of

American Jewish religious life in its expansion and fluidity,
it is best to begin with the early decades of the past century,
when American Judaism was still the expression of a religiously united community. We can then probe the tensions
and new forms of Jewish institutional and personal practice
as they resulted from the needs of Jewish experience and
from contact with American tradition, ideas and events.
That is our concern in this volume, although the scope of the
subject is limited to one current of thought in American
Judaism, which emphasized historical evolution. Out of that
current the Conservative Movement developed in the later
decades of the nineteenth century and in the early twentieth
century. The purpose of this introductory chapter is to describe the prominent factors—both general and Jewish—in
nineteenth-century life, which brought the Historical School
into being, and to define in broad terms the objectives
and make-up of that School before its consolidation and reorganization into the twentieth-century Conservative Movement.

What were the elements in American political and spiritual life that exerted such powerful influence on the formation of Jewish life? Foremost was the concept of religious
equality, which the architects of the American Constitution
set as a foundation stone of American democracy. The classic
formulation of this American idea, framed into the compact
of the United States in the Bill of Rights and passed by the
first Congress, established a new relationship between religious equality and political freedom. It is true that the
formal declaration of law proved to be insufficient, and that
the lag between the law and its implementation was great. It
is also true that the meaning of religious equality—not religious tolerance or religious freedom, but *equality*—called
for continuous clarification, explanation and exhortation in
the state legislatures, as well as the development of a public
opinion. Ultimately, however, the fundamental intent of the
Founding Fathers prevailed; and their understanding of this
relationship as the separation of Church and State became a
basic premise of American life. The corollary result of this

doctrine, which dissociated the government of the United States from any religion, was to guard the young country from turning into a clerical state and to let adherents of different faiths unite into a single nation. The "wall of separation," it turned out, was not a wall against religion. It favored religion for, in a free American society, it placed correlative responsibilities for the advancement of religious expression on the individual, the family and the religious group to which citizens chose to belong.

It cannot be sufficiently emphasized, however, if one is to comprehend the character of America, that although America had decided not to institute an "establishment" or a denominational government, it was nevertheless a religious nation. This was the very first characteristic of America that struck the attention of the young De Tocqueville, upon his arrival in the United States in 1831: "In France I had almost always seen the spirit of religion and the spirit of freedom marching in opposite directions. But in America I found they were intimately united and that they reigned in common over the same country."[1] At least three aspects of this religious American way of life deeply influenced the rising American Jewish community: first, the biblical roots of the American tradition; second, the Christian and particularly the Protestant character of the people; and finally, the tradition of separate and independent religious organization.

The Bible had a singularly meaningful influence on the growth of the American spirit. It was conceived by the American people, in Abraham Lincoln's phrase, to be "the best gift God has given to man." In the American tradition the Bible was the origin of the common faith and served as a cohesive factor for national aspirations. In the most glorious as well as the most trying moments of American history, ancient Israelites of biblical times took on vivid contemporary significance.

But the Bible for America was a Christian testament taught with Protestant interpretation and emphasis. During the past three centuries, "the main thrust of American religion stemmed from the Reformation, and Protestantism in all its heterogeneity must be the object of whatever praise or blame attaches to religious influences in American culture during that period."[2] Protestant thought and forms inevitably affected the organizational structure and activity of the other faiths in America. The dominant pattern of American Protestant organizations was congregationalism, a system of autonomous local religious bodies. American Protestants preferred to leave the decision to found and formulate church policy to the individual conscience. And they were willing to pay the price which this high privilege imposed. They gladly accepted, for example, a double form of taxation: civic taxes to meet the needs of the total community and free-will contributions for their network of religious institutions.

Important social factors, unique to the American environment, also shaped the growth of Jewry in America. A very important factor was that America was a land of immigrants conceptually and in actuality. The extent to which this fact influenced American civilization can be gathered from the approach to American history which maintains that much, if not all, of American history can best be understood in terms of the impact of immigration on the country. It is decisive not only that America was a land of immigrants, but that the immigrants saw in America their best hope for human freedom; and that this land of freedom made newcomers submerge their own cultures in favor of a distinct American culture.

America also sought the complete social amalgamation of its population. In the late nineteenth and early twentieth centuries, social and political thinkers used the terms "Americanization" and "melting pot" to express the need to fuse millions of immigrants into a single united people.

These salient political, spiritual and social elements in American life were posed before Jewry for the first time in its history. How could the American Jewish community, itself a composite of many diverse countries of origin and experience, become part of the land it now accepted as home and still remain organically related to the more than three-thousand-year history of the Jewish people? As a community, American

Jewry was overwhelmed. Many decades passed before it could grasp the basic nature of American society and its implications for the development of an indigenous Jewish way of life in the new world. It was a hundred years and more after the American and French Revolutions before Jews began to understand that the adaptation of Judaism to American democratic society would require ideological and organizational forms completely different from those created in any other country throughout Jewish history. At first, the Jews tended to attribute the communal, cultural and spiritual chaos that pervaded American Jewry in the nineteenth century to the general benefits of emancipation and the apparent difficulty of the Jewish tradition in adjusting to the conditions of "modern" life. Consequently, early Jewish leadership in America, in all the branches of its religious life, thought it could solve its problems by imitating European Jewry—primarily German Jewry. This was to be expected, for most of the leaders were themselves of recent European extraction. Many had participated in the various Jewish religious movements in Europe. On the wider horizon, too, in mid-nineteenth-century America, knowledge, thought and intellectual life followed the patterns of Europe. It was only as America matured that its thought began to evolve out of its own social milieu.

The Jews in America also had to learn the difference between European and American settings. In the area of Religion and State, for example, imitation of the German background could not lead to solutions. Religion in Germany was an arm of the State, and Reform was the passport—many Jews thought—to full participation in German society. But in America, the State was officially indifferent to the faith of the citizen and was concerned with him as a citizen only.

As regards the Protestant way of American religious life, the predominance of the "left" wing of world Protantism in America was a fact of great strength as well as bewilderment for the religious history of American Jewry. Independent congregations, in contrast to the European system of clerical hierarchies, were the controlling unit of authority for almost all Protestant churches. Thus the Protestant-dominated religious concept, which encouraged any religious group willing and able to organize itself without the concurrence of a governmental or religious body, gave rise, for good or ill, to a system of free enterprise in Jewish religious life. Any Jewish group was able to set up its own congregation as it saw fit, without giving thought to the congregations that preceded it. Above all, the new congregations did not fear interference from the organized Jewish community or from the government, as might be the case in Europe. Lacking the authority of an ordained rabbinate, and with a laity unlearned in Jewish letters, congregationalism held sway in Jewish life and congregational autonomy became the rule. The system of a centralized *Gemeinde* was not even suggested as a possibility for American Jewry; and only through many errors and greater trials did American religious Jewry find its path to the national synagogue unions which became the pattern of religious organization by the twentieth century. Considering the diversities, and most often the confusion, of ritual practice, the Jews again had to avoid the influence of sectarianism rampant in the American Protestant religion. How could Jews manage to maintain a basic religious unity amid their own diversity when American religion flourished in hundreds of sects, each one different from the next in clergy, ritual and organization?

The ultimate problem, then, with which the Jewish group wrestled in the United States was the apparent conflict between its environment and the need to maintain its essential group identity. On the one hand, the Jews, like most of the immigrant groups, established strong bonds with America: clear evidence of such deep feelings is found in the pages of the American Jewish periodicals of the last century in English, Yiddish and Hebrew. They express eloquently the need of the immigrant to establish himself permanently in the new land and, conversely, the ability of America to arouse in him the will to dedicate himself to its future. On the other hand, despite the separation of Religion and State, America remained essentially a Christian civilization. While the right to religious differences and even to their perpetuation was recognized, these differences were defined in the narrowest denominational sense. Ethnic and cultural distinctions within the religious framework were discouraged. The ideas of religious pluralism and the acceptance of varieties of religious communities and communions, it must be emphasized, are more recent developments in American life, resulting from great social changes and shifts in the balance of religious affiliations. "The Jewish tradition, like the Catholic," the editors of *Religion in American Life* point out, "has attained free partnership in the American enterprise only in the twentieth century."[3] In the past century, unlike today, the Jews were conceived by many to be a qualitative as well as a quantitative minority in America.

Another difficulty was that the organic interrelationship in Judaism between *Emunat Yisrael*, the Jewish Faith, and *Klal Yisrael*, the Jewish People, was little understood by the great majority of Americans, most of whom never came in contact with Jews and knew about Jews and Judaism only from a few stories and legends taught in their religious schools. The Jews were in fact both a religious and cultural community; as such they differed from other groups in America. All other immigrant groups, such as the Irish or the German, were unlike the majority in many ways, but were part of majority national or religious groups, either in their lands of origin or in their newly adopted country. The Jewish immigrants, however, were a distinct minority in their countries of origin as well as in the new land. This minority status weighed heavily upon them and led many to seek ways of becoming part of the majority, either by outright disaffiliation with the Jewish group or by indifference to their ancestral tradition.

The organized Jewish community, or those who sought to maintain Jewish life in America, individually and collectively, agreed in general on the nature of the problem which faced them. But they did not agree on the means to solve it. Many, like the founders of B'nai B'rith and the various "brotherhoods" which were established in the forties and fifties of the past century, thought that the basic unity of the

Jewish community could be sustained through a network of social institutions. Others felt that philanthropic and benevolent impulses could be the cohesive power. Some argued that Jewish education and culture could cement Jewish relationships. These viewpoints did not necessarily replace religion or religious practice as fundamentals of Judaism, but, it was argued, basic Jewish solidarity could not be maintained on religious principles alone.

The religious leaders argued to the contrary. Recognizing that the synagogue was no longer able to serve the total needs of the community, they supported the development of philanthropic and social organizations outside the synagogue structure. They insisted, however, that there was no alternative but to establish once again the primacy of the synagogue and the Jewish religion in American Judaism. In America, they contended, as in the entire history of Jewry, the religion was the chief expression of Jewish group life and, without its focal and all-pervading influence, the community in America would not survive as a *Jewish* community. The real challenge to Jewish religion in America was to answer the question of the relevance of the Jewish faith to American society in an age of enlightenment, individualism and equalitarian thought, scientific progress and intellectual achievement.

The spiritual leaders had no doubt that Judaism offered an answer to all the questions of the age posed by young and mature alike. Furthermore, most of them agreed that in order to explain this relevance, Judaism would have to take full cognizance of the American milieu and adapt itself to that milieu; otherwise there could be no hope for a continuing Jewish life in America. On that question religious leadership as a whole stood united. It was the measure of accommodation and the method of adaptation that caused the splintering of the religious community into several schools of thought during the middle of the century.

At first, the problem of accommodation was approached from without. Highly localized European Jewish customs and externalities of the Tradition were discarded. Later, methods for explaining Judaism in the language of the people were introduced into religious life. They included a native English-speaking rabbinate, English translations of the Hebrew prayer book, an American Jewish educational system, and the like. But, for many, these were insufficient. Such methods of accommodation had not turned the tide toward more emphatic Jewish observance.

The issue was one of content, not merely form. Therefore, in time three approaches to Jewish religious life arose, each attempting to deal with the central problem and each troubled by the weakening of Judaism in America: Reform, the Historical School and Orthodoxy. All three currents, it must be emphasized, were fluid and went through varying stages of development in their thought and organization. Often, associations with one group or another on the part of lay or religious leaders changed course as new basic issues came up. At times these factions even regrouped themselves in attempts to coalesce organizationally. However, opinions did increasingly crystallize until, in the last decades of the century, the lines became defined and the groups were separated by walls of ideology and attachment to national institutions.

One school of thought, which grew into the American Reform movement and made the greatest headway during the century, explained Judaism essentially as a universal religion that emphasized the ethical tradition as its basic dimension. The eternal moral teachings of Judaism possessed a universal character which all the world, Christianity included, was destined to recognize as the supreme truth. The Reformers held that, in order to fulfill its role in the world, Judaism must constantly keep pace with the changing age, incorporating and reflecting modern developments, without necessarily being bound by the historic evolution and continuity of the Jewish tradition. America was a land where Jews were free to teach their ideas of religion to all mankind. By the term which the Reformers used most, "American Judaism," they meant fundamentally that the ideals of

America and Judaism were one. With this American philosophy of Judaism, they hoped to bring back within the
Jewish fraternity countless contemporaries who had rejected
the traditional view and looked upon ritual practice as
obsolete. Yet despite their most radical innovations in Jewish
practice and interpretation, the Reformers were most careful
not to separate themselves from the living Jewish people,
but to function as part of it. They conceived themselves
to be not a sect, but a party within Judaism.

Orthodoxy, a second school of thought, during the past
century embraced three elements—the Sephardi, the central
European and the East-European interpretations of traditional Judaism. Towards the end of the century it was the
East-European element which prevailed and established the
official movement. Thus, Orthodoxy in America largely took
on the character and forms of that group, differing from the
Reform and Historical schools which were characterized by
western European training and outlook. Above all, that element of American Orthodoxy confined itself at first to its own
circles; only later, as a native Orthodox group developed, did
it enter the struggle in the main arenas of American Jewish
life. Nevertheless, even at the beginning its position was clear,
constant, and always mindful of the great dangers to Judaism
present in the emancipated society of America.

In this Orthodox view, Jewish Law was sacred and supreme,
and while it possessed built-in legal methods to cope with
changing and varied environmental factors, conflict seemed
inevitable. Judaism, the Orthodox group taught, insists on
the adjustment of life to the Law and not the Law to life.
Considering the mode of daily practice of Jewish life in
America, they explained that the revealed Law of Judaism,
as it came down through the ages, had been codified in basic
texts and latterly in the *Shulhan Arukh;* and that Jewish behavior must be in accordance with that code as directed by
contemporary authorized Orthodox courts of law or by individual ordained Orthodox rabbis. Because they believed
that nothing less than the unity of the world under God was
involved in this absolute dedication to Judaism, American

Jews—even those who had strayed from the fold and turned to ideas which were temporarily in the ascendancy—were bound ultimately to return, provided that the core of Jews remained steadfast to eternal Belief.

A third school of thought, the Historical School, was no less inspired by the divine character of Jewish Law, taught by the Orthodox, nor by its moral purpose as stressed by Reform. Indeed, leaders of this group maintained that both these fundamentals of the Jewish tradition come into their fullest significance only when they are viewed as part of the totality of the historic Jewish experience. The Bible, the Talmud and commentaries, the Holy Land, the Hebrew language— these are the seedbeds of the Jewish spirit which nurtured the institutions of Jewish religion and life. Growth and development are inherent in the historical process because they are a response to the demands of life. However, even while affirming the imperative of change and adjustment, the entire Tradition and Jewish experience would have to be explored and studied before specific innovations could be made, so as to prevent the innovation from being at variance with the basic spirit of Jewish legal principles. The exposition of this view was the Historical School's answer to the challenge of contemporaneity. In Europe, the Historical School was shaped by men of great scholarly learning, such as Nachman Krochmal, Leopold Zunz, Solomon J. L. Rapoport, Zacharias Frankel, Heinrich Graetz and others. They used Jewish scholarship as their vehicle for interpreting the present in the light of the past. In America, the rabbinic leaders and laity turned to methods of practical organization and to the building of primary institutions. But the techniques and institutions depended, in the end, on a congeries of ideas and values unique to the School. As we shall explain in detail in the course of the volume, these ideas emphasize the evolving character of the Jewish tradition, the historic experience of the Jewish people as organic to that development, and the acceptance of modernity as a positive force in the growth of that Tradition.

Toward the end of the century these schools of thought became less fluid and they incorporated themselves into three separate religious movements in American Jewry: Reform, Orthodoxy and Conservative Judaism. Each element built its own organization and institutions which consisted of a seminary for the training of a native rabbinate, a union of synagogues and a conference of authorized rabbis. This development did not come about through any preconceived plan or program. Individual positions were fluid and very often contradictory. The conditions of time and place compelled the direction of basic ideas into unchartered institutional forms. Nor could anyone foresee that the shape of events to come would make American Jewry, even toward the end of the century, one of the largest centers of Jewry in history. A difficulty which confronts the student of American Jewish religious history is the possibility of confusing nineteenth-century groups with their respective twentieth-century developments. This confusion must be studiously avoided, for it is just as anachronistic to identify the formative expressions of the religious groups with their respective contemporary twentieth-century compositions as it is to identify American democracy of that period with the democracy of our times.

The purpose of this volume is to discuss the evolution of one of these schools of thought, the Historical School, from its formative period as an approach to Jewish life and tradition in America until its emergence as the *Conservative Movement*. It is not intended to demonstrate the greater ideological validity of the Historical School view as compared with that of the others. And no attempt is made to analyze the structure, conduct and motivations of the constituency of that School from the sociological viewpoint. Furthermore, while the Reform and Orthodox schools are naturally considered, as are the larger areas of American Jewish life in the context of nineteenth-century developments in America, the volume focuses on the ideas, goals and personalities which were joined together to create the Historical School and its institutions. As will become quickly evident from the detail of the book, the interplay of the Historical School's ideas with the ideas of the other schools was inevitable, for practically all of the members of the School, in their struggle to evolve their own views, borrowed freely from the left and the right of the American and European religious trends.

The definition of the name "Historical School" and the delineation of the constellation of ideas to which the members of the School stood committed are essential. The name "Historical School" has fallen into disuse in recent decades: it has been supplanted by the more popular name "Conservative Judaism." In fact, some historians of American Jewry declare the name "Historical School" to be a misnomer even of the nineteenth-century group. They prefer to call it "Conservative," thus interpreting the record of events *a posteriori* rather than out of its origins. Upon considered study of the sources and documents of the period, it seems clear to me that between the two possibilities, with the entire century in mind, the name "Historical School" presents the more accurate description of the pre-twentieth-century "Conservative Movement." It emphasizes the evolutionary character of the idea which only eventually became embodied in particular institutional forms, and includes such differing approaches as the traditionalism of Isaac Leeser and Sabato Morais, the developmental conception of Alexander Kohut and the progressivism of Benjamin Szold and Marcus Jastrow —all of whom identified themselves with this School and its institutions.

Literally, conceptually and historically, this is the name by which the members of the group identify themselves. It is true that the spokesmen of the other schools also emphasized that their ideas were the true continuation of historical Judaism, but they did not use this term as a description of their purpose as a movement. The members of the Historical School did exactly that. For example, the constitution of the Seminary Association in 1887, providing for the establishment of the Jewish Theological Seminary—a document which represented the decades of thought and action which preceded it as well as the aspiration to what was to follow —stated specifically that the purpose of the Association was "the preservation in America of the knowledge and practice of historical Judaism. . . ." And the call of the Association published in the *Proceedings* of the First Biennial Convention of the Seminary was issued to "hundreds of congregations whose members are devoted to the principles of historical Judaism."[4]

The name "Historical School" is also most appropriate conceptually. It emphasizes the distinctive interpretation of Judaism put forth by the movement as a whole. From its inception and through the years of struggle against factions on the right and the left, many of its leaders, both lay and clerical, have rejected the practice of attaching adjectives to the word "Judaism." By selecting the adjective "historical," it was possible to best define the program of the School, to escape partisanship and to embrace the totality of the Jewish past as well as the varieties of contemporary experience. Regardless of the ideological shadings and personal practice of the individual constituent—Orthodox, traditional or progressive—the leaders of the Historical School, who sought to root Judaism in America, were men bound to the spirit and substance of the Jewish tradition. On the other hand, they were also well versed in secular culture and recognized the demands of life. To preserve the Jewish collectivity in America in the encounter between Tradition and environment was a commitment which resulted from their historic consciousness. Therefore they were prepared to accept the principle of the legitimacy of differences within the all-inclusive idea of historical Judaism, as embodied in the Jewish people. The concept of *Klal Yisrael* was expressed frequently in the presentations and plans of the spokesmen of the School.

As is shown in this study, this concept was first discussed by Isaac Leeser who spoke of *Kneset Yisrael* ("catholic Israel") as the ideological and social basis for a religiously unified American Jewry within world Jewry, anticipating in part Solomon Schechter, with whom this concept is identified in the thought of Conservative Judaism. Other leaders of the School in the nineteenth century followed in Leeser's footsteps. In the midst of the struggle against Reform, when a suggestion was made to call the new rabbinical seminary "The Orthodox Seminary," Alexander Kohut decided that the new institution must be dedicated to *Klal Yisrael*. Clearly stating his view of the Seminary, Kohut said, "We do not desire it to be destined for a sect, whether reform, conservative, or orthodox . . ." This view was immediately accepted by his colleagues; they understood the mission of their movement.[5] It was decided from the beginning to unite various groups with different ideas for the future of Judaism in America. The common element which would unite all of them was the idea of a developing historical Judaism. The Historical School in its interpretation of *Klal Yisrael* identified itself with the total experience and commitment of the Jewish people throughout the ages. As a result, when the Seminary was reorganized in 1902, it was called the "Jewish Theological Seminary *of* America," not the "American Jewish Theological Seminary."

Seen in this way, it is possible to understand why and how men whose interpretations of Judaism were as far apart as Isaac Leeser's, Samuel Isaacs', Sabato Morais' and H. P. Mendes', on the one hand, and Benjamin Szold's, Marcus Jastrow's and Frederic de Sola Mendes', on the other, could work together in one direction and for the same cause. Within this framework it was possible for the pioneer leader in American Jewry, Isaac Leeser, who by nature, practice and theology, was a traditionalist, not only to work with the progressivists within the Historical School but actually to lead in the creation of those institutions around which he rallied the rabbinic and lay leaders of various viewpoints in the School. Similarly with the leftists of the School: theologically, Szold and Jastrow were more radical than Isaac Mayer Wise. Yet, when the real test came, they interrupted their tentative working alliances with the Reformers and remained loyal to the foundations and institutions of the Historical group. The Historical School at one time included various strands of American Jewry. Some of them subsequently joined other movements while most of them remained within the School and, despite their differences, worked together to create the Conservative movement.

What then were the basic and uniting ideas which prompted men of such differing modes of practice to remain together in one school of thought and action? Principles crystallized in spite of the different emphases in different periods of the Historical School and in spite of the fact that its members did not systematically articulate any one theology. These ideas, as they emerge from the historical context, can be formulated as follows:

1) The Emancipation and secular Enlightenment must be accepted as significant positive factors in the Jewish present and future development.

2) The equal status of Jews in democratic societies generally, and in the United States in particular, offers new opportunities for Jews and Judaism.

3) *Klal Yisrael* is the historic basis for the unity of the people at all times and places.

4) Judaism can be adapted to changing conditions according to biblical and talmudic teachings in the light of the development of the Tradition in all ages.

5) The traditional *mitzvot,* the precepts, are the basic precondition for the establishment of a Jewish way of life.

It has been pointed out that these principles were not formulated as a platform of the Historical School at any one occasion or even in one generation. They resulted from the collective judgment of many generations. Nevertheless, these principles were the pivot around which all the polemics against other currents, and the discussion within the Historical School itself, revolved. And these ideas make it possible to assess the adherence of individuals and congregations to the Historical School.

It is important to indicate in what respects the members of the Historical School differed from the two other groups which were also taking shape as religious movements. These five principles outline both the points of agreement among the three groups and the points of divergence. The Historical School and the Reform movement were in agreement on the first two points, differed in the interpretation of the third and disagreed about the two others. The Historical School and the Orthodox movement disagreed about the first three principles, and differed in emphasis and practical interpretation on the last two.

Thus, as far back as 1856, Isaac Leeser, the first spokesman of the Historical School, emphasized that traditional faith and Jewish communal existence must be based on the new conditions of modern society: Jewish emancipation, equality of rights, and practical separation of Church and State. These principles became guiding beacons to all members of the Historical School, whether they accepted the authority of the *Shulhan Arukh* in all its details or leaned toward modification in observance of the *mitzvot*. The leaders of the Historical School, unlike the Orthodox but like the Reformers, were willing to accept advantages accompanying the equality of rights and the cultural advances brought by the Enlightenment; they also wanted to benefit from the freedom that came as a result of the separation of Church and State. Unlike the Reformers, however, they were not willing to limit Jewish life so that it might evolve into a "Jewish Church" or to forgo—within the separation of Church and State principle—such questions, concerning the survival of the people, as education, family laws, and specifically Jewish aspects of communal life. Consequently, despite its strict insistence on the principle of separation of Church and State, the Historical School, like Orthodoxy, strove vigorously to maintain the religious, ethnic and cultural unity of American Jewry and its indissoluble tie with World Jewry. With Orthodoxy and unlike Reform, it strove to enforce the authority of Jewish Law. The Historical School believed that the Jews, because of their spiritual heritage, were unique among the nations of the world. It insisted upon the necessity of finding new approaches to Judaism which would maintain the integrity of Tradition and be consonant with the strivings for emancipation and democracy in America.

The opportunity to become organically part of American society along political, economic and social lines is an impressive phenomenon in Jewish history. What is even more impressive and profoundly significant is that in America the Jews were offered the opportunity to express and develop their religio-cultural values to the best of their abilities and to contribute these values, if they could, to the total complex of American civilization. Few parallel situations can be found in the whole range of Jewish experience. To the extent that the Historical School struggled and discovered the meaning of this opportunity by laying the foundations for the Conservative Movement and the contemporary American community of which it is a part, its contribution has meaning for the present and future of Jewish life everywhere.

Part I

Pioneer Efforts
(1840—1870)

Chapter One

Transition: from Unified to Diversified Community (1825-1840)

The character of American Jewish religious life was radically transformed in the early part of the nineteenth century. As American society changed, so did its Jewish community, and it was through the synagogue community that alterations in Jewry were then expressed most emphatically.

The country at large was undergoing fundamental territorial, economic and social changes. America was expanding westward. In 1820 two and one-half million (one-fourth of the population) lived beyond the Alleghenies. By 1830 these "men of the western waters" totaled one-third of the American population of some thirteen million. Entire families began to move with the westward train, plotting out homes in the new regions. The building of the Erie Canal in 1825—marking the union of the Atlantic Ocean with Lake Erie—compressed travel from New York to Buffalo from twenty-six days to six; the price of transporting a ton of merchandise was cut down from one hundred dollars to five. The federal government's keen interest in the development of the West was advanced through the incisive interpretations of Chief Justice of the Supreme Court James Marshall. As he managed to find the legal bridge to span the divisive jealousies of the states, other arbitrary divisions between East and West also began to fade away. The West sent forth its own spokesmen and in 1828, Andrew Jackson, example and choice of the expanding American democracy, was elected President of the United States.[1]

23

The dominant factor in the fluctuating social and economic scene of early nineteenth-century America was the emergence of the city as the major center of residence and occupation. While, in the American occupational structure, the majority of the population still continued to be engaged in agriculture, commercial and industrial pursuits began to involve a new city work force. This was indeed "The End of Arcadia."[2] New York State, particularly New York City, served as a focal point for these changes. Already called the "commercial emporium," New York soon became the greatest port of immigration in the United States. Within the century, New York City was to become the economic capital of America and the gateway to the New World for millions of immigrant Europeans.[3] Describing New York City as "the new capital," Vernon Parrington found that "the romance of expansion was creating there a new psychology, and this new psychology was preparing the city for leadership in the new age that was rising."[4]

The second decade of the nineteenth century was also a watershed in American Jewish history. The New World became, for the first time in Jewish history, a haven for the politically persecuted, the religiously oppressed and the economically uprooted. The Napoleonic wars, anti-Jewish economic and religious manifestations in the southern German States (e.g., Baden, Bavaria, and Wuerttemberg), and crises in Poland forced many Jews to seek refuge on American shores. In literary and social "societies," especially in Germany, Jews learned about the liberty-loving people across the seas. Repeated "invitations to America" in American newspaper editorials and broadsides published and distributed throughout Europe interested these people in emigration. America needed human power for its cities and farms; many Europeans needed a refuge and hope.

The Jewish community in America, consisting of some 3,000 in 1818, doubled its number by 1826 and rose to about 15,000 by 1840. At the same time, the American Jewish settlement rapidly assumed the polyglot character of the country as a whole and consisted of Jews of English, Dutch, German,

Polish, Bohemian, Russian, Spanish and Portuguese origin, as well as those native to America. Meanwhile the real drama of growth, tension and change within Jewish communal life, then completely synagogue-centered, was taking place in a series of isolated but significant acts. These acts brought about the replacement of the monolithic structure of the Colonial synagogue, organized in accordance with the Sephardi *minhag*, and a new form of synagogue life, which differed not only in ritual practice but in organizational method and communal outlook. Most significantly, the principle of diversity rather than uniformity was introduced as the basic principle of Jewish communal order in the United States. In Philadelphia, for example, the first extra-synagogal Jewish organization, the Hebra Shel Bikur Holim Ugemilut Hasadim (Society for the Visitation of the Sick and Mutual Assistance), was organized in 1813. Limited first to members of Mikveh Israel, it developed into a separate entity and in 1820 was opened to non-members of the synagogue.[5] In New York, the first extra-synagogal philanthropic society, the Hebra Gemilath Chesed (later the Hebrew Mutual Benefit Society), was established in 1820 by "eighteen gentlemen who afterwards became members of Congregation B'nai Jeshurun." Five years later a letter (dated October 6, 1825) was addressed by a group of leading Jews, including John I. Hart, I. B. Kursheedt and Mordecai M. Noah, "to the Parnass and Trustees of the K. K. Shearith Israel," informing them that: "we are deputed a committee from a meeting of Israelites held at Washington Hall to announce to you their intention to erect a new synagogue in this city."[6] What began in Philadelphia and New York was repeated and developed elsewhere.

In order fully to understand this radical transition from a small, compact, synagogue-controlled, religiously unified community in the Colonial era to a large, scattered, multi-controlled, diversified and often divided community in the middle decades of the past century, a brief summary of Jewish congregational life before 1825 is helpful.

Some seven congregations were established in various American cities in the approximately 150 years since the first

settlement of Jews in New Amsterdam in 1654; and in direction and structure a common thread of design ran through
all of them.[7]

Though the Jews, primarily grouped in seaport cities
where they were engaged in commerce and trade, came in
close contact with their Christian neighbors, this open contact did not substantially change the basis of religious life
and observance which the Jews had inherited from their
fathers. The synagogue as house of worship was also the house
of assembly and study. The order of prayers was in accordance with the authorized Sephardi *minhag,* and it was followed
as in the past. The members of the congregation were subject
to community opinion. Because community sanction issued
from this central authority, Jewish life maintained its rubric
and character.

The chief of the community was the *parnas,* in law and in
action. He and his associates supervised every aspect of congregational life. Unlimited authority was granted the *parnas*
to punish the unaffiliated and religiously wayward.[8] His rulings were not idle threats: both light and severe punishments
were carried out. Most congregations had two paid officials.
The *hazzan* who was usually a lay person with a pleasant voice
and a slight knowledge of Hebrew, served as reader and
teacher to the young. Second to him was the *shammash,* who
supervised the daily synagogue activities.

In the traditional Jewish manner, congregational concern
emphasized the education of the young. Schooling in Colonial
days was a function of the congregation. While some of the
children attended Christian private schools and others, who
could afford it, received both their general and religious
education from private tutors, most Jewish children were
educated in the synagogue school. The most advanced school
was conducted under the auspices of Congregation Shearith
Israel in New York. From its beginnings in 1755 and until
1800, "Yeshivat Minchat Areb" was conceived within the
general framework of the Colonial educational system. The
parnassim of the congregation arranged curriculum and set
standards and requirements. Cost of maintenance was covered

by tuition fees and community subventions and children of
the poor were admitted without fee. In the beginning of the
nineteenth century, this school was given the same grant-in-
aid that the state offered to religious schools of other denominations. Classes were conducted throughout the year, on
weekdays from ten to five. Studies consisted of "Hebrew,
Spanish, English, writting and Arithmetick." The Colonial
synagogue school, in form at least, was comparable to our contemporary Jewish day schools.[9]

Charitable and social services were also centralized in the
congregation. In general, every congregation possessed a special *zedakah*, or charity fund, which was administered to the
needy. In Mikveh Israel of Philadelphia, part of this *zedakah*
fund grew into an Ezrath Orechim, or Society for Destitute
Strangers. When monies were drawn from the congregational
treasury, the *parnas* and the synagogue board took charge of
examining petitions from the sick and indigent and of dis-
bursing the necessary alms. Messengers from Eretz Yisrael
were also helped on their way from community to community.[10] For Passover, *matzot* were prepared under congregational auspices and their price was set sufficiently above cost
to provide for free distribution of *matzot* to the needy.[11]

As we survey the Colonial synagogue community before
its dissolution in the earlier part of the past century, we find,
in the words of Jacob Marcus, "that a whole community
could receive enfranchisement, could live in a monolithic
political world of strong Christian overtones, could participate intimately in it, and yet remain Jewish in a traditional
sense."[12]

Two primary factors completely altered the Jewish community structure: the expansion of America itself, and the
migration of Jews from Germany and Poland. During the
years 1825-1840 no new Sephardi synagogue was established;
at the same time, according to Joseph Krauskopf's estimate,
some six new congregations were founded, in Cincinnati,
New Orleans, St. Louis, Albany and Easton. A few congregations were also established in Philadelphia and New York.[13]
These very cities in which Jewish congregations were

founded show how closely the expansion of the Jewish community corresponded to that of metropolitan America.

One of the most important results of this congregational development was the consolidation of the German-Jewish group in America and the submergence of the Sephardi community.[14] The Jews from the German-speaking countries, who had come to America in Colonial times and had belonged to Sephardi synagogues, felt themselves sufficiently strong to separate from that community and found synagogues more suitable to their own background. The situation in Shearith Israel of New York is an example of the general process. It had been the policy of the Sephardi leadership to encourage not more than one synagogue per city. For that reason they hesitated in New York, in Philadelphia and elsewhere, to establish a second synagogue in those cities.[15] Nevertheless, they could not deny the need for another synagogue in New York City. As the community grew, Shearith Israel had either to grow—and change—or to admit the right of others to form congregations. Therefore, while we cannot discount the personal and social factors which influenced the split of the congregation (e.g., those who had immigrated earlier looked down upon those who came after them), it was the larger issue which compelled the leaders of Shearith Israel to submit with good grace to the organization of the new proposed synagogue.[16] They realized that their own synagogue building was too small to hold all who would come; and if they admitted the Ashkenazim as members, the original Sephardi families would be overwhelmed numerically. Conceivably, then, the ritual practices of the congregation would be changed because of "the increased number of our brethren, and also the probability of many more coming to reside in the city."[17] Men such as Mordecai M. Noah, who was not an Ashkenazi Jew, supported the new congregation, and the members of Shearith Israel participated in the 1827 dedication ceremonies of the B'nai Jeshurun Elm Street synagogue, the first Ashkenazi congregation in New York City. By 1840, three additional Ashkenazi synagogues were established in the city.

The differences between the Sephardi and Ashkenazi communities were not of an ideological nature. Theologically they were of one view and one commitment—to uphold the Torah through the institution of the synagogue. The difference was in the seat of religious sanction and religious habit. For both communities rabbinic authority came from the "mother" country: the Sephardim turned to the authorities in Amsterdam for interpretation of law and practice while the Ashkenazim of English origin patterned their service after the Great Synagogue in London. Other Ashkenazi congregations, as they were established, turned to the respective authorities in their own lands of origin. Apart from differences in ritual practice, the two communities during the period of transition had much in common. They were united in their recognition of the dangers of individual assimilation and communal disintegration. They worked with combined strength to sustain the fundamental elements of the Tradition and to maintain the synagogue's central position in Jewish life.

Already in the period of transition the signs were evident that the struggle to maintain the all-embracing character of the synagogue would end in failure. Many factors combined to produce this result, of which two were the most significant: the enlargement and consequent decentralization of Jewish areas of settlement, and the new theological and secular views which influenced the mainstream of American Jewish religious life. The first factor caused profound organizational changes in the Jewish communal structure, while the second compelled a division within the ranks of the synagogue-motivated and synagogue-committed members of the Jewish group.

As the population grew and spread over the country, it became increasingly difficult for the synagogue to fulfill all of its educational and social functions. At first the congregations were unwilling to relinquish their authority. But the pressure of decentralization manifested itself ever more strongly, and the synagogue had to relinquish its exclusive control. It could simply not meet the growing total needs of the heterogeneous and undisciplined community. Other institutions and agencies arose to meet those needs.[18] For example, in 1828 the Sephardi congregation Shearith Israel organized the Hebrew Benevolent Society as part of the congregation. Little did the founders suspect that sixteen years later, when the Ashkenazi community would establish a social agency for its constituents, it would be impelled to establish its agency (the German-Hebrew Benevolent Society) apart from the synagogue. That same decade and the next saw the founding of what is now the largest world Jewish order, B'nai B'rith (1843), followed by the Independent Order Free Sons of Israel (1849), Brith Abraham (1859), Order Kesher Shel Barzel (1860) and others. Other philanthropic and social aid agencies, independent of the synagogues, also developed in those years. The Jews were slowly weaned away from the synagogue. The fraternal orders, the *landsmanschaften* and other organizations, which had begun as supplementary agencies to the synagogue, shortly supplanted them in the hearts and minds of their constituents. Even religious schools were founded on a communal rather than congregational basis. In 1838 the first Hebrew Sunday School was founded by Rebecca Gratz, and soon the Sunday School program was introduced to Charleston, Richmond, Cincinnati and New York.

The second challenge to the former undisputed authority of the Colonial synagogue community structure was the division within: the evolution of Reform Judaism, which first began in Charleston in 1824. Reform, after a brief display of color, passed away and seemingly left no trace. Two decades later, however, it rose once again. This time it would remain permanently on the American scene. It is interesting to observe that it was in a sedate Sephardi congregation, Beth Elohim, and not in a German synagogue that Reform was first planted in America. A group of forty-seven members, led by Isaac Harby and David N. Carvallho, were influenced by the developments in the Jewish religion in Hamburg and impelled by the perfunctory order of their own affairs to appeal for a modification of the service. They asked for a shorter, more intelligible and more decorous service. They wanted portions of the service read in English as well as Hebrew and a commentary offered by the Rabbi on the weekly Torah portion. The heads of the community refused to depart from the traditional *minhag*. In protest twelve of the most determined members in the group resigned and formed The Reformed Society of Israelites. Within two years their number grew to fifty. Soon their long-range purpose became apparent. They published a new prayer book, introduced the organ into the service and announced their proposed reforms of Jewish practice as measures to adapt Judaism to the "situation of an enlightened world." Despite their serious preparations the project did not succeed and the monies which were donated for a new building were refunded. Most of the members returned to the fold of the congregation. The dissension in Charleston announced the character of future developments in American Judaism. Counter-religious groups would be contending against Reform. Diversity would reign.[19]

As the year 1840 passed into history, it left the once closed circle of Judaism torn. The dynamism of American life unleashed powerful forces. The Jewish population had grown to some 15,000, most of them immigrants from Germany, Austria and Poland. Their participation in all branches of American life, throughout the country, brought about a basic revolution in Jewish communal life. Alienation from their origins, intermarriage, internal assimilation and, above all, an indifference to the continuity of the Jewish people combined to upset Jewish religious life and its institutions. Even within the synagogue signs of strife and dissension multiplied: there were Sephardi and Ashkenazi rituals, traditionalist and reform attitudes, natives and strangers. The number of synagogue buildings and congregations grew, each acting in independent fashion. From 1840 to 1850 anarchy increased in Jewish communal life: there was a flood of organizations, associations and synagogues, each claiming it alone held the key to Jewish unity.

The crisis which confronted American Jewry in the mid-nineteenth century was a result of the evolutionary forces which began to influence the community from the end of the Colonial period. It was both a communal and spiritual crisis. Consequently, few of those affected understood its profound and deep-rooted nature. In a fragmentary manuscript, Henry Jones, one of the founders of B'nai B'rith, describes the religious crisis in the language and mood of the time:

> The synagogue . . . used to be open twice a day; for a Jew desiring to find a friend, he had but to go there and make himself known by certain signs and tokens; he was sure to find assistance. The sign consisted of a grip given with a full hand and the magical words *Sholem Alechem*. The *Mesussah* on the door-post was the countersign. The *Arbacanphoth* represented the regalia. *Shema Israel* was the pass-word. But now since the synagogue is open but once a week, since the *Mesussah* is to be found at very few door-posts, since the regalia, the *Arbacanphoth*, has almost disappeared from the breasts of our coreligionists, since the pass-word is not given twice a day as it used to be, and therefore has lost its magical power; since to speak plainly, a youth would rather not be recognized as a Jew, and never thinks of visiting a synagogue, it becomes necessary for us to try at least to remedy this evil and show the beauties of our Holy Religion.[20]

In short, the nature of the problem—as the perceptive rabbinic and lay religious leaders in the 1840s saw it—was that the ultimate commitment of Jews to God, Torah and Israel was losing its meaning for the coming generation because of the new way of Jewish life in America.

That religious leadership which grew into a school of thought and common action sought to wed Jewish traditional values with American ideals, and began to search for solutions to contemporary problems. The leading personalities and spokesmen of the Historical School did not form a cohesive group in the beginning and did not always agree with or understand one another. Contradictions and fluctuations frequently resulted from this searching. Gradually, however, the leaders joined each other on the strength of their common viewpoints and struggles to unite opposing solutions. During the first decades, from the forties to the seventies, they worked, not so much as a group as *in* groups and in individual capacities. As we turn to the activities of the School, in education, social welfare, defense of Jewish rights and synagogue organization, we recognize that it faced the difficulties and divergencies in Jewish life without preconceived programs. Rather, it attempted to cope with these problems as they arose while attempting long-range solutions as well. The consequence was a unification of similar minds into the Historical School.

Chapter Two

Education

Fortified by a long tradition of transmitting the Jewish heritage, the leaders of the Historical School of Judaism in the United States were well aware that a proper Jewish educational system would have to be the major instrument for Jewish survival. But in America Jewish education faced a unique situation and past experience could not suggest the appropriate techniques to handle it. What made the American problem so difficult was the fact that it resulted from a great gift of freedom: universal public education. As long as the education of their young was the *exclusive* province of the Jewish community, the Jews were able to train their children in the disciplines of their faith and culture. With the advance of compulsory public education, however, responsibility for the general education of the child became a function of the State, while religious education was relegated to the home and taken up by such voluntary religious groups as responded to the imperative need. Consequently, religious education was reduced to a secondary and, at best, supplementary form of learning. The paradox is that the Jewish community conscientiously supported the public school movement, seeing in it a means for the enhancement of democracy and, in effect, Jewish life. On the other hand, with the Jewish school's loss of status and the limits now imposed on its teaching hours—crucial factors in any educational framework—how could the Jewish community train a Jewishly learned laity? This was the problem posed by

34

public education in mid-nineteenth-century America. Bewildered by this entirely new situation, the Historical School responded with a series of experiments through trial and error.

Elementary Education

The first group of spokesmen for the Historical School held fast to the ancient principle: "Educate!" Isaac Leeser pleaded, "This is the remedy, and without it all talk is in vain."[1] "A synagogue without a schoolhouse is a building erected at the expense of our children," added Marcus Jastrow.[2] "We may not suspend the instruction of children even for the rebuilding of the Temple," Sabato Morais quoted from the Talmud.[3] These statements indicate the direction which these men and their associates chose for the improvement of Jewish life. Within their own ranks and whenever they met with other rabbis and educators of the Reform and Orthodox schools of thought, they emphasized the need for the education of young and old, the establishment of synagogue schools and higher institutions of learning, and the writing of educational materials for the study of Judaism.

In accordance with the traditional Jewish attitude toward education the children were "the guardians of the city." If a proper system of elementary education could be established, there would be greater hope for the Jewish community in the United States.[4] How to accomplish this objective in the context of the emergent public school system and in consonance with democratic institutions was by no means clear.

During the early nineteenth century, public education in this country was in transition. The Free School Society (later known as the Public School Society) of New York, organized in 1805, represented merely the first step of a continuing struggle which lasted seventy years. The cause of free education ultimately won because public opinion was created in its favor. But in the forties of the century, the principle of free and public education was not yet firmly established. Property owners joined with part of the clergy (especially Catholic) to oppose the idea of public schools. In 1849 and 1850 in New York two public referenda were held with respect to state support of education, but the proposal for free public schools was not legislated until 1867. Ultimate success was achieved by men such as Henry Barnard and Horace Mann, leaders of the common school movement, who helped people to understand that democracy depended upon the education of all the people. (It is well to note the interesting correlation of laws both approving free education and granting universal manhood suffrage in the various states of the Union during this period.)

The vast majority of American rabbis, like most Protestants, favored public education for all the American people. Experience taught them that where there were no public schools, most Jewish children were educated in private Christian schools. This condition was also created by the low number of Jewish schools in existence. (It is estimated that there were more than one thousand academies in the United States in 1830, none of which was Jewish.) Leeser was among the first to point out the great danger of this situation. The Christian teachers, he claimed, by inculcating Christian customs and practices, might well convert their students. "If even open apostasy does not follow, there is unfortunately a divided heart, not very favourable to the growth of healthful religion."[5] The rabbis therefore sided with proposals for public education. The government ought to build schools and support them by means of public taxation, they argued. In such schools Jewish children would study the language of the country and other general subjects; formal religion would have no place in them. The rabbis understood the reason for the opposition of various religious groups to public education: each one was concerned for the survival of the principles of its own faith. Christian groups, Leeser pointed out, even the Friends, who have no formal creed, refused to hand over their children to a school conducted by those not of their particular faith or to teachers of doubtful religious opinions. The Jews, however, did exactly that. For the Jews then the argument ran, as for all religious groups, the public school system was the best solution. Divested of all religious instruction, it was the natural means of attaining the common elements of education.

An example of the contradictions which prevailed during this period of transition in American education can be found in the New York situation, where the state aided a synagogue school. Congregation Shearith Israel in New York had conducted its Yeshivat Minchat Areb along typical Colonial educational lines since 1731, when all education functioned under denominational sponsorship. In 1811, the congregation received a subsidy from the state to provide for its poor students.[6] This state aid to a religious-directed school continued until 1870. On the other hand, the public school system, founded by the state, was marked by a Protestant religious character. This united the Catholics, the Universalists and the Jews in opposition to what they considered public religious indoctrination. When the trustees of the Fourth Ward in New York City protested to the Select Committee of the Board of Education that the books used in the public school system taught Christianity, the Committee refused to act in favor of the protest on the grounds that these volumes instilled thoughts of beauty and goodness. More precisely, however, they ruled that the state law *against* the teaching of any particular religious tenet applied only to denominational instruction, not to the general articles of Christian belief. Furthermore, the Jews, even as taxpaying inhabitants of the city of New York, were not to be given as much consideration as Christians for, after all, the Committee ruled, the United States was a Christian country.[7]

During those decades of change in American education when the idea of public education was still in its infancy, the prospect of Christian indoctrination through the public schools troubled the Jewish home. The members of the Historical School first supported Jewish all-day schools, in which Jewish children were to absorb the spirit of Judaism.[8] Later, as the public school system took on a secular character, they accepted public education and began to experiment with forms of supplementary religious education.

Two types of institution developed between 1840 and 1855: schools established by congregations or orphanages for the benefit of the middle and lower classes, and private boarding schools for the children of wealthy families. A good example of the first kind was the school organized in 1851 by the Hebrew Education Society of Philadelphia, in which Leeser played an important part. It soon achieved an enviable reputation. Although a considerable number of children from the various congregations in the city were registered in this school, after some time the largest part of the enrollment was composed of children from the Jewish Foster Home in Philadelphia. This type of school was the forerunner of other schools, such as the school for poor children in New York, of which Samuel Myer Isaacs was one of the founders. The real purpose of this school was to combat the work of Christian missionaries on the East Side of New York.[9] It was established by the Hebrew Free School Association of New York and opened in 1865 with subsidies from the city and the state. This "model" school, the first in the series of nine or ten that were opened at that time, was an all-day school; the others provided supplementary classes for those attending public schools.

Of the second type of institution—the boarding school—established in that period, the academy of Dr. Max Lilienthal, who afterward became a co-worker of Isaac Mayer Wise, was most important.[10] During the six years of his residence in New York (1849-1855), Lilienthal conducted a private school with a traditional Jewish character and earned the profound respect of the rabbinate and laity.[11] Leeser and Isaacs strongly supported this school, publicizing its achievements and extolling its significance. On various occasions, they gained generous financial support for it. They also aided the school conducted for girls by the Misses Palache in New York and the two schools conducted for boys by Adolph Loewe and John Livor. The curricula of these schools were excellent from the viewpoint of general studies, but their main virtue, of course, was that they offered a solution to the problem of Christian indoctrination.[12]

In the course of time, the movement to create public schools for all children gained strength. Connecticut followed New York; by 1871, Rhode Island, Michigan and New Jersey followed them. State after state raised the question of free public education and answered it affirmatively. When the idea of the free public school was finally accepted, most of the congregational schools were abandoned—those which were originally founded for the benefit of the poor and the boarding schools. The process was universal: wherever public schools were established, Jewish all-day schools disappeared. As Rabbi Ishmael teaches in one of his rules for the interpretation of the Bible, a specific example may explain an entire phenomenon. The Jewish educational dilemma of this period and the process of adjustment are illuminated in the case history of the B'nai Jeshurun Educational Institute in New York. In 1852, under the leadership of Dr. Morris Raphall, an earlier decision of the board of directors was implemented and the B'nai Jeshurun Educational Institute was established for "males and females, to give them a Hebrew, English, and classical education." The deeper purpose of the Institute, we are told by a reporter in the *Occident,* is "to make our religion familiar to their children, like household words . . ."[13] Eighty-eight children were registered at the first school enrollment in 1853. The curriculum was designed to meet the standards of the best schools of the time. Soon the Institute had its own building—"the first school built by Hebrews in these United States." The *Occident* reporter commented: "I trust ere long to be able to speak of Rashi and Rabbinical classics, Euclid and Latin classics, as integral portions of the instruction . . ."[14]

Altogether, B'nai Jeshurun took great pride in its school and received praise from other congregations and from leading citizens. But the promise was not fulfilled. The entire program collapsed and, in 1858, the school was discontinued. Waning public support was the apparent cause. The basic reason was the new non-denominational public school system.

The very year of the dedication of the B'nai Jeshurun Institute (1853) was the year in which the city of New York took over the Public School Society. Formerly, the Society had been responsible for the development of public education; its goal was now achieved. This new development, coming after the enactment of a state law (1842) which prohibited the teaching of religion in public schools administered by the city, eliminated the fear of direct Christian indoctrination in the classroom, and Jewish parents were encouraged to enroll their children in the public schools.

"Denominational" education was felt to be a deterrent to the urgent need for the social integration of diverse stocks of immigrants in a cosmopolitan city. It was argued that Jews should be the first to foster the enlargement of American interests. For Jews to continue their separateness in education was to spurn the gift of equality, a gift offered uniquely by America to *all* its citizens. That a desirable Jewish educational substitute had not yet been prepared by the Jewish community was a consideration unanticipated, and the hope was that a proper Jewish supplementary system could be quickly created. This crucial factor in American democratic life compelled the closing of the synagogue all-day school not only at B'nai Jeshurun but in other synagogues as well. And so began a long period of search and experiment in Jewish education.

Responsible Jewish leadership faced the problem with some consolation. At least the problem was clear: if the child was to receive his general education in the public school, new instruments would have to be designed to transmit the religious heritage. But what instruments? The obvious first answer was to attempt the solution suggested by one's neighbors. The religious pattern of the Christian community was adopted, and the Jewish religious or Sunday school movement came into being. The day on which the child was free from public school, Sunday, was to be devoted entirely to learning the language of his people and his religion. Such study was considered a duty for rich and poor alike. Religious training should be available to all, and the poor were to be admitted free of charge. As indicated, the first Jewish Sunday school in America, founded by Rebecca Gratz, became an inspiration for congregations throughout the land. From a report in the minute-book of the Female Hebrew Benevolent Society for 1838, the all-pervading idea of free universal education in a Jewish school finds eloquent expression:

> All who are hungry for the bread of life are welcome to the banquet—all who desire to read the Scriptures understandingly are invited to partake of instruction, given and received with reverence, and at no other charge than attention.[15]

Miss Gratz opened her classes with the verse from Psalms (34.12), "Come ye Children, hearken unto me and I will teach you the ways of the Lord," the verse with which her successors would begin their classes every year. It was not too long after the opening of her school that Rebecca Gratz could record with pride, "Our sisters of New York and Charleston, hearing of the success that has attended our attempt and sensible that much good must result from early lessons of piety, have determined to establish similar institutions in their respective cities."[16] In this effort, Isaac Leeser played a most important role, guiding Miss Gratz and urging her to use the facilities of the Mikveh Israel congregation.[17] Leeser helped publicize the school and urged the development of a network of Jewish religious schools. Undoubtedly his great enthusiasm for this project stemmed from the fact that Leeser himself, together with Isaac B. Seixas, had proposed such an innovation in Jewish education while both were still residents of Richmond.[18]

Not much time had passed, however, before the Historical School proponents of Sunday school education realized their mistake and came to understand that this type of education was only a palliative, and could not conceivably meet the central purpose of Jewish education, namely, the training of an educated Jewish community. If, as a result of a Sunday school education, the child did not understand Hebrew, and gained only parrot-like ability to recite the prayers without

CATECHISM

FOR

YOUNGER CHILDREN.

DESIGNED AS A

FAMILIAR EXPOSITION

OF THE

JEWISH RELIGION.

"Which ye shall command your children, to observe to do all the words
of this law." DEUT. XXXII. 46.

BY ISAAC LEESER.

PHILADELPHIA:
PRINTED FOR THE AUTHOR, BY ADAM WALDIE.
5599.

any penetration into their meaning, and if he did not study the Hebrew Scriptures and the classics of Judaism, what kind of Jewish future could there be for him and for the Jewish community?

The time allotted for Sunday school instruction was not sufficient for the child to gain a good reading knowledge of Hebrew, and it was therefore hopeless to expect any significant progress in the rest of his Jewish studies. As a result, Leeser, Szold, Jastrow, Morais and others—each in his own locale and each at an opportune time—began to urge the creation of a system of Talmud Torah schools under synagogue auspices. There children would study daily after public school classes. The same Jewish curriculum would be followed as in the former all-day schools, with general studies relegated to the public schools. Abraham Rice, rabbi of the congregation Nidche Israel in Baltimore, one of the early leaders of Orthodox Judaism in America, was among the first to found, in 1845, a Hebrew school of this type.[19] In the following decade and in the same city, when Benjamin Szold saw that the private school conducted by Mr. Goldsmith—formerly the most popular in the city—was about to close, he influenced him to combine efforts with the congregation and together build a Talmud Torah designed as a supplementary school. A similar process took place at congregation Shearith Israel in San Francisco, where the afternoon school curriculum included such basic subjects as Bible, biblical Hebrew, catechism and Jewish ceremonials.

The development of the synagogue Talmud Torah was a welcome phenomenon in Jewish education. But once again it was difficult to turn theory into reality. It was a problem persuading the children to attend every afternoon. Therefore, in most of the congregations of the Historical School, students attended twice or, at best, three times a week. Caught between insufficient teaching time and pupils who considered these additional studies a burden, the new supplementary departments were not much better than the Sunday schools. Although the children in the supplementary schools learned more facts than those in Sunday schools, they were far from

being shaped into a generation that could read and understand fundamental Jewish sources—the Hebrew prayer book
and the Bible.

The failure of the synagogue supplementary school could
not be attributed solely to the limitations of teaching time
brought about by the social and general educational developments in mid-nineteenth century America. It seemed that
everything had to be created *de novo* in American Jewish
education. The most glaring defects in Jewish education itself
were the lack of educational materials and of adequate teaching personnel. How could any system develop without books
and teachers? While it is true that American education generally suffered from the same two deficiencies, the situations
were not really comparable. An effective public school system
was a political, economic and social imperative supported by
the total community and encouraged by the most talented
minds. In the fifties, for example, it is true that teachers in the
state of Pennsylvania were paid an average monthly wage of
$24 for men and $16.60 for women, and children were taught
in bare one-room schools. Horace Mann could nonetheless
rise at a convention of the National Education Association in
Cincinnati in 1858 and speak with some truth about the future of American education: "A brighter day is dawning, and
education is its day-star."[20] Christian religious education, also
inadequate in these two key areas, nevertheless benefited from
an inheritance of personnel from the mother country and
older American communities, as well as a method for the
preparation of teaching materials for the children. Nor did
it have to cope with the vast complex of Hebrew language
and text requirements. The Jews, however, could not easily
import their teaching tools, nor was trained personnel available. Both had to be designed and produced here.[21]

As we first examine the problems which ensued from the
lack of textbook materials, it should be recalled that for the
Jews, who had a long and honorable tradition of early childhood training—they were the first to introduce universal public education (as early as the first century before the Common
Era)—the need for children's textbooks was an entirely new

phenomenon. Originally, the child learned Hebrew reading and prayers from the *siddur;* he acquired his people's commitment and faith from the Pentateuch; and he received wisdom and a way of life from the Talmud and Commentaries. Child and adult were people of *The Book.* Motivation for study and interpretation of the texts for daily life were absorbed from a tightly structured and all-enveloping community. The Jewish way of life revolved about the teachings of Scriptures, Talmud and Commentaries and therefore they were the best possible children's books.

Early American Jewish education in the Colonial Period relied mainly on improvisation of the traditional forms of education, based on the prayer book and the Pentateuch. The child learned mechanical reading from the prayer book, and then was introduced into the narrative portions of the Pentateuch. That was the sum of his Jewish education. Study books and appropriate Hebrew texts for the purpose of teaching were rare. In most cases, parents did the best they could to teach their young out of their own limited resource of Jewish knowledge. But the living community did its share too. Although there was not much substance to the Colonial Jewish community, a coherent Jewish community was manifest.

In the early decades of the nineteenth century, the communal framework also was shattered. As the Jews broke out of the compact Colonial communities in increasing numbers and became part of the free American environment in towns and cities throughout the land, Jewish communal life was reduced to group ritual expression, to Sabbath and festival synagogue prayers. The individual home could not cope with the need to train the child in formal belief, especially since the child now asked "why" before he learned "what." The religious school, it was hoped, would answer the "why" and somehow relate the basic historic ideas of Judaism to the growing American child in his own idiom, in English primarily, and sometimes in German when it was the language of the home. Hence the proportionately amazing number of books produced during this period of the catechistic variety,

in which were combined the elements of Jewish history,
Bible study, belief and practice. Without their own pedagogical devices, the Jews quite naturally appropriated those
of their neighbors. In this instance, it was the catechism which
was the prevailing form of Christian religious teaching.
Virtually every religious leader produced his own version of
a catechism.[22]

That the core of the problem was the crumbling Jewish
community structure which resulted from expanding freedom
is further demonstrated by the fact that the first Jewish
catechisms were written in West-European Jewish communities where reforms had been initiated to halt the tide of
communal disintegration. Leeser, who was the first to introduce such a catechism in the United States, copied his text
from a German Jewish source. He translated from the German *Instruction in the Mosaic Religion* by J. J. Johlson
("teacher of an Israelitisch School at Frankfort-on-the-Main")
and published it in 1830. Because Leeser was not very pleased
with the contemporary Reform overtones of this work, he
issued a catechism of his own composition in two versions
(1839): one designed "as a Familiar Exposition of the Jewish
Religion," and the other as a manual for home and school.
These volumes also were patterned after a German catechism,
that of the rabbi in Hamburg, Dr. Klee.

A. S. W. Rosenbach's essay on "Early American Jewish
School Books" transmits a feeling of the content and literary
texture of these efforts. Most of the writing was formal and
stolid. But occasionally, a charming and creative line breaks
through—even though the form may not pass the critical
examination of a twentieth-century textbook reader. The
following quotation is from Mrs. Eleazar Pike's verse catechism, *Scriptural Questions for the Use of Sunday Schools
for the Instruction of Israelites,* by which she taught the
uninitiated at the Philadelphia Sunday school of Rebecca
Gratz:

Q. Who formed you, child, and made you live?
A. God did my life and spirit give.

Q. Who keeps you safely, can you tell?
A. God keeps me safe, and makes me well.
Q. Has God made known the way of truth?
A. The Bible is the guide of youth.
Q. What should you feel towards God above?
A. Honour and fear and grateful love.
Q. Does God know all you do and say?
A. Yes! and my thoughts, too, night and day.
Q. Have you an evil heart within?
A. Yes! or I should not often sin.
Q. How does your heart its evil show?
A. By sinful words, and actions, too.
Q. And does not sin God's anger move?
A. Yes! for I sin against His love.
Q. Must you repent, with humble heart?
A. Yes! and from every sin depart.

These couplets made a vivid impression on young minds. As Rosenbach recalls, he knew an old lady who remembered them seventy years after she learned them.[23]

Without underestimating the catechism form as a method of motivation in that period of Jewish education, it should not be confused with content itself, just as reading-readiness is not the ability to read. Catechisms were but a preface to Jewish education. The next step was to teach Hebrew, so that the child could learn to read and understand the Bible in the original. Here religious leadership came face to face with the problem of transmitting the tradition of language and learning.

The first Jewish textbook to be published in this country was *Maf-teach Le-shon Ivrit: A Key to the Hebrew Tongue,* amply described on the title page—

> containing the Hebrew alphabet with the various vowel points: accompanied by easy lessons of one and more syllables, with the English translation affixed thereto, so that the learner may understand as he proceeds. To which is added an introduction to the Hebrew Grammar with points, intended to facilitate the scholar in his progress to the attainment of the primitive languages. By the Rev.

E. N. Carvalho, Professor of Hebrew and Chaldee languages, Philadelphia. Published for the use of his pupils, William Fry, Printer, 1815.

Carvalho served as instructor and *hazzan* in several Sephardi congregations in the first and second decades of the nineteenth century: Shearith Israel in New York, Beth Elohim in Charleston, and finally in Mikveh Israel in Philadelphia. But his volume was for the mature student.

The second book for the teaching of biblical Hebrew appeared in 1834: Joseph Aaron's *A Key to the Hebrew Language and the Science of Hebrew Grammar Explained* (with points). Not until 1838 did the first elementary text appear, again the work of Isaac Leeser: "*The Hebrew Reader:* Hebrew and English. Designed as an easy guide to the Hebrew Tongue, for Jewish children and Self-Instruction." This flimsy text, marked "no. 1, The spelling book," seemed a great step forward, and served for a long time as the model for other "Readers." But the skimpy unattractiveness of the pedagogic literature can be recognized from Dr. Aaron Klein's listing of all types of educational publications: four volumes between 1766-1829, of which two are translations of the prayer book; a miscellany of ten books between 1830-1839; and another twelve assorted titles until 1850.[24] Altogether an inventory of twenty-six volumes—not all of them accessible—for the use of Jewish children, youths and adults comprising an estimated population of 50,000 in dozens of communities in the United States.

Adult Education

While the need for children's textbooks held the highest priority, the members of the Historical School knew, of course, that the educational enterprise could not be limited to the child's bookshelf. Judaism teaches that all of man's life ought to be a process of growth, of acquisition of new intellectual and spiritual values. Education does not come to an end at a definite age or time of life. Moreover, the rabbis

מורה דרך

ללמד את נערי בני ישראל דרכי לשון עברית

THE

HEBREW READER:

HEBREW AND ENGLISH.

DESIGNED

AS AN EASY GUIDE TO THE HEBREW TONGUE,

FOR

JEWISH CHILDREN AND SELF-INSTRUCTION.

NO. I.
THE SPELLING BOOK.

BY ISAAC LEESER.

PHILADELPHIA :
PRINTED BY HASWELL, BARRINGTON, AND HASWELL.
1838.

had sound pragmatic reasons to explain the urgent need for a continuing education. If they could not sway their congregants to pursue Jewish studies for their own good, they hoped to influence them for the good of their children. As long as ignorance of Jewish tradition remained the permanent condition of parents, they argued, and as long as parents did not recognize the need for Jewish education in their own lives, they could not exert a beneficial influence on the training of their children. "Home teaching" was the phrase Raphall liked to use.[25] Once again, they were plagued by a lack of teaching materials.

Adult education was not, in those days, the elaborate scheme of classes and institutes that it is today. In the main, it consisted of weekly evening sessions at the respective congregations. Leeser organized such courses while he was still rabbi of Mikveh Israel and later at Beth-El-Emeth. One of the most popular courses was the Bible. Occasionally, these classes were attended by as many as a hundred people, most of them young adults. In one of his reports, Leeser echoes the familiar plaint of contemporary rabbis who have to explain their dwindling adult class attendance: "The general inclemency of the Thursday evenings during the winter has materially interfered with the undertaking, add to which that the prevailing diseases, which have invaded many a household, have often detained those who otherwise would have been present." Sabato Morais, too, held such weekly classes at his congregation.[26] This pattern spread until it extended in the course of years to the whole country. Besides the formal courses, announced in the beginning of the year, there were private gatherings, not regularly scheduled, in the homes of rabbis. Morais especially distinguished himself as a teacher of adults. Everyone who knew him found in Morais a gifted teacher and whoever wished to do so could visit him at his home and learn Torah from him.

With the participation of Leeser, Raphall and Isaacs, a plan was drawn up to visit the cities of America for the cause of adult enlightenment; and these men used every opportunity to teach Torah in public or in private. Leeser traveled about 30,000 miles in his lifetime, faced with difficult mid-ninetenth century conditions, to spread the message of Judaism. Raphall was invited throughout the country to deliver his popular discourses on the history and literature of Israel. Isaacs, too, lectured widely. Writing to the editor of the *London Jewish Chronicle* in July 1851, Isaacs had this to report about Jewish life in the Midwest.

Having been invited to consecrate a synagogue 1100 miles from here, I expected to find some few families in Chicago, one of the leading cities in Illinois; but I certainly was not prepared that, after leaving Buffalo, I should see any of our race; yet it is remarkable that not a village on my route was without an Israelite, much less the towns such as Detroit and Ipsylanti, each containing twenty families. Ralmazoo [Kalamazoo] and Marshall ten, and others in proportion; and all these are destined to be congregations; but where are the ministers to be found to guide them in the way they should go?[27]

As these leaders became acquainted with Jewish communities both large and small, they were saddened by the abysmal ignorance exhibited by the masses of Jews concerning their religion. They therefore decided that, since there were no rabbis and no teachers, they should at the very least supply reading material to adults for self-education. In 1844, Leeser estimated, there were no more than eight Jewish devotional books for English-speaking Jews. "It thus happens, that many families must be entirely without a single volume which they can use for religious reading, or put in the hands of their children as guides to eternal life."[28]

Leeser suggested organizing a society to provide in English a literature on Judaism: the American Jewish Publication Society. He tells about the growth of this idea in one of his articles in the *Occident*. It was his custom each year to send letters to some of his friends in the South (especially Richmond) concerning this matter, but they reacted unfavorably to his suggestions. In 1844, two members of his congregation in Philadelphia requested him to supply them with a very expensive book for which they were willing to spend a great

sum. Leeser proposed that they reprint the book, and they
did. From this small experiment arose the idea of the Jewish
Publication Society, so that "a mass of good reading" could
be placed even among the poorest families. Leeser prepared
a plan, eighteen paragraphs in length, for the undertaking
and published it under the title "Cheap Religious Publications."[29] The plan was well received. His letters to the South
finally bore fruit and a branch of the Publication society
was organized in Richmond.

Strangely enough, the Jewish Publication Society was
founded without difficulty. A group of communal leaders
in Philadelphia undertook the responsibility of holding office
in the Society and its first years were crowned with success.[30]

By way of a digression, it is interesting to note the magni-
tude of the problem of obtaining books. The importation of
Anglo-Jewish books from England was highly expensive.
When Leeser began to print books locally he lacked the
proper materials. He had to go about and obtain paper and a
printing house, create type and teach the printers the Hebrew
alphabet. He frequently set the Hebrew type himself.

The Jewish Publication Society issued several books, adap-
tations of volumes published abroad. Soon difficulties
mounted. Leeser wrote:

> The enterprise is not a local nor a personal one; . . . that
> the rich have not stepped forward to endow our treasury
> with the requisite funds, in the absence of subscribers, is
> no cause of blame to us. But if we Jews had among us a
> tithe of the zeal of the Christians, who spend their thou-
> sands in tracts, prayer-books, and Bibles for gratuitous
> distribution all over the land, we should not have been
> compelled to wait for the slow incoming of the individual
> subscriptions.[31]

In spite of these unremitting appeals, the interest of the public was not aroused. The support necessary to cover losses was
not forthcoming. When a fire broke out in 1851 on the property where the stock of books was stored, public excuse was
found to dissolve the Society. The flames consumed the books
and the organization, but not the fundamental need. Almost

a quarter century was to pass before another attempt was made, unsuccessfully. But in 1888, the third Jewish Publication Society was established and it endures.

Attempts to Found Institutions of Higher Jewish Learning

Common to these several pioneering efforts to produce adequate text materials was their failure. But in that very failure were the seeds of experimentation and, more important, the understanding that the crisis of Jewish education was not in the small quantity of study books but in the lack of teachers. The solution to Jewish education was not to be found, therefore, in the creation of textbooks, but in the creation of the creators of those books. Teaching is possible even without good textbooks, but what can be done without teachers to transmit the Torah from generation to generation? If the classroom was to be the handmaiden of the home in transmitting the religious heritage, it required personalities who could stir the imagination of child and adult alike.

The *hazzan*, or sexton, could not fulfill the demands of the teaching office. Voluntary teaching, which was the custom in those days, was scarcely adequate. Hebrew teachers had to receive a salary to constitute a profession. If real pedagogues were not readily found in America, they had to be trained by Hebrew educational institutions. Judaism could not be expected to flourish without a proper system of Jewish education —and that very system would then produce its own teachers.

The organization of an educational system which could produce its own personnel was proposed by Louis Salomon of congregation Rodeph Shalom in Philadelphia and Isaac Leeser. The plan was presented to a group of representatives of synagogues in the county of Philadelpia in 1841 as part of Salomon's and Leeser's long-range plan to form a religious union among the Jews of the United States.[32] We shall treat the general proposal in a later chapter. Here it is pertinent to summarize several sections of Article II, subtitled "The

Schools." In this section, Salomon and Leeser proposed that schools be established for both sexes in every major town where the Jews resided, and that the teachers be paid out of a local fund, not directly by parents; that a local board of education be established; that the Jewish studies consist of Hebrew, Bible and an introduction to Talmud; that the general studies be as all-embracing as in any other good private school; that a formal board of supervision be appointed. The most significant suggestion in this section, however, was paragraph five, which called for the creation of

a High School for education in the higher branches . . . where young men are to be educated in such a manner, that they may be fit for the office of Hazan, lecturer and teachers; and young women be educated for the high calling of female instructors.[33]

This novel suggestion may have had several other antecedents among the Jews in the United States, but only one is known. In 1821, Moses Elias Levy, who dreamed of a great settlement of Jews in Florida, received the endorsement of a New York committee to establish a higher school of Jewish learning in Florida, to be supported by the national Jewish community.[34] Levy's broadside did not awaken much interest at the time. It did plant a seed in M. M. Noah's active mind, and he virtually repeated the same proposal in an article in the *Occident* called "Hebrew College."[35] But nothing came of that either.

Leeser did not separate suggestions from deeds. A proposal was a prelude to action. Continuing to complain in the pages of his paper about the critical state of affairs in Jewish education, he soon tried a new tactic, a more pointed approach, one which came to him even as he worked on the implementation of his plan. He came to the unanticipated conclusion that the answer to the question of personnel was not at the roots, in a network of elementary schools, nor even on the high school level, but at the very top of the educational ladder, in a rabbinical seminary. He discovered that the educational process works in reverse: only by establishing a school for the training of rabbis, who in turn would develop well-organized synagogues, would it be possible eventually to create good schools. Since it was impossible for rabbis recently emigrated from Europe, for whom English was a foreign language, to influence the youth of this country, the only possible solution was to found an institution of higher Jewish learning for the training of rabbis. The available rabbinic manpower, Leeser pointed out, was appallingly small.

In the forties, there were some sixty men serving throughout the United States as rabbis and *hazzanim*.[36] Of the entire roster, only two were definitely known to have received rabbinical ordination—Max Lilienthal and Abraham Rice. According to Isaac Mayer Wise in his *Reminiscences,* most of those who officiated as rabbis and *hazzanim* could not read unvocalized Hebrew, not having been trained adequately as rabbis or teachers.[37] Leeser did not think it mattered whether the seminary was established in England or the United States; all that mattered was that it should be conducted on the basis of correct pedagogical principles, and that the students be taught both the general sciences and Jewish studies. Furthermore, he suggested, the school should be given proper academic standing, by applying for a collegiate charter to enable it to confer the usual academic degrees:

> The entire freedom with which we could develop a perfect system of Jewish education uncontrolled by governmental influence is a mighty reason why we should endeavour to secure a college for our selves, since in no European country, except England, could we hope to be so favoured.[38]

In 1847 when Leeser announced this program in public, he was a man whose voice reached few ears. Nevertheless, he found a little support. The first organization to concern itself with founding an institution of higher Jewish learning was the "Hebrew Education Society of Philadelphia." It attempted to realize Leeser's proposal by obtaining from the state of Pennsylvania a charter to teach religious and secular subjects in one of the cities of that state. The charter was granted in 1849. Realizing that the time was not ripe for such an undertaking, the incorporators nevertheless hoped that the Jewish community would begin to prepare for the future: "It is left to the Israelites of America to say whether it shall be merely a legislative grant, or be employed for the advancement of our religious interests."[39]

Another ray of hope came from New York in 1852 when Sampson Simson, Benjamin Nathan and Henry Hendricks initiated an effort to establish a "Jewish Theological Seminary and Scientific Institute for the training of Rabbis and Teachers for the Jewish Congregations in North America conformably to their law, ancient doctrines and traditions." Simson, the founder of the Jews' Hospital (later Mount Sinai) contributed a tract of land in Yonkers to this enterprise. He turned over the responsibility for the project to a board of trustees, but they lacked the ability or the interest to carry the project forward.[40]

The idea of higher Jewish education was pushed ahead by Isaac Mayer Wise, a man of deeds as well as of vision, in the form of the Zion Collegiate Institute.[41] Wise had first broached the subject publicly in 1848, and he returned to it in 1854, spelling out the underlying objectives of such an institution in an article in the *Asmonean:*

> We must have an educational establishment of a higher order to train up men who will be able to defend our cause, to expound our law, to inspire our friends, to silence our enemies, and to convert our opponents.[42]

The founding organization of the Zion Collegiate Association was quickly set up in his home city, Cincinnati, the following year. Branches of the Association followed in Louisville, Cleveland, Baltimore, Philadelphia and New York City. His original notion was to create a series of supporting branches, and then determine where to place the school or even several schools. When Wise saw that the Cincinnati membership exceeded in number that of the other cities, he opened the first institute there. As it turned out, this proved to be a mistake. Other cities were envious and opposed his procedure as opportunistic. In addition, others who generally opposed his ideas began to criticize him openly. The Orthodox, represented by Bernard Illowy, then of St. Louis, did not give Wise a moment's peace.[43] Wise was strong enough to counter the opposition, but he could not contend against communal apathy and the lack of financial support. These factors caused him to abandon the school.[44] Wise tried again. He made two other suggestions: to found a school for young men in America and to send selected students to Europe for advanced religious studies.[45] But these proposals did not evoke further interest.

A decade passed, and the idea of higher Jewish training continued to find only sporadic support. A positive sign came from Baltimore, this time stemming from young people and not from communal leaders. The Hebrew literary societies of Baltimore organized themselves with a common aim—to found the National Hebrew College for the religious education of the new American generation. Declaring in the preamble of their official resolution of January 19, 1864, that ". . . the Hebrew Literary Associations of the United States are mostly composed of young men, who are in duty bound to take the initiative," they resolved to unite the Hebrew literary associations of the United States, to spare no efforts to attain this aim and to request the aid of the most important rabbis and communal leaders. They further proposed calling "one grand National Assembly" as soon as the approval of the various cities had been obtained. However, this lofty aim like others, remained only a good intention because there were not many societies and these consisted of young people who could not implement their plans financially.[46]

It was now a New York group's turn to make the attempt. The initiative of the members of Reform congregation Emanu-El, under the leadership of their rabbi, Samuel Adler, led to the founding in 1865 of the Emanu-El Theological Seminary Society. Its purpose was to create an institution for "the education of Jewish youth, on the basis of reform." The lack of a native American rabbinate was urgently felt; but whereas Leeser and Wise in their efforts had envisaged a remedy for the entire Jewish community, the limited aim and organizational base of the proposed Emanu-El Theological Seminary hindered the undertaking from the start. Not only was it restricted to the training of Reform rabbis, but the stipulations in the by-laws declared that the majority of the board be limited to members of congregation Emanu-El. Although a board was formed, membership solicited, funds raised and periodic meetings held, public response was scanty and students were not to be found. David Einhorn, elected the following year as an honorary board member of the Society, suggested that the name Emanu-El be removed from its title in a move to broaden its base. The name adopted was The American Hebrew College of the City of New York, and the usual circular was issued for national distribution to solicit funds and support.[47] The change of name and scope did not help. In fact, it was a hindrance, for now even the Emanu-El congregation ceased to undertake direct responsibility. In 1872 the association resumed its original title and limited its purpose to helping worthy rabbinical students by providing stipends to continue their studies. A few years later, in 1876, before its final demise, a member of the Historical group was brought into the association's work. Henry S. Jacobs, then serving as rabbi of B'nai Jeshurun in New York, who had been concerned very deeply with this undertaking, was elected secretary of the committee. Again the name was changed, to the Hebrew Theological Seminary Association to indicate the greater latitude of program. Classes were held for several terms, but the project petered out.[48]

Another attempt was made in 1866, by the Order of B'nai B'rith, when it first began to develop its unique program for educational work among American-born youth. Benjamin Franklin Peixotto, Grand Saar of the Order, published a plan for the founding of a novel institution, an American Jewish University in America. A circular was sent to all its lodges, the members of which totaled 7,000 at that time. The simple proposal was that each member contribute $10, so that a fund of $70,000 could be collected at once, representing a sizable sum which would undoubtedly suffice for founding such a school. In this case there was intense interest and discussion, and it seemed as if the proposal would be accepted. But the Constitution Grand Lodge, the highest authority of the Order, rejected the suggestion, and it was abandoned.[49]

Maimonides College

Having briefly surveyed a succession of failures to found the first higher school of Jewish learning in this country, we come now to the grandest failure of them all. The "grandeur" consisted in that it was not really a failure. Maimonides College survived for six lean and difficult years. It had fewer than five students in any given year, and only three of these students entered the calling of rabbi or teacher. Yet, in retrospect, it was that indispensable first: a higher school of Jewish learning actually in existence. And it was virtually the same men of the Historical School who, having lived through an experiment that failed, tried again later, this time with greater success, to create the Jewish Theological Seminary in 1886.

The vision of Maimonides College was that of Isaac Leeser. He established the school in the last year of his life, serving as its first provost, even as his energies were ebbing. But he was not alone. Surrounding him were a group of lay leaders; foremost among them, Moses A. Dropsie, a former pupil of Leeser, as well as rabbinic colleagues of the Historical School who saw in the organization of the college a vindication of their faith in the American Jewish community and a happy augury for its future.[50]

Over the years, Leeser had sustained continuous propaganda for the cause of a Jewish institution of learning. Finally, his words fell on receptive ears. In November 1864, the supporters of the idea succeeded in calling a gathering "to take into consideration the propriety of founding a High School, for the training of young men to the Ministry, under the charter of the Hebrew Education Society." Dropsie was the chairman of the meeting, and in his opening address sketched the educational situation in America with dark and gloomy colors.[51] A formal resolution was introduced to immediately establish a theological faculty, and Leeser rose to explain the concrete suggestion. He examined the status of Jewish education in America, pointing to Europe and showing how seminaries were established there for the education of native-born rabbis equipped to spread knowledge of the Torah among the people.

It was decided on the spot to establish a theological faculty in accordance with the provisions of the Hebrew Education Society charter. The participants in this meeting also decided to begin collecting a fund for the college; they felt that they were witnessing "the dawn of a new era for American Judaism." Among those present was Sabato Morais, who "arose and offered, in a few appropriate remarks, his services to teach any branch for which his services might be deemed efficient." Leeser followed with a similar offer. A committee of twenty-one was appointed, its members serving as trustees of the undertaking, with Mayer Sulzberger, another devoted student of Leeser, serving as one of the two secretaries of the committee. There was no explicit mention of the city in which the college was to be founded, but the implicit understanding was that it would be Philadelphia, the place where the idea had originated.[52]

Funds were not available as readily as had been anticipated. This time, however, the lay leaders showed more determination. They collected some endowment money and then turned to the Board of Delegates of American Israelites, which had been organized in 1859 as a national association of Jewish communities, to assume responsibility for the college. With such moral and financial assistance, which the other educational attempts had lacked, hope of success was high. Dropsie, Leeser, Morais, Jastrow and Sulzberger had a hand in the decision of the Board of Delegates. Other key leaders in the Philadelphia community were Abraham Hart, *parnas* of the Mikveh Israel congregation and president of the Board of Delegates, and Isidore Binswanger, a business leader who spoke with great enthusiasm at the founders' meeting in Philadelphia. Of those most active outside Philadelphia, the most important was Samuel Myer Isaacs, whose influence in the community as one of the organizers of the Board and as editor of the *Jewish Messenger* contributed greatly to the merger of New York and Philadelphia forces in favor of the undertaking. Isaacs, who was a firm supporter of Leeser throughout the years, had proclaimed the need to establish a Jewish institution of higher learning on many occasions and actually carried out a campaign in New York similar to that of Leeser.[53] On August 1, 1866, the Board of Delegates issued a circular to the presidents of all participating congregations, in which the college was described, as to its purpose, structure and place.[54]

In addition to a college fund of $5,000, established by the Board of Delegates with the participation of a number of congregations, eight resident scholarships of $300 each were announced. The Board published another circular proclaiming the opening of the institution, the names of faculty members, courses, and admission requirements.[55] The list of the faculty (a group of names which in itself defined the character of the new school) headed the announcement:

Rev. Isaac Leeser, Professor of Homiletics, Belles-Lettres and Comparative History.

Rev. S. Morais, Professor of the Bible and Biblical Literature.

Rev. Dr. M. Jastrow, Professor of Talmud, Hebrew Philosophy and Jewish History and Literature.

Rev. Dr. Bettelheim, Professor of Mishnah with Commentaries, Shulchan Aruch and Yad Ha-Chazakah.[56]

Rev. L. Buttenwieser, Professor of the Hebrew and Chaldaic languages and of the Talmud.

Those who remembered past failures could hardly believe that, despite all the obstacles which had in the past barred the way, the new venture could be realized. And before long, the critics, new and old, appeared. Jonas Bondi, editor of the *Hebrew Leader*, had long felt that the main task of such an institution should be the training of teachers and not rabbis. In Europe, he emphasized, he had proposed precisely the op-

posite, namely the training of rabbis, because teachers' seminaries were already in existence there. But in America the
first concern should be for teachers.[57] Bondi approved the
forward step taken by the Board of Delegates, but continued
to warn that the college should limit itself for some years to
the training of teachers.[58] In this connection, it is interesting
to note that Sabato Morais, even at the founding session of
the college, took the identical view. But he bowed to the
wishes of the majority, especially to those of the determined
Leeser.

Despite planning, enthusiasm and earnest leadership,
Maimonides College was not able to evoke a real interest in
the American Jewish community itself. Samuel Myer Isaacs
pleaded with his readers to extend a helping hand. He put his
finger on the real problems of the college: students, scholarships and endowment.[59] Writing in a different vein on another occasion, Isaacs added:

> Our brethren are reputed to be practical men, yet it is
> apparent that they have not judiciously met the question of
> providing a ministry for the future. . . . The sessions of
> Maimonides College have, thanks to the energy of the
> Hebrew Education Society of Philadelphia, and the in-
> defatigable attention of the able faculty, been maintained
> without interruption (save for the customary vacation) for
> eighteen months; and while the students have made most
> gratifying progress, and several eminent gentlemen have
> cheerfully accorded their valuable aid, only two congre-
> gations in the United States have agreed to sustain the effort
> by material assistance.[60]

The college had not gotten off to a good start; soon it
began to falter. Nevertheless, the founders did not lose heart.
When, however, Isaac Leeser, the organizer and leader of
Maimonides College, died, it was inevitable that the
college would have to close its doors.[61] Morais was offered
the position of provost, but refused. Jastrow took the assignment officially, but lacked the ability to keep the school alive.
Two of the three remaining students, David Levy and Marcus
Lam (the third student was Samuel Mendelsohn), left the col-

lege to take up positions in other communities, and all hope faded. The college died then and there, early in 1873, for lack of students. The official closing was two years later, when the Board of Delegates formally withdrew its support. The Hebrew Union College, under Wise's brilliant leadership, opened that year in Cincinnati, and managed to attract the aid of many in the Historical group, including Sabato Morais, the most traditional of them all.

Maimonides College had come to an end. After a brief period of existence, it was closed, having trained three students—the first three students to be prepared for the rabbinate in America.[62] In 1875, it was said, Maimonides College faded from the American scene. But did it, indeed, fade away?

Cyrus Adler, who later became a central figure in the reorganized Jewish Theological Seminary and its third president, describes how he himself was a link in the human chain of the tradition of Maimonides College: "In the same building in which the [Hebrew Education Society] school was housed, there was also carried on the work of Maimonides College, . . . and there the older students, David Levi[y] and Marcus Lam, used to carry me about on their backs . . ."[63]

What the students lovingly did for Cyrus Adler in his early years, the members of the faculty did for him and others in his adolescence and later. Adler tells in his autobiography how the pain and anguish at the failure of the college was transformed into quiet determination, which moved the former members of the faculty "to give instruction without compensation to any boy who wanted to learn." In the late seventies, without benefit of sponsorship or organization, boards or fund-raising machinery, a small coterie of Philadelphia rabbis trained a group of young scholars who, in erudition and accomplishment far outranked the three graduates of Maimonides College. The instructors were Morais, Jastrow, George Jacobs, and Samuel Hirsch, the last being one of the leading Reform rabbis in Philadelphia. Except for the Hebrew Union College, which was devoted to the training of rabbis, there was no other institution for higher Jewish learning in the United States. The students met with their teachers four evenings a week. Out of these informal classes came such leading personalities in American Jewry as Joseph Jastrow, Charles I. Hoffman, William A. Rosenau and, of course, Cyrus Adler.[64]

In this way the ideal and reality of Maimonides College lived on. Eleven years later when these men, joined by their associates in the Historical School, founded the Jewish Theological Seminary of America, they inscribed in the opening announcement of the new institution the legend that had been inscribed upon the entrance of Maimonides College: "To learn and to teach, to heed and to do." And in 1908, Louis Ginzberg published his *Geonica,* inscribing on the title page: "To the memory of Isaac Leeser, Founder of the First American College for Higher Jewish Learning, this first publication of the Jewish Theological Seminary is dedicated."

The Changing Communal Order

The middle decades of the nineteenth century marked the final passage of American Jewry from a coherent community to a diversified communal structure. In the earlier period the community had been dominated by and coextensive with the synagogue. With the growth of German immigration and the strong westward movement of Jews, the synagogue ceased to be even the center of community life. The needs of Jews in the growing cities and towns of the country were new and complex. A variety of independent institutions assumed the responsibilities for philanthropy, social welfare, aid to Jews in the Diaspora and in the Holy Land, as well as the defense of Jewish rights at home and abroad.

It is remarkable that religious leadership generally encouraged, and in many instances initiated, the processes of communal change which, after all, weakened the synagogue hegemony. The leaders understood this trend to be both desirable and inevitable. They drew a line of distinction between the spiritual needs of the individual and his family, and the requirements of the Jewish community as a whole. At a much later period, when the mass immigrations had grown even larger, community leadership was fractionalized and a distinction drawn between institutions specifically religious and communal. In the beginning, the men of the synagogue conceived it to be their responsibility as religious leaders to go beyond the synagogue and create the necessary insti-

tutions for the satisfaction of communal needs. As we trace
the role of the Historical School in the development of these
extra-synagogal institutions, we learn much about its evolving attitudes and the type of communal life it envisaged for
the Jewish group in America.

Social Welfare

When Peter Stuyvesant informed the Jews of New Amsterdam in 1655 that they might travel, trade and live there, he
made it conditional on their agreement that "the poor among
them shall not become a burden to the company or to the
community, but be supported by their own nation."[1]
Actually, neither Stuyvesant nor the Dutch West India Company had cause to worry. From earliest times Jews have never
ceased to care for their needy. Built into their communal
consciousness was the fulfilment of the biblical injunction
to not *shut thy hand from thy needy brother* (Deut. 15.7).
And as it turned out American Jewish history added another
significant chapter to a long history of Jewish philanthropic
achievement. For the student of modern Judaism, this aspect
of American Jewish life is of particular interest because, in
America, the Jewish talent for charity and communal philanthropic inventiveness has been more intensively exercised
than any other gift which the Jews as a group may possess.
It turned out to be a major contribution that American
Jewry made to American philanthropy in general. The first
voluntary type of association to be established as a permanent
charitable federation was the Associated Jewish Philanthropies of Boston in 1895. Together with other Jewish federa-
tions, this form of association became the model for the
non-sectarian community chests of the twentieth century.[2]
   The Jewish urge to give and to help one's fellows was
greatly enhanced by continuing strong emphasis on religious teachings in the American environment. Religion
was a dynamic factor in the history of American philanthropy. For example, just as general American philanthropy

in the Colonial period was "church-related," Jewish charity was synagogue-centered. During the nineteenth century most of the social welfare agencies, Christian as well as Jewish, grew out of organized religious initiative, but did not necessarily function under religious auspices. Subsequently these agencies became communal, civic, foundation or local governmental responsibilities. But, despite a continuing pattern of structural change, underlying religious teachings inspired the new as they had inspired the old. Most important, as Merle Curti has explained in his analysis of the philanthropic impulse in American life, religion in its American forms has contributed to the American *habit* of giving.[3]

In the Colonial era, the need for organized Jewish charity was negligible. The Jewish immigrant who required financial support was only in need temporarily. With the exception of the physically or mentally ill, synagogue authorities in the main Jewish communities could cope with individual requests and, within a short time, a person who once required assistance became a source of support for others. The usual practice was the establishment of a special charitable fund apart from the synagogue treasury but distributed by the synagogue leaders as a communal service. The first charitable institution in New York, named Kalfe Zedakah Matan Baseter (Charity Funds, "Anonymous Gifts"), was organized at the Shearith Israel congregation in 1798 by its *hazzan*, Gershom M. Seixas.[4] The seeds of civic philanthropic responsibility on the part of the lay leaders of various American religious groups were also planted in that early period. A striking example of Jewish initiative was Mordecai Sheftall, a leader of the Mikva Israel congregation in Savannah, who served as president of the Union Society (*Union* applying to "opposites in modes of worship") founded in 1750, probably the first type of civic philanthropic cooperation in the United States.

The situation remained basically unchanged until the 1840s, when an unprecedented number of obligations fell upon the Jewish community. From then on, those who participated in the creation of hospitals, orphanages, loan societies,

and aid for the widow, immigrant and indigent, did so as individuals rather than as officials of religious organizations.
In the course of time the influence of the synagogues on the
organizations which they had helped to found began to wane.[5]
Names, like habits, linger on. It is interesting to recall that
many charitable societies, originally organized by synagogues,
kept the names of parent organizations even after their functions were changed and they became independent. Moreover,
the slow detachment of these organizations from the synagogue structure did not mean that the individual members
of the synagogue had to relinquish their interest in and responsibility to communal social welfare. In the administration
of charity, for example, lay leaders and rabbis of congregations began to shoulder a double responsibility: to the
synagogues and to the new institutions. Marcus Jastrow once
said about Sabato Morais that he was associated with every
Jewish charitable organization in Philadelphia, either as
founder, administrator, or supporter. This applied to most of
the rabbis in America. With no Jewish public centers, the
rabbis' homes served instead. In the spirit of *blessed be he that
cometh in the name of the Lord* (Psalms 118.26), they kept
their doors open so that the poor would always be welcome.[6]

Also significant in the transition affecting Jewish welfare
agencies, was that even when a union of charitable societies
was created most such organizations were local and municipal
rather than national in character. The maxim that "charity
begins at home" (the counterpart of the talmudic injunction,
"The poor of your own city take precedence") was quite literally carried out: each city cared for its own poor. Unlike educational institutions and religious movements which came to
be organized nationally, social services remained provincial.
On the other hand institutions for social welfare grew out
of self-evident necessity, without having to suffer the debates
which hindered other enterprises. Whenever an institution
hit on some new method for charitable work, it was imitated
and adopted by other cities. The widest field of agreement
throughout Jewish life was reached in philanthropy.

Jewish Hospitals and Orphanages

Before Jewish hospitals had come into being, the Jewish sick were received by Christian hospitals where, frequently, zealous Christian missionaries baptized dying patients who had no relatives to "save" them. Thus the builders of Jewish hospitals in three cities (Cincinnati, Philadelphia and Baltimore) explained the need for such hospitals on the grounds that the Christians attempted to convert the sick to their faith, and that a Jew could die in such hospitals without the presence of a coreligionist.

Leeser was one of the first to agitate for a Jewish hospital in Philadelphia. This position, which he adopted in 1864, represented a change from his previous viewpoint.[7] He had originally opposed any "squandering of money" for purposes other than those of an educational nature. But when he saw that the hospitals were furnishing an opportunity for missionary enterprise, he advocated the building of Jewish hospitals. There were some men, like Bernard Felsenthal, the Zionist Reform rabbi of Chicago, who took issue with this stand. Felsenthal urged that it would be a waste of money to build Jewish hospitals when Jewish wards in general hospitals could easily solve the problem.[8] Exclusiveness on the part of Jews, he reasoned, would lead their Christian neighbors to behave similarly. A Jewish kitchen in the ward might resolve the existing difficulties.

Leeser opposed this solution as too facile. He argued that Jews would still have to submit to general regulations prevalent in these hospitals and that total Jewish ministration would be denied them. *Kashrut* was a specific example:

> We are well aware that these laws are sadly neglected in everyday life, and that many in health pay no attention to their food, holding everything permitted. But this is no excuse for making it obligatory on those suffering in body and mind to eat what is prohibited, by sending them to institutions where it is impossible to obtain permitted things.[9]

The danger of exclusiveness could be met, it was agreed by the advocates of Jewish hospitals, by following the Jewish teaching that "for the sake of peace" all those who are sick should be visited, not only one's own. When the Jewish hospital of Philadelphia was founded, the following inscription, expressing the ancient dictum in a contemporary American idiom, was placed at the entrance: "This hospital was erected by the voluntary contributions of the Israelites of Philadelphia and is dedicated to the relief of the sick and wounded without regard to color, creed and nationality."

In New York, the leading members of congregations Shearith Israel and Shaaray Tefila, under the leadership of Sampson Simson and with the assistance of Samuel Myer Isaacs, concerned themselves with the same problem. In 1852, they organized the "Jewish Hospital in the City of New York."[10] The plot for the hospital building was received from Simson. A board of nine members was appointed to direct the hospital, and membership in the supporting association cost five dollars. The laws of *Kashrut* were scrupulously observed as were other religious duties insofar as such observance was practicable. The organizational form of this institution illustrates that of other Jewish hospitals founded at the same time.

It was not only the physically ill, however, who were in need of help. Widows and orphans also needed aid. Jews, whom the Talmud likes to call "the compassionate, the descendants of the compassionate," concerned themselves with such problems as reflected their traditional generosity of spirit. Once again the work was not developed in a systematically planned fashion. But time and experience helped introduce order. While there are earlier Jewish charitable organizations, the first incorporated Jewish charitable organization in continuous existence in the United States (founded in 1801) was the Hebrew Orphan Society of Charleston. In the official act of incorporation the Society was called Abi Yetomim Ubne Ebyonim, or Society for the Relief of Orphans and Children of Indigent Parents.[11] In its earlier years, the Society did not run an orphanage; but as the needs of the children grew more urgent, a home was built.

Such was the practice in other cities as well. In Philadelphia, Rebecca Gratz and Isaac Leeser worked jointly and in 1855 established the Jewish Foster Home of Philadelphia with the following purpose, stated in the preamble:

... Wherein orphans, or the children of indigent Israelites, may be rescued from the evils of ignorance and vice, comfortably provided for, instructed in moral and religious duties, and thus prepared to become useful members of the community.[12]

After a time, however, Leeser, observing unexpected defects in the orphans' home, arrived at a very progressive conclusion which became a fundamental concept in later social work—to provide board and lodging for orphans in private homes at the expense of the community. In that way, orphans would be brought up in the congenial atmosphere of a family, knowing the love of a father and mother, and they would therefore become normal, healthy individuals, good citizens and good Jews. There was much that was considered radical in Leeser's proposal. It is hardly surprising that the suggestion was not adopted immediately. Meanwhile, orphans' homes similar to the one in Philadelphia were founded in New York, New Orleans, Baltimore, Cleveland and San Francisco.

Absorbing the New Immigrants

A most persistent problem in those years was immigrant absorption. Wave after wave of immigrants continued to come to America, seeking relief from the revolutions that had shattered their homes and a share in the promise of the New World. It was a national American problem. During the decades of 1840-60, approximately 200,000 newcomers arrived from Europe each year.

The American Jewish community experienced, for the first time, what was to become a permanent aspect of communal life until 1924—the unending problem of mass immigrant

absorption. During the Colonial period and up to the 1840s,
Jewish immigration was a personal sort of immigration, each
individual's and isolated family's arrival motivated by a private decision. In 1836, following the Bavarian control-of-
marriage law and other economic and personal status restrictions, the Jews of that province and other German provinces
began the process of Jewish "mass emigration" to the United
States. By "mass emigration," to use Nathan Glazer's formulation, is meant "a movement of whole families and groups
of families, from a single locality or country, owing to influences which affect an entire community, and the individual
through the community."[13]

To some extent emigration was stimulated. Now and again,
after the Napoleonic Wars, individuals, ship agents and large
city newspapers in the United States published "Invitations
to America" and plans for the amalgamation of European
Jews into American life. In Europe various organizations
were founded, such as the *Nordamerikanische Kolonisations-
gesellschaft* in Stuttgart.[14] A movement developed on the
Continent to help those who ventured to leave, since the
transportation of families and whole segments of communities required master-planning at the points of origin. The
Cleveland Plain Dealer reported in 1846 that "a large number of Jews recently left Germany for the U.S. A German
paper says they exhibited a very different appearance from
the squalid poor that usually emigrate to this country. Ele-
gant carriages conveyed them to the place of embark-
ation . . ."[15] We know from other sources that the entire community that stayed behind usually participated in the preparations for a farewell, contributing something for the trip.
A small pocket-size prayer book, dated 1842, offers further
evidence of the spiritual blessings that were sent along. Published in Fuerth, the book's title page reads: "Prayers for the
whole year . . . for those who travel by land and for those who
cross the seas, for the voyagers to the land of America, may
Heaven protect them!"[16]

In truth, the immigrants needed their prayers as much
as their stocks of clothing and personal effects. Upon arrival,

תפלה

מכל השנה

מנחה קטנה

לטולכי דרך ולעוברי ימים להנוסעים

למדינת אמעריקא יע"א

אייגע מיניאטור אויזגאבע

אויף פיינער פערל שריפט.

פיורדא

בשנת תרט"ז לפ"ק

Verlag von S. B. Gusdorfer.

Druck von Zürndorffer & Sommer

in Fürth. 5615.

even their most elementary need—shelter—was lacking. The
Jewish community in the United States was the least prepared of all to cope with this tidal wave. All it could do was
to respond instinctively to human need. And it did. Numerous *ad hoc* agencies sprang up, most of them organized by the
congregations. The watchword was *benevolence,* the American translation of Simeon the Righteous' third principle for
world order: *Gemilut Hesed* (lovingkindness). There were
Hebrew Benevolent Societies and German Benevolent Societies, Female Hebrew Benevolent Societies and Bachelors'
Hebrew Benevolent Societies, Young Ladies' and Young
Mens' Benevolent Societies—all established to serve the immigrant.[17]

The major task of these societies was to help the new immigrant adjust to his new conditions: to disembark, to be
supplied with clothes, to find shelter and work and be introduced to American life. But these organizations did not always succeed in achieving their goals. They were staffed
primarily by inexperienced volunteers. Even worse, a benevolent society often came into existence not so much for the
benefit of those in need as for the social prestige of the organizers of the society. Invariably, reports of the work gave more
space to listing and congratulating the solicitors than to explaining the pressing needs which brought the society into
existence.

The synagogues associated with the Historical School did
their share in the communal effort. Several approaches
evolved, not necessarily mutually exclusive, for the amelioration of the immigrants' dilemma. Some men, like Sabato
Morais, preferred to concentrate on their private projects to
fulfill the *mitzvah be-gufo*—to help directly and personally;
others (for example, the lay leaders of the three synagogues
in New York) suggested the coordination and expansion of
the various synagogue charity bodies already in existence to
meet the emergency; still others (for example, Leeser and his
followers) looked beyond the immediate crisis and saw in the
new social situation an opportunity to strengthen the grow-

ing American Jewish community by the creation of fundamental and far-reaching programs.

Within the synagogue itself, most of the work properly fell
to the rabbi. A good example of the personal relations developed by a rabbi in this type of activity may be found in
the work of Sabato Morais. In one of his letters to the members of the congregation, Morais explains that poverty is on
the increase in the city of Philadelphia. He therefore requests
that they

> appropriate a sum, which they may deem sufficient, author-
> izing one or two persons in whom they place confidence,
> to investigate all cases which are brought under their no-
> tice so that after having ascertained as far as human knowl-
> edge can, the deserts of the applicants, they may grant the
> latter such means as, while saving them from destitution,
> may enable them at the same time to pursue their calling
> reputably.[18]

The board gave him a sum of $300, supplementary to the
regular allocations, as "a special poor purse placed at the disposal of the Hazan, to bestow as he may deem proper."[19] This
is perhaps the first recorded instance of the rabbi's charity
fund which has become part of synagogue life today; and
Morais' action was an important first move to consolidate
charitable work in the community of Philadelphia. In another
letter to the congregation, Morais details some of his dis-
bursements: tools for gainful employment, goods for trade,
rented quarters for those who could not work because of the
difficult winter, clothes for the children, medical attention
for the ill.[20]

Consoling as such personal attention was to the needy, a
community clearly could not depend on individual practi-
tioners of charity. Nor were the funds ample. In New York,
in 1837, even before the larger flood of immigrants came
upon the city, the lay leadership of its three congregations—
Shearith Israel, B'nai Jeshurun and Anshe Chesed—formed
a joint committee of the Hebrew Benevolent Societies in connection with their respective synagogues. Anticipating the
sums of money needed to meet the arrival of many immigrants

"now on their way to this country, and mostly bound for the port of New York," they cited the verse in Deuteronomy (15.11): *Open thy hand wide unto thy brother, to thy poor, and to thy needy, in thy land.*[21]

Leeser, for his part, did not believe in temporary measures. He sought basic solutions. At first he called for a better system by removing the responsibility from individual congregations. Leeser also made additional suggestions which have become basic principles in social work today. He pointed to the anarchy that reigned in the distribution of money—too much being given at one place, too little at another. He demanded a central agency that would properly distribute the funds and keep accurate records of its transactions.[22] He detailed the plan of an endowment fund for charitable purposes and the nationalization of the service agencies.[23] On his initiative the United Jewish Charities was organized in the city of Philadelphia. In addition, Leeser encouraged the establishment of free loan societies; he insisted above all, in the spirit of Maimonides' rules of philanthropy, that the individuality of the poor must not be thwarted. The money given to the immigrant had to be for the purpose of enabling him to help establish himself economically.

In spite of all efforts, poverty and overcrowding grew in the cities. The problem of immigrant aid ceased to be local and became national in scope. Jews were often deprecated as nomads who did not know how to work the land. And older residents feared the establishment of ghettos in the Jewish neighborhoods of the larger cities. As a result, the more progressive leaders—long before the Galveston and the Industrial Removal projects—began to work out basic plans for the removal of immigrants from cities to the towns and villages of America. Some thought was given to the development of agricultural settlements. A rural population, it was felt, could more rigorously observe the Sabbath and lead a higher moral life than people in the cities. This mood fitted well with the general idealization of rural life which was part of progressive nineteenth-century thought. In the course of time, it was hoped that Jews would be able to establish small independent settlements which would be model communities in the western hemisphere. The ever-active Leeser, who was very much in favor of agricultural settlement for the Jews, nevertheless was among the chief opponents of the idea of establishing exclusive Jewish colonies in the United States. He believed that Jews must live within the general framework of the American economy and society like any other religious group. He was opposed to special Jewish settlements such as the one called Ararat which had been the suggestion of Mordecai Noah. Leeser felt that Jews should associate with, influence and be influenced by their Christian neighbors; although it would be well, from the viewpoint of Jewish life, he added, if the Jews could constitute a majority in some of these communities.[24]

A leading propagandist for the idea of Jewish agricultural settlements in the United States was Simon Berman, who came to America in 1852 and interested Raphall and Leeser, as well as a number of laymen, in his enterprise. Dr. Raphall agreed to call an organizational meeting at his home in order to discuss these problems. Berman proposed that a society for Jewish agricultural settlement in New York be established and function on the basis of 2,000 subscriptions at $25 each, in addition to higher individual contributions. He also urged that an influential member of the Jewish community lend his name and prestige to the organization. In a book published in Europe in which he pictures Raphall as the "most famous and esteemed preacher in all of America," Berman described the vicissitudes encountered by his plan, which was not carried out.[25] Berman left New York and did not return until 1860. Again a meeting was called in the home of Dr. Raphall and it was decided to organize a board of directors. These decisions, too, came to nothing.[26]

Many attempts at agricultural settlement were made in this period, but none was sustained. The settlements slowly declined and ultimately disappeared. Not until the twentieth century, with the organization of the Jewish Agricultural Society, did farming take hold of the imagination of small groups of American Jews, and even then, with limited success.

Overseas Aid and Activities for Eretz Yisrael

If the Jews of America felt an obligation toward the needy among their brethren, this sense of responsibility embraced primarily those who had emigrated to this country. Most of the Jewish communities overseas were well organized and continued to care for their poor as in the past. Even in Russia, where the internal authority of the communal Jewish councils had been weakened by the Russian government, the Jews supported a network of communal Jewish institutions through supplementary taxes, in addition to those they paid to the government. The Jewish community in America, too, was fully occupied with the problems of its own growth. Small Jewish communities here had to be considered first.

Special requests from Europe did elicit a response now and then, such as the appeal of Jews College in London for support in 1857. S. M. Isaacs, the *hazzan* of Shaaray Tefila, who was of English origin, came to its aid. But such requests were quite infrequent. More often, appeals came from the Jewish settlements in North Africa, the Middle East and the Far East. From time to time, these foreign communities dispatched messengers who traveled throughout the United States. Such activity was not centrally organized: the messengers were satisfied to obtain small contributions and then proceed on their way. The Jewish communities in China, however, were exceptional. The attempts of missionaries to convert the few Jews remaining in China were discussed at public meetings in this country. In his monthly magazine, Leeser published information about the situation as described by missionaries and the sums which the missionaries spent for their work. He pleaded that Jews send representatives to "Judaize" the few remaining Jewish Chinese. He contemplated a mission to China and other parts of Asia and Africa:

> We hear much of the misery of our people in many lands, of their sorrows in Africa, of their hardships in Palestine, of their persecution in Persia, where many have become compulsory Mahomedans, of the oppression in Russia, where many have been driven to acknowledge the Christian faith by an outward profession, which the tyrant of Muscovia renders irrevocable; but they all, to our views, are of less immediate weight than the absolute helplessness of the Chinese Jews, that handful of the faithful in the centre of half-civilized heathen, ready as are the missionaries of various denominations to rob them of the little remnant of their everlasting hopes . . . How delighted should we be to learn that some adventurous pious youth had started on the mission of mercy to carry instruction and a renewal of hope to our brothers in China.[27]

His suggestions succeeded, for a while, in arousing some interest. A Hebrew Foreign Mission Society was organized in 1853 and, as might have been expected, the first substantial contribution came from Judah Touro.[28] Lack of contact and continuing purposefulness soon forced the group out of existence.[29]

While the Jews of America could not cope with urgent requests from the distant communities of world Jewry, appeals from the Holy Land fell into another category entirely. The love and dedication of generations had its effect even upon people who were culturally and geographically far removed from Palestine. Printed circulars in Hebrew had found their way to responsive Jews in Colonial times and direct contact with the Holy Land increased as the Jews in America grew in number and strength.[30]

Members of the Historical School occupied a very important place in all kinds of activity for the benefit of Eretz Yisrael. Some were motivated by the traditional belief in the coming of the Messiah, while others were moved by the desire to provide a place of refuge for those leaving Europe.[31] During this period questions connected with the transmission and distribution of money to Eretz Yisrael (rather than with social and political implications for the restoration of the Jews in the Holy Land) aroused the greatest interest. Mordecai Noah's political formulation of America's role in any possible Restoration was still in the nature of a "discourse." The problem at hand was to give practical aid to the residents in Zion. Any Jew of the Diaspora, whether religious or not, felt it incumbent upon himself to give financial support to the communities in Jerusalem. Whoever appealed on their behalf was not turned away. And such appeals were not lacking.

The settlements in Jerusalem had sent representatives to the United States as far back as the eighteenth century. Among the first of these were Moses Malki (1759) and Hayyim Isaac Carigal (1771). Their success stimulated others. In their wake came many frauds and swindlers who proceeded to appropriate for themselves the money they had collected. Furthermore, echoes of the disputes about the division of the sums collected reached America. Sephardim quarreled with Ashkenazim and Ashkenazim among themselves. In addition, Jews in America began to realize that the salaries of the solicitors and the expenses of their journeys were deducted from the contributions, resulting in losses to the inhabitants of Jerusalem. American Jews, not wishing to see their money squandered and attempting to secure transfer of all the collected money, organized the *Hebrah Terumat ha-Kodesh* (Society for Offerings to the Sanctuary) in 1833 under the presidency of Israel B. Kursheedt, one of the outstanding figures of congregation B'nai Jeshurun in New York City. The purpose of this society was to make annual collections among its members and then transfer the money directly to the inhabitants of the "four holy cities": Jerusalem, Hebron, Safed and Tiberias. In this way they hoped to put an end to the unnecessary expenditures of various solicitors. When a sizable sum had been collected, it was transmitted directly to Rabbi Hirsch Lehren, the original founder of *Hebrah Terumat ha-Kodesh* in Amsterdam, who was to transfer and allocate the monies at his discretion.

In time of peace it might have been possible to supply all

needs from European sources, without resort to aid from the United States. But when revolutionary disturbances engulfed European Jewry, collections failed. The revolutionary years of 1848-49 in Europe substantially reduced the contributions of European Jews for Eretz Yisrael. Once again, the Jews of Eretz Yisrael turned to their coreligionists in free and peaceful America. Two messengers, Joseph Schwarz and Zadok Levy, were dispatched in 1849. Joseph Schwarz was the first modern scholar of Palestinography whose works are still consulted. Isaac Leeser translated his first volume into English in 1850 and called it *Descriptive Geography and Brief Historical Sketch of Palestine*. The two distinguished emissaries were welcomed by the eager American leaders. Their mission, according to Isaac Leeser's testimony, was to help set up a society which would collect annual contributions. Leeser explained that, unlike the situation of 1833 when the *Hebrah Terumat ha-Kodesh* had been organized, "communication by steam-packets has made every country easily accessible, and commercial connexions have now been formed all over the world, so that remittance can be made promptly from here to Palestine, in a manner formerly impossible."[32] The two messengers issued proclamations in the name of the inhabitants of Jerusalem. Leeser calculated that, if each of the forty organized congregations in the country were to contribute from ten to twenty-five dollars annually, it would be possible "to protect the poor of Palestine, and to snatch them from the necessity of receiving aid from the missionaries, those inveterate foes of our religion."[33] He announced the formation of a committee of eight that would receive donations.[34] But the proposal by Leeser and his friends was not realized for two reasons. First, the Jews of America were not yet experienced in the collection of funds. Therefore they responded to immediate needs instead of planning for the future. Second, each faction in Eretz Yisrael felt it necessary to protect its own interests by sending its own messengers.

In the same year, 1849, Rabbi Aaron Selig Ashkenazi, a representative of the chief Ashkenazi group who called them-

selves the *Perushim* of Jerusalem, arrived in America. Rabbi
Ashkenazi, systematic and enterprising, succeeded in rallying wide support although many forces on the American
Jewish scene were opposed to his method of operation. One
of his main achievements was to attract Samuel Myer Isaacs
to his project. Leeser, who was generally opposed to the system of messengers, agreed to aid Ashkenazi's mission only on
condition that all the money collected would be transferred
to Sir Moses Montefiore in London, while Ashkenazi himself would receive limited funds for his own expenses.

In the course of time, Isaacs became the mainstay of all
efforts on behalf of Eretz Yisrael and was held responsible
for this work by the American Jewish congregations. He was
in constant correspondence with Moses Montefiore, with
whom, as an English Jew, Isaacs felt a special sense of kin-
ship. Isaacs transferred the funds to him for distribution.
Before long, Isaacs began to investigate carefully the private
affairs of the messengers, a step which Ashkenazi disapproved
of. Isaacs complained about the disproportionate expenses
of the messengers, and in the *Asmonean* of the 26th of April,
1850, he announced:

> Notice is hereby given. To the Presidents and Members
> of the various Societies organized throughout the United
> States, in support of the mission of Rabbi Aaron Selig for
> the Poor of the Holy Land, *not* to pay any *monies* what-
> ever either to Messengers or through any channel except
> through the only accredited agents (Isaacs, Noah and
> Micholl).[35]

But Rabbi Ashkenazi did not rest either. Instead of opposing Isaacs publicly, he sought a device to win power from
the hands of his opponents and at the same time benefit his
mission. He transferred the presidency of the committee
that was to receive funds from Isaacs to Morris Raphall who
had just arrived from London, and whom he knew to be a
person active in such overseas matters. But Raphall, as a new-
comer, did not understand the motives behind this scheme,
and accepted the presidency.

Isaacs, however, did see through these machinations and they angered him. He felt himself responsible neither to Rabbi Ashkenazi nor to any messenger—but to the Jews of Eretz Yisrael, the beneficiaries of the aid, and to the Jews of America, its donors. In order to make sure that not a trace of misunderstanding was left, he announced his intentions in public:

> The system of encouraging messengers from the East has, for years, been productive of evil; it has fostered mendicancy, it has destroyed harmony, and robbed the poor pilgrims of hope, located on Holy Ground, of a portion of the liberal means the Jews of America contribute towards their support. It cannot be too generally known, nor too widely disseminated, that a fourth part of the sums collected by messengers, swells the pockets of the employed, exclusive of his travelling expenses and what he gathers on his own private account . . . Urged thereto by some valued friends in Europe, I have devoted my time to the subject, and have transmitted large sums to the houses of Montefiore and Lehren. In all cases requiring the amount to be distributed amongst *all* the poor, instead of fostering sectional feelings, the result has been highly advantageous to the recipients, no expense is incurred in the transmission, and the poor man obtains the whole of his due. Let us then urge congregations to *discountenance all messengers*.[36]

Isaacs' firm stand and strong statement brought about an improvement. Members of the Historical School, a majority of the congregations in New York and in Philadelphia, participated in a meeting in New York. Their purpose was to decide the division of the money in the future.[37] The main spokesmen were Isaacs and Leeser. In charitable matters for Eretz Yisrael, to adapt a talmudic view, they deemed direct work preferable to work through intermediaries. It was therefore clear from the outset that the inhabitants of Israel would gain if the expenses of the messengers were eliminated.

Plans for systematization had little effect. Somehow the Jewish public could not be made to fulfill its obligations to the indigent of Eretz Yisrael without hearing the pathetic and heartrending accounts of the messengers as they described the poverty and suffering. Nevertheless, in 1854, Isaacs succeeded in collecting a fund of $5,000 for the relief of famine-stricken areas in Eretz Yisrael. One year earlier he had organized the North American Relief Society for Indigent Jews in Jerusalem and Palestine, of which he became treasurer. The Society benefited from bequests by Judah Touro to the sum of $10,000 which, when invested, yielded an annual income of $700. This sum was sent directly to Jerusalem. A contribution by Moses Montefiore was added to the income from Touro's legacy. With this money a row of houses for the poor was built in 1860 outside the Old City's wall, thus creating the first residential quarter of the new Jerusalem, Yemin Moshe.

It is therefore no surprise that the various settlements of Eretz Yisrael continued to send messengers in an attempt to stimulate the generosity of American Jews. In 1861, Abraham Nissan Ashkenazi was dispatched. Isaacs and Raphall, the loyal old friends of the cause of Eretz Yisrael, though pained by the failure of their ideas for better organization, could not, as faithful supporters of the Jewish settlement, withhold their help. Despite the economic depression which hit America on the eve of the Civil War, many rallied to the cause. Isaacs' weekly publication, the *Jewish Messenger,* was an important vehicle for bringing the mission of Ashkenazi to public attention. But when Isaacs saw that Ashkenazi was conducting himself as others had previously, he pleaded with him to leave America and once more tried to establish a central organization. And again his effort was unsuccessful.

In 1867 the Jews of America witnessed a significant development in requests from Palestine. A group of twelve persons, former American Jews who had settled in Eretz Yisrael, complained that neither the German nor the Russian Jews wanted to give them a single cent of the money that had been received from America. They further complained that the Jews of the United States had no knowledge of the existence of an American Jewish settlement in Jerusalem.

The American consul in Jerusalem, Victor Beauboucher, sent the following letter to Rabbi Max Lilienthal in Cincinnati and Samuel Isaacs in New York:

> The number of American Jews residing in Jerusalem is very limited, a dozen altogether; but these unfortunates are the most miserable of all and do not receive pecuniary succor from any one, the German committees never having given a cent, and those of America perhaps do not know them at all.
>
> I have done all I could to relieve these poor people ever since two years that I am in Palestine: and seeing their increasing misery, I this day address myself to you, in order that something may be done in their favor by the Committee of which you are a member.
>
> One of them, Benjamin Lilienthal, whom I know as an honest man, left yesterday for the States, and will be able orally to make to you the lamentable narration of the position of his co-religionists and fellow-citizens in Palestine. I have remitted to him the necessary recommendations for the success of his travel, and beg you to receive him with the attention due to a good and honest father of a family . . .[38]

Every aspect of America-Eretz Yisrael relations reveals how deeply involved the Historical School was in the destiny of Jerusalem. Not only the rabbis, but also the members of their congregations, aided each new enterprise and were among its organizers. In addition to their endeavors to supply the perennial needs of the inhabitants of Jerusalem, they were concerned with the long-range development of the Jewish settlement in Eretz Yisrael. Many of the appeals of Leeser and Isaacs expressed the hope that the day would come when Jerusalem would be so firmly established that it could care for its own needs and redeem itself by its own efforts. The members of the Historical School did not believe that Eretz Yisrael could be rebuilt without hard, exhausting labor. In the eleventh volume of the *Occident* (1853-4), Leeser wrote three basic articles about Eretz Yisrael. In them he discussed the possibility of agricultural development of the land. He wished to see the inhabitants of Jerusalem as farmers, vine-growers and workers of the soil. He was therefore very happy when Gershom Kursheedt, president of the Society for Offerings of the Sanctuary and the executor of Touro's will in matters connected with Eretz Yisrael, returned from the Holy Land and gave an account of the position of manual labor there. The widespread opinion, he said, that manual labor was not acceptable to the Palestinian Jews, was erroneous. On the basis of this information, Leeser proposed that the workers in Israel begin to build their own institutions: libraries, hospitals and the like. From the profit made in this way, they could conceivably expand their building activities. He wrote:

> Let it not be imagined that Palestine even now is what it was twenty years ago; on the contrary, many changes for the better have taken place already, and the arts of European civilization, and the requirements, luxuries and comforts attending them, are gradually making their way, at least in Jerusalem.[39]

Leeser wanted to see the establishment of agricultural settlements in Eretz Yisrael. The Jews of the diaspora ought not to go to Israel to die in the Holy Land or to live on charity. The aged and the sick should not be sent, but rather those who were able to work. At the time Isaacs and Raphall were attempting, in the face of apathy, to collect money for the needy in the Holy Land, Leeser began to work in other directions. In 1853 he supported the effort of Moses Sachs to organize an agricultural settlement in Jaffa. He served as president of the central committee in America whose aim was to collect a fund for the support of this undertaking. Isaacs followed his colleague and presently he, too, writing in various articles, began to demand that those who were actively working for the support of Eretz Yisrael should be more interested in contributions to agricultural funds than in charitable aid. He appeared before the Board of Delegates with such a proposal, and was also largely responsible for convincing the Board of Delegates to apportion a fund for an agricultural school in Jaffa.[40]

What moved the builders of the Historical School in the United States to such intensive efforts on behalf of the Jewish settlement in Eretz Yisrael? The foundation of their belief in the Restoration is, of course, expressed in the Tradition which they taught their generation. Certainly ample consideration had been given to the prospects of such a "Return," not only in Jewish circles but also in Christian religious groups. A characteristic volume was Ethan Smith's *View of the Hebrews,* "exhibiting the destruction of Jerusalem; the certain restoration of Judah and Israel. . . ." Published in 1823 in Poultney, Vermont, it answered with an unqualified Yes the question whether the Jews were literally to be restored to Palestine.

Echoes of the same practical hopes, from a geopolitical viewpoint, also were heard in those days. W. H. Lynch, U.S.N., Commander of a United States Expedition to the River Jordan and the Dead Sea in 1847-48, included a political prognosis in his naval report:

> The Muhammedan rule, that political sirocco, which withers all before it, is fast losing the fierce energy which was its peculiar characteristic, and the world is being gradually prepared for the final dismemberment of the Ottoman Empire.
>
> It needs but the destruction of that power which, for so many centuries, has rested like an incubus upon the eastern world, to ensure the restoration of the Jews to Palestine.[41]

In this context, one can better understand Mordecai Noah's famous *Discourse on the Restoration of the Jews,* which he delivered in 1844 before an audience diverse in background and religious faith. Having suffered a stunning defeat in 1825 when he tried to found a city of refuge for the Jews on Grand Island, near Buffalo, New York, Noah came to understand, as did Theodor Herzl almost a half century later, that only Eretz Yisrael would be acceptable as the Homeland of the Jewish People. There they could gather once again to fulfill the ancient prophecy of the Return.

Leeser, too, slowly came to embrace the conviction that the dream of the Return was a practical reality. Beginning as a practitioner of charity for the needy in the Holy Land, he moved on to a more constructive program. He began to consider the twofold goal which was much later to be defined as Zionism: the practical building of Eretz Yisrael as the home of the Jews, and the dedication of the Land to the spiritual and cultural regeneration of the entire Jewish people, in the Diaspora as well as in Eretz Yisrael. His words, haltingly but surely, point the direction which the Historical School took in later decades:

> Will this dream be speedily realized? We cannot tell indeed; events occasionally creep slowly over the face of the world; but at other times they rush rapidly forward, and one great development follows closely on the heels of the other. The same may be the case with the now apparently distant restoration of Israelites to Palestine. . . . Is it then so unlikely that an effort will be made to place in Palestine and the countries immediately north, south, and east of it an enterprising race, which shall keep it as a highway of all nations, and thus prevent the occupation of it by any great power, to become a clog to the commerce of the world? . . . whereas, possessed by Israelites, feeble as they would be politically, disinclined to control others if they even could, it would be a highway of nations, and men could meet there to exchange the products of all climates in perfect security, and without injury to any other land or government . . . One thing is certain, whether our views be realized or not, whether speedily or tardily, that it is no silly wish for us to pray for a national restoration, if we have any love for the triumphant though peaceful rule of our religion over our people, and to free them from the moral and physical yoke which will necessarily rest upon us, while we have a permanent home nowhere.[42]

As we review the thoughts and actions of the members of the Historical School regarding Eretz Yisrael, we learn about their understanding of Judaism as well as their understanding of Zion. The Return to Zion was integral to their Judaism. Moreover, they had an unusual insight into the American spiritual tradition with respect to Zion. They knew that every American regarded himself as possessing a portion in Zion, and that the dream of the Restoration was part of the thought-pattern of America. As America was a highway of peoples, so the Holy Land, in the age of a third Jewish Commonwealth, could become, to use Leeser's phrase again, a "highway of nations."

Civil Rights

The areas of social welfare and overseas aid were not the only ones that required extra-synagogal initiative and coordination. The need for new communal structures became manifest, in a special sense, through the questions of civil rights at home and abroad. For the first time, however, in 1859, the transfer of responsibility from the synagogue culminated in the organization of an authoritative national body—the Board of Delegates of American Israelites. The members of the Historical School played a leading role in the formation of this significant union. We can learn a good deal about their views of America and Jewish life in America by describing their part in the total effort.

During the period under discussion, the Jews of America came to realize that even in free America it was necessary to guard and defend their rights. From its beginning this country had taken care to mark the boundaries between government and religion. The Constitution guaranteed personal liberty and freedom of religious expression for each citizen. But liberty is one thing, equality another. Liberty could be granted; equality had to be achieved. In times of dominant states' rights, national governmental intent was not always realized in local situations, especially when the "spiritual conscience" of the general citizenry was involved.

Such a cleavage existed between federal design and state laws in the domain of religious freedom. Many Americans believed that the United States was a Christian country and that, therefore, Christianity in its Protestant form should rule supreme in America.[43] Some wished to give explicit legal recognition to Christianity. In 1864, the Presbyterians, meeting in Cincinnati, suggested to Congress that it proclaim the United States "officially" a Christian country. Although all attempts failed to amend the laws of America to recognize the divinity of Jesus and to recognize Christianity as the religion of the country, prejudice brought about discrimination in law as it was practiced. After years of unceasing labor, Jews succeeded in erasing discriminatory statutes, but they did not always succeed in changing the sentiments of many Christians.

Most Jewish factions worked together in defense of Jewish rights. The first task was to wipe out discriminatory legislation in the states where such laws still existed. These laws were remnants of Colonial days. Some states, such as New Hampshire and North Carolina, maintained that only Christians were permitted to hold public office. Isaac Leeser published a letter on this subject in one of Philadelphia's newspapers:

. . . It is a melancholy fact, that in North Carolina, one of the original thirteen States, and the one which claims to have shed the first blood in its resistance to British aggression, and to have put forth the first declaration of independence from the mother country, the principle of universal equality of all religious persuasions has not yet been acknowledged. Are you perhaps aware, Mr. Editor, that one of our persuasion cannot hold any office of profit or trust in North Carolina? It seems hard to be believed, but still it is so, though it is not quite four years that the writer of this, having asserted the fact in an address which he was called on to deliver before a mixed audience of Christians and Israelites, could scarcely obtain credence that so unjust a clause existed in the organic law of the State. Investigation, however, proved, that Israelites, for no other reason than their profession of faith, were excluded from all political offices of profit in the Old North State, as it is so generally called, while there is but another in the whole Union where a similar disqualification exists, and this is New Hampshire. The same was also the case formerly in Maryland and Massachusetts; but in these states amendments have been engrafted on their constitutions removing the obnoxious clauses.

The idea that America was a Christian country also prevailed in American education. It was debated whether to
introduce reading of the Christian version of the Scriptures
as a subject of study in the public schools. The clergy were in
the vanguard of those who demanded its inclusion. Jews opposed it, especially when they saw that Christians would not
be satisfied with the reading of the Hebrew Scriptures but
would also attempt to teach the New Testament. Marcus
Jastrow discussed these proposals from the point of view of the
general American public:

> ... Religion and Government, or, to use the current terms,
> Church and State, in order to remain pure and free, each
> in its own dominion, must be kept separate from one an-
> other, and naturally guard themselves against intrusion.
> ... To keep political government free and pure, it must
> beware of making religion the handmaid or the handmill
> to grind its corn ...
>
> Let us guard the border lines which the framers of our
> Constitution have drawn, and recall to the memory of
> both neighbors the warning, "Do not remove thy neigh-
> bor's landmark which they of old time have set in thine
> inheritance." Attempts at displacing these landmarks have
> been made in our Country from time to time. They have
> been unsuccessful thus far. The plans to Christianize the
> Constitution and secularize Religion were shattered on
> the rock of the people's sound political sense which refuses
> to turn to folly again.

The Sunday Laws, by which the State undertook to enforce
the Christian Sabbath, were the most irksome example of the
tie between Church and State. How is it possible, argued
the Jews, for the government to restrict the personal rights
of its citizens and to force upon them its selection of the
"proper" hours for rest and work? Who gave a Christian judge
the right to permit or prohibit a Jew from working on Sunday? Did the Jew demand of the Christian that he should not
work on Saturday?

Members of the Historical School appeared before the

American public with the following legal arguments against
the government:

1. The officials in the House of Representatives, who had
voted for Sunday Laws, had been elected by the people. Yet
the laws they were enacting were based upon their own
religious backgrounds and points of view. They neglected to
take into account the feelings of those adhering to other
religions.

2. The government does not have the power to regulate the
hour at which a citizen may work.

3. A Christian judge does not have the power to decide
whether a Jew may desecrate his Sabbath by working or not.

4. Jews do not have the right to demand of Christians that
they cease working on Saturday, nor Christians to demand of
Jews that they do not work on Sunday.

5. The Sunday Laws constitute direct discrimination
against Jews and members of the Seventh Day Adventist
sect.

Nonetheless, Sunday Laws were found in the statutes of
various states. Those Jews who were concerned with defending their rights had to be constantly on guard. The struggle
carried on by Leeser against the verdict of the Supreme Court
of the state of Pennsylvania in 1848 provides a good illustration. One of the presiding judges expressed the opinion that
Sunday is a "political institution" which had always been
accepted as the law of the land, together with all other laws,
by political authority. Another judge took the stand "that the
Pennsylvanians are a Christian people and State, and that
over all the length and breadth of this great nation, the
Christian Sabbath is recognized and guarded by the law as a
day of sacred rest. Our national Congress recognizes it."
Against these opinions of the judges Leeser came out with a
penetrating statement:

It has been wittily said that words were invented to hide
our thoughts; most men believe the contrary. But if the
Constitution of Pennsylvania declares Sunday-keeping,
trinitarian Christianity, to be the foundation of the social
compact, then for one, we do not profess to know the mean-

ing of words, and we shall then have to resort to the Supreme Court, not alone to expound to us what is the law of the land, but to teach us the meaning of ordinary words. For we hold it as self-evident, that no matter how learned a man may be, and we do not impugn the superior knowledge and learning of their honours who compose the highest court in this State, it is not requisite to resort to them or their tribunal to be told the definition of names—of natural objects, nor of the simple elements of arithmetic; and if an ox be an ox and not a mule, and if twice four be eight and not nine, there are, in the words of the Declaration of Right, no earthly supports for the opinion that Christianity is the law of the land. Is it the only religion which believes in the existence of a God and rewards and punishments? Was it the first which announced these pillars of society and built upon them a state governed by laws and laws only? Is it so harmonious in its views of the being of God, that it can claim any prerogative about its own tenets in opposition to the other followers of the Bible? Does the Constitution exclude Mahomedans from the rights in the State? If so, we do not understand plain, simple words, and we yield to the superior wisdom which discovers a negative in an affirmative, and renders yes into no, or no into yes, not according to the sense of the writer, but according to the arbitrary will of the interpreter. And it is against this assumption that we, as a defender of Jewish ideas, which we deem compatible and identical with the laws of social order and happiness, most earnestly protest.[44]

With each new instance the defenders of Jewish rights were forced to begin from the beginning. But in the end they obtained their explicit rights. They succeeded in getting laws passed in New York, Maine, New Hampshire, Vermont and other states, making it possible for Jewish citizens "who observe the 7th day of the week as a holy time" to conduct business on Sunday, the Christian day of rest.[45] In general agreement was obtained, ruling that Sunday Laws—based on religious grounds—had no place in America.

If the men of politics had the temerity to legislate in the interest of sectarian religion, why should the religious sects hesitate to spread a net of missionaries over the entire United

States? Indeed, missionizing the Jews wore subtle and devious disguises. Leeser pointed this out by saying that the Christians, unable to surmount Judaism by any other means, found words of brotherly love more tempting.[46] To counteract the effect of Christian missionaries, Leeser proposed to dispatch Jewish teachers, preachers, and leaders to the danger zones and so fight the attack internally.[47]

But they would have to face the danger from without, as it was embodied in the American Society for Meliorating the Condition of the Jews, an organization which, after a long period of inactivity, began to function again in the 1840s and published a periodical called the *Jewish Chronicle*.[48] The plan of these missionaries was to enter poor Jewish homes, bribe the inhabitants with a little money (sometimes as little as a quarter), and then begin talk of the "Messiah."[49] The Society had its headquarters in New York. Samuel Myer Isaacs warned that the number of Christian missionaries was increasing. Although he knew that "paid agents" would not succeed in capturing many souls, he feared the effect of the intolerant teachings of the missionaries would penetrate the consciousness of the American people and not even the education of many generations would be able to eradicate it.[50] Jewish leaders had little fear of individual missionaries and professional converts from Judaism, but they were deeply frightened of the Jewish missions conducted by official Protestant denominations. From time to time an official Protestant leader appeared who believed that he would save his own soul by "saving" one Jewish soul. In 1849 a new secretary to the general council of the Presbyterian Church was elected; he planned to bring all Jews in America into the fold of Presbyterianism. He issued a proclamation in which he pronounced that Jews must join his church if they wished to ease their burdens.[51] Leeser printed an article by Isaac Mayer Wise in the *Occident* which constitutes an important answer to the threat of the missionaries, contrasting the values of Judaism with those of Christianity.

If it was possible, from time to time, to wipe out a negative law or to nullify the attempts of some missionary sect, it was not always possible to overcome the prevailing idea that the United States was a Christian country. That notion insinuated itself into the phrasing of various official proclamations, especially those setting forth the meaning of Thanksgiving Day. Actually, this holiday was never conceived either as an official religious or even a national celebration. Early in American history, Congress began to request that the President and the executives of various states issue Thanksgiving proclamations. Washington was the first to issue such a proclamation. Jefferson, on the other hand, did not do so, refusing to leap over the "wall of separation" between Church and State. His fears were well grounded. State and federal officials of the Protestant faith singled out the day as set aside exclusively for Christian Americans. But Jewish spokesmen did not remain silent. Believing in the rightness of their cause, in the justice of American law, and in the fairmindedness of their fellow-citizens, they took every issue to the public, stating their case openly in the press and voicing their opinions from every available rostrum. On one occasion, in 1849, when Governor Hamilton Fish of New York seemingly addressed his Thanksgiving Day proclamation only to the Christians, ten synagogues in New York refused as an act of protest to have any Thanksgiving Day services. Leeser commented that even though such silent protest has its place, silence itself would not suffice. He wrote:

> . . . The Israelites of the state at large ought to have remonstrated with the Governor in energetic terms, and thus induced him not to forget the Israelites another year; and we state it merely as our opinion, that though a captious fault-finding and a constant nervousness to take offence should never be manifested by Israelites, as unbecoming and unmanly, at the same time no public insult, either of omission or commission, should be passed over in silence; for we ought to take good care of our rights and never allow them to be tacitly violated.[52]

The following year Governor Fish omitted any reference to Christianity in his proclamation.

In 1868, another such incident occurred and evoked a

response from members of the Historical group. The Thanks-giving Day proclamation of Governor John W. Geary of Pennsylvania excluded the Jews from participation in Thanksgiving Day. The governor, in his proclamation, called for giving thanks to God "with Christian humility." He prayed "that our paths through life may be directed by the example and instructions of the Redeemer, who died that we might enjoy all the blessings which temporarily flow there-from, and eternal life in the world to come." The rabbis of Philadelphia, among whom were Bettelheim, Jastrow and Morais, were greatly aroused. They consulted with each other and prepared an answer in which they informed the congrega-tions of the unprecedented occurrence and pleaded with the citizenry to protest to the governor.[53]

In this instance, strong protest did not help. The spirit of the first amendment of the Constitution did not yet reign in the state of Pennsylvania. Sabato Morais received letters from Christian clergymen who expressed their amazement at his having forgotten that Pennsylvania was a Christian Com-monwealth. Where did he find the audacity to protest? Morais adopted a sarcastic tone and apologized for his "error." It was true, he said, that when he objected he had been under the impression that America was a land of freedom of religion. But he had learned that in this state where the Sunday Laws were still on the books, no Jew had the right to complain about infringement of his rights. On the contrary, he had to be thankful for the crumbs of human rights which were thrown to him from the table.

In the course of time signs of progress appeared. The elected representatives of the people realized the justice of the Jewish protests. Laws that discriminated against the Jews were slowly stricken from the books. Jews and Christians came before the courts as persons with equal rights and responsibilities. Slowly, the American people learned that the framers of the American Constitution had done well to pro-tect the freedom of the individual.

Defense of Jewish Rights Abroad

The Jews of America did not restrict themselves to activities on their own behalf. Paradoxically—and this is a pattern which has continued—it was the need of Jews overseas that brought domestic union into being. Whenever the news of persecution, whether by Church or State, reached them, American Jews were prepared to come to the aid of their brethren. At first the various factions could not agree on common action, but in time, the communities united in the binding cause of Jewish defense.

In 1840, the Damascus slander occurred. When first news of the incident arrived in the United States, the Jews of America, like their brothers in Europe, were aroused. A Franciscan Father had mysteriously disappeared and the French consul in Damascus, Ratti-Menton, upon the advice of certain monks, conducted an investigation. A Jewish barber was tortured until he "confessed" to the murder and he implicated others as well. Thirteen prominent Jews were thrown into prison and tortured as a result of the "confession"; three of them died. The libel stirred consternation throughout the world. Large protest meetings were held in New York, Philadelphia and Richmond, demanding intercession by the American government with the government of Turkey in order to correct the injustice.

The real achievement of this official Jewish reaction in America is not to be measured by its practical results. (It was another Jewish delegation, headed by Moses Montefiore, that succeeded in this case.) Its significance is that for the first time local Jewries were united for the defense of Jewish rights on an international level. Yet key lay-figures of synagogues associated with the Historical School were in the forefront of action. Especially noteworthy is the role played by Israel B. Kursheedt who conducted the first public protest meeting organized by New York Jewry at congregation B'nai Jeshurun and, together with Theodore J. Seixas, drafted a letter to President Van Buren urging him to condemn the incident.[54]

Among the rabbis, the personality of Isaac Leeser stands out
as a powerful force. Out of a crescendo of discussion in the
Jewish press came Leeser's decision to found the *Occident*
for the dissemination of Jewish news and the encouragement
of organized national Jewish action.

The second serious incident relating to disabilities of Jews
abroad, and which rallied American Jewish opinion, was the
proposed Swiss-American treaty in 1851. Swiss Jews had long
suffered under the illiberal decrees of the Swiss government.
Several of the Swiss cantons were closed to Jews. Each canton
had the right to decide whether Jews who were American
citizens were to be admitted or not. The Jews of America felt
helpless in the face of this discrimination as long as the government of the United States took no interest in the matter.
But in 1851, a furor was created in Jewish ranks when the
question arose whether to ratify a treaty between America and
Switzerland, one of whose provisions was that only American
Christians might live in Switzerland. A flood of letters descended upon the senators in Washington.[55]

Leeser painted the truth in clear colors. If the treaty were
ratified, he said,

> [it] would exhibit an American citizen in a new light as
> invested with a peculiar religious or denominational char-
> acter before he can with safety leave the shores of his coun-
> try. . . . As American citizens we indignantly protest against
> the ratification by the Senate of the United States of a
> treaty containing a provision which strikes at the very root
> of the religious liberty of one hundred thousand American
> citizens.[56]

In 1854, a representative national Jewish committee was
formed and a petition was submitted to the Senate. Christians
and Jews united in common effort and newspapers throughout the country associated themselves in this cause with
their fellow-citizens of the Jewish faith. The question persisted for about fifteen years when some changes were introduced. It was finally settled in 1874: a new Swiss constitution
established religious liberty.

The victory, like all solid blows for liberty, was not only a victory for the Swiss Jews. It taught American Jews something about their own country: The United States government responded to the just complaints of its Jewish citizens. Summarizing the entire affair, Leeser wrote:

> Had the first step not been taken here, it is likely that neither American nor European governments would have troubled themselves about us. "Those who wish to be free must themselves strike the blow." Let us be grateful that it has been done and one more land is open for the wandering sons of Israel.[57]

These activities were further steps in the attempt to unify American Jewry in defense of Jewish rights. The incident that crystallized the organization for unity was the Mortara abduction case in Italy. A Jewish child had been baptized secretly by his Christian nurse and, on the strength of this action, he was taken away by the Church authorities and placed in a Catholic home where he was to receive an education proper for a "Christian soul." All this had been done with the knowledge and approval of the Pope.[58]

When the abduction became known publicly, violent protests arose on both sides of the ocean, especially in England and America, but to no avail. The Jewish congregations in America were moved to action by Sir Moses Montefiore who, as Bertram Korn correctly points out, "was more successful in gaining the support of the Jewish congregations in America, in many matters of overseas philanthropy and the defense of Jewish rights abroad, than was any local leader."[59] Isaacs, Leeser and Wise used their respective periodicals as the foci for information and direct organization of meetings throughout the country. Public protest meetings were organized in Philadelphia, New York, Syracuse, Richmond, Rochester, Baltimore, Memphis, Mobile, New Orleans, and other cities. Communications were directed to President James Buchanan and Secretary of State Lewis Cass.

Members of the Historical group were active in the leadership of the protest movement. In New York delegates of twelve congregations assembled in the home of Morris Raphall and constituted themselves a permanent committee called the Executive Committee of the Representatives of the United Congregations of Israelites of the City of New York. It was the first of its kind in that city. In Philadelphia a delegation was chosen to call upon President Buchanan and ask him to intervene in defense of human rights as had President Martin Van Buren at the time of the Damascus slander. The President, however, "smilingly replied, 'It happened when I was not President.' " The forceful pleadings of the delegation could not move the President: he feared that any intervention affecting the internal affairs of another government would establish a precedent and give other nations the right to interfere with the internal affairs of the United States. Although Buchanan claimed a sincere interest in the affairs of the Jews, the delegation could accomplish nothing and ended its efforts. The Jews of America were astounded. Leeser printed a complete account of the visit and rebuff. Morais, too, denounced this injustice in public and, as a sign of protest, excluded the customary prayer for the government on the Sabbath.[60] It is significant that, despite the stream of articles against the Catholic Church and the attempts of the Know-Nothing group to promote its own interests through the affair, the Jews did not transpose their resentment into an anti-Catholic movement. They sought religious liberty for themselves and others, and it was through this issue that they drew their line of battle.[61]

From the agitation surrounding the Mortara case, American Jews learned an important lesson. In 1859 two resolutions were adopted by the Executive Committee of the Philadelphia Israelites, which showed they had come to realize that the time for proper organization had arrived:

> RESOLVED, That this committee regret the answer of the President, and are of opinion, that had our plan been adopted of acting in union all over the United States, and of petitioning the Executive in proper form, delegates from different sections could have gone to Washington with tens of thousands of signatures, including governors of States, members of the Senate and House of Representatives, and the most influential names of the different denominations,

which would probably have insured for our efforts, in a cause common to all Israelites, a success far different from the deplorable results consequent on the separate action which we have witnessed.

RESOLVED, That this committee recommend that the different congregations throughout the Union take into consideration the propriety of electing delegates to represent them in future, so as to form a body similar to the Board of Deputies of British Jews in London. For united, we can accomplish almost everything; otherwise, nothing.[62]

The Board of Delegates of American Israelites

The storm that broke over the Mortara case resulted in the organization of the *Alliance Israélite Universelle* in France; it also awakened the Jews of America to action. The formation of the Board of Delegates of American Israelites was a direct and immediate result of the incident, although its prompt emergence was due to the groundwork that had been laid for it years earlier. Far-thinking individuals of the American rabbinate and laity had long recognized the need for uniting forces against the enemies of Jewry, who were spreading insidious propaganda in America and overseas.

In England the Board of Deputies had been in existence for some time. When it came to defending Jewish rights, England was far ahead of the other countries of Europe and America. Several English Jews in America, influenced by the sentiments expressed in the *Jewish Chronicle* of London, felt that Jews in the United States could better cope with their disabilities if they were similarly organized.[63] Samuel Myer Isaacs, a Jew of English background, and one of the early architects of the Historical School in America, was the principal organizer of the Board of Delegates.[64] Isaacs influenced his congregation, Shaaray Tefila, to take the initiative, and as a result of its invitation, in 1859, 25 congregations, 11 from New York and 14 from other cities of the United States, gathered "for the purpose of conferring with

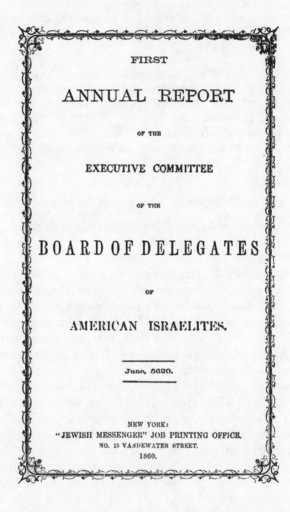

FIRST

ANNUAL REPORT

OF THE

EXECUTIVE COMMITTEE

OF THE

BOARD OF DELEGATES

OF

AMERICAN ISRAELITES.

June, 5620.

NEW YORK:
"JEWISH MESSENGER" JOB PRINTING OFFICE,
NO. 15 VANDEWATER STREET.
1860.

the officers of other Congregations as to the best mode of
adopting a plan for the establishment of a Board of Representatives of the Israelites of the United States."[65]

This was an historic meeting. For the first time in the
annals of American Jewry, after many articles and speeches,
a forum of unity was achieved. There were Germans, English,
Poles and also many Sephardim. The only factions absent
from among the various strains of American Jewry were the
extreme Reformers and some of the older Sephardi congregations. Advocates and supporters of the Historical School
took the lead. On November 27, 1859, 46 delegates representing 25 congregations in 14 cities met at Cooper Institute in
New York and created "The Board of Delegates of American Israelites."[66]

The basic purpose of the new organization as it was expressed at that meeting was

> to gain statistical information, to promote education and
> literature, to further the cause of charity, to watch over
> occurrences at home and abroad relating to the Israelites,
> and to establish a "Court of Arbitration" for the settle-
> ment of disputes between Congregations, &c, without re-
> course to litigation.[67]

For Leeser, the plan was minimal. Despite his strong pleas
to exploit this rare opportunity to realize more constructive
purposes, his suggestions were rejected. The first Executive
Committee elected at that meeting consisted of Henry J.
Hart of New York (a member of Isaacs' congregation), president; Isaac Leeser and John Marks of New Orleans, vice-
presidents; G. N. Herrman of New York, treasurer; and
Myer S. Isaacs, son of the founder, secretary.[68]

The founding members of the Board, representing, as
they did, only a limited number of "moderate, traditional
congregations," mainly of a conservative religious character,
certainly expected critical reaction to their work.[69] However,
they did not anticipate the attacks out of personal animus,
which came from the Reformers of both extreme and moderate factions. Wise, who felt that his stature had been dimin-

ished because the meetings were held in New York and
because he could not attend them, criticized the Board of
Delegates.[70] But David Einhorn, the spokesman of radical
Reform, gave no pretext for his disagreement. He was opposed fundamentally to the basic idea behind the Board.
Einhorn used an argument that he hoped would raise
many fears: Jews should appear before the American public
as citizens of the United States, not as Jews. The Reformers
felt, moreover (and Einhorn expressed their views), that
the purpose of the Board would be to set up a "hierarchy
which would bind in degrading fetters Judaism and its followers in this land of liberty, and assume functions which
plainly meddle with civil relations." The Board, he continued, would widen the existing breach by establishing a
clerical body "to check the universal transgressions of the
laws, such as the desecration of the Sabbath and the viola-
tion of the Dietary laws."[71]

The Board took account of this sharp criticism and answered it point by point. Its first announcement, in the form
of a circular, made it perfectly clear that it had no intention
of meddling in the internal affairs of the various congregations. The problems with which the Board was to concern
itself were seven in number: education, statistics, a Jewish
arbitration court for internal disputes, the strengthening
of charitable institutions, the creation of a center to exchange information and ideas, the establishment of ties with
World Jewry, and the defense and protection of Jewish life
at home and abroad. Isaacs' and Leeser's influence is apparent in these resolutions.

As one looks back on the formation and history of the
Board of Delegates, one sees the beginning of a pattern in
American Jewish life which has lasted into our own time:
Unity in Jewish organizational life was achieved by the
pressure of overseas needs and by emergencies facing the
Jewish people as a whole, rather than by the desire for
representative government to raise the standard of conduct
in domestic Jewish group life. Consequently the forum of
unity, built on the needs of emergency, never lasted beyond

the end of the external pressure. Another parallel: in America sectarianism was rampant, cultural and civic groups prided themselves on their proliferation, and the Jews were no different.[72] Abraham G. Duker, by contrast, draws a parallel from other Jewish communities before the rise of modern Jewish nationalism, in which the establishment of central organizations as the authoritative representatives of the Diaspora communities (for example, the frequently cited Council of the Four Lands in ancient Poland) was predominantly the result of outside pressures rather than voluntary action.[73] Whatever the historical analogue, general or Jewish, the fact is that the Jews in America, under pressure to defend and protect Jewish life abroad, have organized expertly and often achieved nearly total participation. But regarding the first six planks in the platform of the Board, organization on a national scale was fractional and competitive.

In 1878 (immediately prior to the Board's absorption by agreement into the Union of American Hebrew Congregations), the President of the Board, Myer S. Isaacs, wrote in the Financial Report:

> The usefulness of the Board of Delegates for uniting American Israelites in self-defence has happily not been severely tested. It has been occasionally requisite to remind the National and State Governments of a discrimination against the Jewish religion or Hebrew citizens: rarely has a substantial wrong been committed under form of law or in hostility to the intelligent spirit of American legislation.[74]

Several important incidents of such action, to attain complete religious equality, occurred. The members of the Historical School were most directly involved as a religious group. The events occurred during the first few years of the Board, corresponding to the most crucial decade in American history—the years of the Civil War.

One of the most important questions that concerned the Board was the problem of providing military chaplains at the very beginning of the Civil War, from 1861-62. It should be noted that the struggle to achieve equality in the chaplaincy was fought in the North. In the South there was no legal block against such an appointment; the Confederacy in this regard was more liberal than the Congress in Washington. From their beginnings in 1755, all army chaplains of the United States until the Civil War were Protestants. Not until 1850 were Catholic priests appointed to military posts; their right to serve as army chaplains was first granted during the Civil War.

This history of the right of Jewish chaplaincy to be recognized in the American armed forces is comprehensively described in Bertram Korn's volume *American Jewry and the Civil War*.[75] For our immediate purpose, two approaches which the Board made to the authorities in Washington bring us to the heart of the matter. On the 22nd of July, 1861, Congress passed a law stating: "The chaplain ... must be a regular ordained minister of some Christian denomination ..." Thus Jewish soldiers were not allowed Jewish chaplains. The Board therefore prepared a petition which was presented both to the House of Representatives and to the Senate:

Your Memorialists respectfully submit, that the body of citizens of the United States, whom your memorialists represent, numbering not less than two hundred thousand, are unexcelled by any other class of citizens in loyalty and devotion to the Union; that thousands of them have volunteered into the Army of the United States ...

That the said Acts, inasmuch as they establish "a religious test as a qualification for an office under the United States," are manifestly in contravention of Section 3, Article VI of the Constitution, and Article I of Amendments thereto.

Your Memorialists, therefore, respectfully pray that your honorable body will take this, their memorial, into favorable consideration, and that you will, in your wisdom, cause the Acts of Congress, approved July 22d and August 3d, 1861, respectively, to be formally amended, so that there shall be no discrimination as against professors of the Jewish faith in the several laws affecting the appointment of chaplains in the service of the United States.[76]

In addition to the Memorial, the Board sent Arnold Fischel as a special delegate to Washington. The following quotation from the report of the committee illustrates the success of the mission:

The committee addressed the President of the United States, urging the appointment of a Jewish chaplain to each of the grand Military Departments; the Executive (Abraham Lincoln), while informing them of his inability to provide in that way for the spiritual wants of Israelites in the camps and hospitals, declared his intention "to recommend to Congress to modify the laws to which the Israelites objected." That this course was not without effect, is evidenced by the prompt action of the Senate Military Committee, by whom a bill was forthwith reported, securing to Jewish soldiers the rights they had been denied.

The amendment read as follows:

That no person shall be appointed a chaplain in the United States army who is not a regularly ordained minister of some religious denomination, and who does not present testimonials of his present good standing as such minister, with a recommendation for his appointment as an army chaplain from some authorized ecclesiastical body, or not less than five accredited ministers belonging to said religious denomination.[77]

On the basis of this change in the statute, rabbis could be commissioned as regimental chaplains or as hospital chaplains. Jacob Frankel, minister of the Rodeph Sholom congregation of Philadelphia, was appointed on September 18, 1862, to be the first Jewish chaplain in the hospital division of the American army. This act created a precedent for the future.

Two other events, distressing to Jews, occurred during the Civil War: the anti-Jewish letter of General Grant and the report of General Benjamin F. Butler.[78] Both generals unjustly condemned a group on the basis of the actions of some individuals. The Board of Delegates protested on both occasions and the generals apologized. After the war, as President and later private citizen, Grant repeated his regret of the "order" which he claimed was written "without reflection."

These are instances of the way in which the Jews of America, organized in the Board of Delegates, proceeded in their defense of Jewish rights. Alert to signs of discrimination, the Board well knew that it could establish its claim on the basis of liberty guaranteed to Jews by the law of the land. And every victory was a victory for democracy itself.

Identification with American Thought and Society

Even as American Jewry labored to gain full equality for Jews and Judaism, they were grateful for the refuge they found as individuals, and the sanctuary offered their people in America.[79] The members of the Historical School cherished a strong love for America and for its heritage. But they did not consider it necessary, like many of the Reform group, to proclaim America as Zion and the particular city in which they lived at the time as Jerusalem (according to the slogan first raised by Gustav Poznanski at the dedication of the Charleston synagogue in 1841).[80] They did see in America the hope of mankind, a country in which justice and right ruled. They transmitted this feeling to their congregations. Morris Raphall summarized their faith with these words:

> The United States of America, are the only true Republic now in existence, the only real great democracy that the world has ever seen, accordingly in these United States, all citizens are perfectly equal. Talents, virtue, public esteem, confer the only titles to dignity and exu[a]ltation. The Jew, therefore, whose abilities, energy and high integrity may gain for him the confidence of his fellow-citizens, can rise to stations of great public trust. He may even eventually be called to fill the highest office that Freemen can confer, and which in a few years

more will be the first in the world, the Presidential chair of the United States.[81]

Isaac Leeser repeated time and again that the inhabitants of America ought to thank God daily for their good fortune. He introduced a new and beautiful note into his thanksgiving. "This country," Leeser wrote, ". . . is emphatically the one where Israel is to prepare itself for its glorious mission of regenerating mankind."[82]

The leaders of the Historical School opposed the "official" recognition given to the German language by many American Jews of German extraction. They strove to unite their congregants with the spirit of America by absorbing the English language and spirit of the country. Although Szold and Jastrow preached in German during their first years in America, this was deemed temporary. Leeser opposed the use of the German language vehemently, preferring English as the language for sermons and for teaching in Jewish schools. "The country," he said more than once, "is essentially English in its tastes, habits and predilections, and it appears to us absolutely requisite that Jews should conform as nearly as possible, consistent with their religion, to the manners of the people among whom they live."[83]

Like the rest of the population, the Jews' loyalties were divided in the Civil War. It was reported that in the South, Jews participated in the war effort in a proportion far above their actual numbers.[84]

One of the incidents that deeply disturbed the Jews of the North was a sermon by a member of the Historical School, Morris Raphall. It was inevitable that the clergy and spiritual leaders of America should express their opinions of the moral aspect of slavery. The clergy was divided on moral grounds as was the country in its political views. The North had its great Abolitionist preachers who found an ample supply of texts in the Bible to sustain their argument. In the South, the language of religion seemed to parallel the language of slaveholders. The Baptists, for example, apologized at first for slavery, then gave it tacit acknowledgment; finally, a defense was made on the basis of Scriptures.[85] Among Jews, however, even among those who sided with the Confederacy, not a single ordained Jewish clergyman spoke out in defense of slavery in America until Morris Raphall raised his voice. On the fast day proclaimed by President Buchanan on January 4, 1861, Raphall delivered a lecture on the topic, "Bible View of Slavery." The sermon was included in a book entitled *Fast Day Sermons,* a volume containing sermons by ministers of different faiths, reflecting both the Northern and Southern viewpoints on slavery and related issues of the day.[86] The impression spread in America that such was the official view of Judaism on this difficult question. In his sermon Raphall argued that according to the laws of the Bible, possession of a slave was not considered a sin and, since the Bible was the only source of Divine Law, it was not correct to say that Divine Law was opposed to slavery. Raphall did not intend to approve or disapprove of slavery in America; he intended to deal with this question from the point of view of the Torah. The timing of his statement caused consternation, and many took his words as an approval of slavery.[87]

Most rabbis and other learned Jews did not react to his viewpoint in silence. In spite of the attempts of David Einhorn and Michael Heilperin to refute Raphall, the historical fact of slavery in the Bible could not be contradicted. However, they expressed their amazement at Raphall's words, and criticized him for leaving himself open to misinterpretation and for presenting a false idea of the biblical concept of slavery. Actually Raphall sided with the Union (his son became an officer in the Union Army).[88] Nevertheless, his words could not be eradicated and, since they were delivered in public, no explanations ever sufficed.

One member of the Historical School, Sabato Morais, did place his position in jeopardy because he was willing to take an open stand against slavery. The other members of the group were less forthright. Samuel Isaacs had always been opposed to slavery in America and wanted to expound his opinions in public, but deferred to the officers of his congregation who felt that a religious leader should not express opinions of this kind from his pulpit. Outside the confines of his synagogue, in the community at large, and especially through his own newspaper, which commanded country-wide circulation, Isaacs spoke eloquently and militantly for the Union. On one occasion the *Jewish Messenger* became the butt of a "terrible censure." The leaders of the Hebrew congregation of Shreveport, Louisiana, incensed at an article entitled "Stand by the Flag!" sent the paper a strong letter of condemnation. This censure, while it had little impact on the newspaper (as Isaacs wrote, "we have only one subscriber in Shreveport, and he has not paid for two years") expressed the reaction of the Southern Jews to Isaacs and his paper. Isaacs was declared "an enemy to our interest and welfare." The resolution further stated:

> RESOLVED, That while we mistook your paper for a religious one, which ought to be strictly neutral in politics, we shall from this [day?] out treat it with scorn, as a black republican paper, and not worthy of Southern patronage; and that, according to our understanding, church and politics ought never to be mingled, as it has been the ruination of any country captivated by the enticing words of preachers . . .[89]

A third member of the Historical School, Isaac Leeser, who had served and lived in the South, was a neutralist. Agonized by all the bloodshed, he tried to explain each side to the other.[90]

Morais, in writing and speaking, supported the cause of Negro freedom with all his strength. From the day of Lincoln's election, Morais preached against slavery and was prepared to sacrifice his private interests for the liberation of the slaves. His freedom of speech did not last very long. Influential members of the congregation expressed sympathy for the Confederacy. Their protests against Morais' "political" speeches grew in intensity. In 1864, when Morais spoke in praise of Maryland's abolishment of slavery (Morais referred to it as Merry-Land), the animosity of these members of Mikveh Israel reached a peak. A new *parnas*, one of Morais' opponents, was then at the head of the congregation. In December of that year, the board of trustees decided

to silence Morais by forbidding him to deliver his weekly
sermon without first obtaining permission in writing from
the *parnas*. Morais began to agitate against this rule and
found many supporters. After some months the board abolished the ruling, and Morais was permitted to deliver one
sermon a month on a religious topic. At the end of the war,
he was permitted to deliver weekly sermons, but from this
point on he was required to preach *only* on "religious" topics.
The official letter in which Morais requests permission from
the board to preach regularly is preserved in the archives
of the congregation:

> . . . I would now respectfully ask that you allow me, in my
> capacity as lecturer to address the congregation, whenever
> I deem it fit, before the chaunting of the last Hebrew
> Hymn in the morning service for the Sabbaths or Fes-
> tivals . . .[91]

Morais' struggles for the ideals of the Union were not
hidden from the authorities, and he was honored by being
appointed an honorary member of the Union League Club
of Philadelphia.[92]

It is impossible to end this summary of the participation
by rabbis of the Historical School in American life without
referring to their deep love for Abraham Lincoln, in whom
they saw the living symbol of the spirit of America and the
ideal of real justice and freedom. For these rabbis as for
Walt Whitman, Lincoln was "the grandest figure on the
crowded canvas of the drama" of their century. They never
ceased to extol and laud him. They praised Lincoln's deeds,
all of which they felt were "for the sake of heaven" and they
esteemed his perfect simplicity, the purity of his soul, his
ideals which embraced all of mankind, his compassion, his
consolation of the stricken and, above all, the seal of truth
that was imprinted upon his manner and speech.

When the news of the President's assassination was received on the Sabbath of the 15th of April, 1865, Morais
arose and, shaken, raised his voice in prayer for the dead
leader.[93] All his fellow-rabbis eulogized the President. Leeser

was invited to Washington to represent the Jews. Benjamin Szold, in praising Lincoln, said that the day of his death should not only be a day of sorrow but one of joy, in thanks for having had such a great leader at this crucial period, and for having had the opportunity to live when such a man lived.[94]

What Lincoln meant to the nation and all men, in all lands, will continue to be expressed wherever the meaning of freedom is discussed. In one fragment of memory, Nina Morais describes an infant's recollection of the period and thus summarizes for us the impact of the man and his times on one household:

> There was once a child, who almost an infant, went to the public school with a picture of Lincoln upon her breast. Almost her first recollection was that of her father's weeping for Lincoln's death, and of being led to gaze on the features of the martyr President. This man Lincoln was her childish ideal, her American hero, her heritage against all the world. Her father suffered for holding political opinions adverse to his interest; she, too, among the children of the school. Could this child believe that she was not an integral part of the American nation? She was taught—and under rabbinical rule be it emphasized—to love all her little friends, Christians and Jews alike. With both she celebrated the national holiday, with both, made lint for the soldiers, and brought her lanterns to hang out after Union victories.[95]

Chapter Four

**Uniting
the
American
Synagogue**

In the realm of Jewish education, the leaders of the Historical
School believed the synagogue should retain primary responsibility, but share authority with other communal forces.
In social service and Jewish mutual aid activities, these
same leaders advocated the transfer of authority to communal
agencies; they accepted a secondary role for the representatives of the synagogue. When it came to religious life
and institutions, however, they could relinquish neither
authority nor responsibility to other agencies. During the
period under discussion, the Historical School worked to
establish a united, traditional American Synagogue as the
cornerstone of the Jewish communal structure.

Although in the middle decades of the nineteenth century
the Historical School sought, and almost achieved, a program
of religious action in common with the leaders of the Reform group, the foundation of that program was too unstable
to withstand the pressure of attacks from without and, as
we shall see, of basic division within. At this time, two distinct camps grew up in the Historical School, just as two
tendencies evolved within the Reform and Orthodox groups.
These groupings were informal, created by a willingness to
compromise. Jewish religious leaders of all trends had to take
into account both the times and the land where their people
had chosen to come. All of them sought to find the direction
of continuity in the midst of change. They differed in their
appraisal of the times, in their interpretation of continuity—

and in their decision to resist or submit to change, for the sake of that continuity. They also differed in the determination of immediate program and method even when they accepted the same objectives. It was a time of great flux, of unusual experimentation, of rapid association and equally rapid dissociation. Personality played a dominant role. Trends had not yet coalesced into movements nor movements into institutions. Intention and conviction moved people more than philosophies and tradition.

A great deal of ferment in Jewish religious life corresponded to the idea of change which moved the American spirit. Henry Steele Commager uses the term *tradition* to describe the American habit of change and reform, a tradition whose sources are embodied in the American environment and historical experience.[1] The great personal uprooting of the immigrant made all the changes that followed it comparatively insignificant. Democracy was the prevailing structure but, within this structure, the individual was free to move from place to place, from institution to institution, from loyalty to loyalty.

"The period from 1830 to the Civil War," Commager writes, "was the great reform generation of American history. In these decades every institution was called before the bar of Religion and Reason, and made to justify itself."[2] The religions of America—including Judaism—were profoundly affected by the national, divided temper. But, as William Sweet has explained, the splintering and multiplicity of religious denominations in the United States—by the middle of the nineteenth century there were over a hundred groupings—was also determined by historical, sociological and legal factors.[3] Several reasons can be given for the splintering into denominations. In the first place, the American population represented many of the populations of the world; they were people who brought with them their own divisions and differences. Furthermore, religious liberty was established, a majority religion was unavailable, and the private conscience was held sacred. All these causes brought forth a multiplicity of sects. The extreme individualism of the American frontier in those decades also helped to nurture indigenous American religious movements, such as Mormonism and Seventh Day Adventists. Consequently all religious groups turned away from abstract theology and rigid doctrine, and depended upon organization and mutual accommodation.

To forge a united Synagogue as the institutional embodiment of traditional Judaism in America, and to lessen the emphasis upon "the synagogues" was Isaac Leeser's lifelong ambition. As the moving spirit of the Historical School, Leeser applied his great organizational faculties and his gift of tact to the task of bringing together dissident forces by means of a program of religious union. First he sought to combine the differences between the long-established native American Sephardi community and the immigrant Ashkenazi settlement. Actually, these differences, which stemmed from their respective European ethnic and cultural backgrounds, were minor compared to the common aspects of the two groups —especially since these differences faded away in the now native land of their children.

Most of the thirty congregations that existed in America in the 1840s were traditional both in congregational practice and liturgy. These congregations were very similar to one another even in such organizational matters as their way of imposing taxes. Leeser pointed to the futility of imposing divisions upon American Judaism on account of trivial minutiae. He put his case simply. The fact that European communities were divided could be attributed both to governmental oppression and established local influences "vested in the ordinary rabbinical courts and in the consistories which have elsewhere the supervision in church matters."[4] In America, however, where the government did not interfere with internal Jewish affairs and where the congregations were not yet well established, there was no reason for quarrels and divisions to arise over unimportant matters. The faith of Judaism was more important than one's accident of birth in America or Europe. If the new immigrants brought different customs with them, these customs were to be subordinated to prevailing practices. The brotherhood and unity of Israel were more crucial than the perpetuation of secondary local traditions. The wealthy inhabitants ought not to separate themselves from the poor immigrants; in America the individual was more important than his wealth. Let the wealthy contribute their money and the poor their work, he said.

Leeser emphasized that the differences in the prayer ritual also were not great. This turned out to be the knotty point. If the divergences had been between essentials, it would perhaps have been easier to effect a compromise. "But the distinction is almost so inappreciable, that each party fears of being swallowed up by the mass, if it do not persevere in all the minutia which old custom has brought down."[5] What, then, was to be done? Leeser looked forward to the day when all Jews would follow the same order of service, the Ashkenazi *minhag*. The number of German immigrants in America was growing rapidly, and the Sephardi influences were diminishing. Yet the oldest congregations in America followed the Sephardi prayer service and, since this service had been accepted for more than a hundred years, Leeser felt that all synagogues should for the present follow the Sephardi service.[6]

Meanwhile, small differences multiplied to bring about a state of anarchy. Each congregation in the New World established its own customs without considering those of any other congregation. Leeser deplored this unfortunate development:

It is an evil certainly that, in small communities especially, Israelites do not unite to form one large respectable Synagogue, in place of weakening their strength and wasting means uselessly in keeping up separate establishments for the Portuguese, German, and Polish customs. But it is a far greater evil that that there should be no unity of feeling where Synagogues of the different denominations do exist; or that different towns do not combine to effect a general object, because the imaginary lines of separation place, as they aver, an insurmountable obstacle in the way of a union of the disjointed members which now constitute our American congregations. But how short-sighted are all who think and act so; who suffer themselves to be led away by petty motives and little views, which are a disgrace to thinking manhood![7]

Proposals for Congregational Unity and Practice

Attempting to unify Jewish life, Leeser began to speak of *Kneset Yisrael,* the community of Israel, or "catholic Israel." "What is it that all desire? is it not the welfare of the church of Israel, the assembly of the faithful, the *Kneset Yisrael?*"[8] Consequently, it was necessary to create a federative union, or a union of congregations, which would concern itself with those matters that transcend the local concerns of individual congregations: general religious questions, Jewish rights, and the like. While this organization was to enjoy general authority, it would not be allowed to interfere with purely internal matters of the member congregations. The problems and details of the synagogue service would remain in the hands of the congregational leaders, not the central organization. It is interesting that Leeser, himself an immigrant to America, proposed a federative democratic structure reflecting the organization of the country as a whole.

It will be recalled that Louis Salomon and Leeser had called a meeting as early as 1841 to found such an organization.[9] The program consisted of three parts:

1. The founding, in America, of a congregational body of Jews which was to supervise all spiritual aspects of each congregation's life.
2. The founding of proper schools.
3. The calling of regular meetings of the heads of congregations for the development of common undertakings.

This document is of inestimable value in understanding the movement for American congregational unity. It reveals the desire of its authors to unite Jewish congregations in America and work together with all factions for the welfare of Judaism. By these means they hoped ultimately to correct the ignorance and indifference of masses of people to their religious heritage. The idea for unification was born in the minds of Salomon and Leeser and nurtured by the representatives of three congregations: Mikveh Israel, Rodeph Shalom and Beth-El—all in Philadelphia.[10]

Their intention was to obtain the consent of other congregations throughout the country. Every congregation received a copy of the suggestions and was invited to a national meeting. Leeser, anticipating that the letter might elicit negative results, came to New York in order to prepare the foundations. He turned to the *parnas* of Shearith Israel, at that time the strongest congregation, and invited him to participate. The *parnas* refused the invitation, fearing that the influence of the Sephardi congregations would be further reduced because the Ashkenazi congregations were in the majority. The plan therefore came to nothing. Strong opposition also came from the Reform group. Congregation Beth Elohim of Charleston, S.C., voted in a resolution against the plan, not only denying its practicality but generalizing that "all conventions, founded or created for the establishment of any *ecclesiastical authority* whatever, . . . are alien to the spirit and genius of the age in which we live, and are wholly inconsistent with the spirit of American Liberty."[11]

Instead of sustaining his original effort to establish a superstructure, Leeser and his friends thought it possible to achieve the desired unity in religious life by means of small reforms within each synagogue. They agreed that careful attention should be given to the criticisms directed against them, and that they should introduce as many changes as were possible and consistent with tradition. They limited themselves to four kinds of change: improvement in synagogue decorum; introduction of new rituals; use of English and creation of supplementary readings for the service; and recognition of the new role of women in the traditional synagogue.

The question of order and decorum in the service was most important. The new immigrants conducted their service, as had been their custom in the old country, with a cantor of the European type; the selling of religious honors; many special blessings for the congregation's members; constant coming and going during the service, and the like. These "customs" and manners were appropriate in Europe, but they did not suit American conditions. The members of the Historical School wanted to change this pattern of synagogue conduct. Isaacs, for example, understood that if he proposed the abolition of public pledges in the synagogue, he would be asked how the synagogue could be supported without this income. He therefore suggested one annual contribution instead of small weekly ones. Not only would this add dignity to the service of the synagogue, but the congregation would no longer have to depend on intermittent support.[12] Isaacs informed Leeser of the important good news in his congregation:

Sir:
It affords me pleasure to be enabled to communicate to you, and to ask its insertion in the *Occident,* that on Sunday, June 30th, a general meeting was convened of the members of the Elm Street Synagogue, and to their credit be it written, a resolution passed unanimously, that from and after the 1st of September next, the *mitzvot* which have hitherto been sold, shall thenceforward be distributed in rotation amongst electors and seat-holders. The advantage of this alteration must be manifest at a glance, visited as our shrine is by different denominations; it will remove that which ever evinced an unhealthy appearance, whilst at the same time the poor man worshipping will participate with the rich in the honours of the Synagogue. I cannot speak too highly of the members in thus voluntarily relinquishing an annual revenue of $600, in order to meet the exigencies of the times, and in some measure to revert to our original simplicity. This may be considered reform, and to that extent I avow myself a reformer. I would improve all the temporalities, but I would not touch our liturgy; I would give less to man, more to God.[13]

These questions were taken very seriously by the members of the various congregations. Readiness for or resistance to such changes may have spelled the difference between a congregation's going into the Reform camp or being internally split. Therefore, hours were given over to debating these proposals. Israel Goldstein records an example of "excessive zeal" for decorum in congregation B'nai Jeshurun in 1840. A resolution was passed ruling that a hat and cloak must be worn by the *shammash* (sexton) but he refused to abide by the resolution. "It was only after the hat and cloak were brought and exhibited on the person of the Shamas before the meeting, that the resolution was rescinded."[14] In Marcus Jastrow's congregation, Rodeph Shalom of Philadelphia, it was made clear "that none but clean and perfect Talithim [prayer shawls] are allowed, which must be worn in a respectful manner." In the same congregation, there is also recorded a resolution which permits the president of the congregation to fine anyone from 50 cents to $5 for disobeying regulations governing the congregation.[15]

Not only by changing old habits, but by permitting innovations, did the members of the Historical School attempt to improve the services. Whenever opportune, they borrowed ideas from the moderate Reformers. Members of the Reform rabbinate began to create new ceremonies. Confirmation, one of the ceremonies introduced in that area, was practiced for the first time in America by Dr. Lilienthal in congregation Anshe Chesed. The boys had to be twelve years old, the girls eleven. It is to be emphasized that the originators of this ceremony did not want to abolish the traditional Bar Mitzvah.[16] Members of the Historical School, excluding Raphall and Isaacs, accepted this custom and it spread throughout the country. Opposition to the innovation was aroused, not so much by the ceremony itself, as by its Christian Protestant source. Raphall, Isaacs and Leeser were skeptical about the borrowing of "strange fruits." Leeser vacillated. In the very first volume of the *Occident,* he reports the first confirmation ceremony "among American Israelites" held in connection with the Sukkot festival.[17] He explained later that although he was not opposed to its introduction into congregational life—for "many wise and good men" maintain its propriety—nevertheless he was still waiting for proof that this "new ceremony adopted from the Christians" would have beneficial effects on Jewish education.[18] In the course of time, virtually everyone was won over to the constructive effect of this ceremony, and it came to be conducted on Shabuot, the festival of the Giving of the Torah.[19]

Another practice that was accepted by all factions—an innovation which had been introduced in Europe—was the prayer for the welfare of the government. It quickly became a permanent feature of most synagogues.

Decorum in the service and the addition of some new ceremonies did not solve the problem of a general indifference to the synagogue. The treasures of the Torah were being forgotten and the Hebrew language was not understood. The people used translations. The rabbis realized this and reluctantly introduced English into the service, first by translating individual Hebrew prayers and afterwards by introducing new English prayers into the liturgy.

But the greatest innovation, a "revolution" at the time, was the regular English sermon introduced by Isaac Leeser and thereafter observed by other preachers in America. Because he introduced the English sermon as part of the Sabbath service, Leeser was considered a Reformer by the extreme Orthodox, and he writes in one of his articles:

> It [the first sermon] was a painful experience, the issue of which I greatly dreaded. . . . Since the year noted above, the custom has extended almost everywhere, and no congregation thinks itself thoroughly organized without a preacher.[20]

Samuel Myer Isaacs, Leeser's faithful friend, quickly accepted the innovation; and his many successful appearances at various congregations stimulated the demand for English preaching elsewhere. His appearance at Anshe Maariv in Chicago caused that congregation to invite a rabbi who could preach in English. Congregation B'nai Jeshurun in New York made a similar decision when it invited Dr. Raphall in

1849. He was the first rabbi in New York to preach regularly in English on the Sabbaths and festivals. Jastrow was asked by his congregation, Rodeph Shalom, to deliver an English sermon at least once in every four weeks.

English preaching found eager listeners, which in turn emphasized the lack of religious literature in English. As was pointed out in the discussion of Jewish educational materials, not even elementary works were available. The members of the Historical School began to fill this void in what seemed to be the easiest way—by translating the classics of Judaism. Leeser, for example, took Moses Mendelssohn as his model, in an attempt to do for his generation what Mendelssohn had done for his. To this end, Raphall and Szold translated the prayer book and the Bible.

As they proceeded in search of ways to attract the disaffected and disinterested members of the community to the Synagogue, the members of the Historical School began to concern themselves with the modification of a major practice —the exclusive attention given male members in the traditional synagogue. Once again the Historical School was indebted to the Reformers for their criticism of American synagogue practice, which excluded any significant participation of women. The Reformers argued that conditions had changed: women in America were beginning to assume new educational responsibilities in the home, and they were becoming an important influence on cultural activities in the community. Leeser and Raphall had long understood this. Leeser had written as early as 1844:

> The females too belong to Israel, and they also must be taught, that they may understand and observe the law . . . there are a thousand opportunities when man's voice is not heard, when the admonition of the highly endowed and eloquent will remain without effect. . . . There is so much given to women, especially the women of Israel, that we may freely say with a great writer of modern days, whose name we do not now remember, "that we are always what women make us." When the child first begins to think, it is his mother who infuses into his mind the first

ideas. Does he show symptoms of a development of the
power of speech? It is the mother who teaches him to lisp
the first words. Is he able to learn something of God? It is
the mother again who instructs him concerning the great
Being who is the Creator of all. . . . She ought to be deeply
and early impressed, nay penetrated with a profound respect for the Divine ordinances, and be carefully instructed
in the duties which are demanded of us as Israelites, and
be thoroughly initiated in the books of revelation which
contain the basis of our holy faith. . . .[21]

He was particularly anxious to see women supplied with an
English text supplementary to the Hebrew prayer book.
While he never swerved from the position that the basic form
of prayers should be in Hebrew, he nevertheless stated that
"it is erroneous to assert that Israelites are opposed to the
use of prayers in the language of the various countries."[22]
Morris Raphall confirmed Leeser's views. In his preface to
the volume *Ruhama: Devotional Exercises for the Use of the
Daughters of Israel,* which he translated and edited, he describes the need for religious readings and meditations for
women. "In this young country," he writes, "where Hebrew
educational institutions for both sexes are in their infancy,
and where, while boy's schools are few, girl's schools can
scarcely be said to exist; but where nevertheless woman's
pure heart is unchanged—glowing with the same pious aspirations, and longing for the same prayerful outpourings, it
is imperative that attention be paid to these lacunae as well
as to others in the framework of the Synagogue."[23]

Of all the changes and reforms adopted internally by the
members of the Historical School, the most profound was
the recognition that women deserved a more significant role
in the life of the synagogue. Although that role was not easily
or quickly defined, the very acceptance of women as participants in synagogue life wrought a quiet revolution at the
time and subsequently changed the character of the traditional synagogue in America.

Wise and Leeser Cooperate for a National Religious Organization

While they continued to work for basic unity by paring down external differences and by adopting in their synagogues changes and modifications which were within the framework of Jewish tradition, the leaders of the Historical School understood that organizational structure was imperative for a national synagogue movement. The goal, of course, was not unity alone. Unity was the means to defeat the common enemy, Jewish ignorance and apathy; and to rally the people to Jewish life and service. For that purpose, every resource needed to be enlisted. Within the Historical group, Leeser was tireless in his attempt to create institutional unity.

In 1848, Leeser received support from an unexpected source. The editorial office of the *Occident* received a letter from Albany, New York, in which Isaac Mayer Wise penetratingly discussed the idea of unity.[24] He praised Leeser's ideas and promised to support them. In only one sentence is there any indication of a possible future conflict of opinion between himself and Leeser:

> It is lamentable, but true, that if we do not unite ourselves betimes to devise a practicable system for the ministry and religious education at large—if we do not take care that better educated men fill the pulpit and the schoolmaster's chair—if we do not stimulate all the congregations to establish good schools, and to institute a reform in their Synagogues on modern Jewish principles—the house of the Lord will be desolate, or nearly so, in less than ten years . . .

Leeser responded to this prophecy by stating he certainly supported the proposal to establish a national synagogue organization in America. "But we say, in all candour, that any Synagogue reformation, except such a one as looks to raising the standard of decorum and propriety, cannot be supported by us or our journal . . ."[25]

Differing from Leeser tactically, Wise thought that it would be more useful if the rabbis met first in order to ex-

THE OCCIDENT,

AND

AMERICAN JEWISH ADVOCATE.

A MONTHLY PERIODICAL

DEVOTED TO

THE DIFFUSION OF KNOWLEDGE

ON

Jewish Literature and Religion.

EDITED

BY ISAAC LEESER.

ללמוד וללמד לשמור ולעשות
"To learn and to teach, to observe and to do."

VOL. I.

PHILADELPHIA:
PUBLISHED AT 118 SOUTH FOURTH STREET.
5604.

change opinions and prepare the groundwork for a meeting of congregational leaders. Leeser at once recognized the cogency of Wise's suggestion. But other traditional rabbis of the Historical School and those among the Orthodox group did not agree with him. They were afraid of Wise, whom they suspected of radicalism. They asked: How could they, rabbis faithful to Tradition, sit and act with a man whose every desire was to destroy what they were working to preserve? For the sake of unity, Leeser was willing to overlook many of Wise's Reform tendencies. He pleaded with his traditional colleagues not to fight the Reformers.[26] He believed what Isaac Wise had explicitly written:

> I am a reformer, as much so as our age requires; because I am convinced that none can stop the stream of time, none can check the swift wheels of the age; but I have always the *Halacha* for my basis; I never sanction a reform against the *Din*. I am a reformer, if the people long for it, but then I seek to direct the public mind on the path of the *Din;* but I never urge my principles upon another, nor do I commence to start a reform in a Synagogue.[27]

Leeser had always thought that unlimited immigration had brought Reform to these shores.

> Now, as far as the American Israelites are concerned, it was a long time before they felt the contagion. Separated from the old world by the Atlantic, they pursued for a long time a course of godliness according to the best light accessible to them; they were not learned, it is true, neither in Hebrew nor other knowledge, but their heart was true with God, and they strove to do all in their power for the glorification of the Holy Name. But, with an increase of immigration from Europe, persons tinctured with all the modern heresies have mingled among us, and we daily see the effects of their working in our midst. They often decry the ancient usages, and their irreligious conduct is an ample evidence of the spirit within. The profanation of the Sabbath, the eating of forbidden things, the unjewish household, the omission of the covenant of circumcision, and the intermarriages with gentile families, have been chargeable to European immigrants to as great a degree as

to native Americans, though the former have had for the most part greater opportunities of obtaining religious knowledge than the latter. In addition to the open violations we have just mentioned, reform notions of the ultra kind have been brought over to this country chiefly from abroad, or have been excited by foreign example.

In order to turn American Jewry back to Jewish tradition, Leeser was ready to work with everyone. In Wise he found a man who not only spoke boldly but also thought boldly. Leeser and Wise joined each other on the platform of "the demands of the times." Wise at one point frankly wrote to Leeser that he regarded him as "my best friend in this world of flattery and falsehood, since you never hesitate to tell me truly, what you think about."[28] Paradoxically, the association of Leeser and Wise, set against various extremists, points up the tragedy that befell the Jews of America in the nineteenth century when the two men parted company. If these dedicated personalities could have cooperated in later years as they had earlier, the institutional unity of Judaism in America might have been achieved.

Leeser fully recognized the threat that an unrestrained Reform movement posed to the character of American Judaism. The Reformers began by criticizing the lack of order in the synagogue and the length of its prayers, and emphasized the need for English sermons and equality of the sexes—criticism which was accepted by the Historical School. But they ended, as in Charleston, by denying faith in the Messiah and the resurrection of the dead and by eliminating any reference to the Land of Israel. Not all Reformers, however, were as extreme as the congregation in Charleston. Reformers like Wise and Lilienthal appeared to be quite moderate; this in time led the members of the Historical School to think that, with the proper influence and cooperation, they could be made to return to the path of Tradition. Thus Leeser supported the proclamation, issued by Wise and Lilienthal, to call a meeting to discuss unification. Leeser became temporary secretary of the board that was to prepare the meeting.

Wise and Leeser set the time of the meeting for June 1849;

they began to preach and write about the centrality of the synagogue in the American Jewish community. In their writings a change from the original proposals of 1841 can be observed. Leeser was influenced by Wise's suggestion of a national synod in which both rabbis and lay leaders would participate. Eight congregations were receptive to the circular that was sent, but the planners wanted to wait until twenty had responded. Again, New York was decisive.[29] Wise tried to use his personal influence with the Reform synagogues. Temple Emanu-El was opposed to the idea. It feared that the synod would interfere with the development of Reform. Many others expressed similar opposition. Wise did not succeed in achieving general agreement, and he accused the various congregations of opposing him, primarily out of a desire to retain their autocratic rule.

S. M. Isaacs worked with the two planners to encourage the participation of the New York synagogues. Writing in the *Occident,* Isaacs laments the state of indifference, which he believed could lead to catastrophe:

> Alas! alas! that it should be so with a number of our coreligionists; that they should imagine the Synagogue and the charnel house the only prerequisites to attain the key to immortality. . . . We will endeavour to discharge our duty, if not ably, at least fearlessly. Reform and anti-Reform will not escape our lips; there is a broad platform we can occupy in common, without in any way unfurling separate standards. Our advice will be, let the Synagogue alone, let us employ our energies to beautify and adorn the exterior; not to touch the worship but to improve the worshippers; and this will be a fruitful theme for all. Away then with childish fears of danger; we can see nothing but benefit from meeting—the danger we apprehend is lethargic indifference. We for one are unwilling to waste time on the couch of indolence . . .
> We cannot prosper religiously as Jews, unless some great effort be now made to retrieve our condition. The whole church is out of order; instead of a commonwealth we have fifty distinct republics. Synagogues are crying aloud for ministers, and there are found none to respond to the call,

Jewish children are hungering for religious food . . . and
there is none to supply the desideratum; and this in free
and happy America! Where are our collegiate establishments? where our theologian institutes?[30]

Events in Europe added another reason for further indifference. Following the liberal revolutions which were sweeping Europe in 1848, a new society, called the Society of the
Friends of Light, was organized in America. Jews and members of all Christian sects were accepted into it. One of the
purposes of the Society, though not stated explicitly, was the
elimination of boundaries between various world religions.
Many of the former persecuted liberals of Europe, such as
Wise, looked with favor on this new religious utopianism.
And even those who did not were weakened by the movement in their work for such a "small matter" as a Jewish
synod. Wise himself almost decided to return to Europe.[31]
The hour for the synod proved to be inopportune. Up to the
time that was originally determined for the meeting, only one
congregation in New York responded—Shaaray Tefila. Of
necessity, the meeting was postponed indefinitely.[32]

Those who believed that a synod would solve the problem
of Judaism in America stood firm.[33] By 1855, there were 110
synagogues in the United States. Statistics cited by Leeser
reveal the potential communal anarchy perceived by the organizers of the conference.[34] In spite of two failures, the advocates of the Synod refused to give up, and prepared a third
attempt, calling a "Synhedron" of all rabbis in the country.
This third attempt was realized because of the untiring efforts of Wise, who succeeded in convening the Cleveland
Assembly in 1855 under the slogan *Shalom Al Yisrael* (Peace
be unto Israel).[35] Not many promised to come, and those
who did were mostly Reformers. Leeser was the only important exception. At first, even he did not want to associate himself officially with the assembly. He wanted assurance that
the assembly was ready to unite on the basis of his conditions,
namely, that the members of the organization were willing
to accept the Tradition as the basis for their work. The
Orthodox rabbis veered away. Illowy would not meet with

Wise. Altough he signed the original call, he did not come; and Abraham Rice, who wanted to prohibit anyone in his congregation who violated the Sabbath from being called up to the Torah, certainly boycotted the conference. On the other hand, not many eastern Reform congregations were represented because of the sharp competition for power between the leaders of Reform from the East and the West. The extremists among them, led by Einhorn, were not willing to tolerate Wise's compromises with the traditionalists. In spite of all this, the assembly did meet.

Wise was elected chairman, Dr. Elkan Cohn, minister of congregation Anshe Emeth, Albany, New York, vice-chairman, and Dr. Lilienthal, secretary. The proceedings were conducted in German. Leeser abstained from voting because he preferred to remain noncommittal until he could discern the trend of the meeting. After asserting that a Jew could not be read out of Judaism—whether the prayers he recited were many or few, whether the synagogue he attended had an organ or not, whether he observed or did not observe the second days of the festivals—Dr. Wise presented some basic principles without which, he felt, there could be little progress:

1. The first conference of American Rabbins acknowledge the Bible which we have received from our fathers as the revealed word of God, given to us by divine inspiration.

2. . . . . the Talmud contains the logical and legal development of the Holy Scriptures, and . . . its decisions must guide us in all matters of practice and duty.

3. . . . this conference and all future Synods will act according to these principles.

4. . . . the illiberal assertions contained in the Talmud are not of the kind referred to, and have no binding force on us.[36]

It is not known whether Wise unwittingly glossed over the contradiction inherent in the second and fourth principles or introduced the latter in order to excuse actions which contradicted the former. It is known, however, that these words did make an impression, especially on Leeser, who announced that he was ready to become a member of the organization. He also expressed regret that many of his friends, who were traditional rabbis, were not aware in advance of Wise's basically conservative stand. Had they been aware of it, they would all have participated in the assembly without fear of compromising their traditional beliefs. Leeser even suggested that it would be worth while to adjourn the meeting immediately, so that the opinions of Wise could be given widespread publicity, and the following summer call a new meeting with much wider participation. This suggestion was postponed until the next day. Leeser's joy exceeded his amazement when he saw the representatives recite the *minhah* (afternoon) service led by a Reform rabbi praying for the coming of the Messiah and the resurrection of the dead.

Although Leeser agreed with Wise's formulation, on the next day he proposed a correction of Wise's second principle so that no misunderstanding could occur. Leeser's proposal read: ". . . that the Talmud contains the divine tradition given to Moses, and that all Israelites must decide all questions according to its decision." In explanation of his proposal, Leeser added some comments which reveal very much about the thinking of the Historical School. He said that the words "Orthodox" and "Reformers" sounded harsh in his ears. He used the terms "Catholic" and "Reformed" Israelites. "Catholic" Israel would be the term applied to all Jews who accepted the authority of the Talmud, and "Reformed" to those who denied this authority. Leeser wanted Wise and his colleagues to publicly state that they belonged in the first category. The substance of Leeser's proposal was accepted, but in a somewhat changed form. The last paragraph asserted that the Talmud contained the traditional, "logical and legal exposition of the sacred Scriptures . . ."[37] At this point, Leeser had to leave for home; but because of his success, he left with the conviction that harmony was about to visit the Jews of America.

Next day, the meeting reconvened and adopted a number of resolutions that contradicted the gathering's original principles. It was decided to call a regular synod, to appoint two committees to prepare a new prayer service, to organize Zion Collegiate Associations in all cities of the United States, and to condemn all-day schools because the public schools, coupled with supplementary religious education, were sufficient.[38] Leeser heard of these proposals in New York; but he still believed, in spite of his disappointment and on the basis of the first principles that were adopted, work with the Reformers could continue.

The strongest opposition to the results of the meeting in Cleveland did not come from the right. On the contrary, Leeser and Wise both received the approbation of the Orthodox. The extent of the hopefulness of the Orthodox can be gathered from a long letter in Hebrew by Bernard Illowy published in Leeser's *Occident* and in Wise's *American Israelite*. Illowy calls the rabbis assembled "Shepherds of Israel" and Wise "chief shepherd." But, recognizing the discrepancy between Wise's words at Cleveland and many of his actions, Illowy urged Wise to practice as he preached. Illowy's statement spelled out the position of the infant Orthodox movement in America.[39] A storm gathered on the Reform side. Einhorn and his followers felt that Wise had no right to enter into a compromise with the Orthodox and their "talmudic ideas." This was not their interpretation of Reform.[40] Wise offered excuses. The Talmud, he argued, had amended biblical laws, rescinded some, and invented others. Therefore there was no danger in following the spirit of the Talmud.[41] In putting forth this argument Wise showed that he did not understand the extreme Reformers. They wanted to strike out any mention of divine authority.[42] Wise and Lilienthal were not extreme Reformers. Their intention was to work toward gradual Reform, and they were suspicious of extreme Reform because of its consequences in Germany. Wise's moderation is evident in that one of the editions of his prayer book, the *Minhag America*, is all Hebrew without a single prayer in English translation.[43] A division split the ranks of Reform, with criticism centering on Wise.

But Leeser demanded continued activity. Where were the

minutes of the gathering? When would a second meeting be called? When would the promised synod come into being? A good beginning had already been made, now it was necessary to go further. With his vivid imagination, Leeser had seen in the Cleveland conference a single step toward the creation of a Jewish legislative world authority "like the ancient Sanhedrin at Jerusalem." In this way, the Torah would be returned to its original place in the hearts of Jews.[44] Leeser continued to envision the "necessary result" of the Cleveland meeting: America was to be the pathfinder for the Diaspora. There were observant Jews in other countries. Perhaps the Chief Rabbi of Britain, the Dutch rabbinate, the heads of the traditional congregation in Germany and the representatives of France would unite with the rabbis of Russia and Eretz Yisrael to save the faith? That would be the only way in which the needed innovations could be made. The Jews of America alone could not make decisions without the participation of Jewry in all parts of the world and in Eretz Yisrael. And until the election of an authorized higher *Bet Din,* no innovations could have any validity.[45]

These had not been the intentions of Wise and Lilienthal in calling the Cleveland meeting. They were seeking the exact opposite, the creation of a uniquely American Judaism —a *Minhag America.* Wise's new prayer book, on which he had been working ten years, was finally published.[46] The ideas expressed in it and the customs introduced by these moderate Reformers in their synagogues convinced Leeser and his friends, beyond doubt, that a national religious organization could not bring American Jewry closer to its original objective—a return to Judaism. A second meeting was not called, and the Reformers continued reforming. The Cleveland meeting marked the beginning of division, not unity, in American Jewish religion.

Two Trends in the Historical School

In the years following the Cleveland conference, which was to have brought "Peace in Israel," four factions emerged in American Jewry: the Orthodox, the Historical School, the moderate Reform and the extreme Reform. The history of the two middle factions concerns us most directly. For approximately three decades after the Cleveland meeting, their development is related one to the other. At times they joined their efforts in specific areas of religious activity; at other times they stood apart. But while they had given up the possibility of a "united front," each nevertheless hoped that through specific cooperative ventures it would convince the other group of the validity of its ideas.

Argument within the Historical School continued. Leeser's tactics were challenged. How should the Historical School react to Wise and his colleagues? Opinions were divided. Some advised opposition; others reconciliation. Two trends therefore began to take shape: the right wing, or the traditionalists, which included Leeser, Isaacs, Raphall and Morais; and the left wing, or the progressives, which was consolidated after the arrival of Szold and Jastrow.

The first decided to oppose any appearance of Reform, while the latter, in spite of their disagreement with many of the actions of Wise and his group, felt it was better to overlook the unacceptable reforms in order to maintain a pattern of unity.

Leeser and his associates criticized the Reformers, whose fear of agnosticism and irreligiousness, they said, took priority over their religious beliefs. The Reformers' intention, they charged, was to "deform," not reform, Judaism. It was a privilege to be born a Jew, proclaimed Leeser. For this privilege many had given their lives and now these "false prophets" appeared and wished to substitute strange notions for the sacred Law.

The Cleveland meeting, which Leeser had helped bring together, now became a target for derogatory attacks and its decisions were held up to contempt.[47] Reform was bankrupt, the traditionalists claimed; Reform did not solve the question of attendance in the synagogue, it did not increase synagogue membership and it did not deepen religious sentiment in its followers.[48]

The decisive separation came with the beginning of public

participation in the disputes. Many of the details of the theological and talmudic questions were not clear to the average layman. Nevertheless, the general outline of the argument was understood. The followers of Reform discovered that Reform Judaism permitted a lifting of the "burden" of the *mitzvot* and consequently allowed an easier integration with the life of America. The liberal-minded congregations responded by adopting proposals put forward in the rabbis' debates. The arguments within congregations between Reformers and traditionalists were often petty, and sometimes so acrimonious as to lead to physical violence. The organizers of congregation Beth El of Detroit, for example, had enacted a provision in 1850 stating that the congregation could never abandon the Ashkenazi service; but the Reformers found a way of introducing their reform by devious methods. The question of family pews was being debated in the congregation, and the official vote was not conclusive. On the day before Rosh Hashanah, several members of the Reform faction entered the synagogue and removed the seats from the women's section. The next day there was no choice but to let the women sit with the men, "and the women never gave up the privilege."[49] In congregation Adath Israel of Louisville, Kentucky, it was the traditionalist group that threatened violence. When, in 1849, it was proposed to install an organ, the Orthodox faction actually threatened to burn down the synagogue. After some years, the threat was forgotten and the organ installed.[50]

The right wing of the Historical School was determined not to permit the slightest infringement of Jewish laws and customs, especially those authorized by Scripture. But Leeser was expected to propose a positive program, and it was soon forthcoming. He proposed a strong union of those who adhered to Tradition, with the associated congregations on the right wing of the Historical School as its core. The Reformers, according to Leeser, clearly understood their mission and their power, and they worked in unison in order to achieve their goals. He urged the congregations of the Historical School to wake up and choose powerful voices to represent them. It was not possible to observe the Divine commandments and at the same time neglect the world, letting it go its own way, wrote Leeser. The hour demanded union. Characteristically, Leeser's approach was to preserve communication, if at all possible; he was prepared to admit the Reformers into this union, but without the right to vote on religious questions.[51] Until the establishment of this union, however, each individual was to do his part in the war against Reform.

In New York, Morris Raphall was recognized as one of the pillars of the more traditional group in the Historical School. He, S. M. Isaacs and J. J. Lyons composed a formidable group. Morais, too, entered the fray, supporting Leeser in Philadelphia. The Reformers were called a "Jewish Protestant Church," thus clarifying the main theological issue under discussion between the moderate Reform group and the Historical School. This was a theme that Leeser had developed at one time, when he said that Reform conceivably could break up Judaism into many sects as was the case in Protestantism, because each leader wanted to be a Luther, a Melancthon, a Zwingli or a Calvin.[52] But while Leeser's anxieties were, in this regard, organizational, others, like Morais, perceived the true ideological and theological differences. Wise, as Jacob Marcus has written, "was an eighteenth-century European liberal on nineteenth-century American soil."[53] His thinking was shaped by the Enlightenment and the ideals of the Emancipation. Wise discerned a distinctly American formulation of the Jewish tradition in the light of these European ideas. The thoughts expressed in his volume, *Cosmic God,* published in 1876, are not unlike those of his American Protestant contemporaries, such as John Fiske's *Outlines of Cosmic Philosophy* (1874) and similar writings of McCosh and Le Conte.[54] The Historical School, on the other hand, avoided Protestant theological views. Its members sought to root Jewish traditional beliefs in the American soil and in the American situation, while taking full cognizance of the thoughts and needs of the times. When they differed among themselves, it was not in objective, but rather in the kind of adaptation necessary to achieve the objective.

This conflict developed and spread to every state. Even the dead were not exempt. Some congregations, affiliated with the Historical School, refused to bury Reform Jews in their cemeteries; they considered them outcasts and heretics. The champions of the contending groups, Wise and Leeser, at times forgot that they were spiritual leaders. Leeser, in speaking of his old friend, announced publicly that he never read the *Israelite* because "its praise is defamation, and it is a mark of respectability to be covered by its poison.... I. M. W. may continue, for all I care, to be the greatest man living in his own estimation; but this much I will maintain, that if I need any information I shall never go to Cincinnati to obtain it from the man who has caused more disturbance and heartburning than any other Hebrew within the limits between the Atlantic and Pacific."[55] Dr. Lilienthal, Wise's ally, was also attacked though with greater temperance. Nor did either of these lack the power to retaliate.[56]

The approach of Szold, Jastrow and the others of the Historical School's left wing, differed considerably from that of the right. They maintained good relations with Wise and Lilienthal and the other members of the moderate Reform movement, and they were very much impressed by the seriousness of their words. They were stirred by Wise's fight for the observance of the Sabbath in Albany, and his success in this regard in Cincinnati where, with the help of Lilienthal, he induced thirty-seven places of business to close on the Sabbath.

From the time of their arrival in America, Szold (1859) and Jastrow (1866) had been the leaders of the moderate Reform movement in the ranks of the Historical School. Their endeavors brought them the suspicion of both camps. The extreme Reformers, such as Einhorn, considered them Orthodox; and the traditionalists, whether in the Orthodox ranks or in the Historical School (for example, Isaacs and Morais), considered them Reformers.[57] But Szold and Jastrow, who had not suffered the disappointments of the abortive cooperation of the Reform and Historical School, entered the battle fresh, and did not heed these barbs. To the Orthodox, who argued that Judaism needed only one reform—to stop making reforms—they replied that blind Orthodoxy could not exist in America. They insisted that it was not the survival of the *Shulhan Arukh* that was essential, but the survival of Judaism. It was therefore wrong to confuse slight changes with major ones. There are permanent principles of Judaism, but there is, too, a hierarchy of values. They warned the Reformers, on the other hand, not to accept the reforms of the *Sinai* (Einhorn's periodical) as divine revelation. Before destroying one must think of building, and German Reform was built on a foundation of sand.

Orthodoxy and ultra-Reform had become allies, they thought, in turning the youth away from Judaism. The problem of Jewish youth in America, they contended, was the choice between an opaque Orthodoxy and an extreme Reformist stand on the one hand, and a temperate fusion of Tradition and progress on the other.

In the opportunistic nature of Wise's Reform, too, they saw no permanent future. Therefore, they attempted to cut a new path. On the whole they accepted the approach of Zachariah Frankel, Solomon J. L. Rapoport, Michael Sachs, and the school of Breslau which so effectively counteracted the influence of the radical rationalism of Samuel Holdheim and his associates upon the Jewish youth in Germany. A summary of this view can be found in an article, defending Jastrow, which Szold wrote when Jastrow was attacked by Samuel Hirsch, an extreme Reformer.[58]

Szold granted authority to the living person, the rabbi, instead of to the written law. Every rabbi may attempt to better the condition of his congregations by reforms, providing his intentions are sincere:

> Reform does not yet have any fixed dogmas. The definition of its contents and limits must therefore be left to the insight of the rabbis who must reckon with the

needs of the congregation. They may introduce those reforms which they are convinced will sooner or later give
to the congregation an enlightened understanding of the
deeper contents which lie in Judaism.

But Szold made one condition: that the reforms enhance,
and not destroy, the Judaism of the life of the congregation
and its congregants. Such constructive reforms were good
even if they were of doubtful legal status, because their
purpose was to bring the people to a greater observance of
the precepts. It was therefore improper for one congregation
to compare its reforms with those of another. Such an approach would not produce any harmful effects as long as the
rabbis of the congregations were pious men who understood
both the sources of Judaism and the spirit of the times. It
was likely that with time all the individual and local reforms
would be combined into an harmonious whole. Szold argued
that it was not right to speak against this or that act of
Reform, since it was permissible at times to approve something for others which one would not approve for oneself.
The main task was to find the historical or logical reason for
Tradition. And if this proved impossible, individual *mitzvot*
might have to be adjusted to the demands of the time.[59]

Even though religious reforms were necessary, it was not
right for the rabbi to be subordinate to the will of the laity.
"Judaism has two basic principles," Szold wrote, "one is
mobile, the other is static. Only through the fusion of both
elements will we discover the golden mean."[60] Therefore,
explained Szold, he chose the middle path between the two
extremes. This middle position was not, in his opinion, a
compromise. On the contrary, the indispensability of the
mitzvot to Judaism must be affirmed. The Torah with no
source is no Torah; Reform should aim at the maintenance
of *mitzvot* and not their abolition. Growth does not come in
a leap, through radical changes or the abolition of customs,
but rather by adapting the *mitzvot* to the contemporary situation.[61]

Szold's and Jastrow's ideas about the nature of Reform
were given practical application. Both felt the need for a

new *siddur* (prayer book) in which ideas on God, the Torah, Israel, and mankind might be expressed in prayer. The need to change the prayer book had long been felt. American Jews were not willing to pray in a language which they did not understand, even though it was "a holy language." Many could not even read Hebrew. And when the prayers were translated and, more often, paraphrased into German, there were objections to the contents. "Modern" worshipers insisted on prayers that were in the "spirit of the times," and they objected to prayers that spoke for bygone ages. Many rabbis tried to meet the expressed needs of their congregations. The *American Jews' Annual* of 1888 reports that in 1855 there were nine Reform congregations in the United States using six different prayer books. The abundance of individual prayer book production in congregations which veered to Reform was characteristic of this epoch, for rabbis felt entirely free to create their own forms of worship.

The first prayer books were mainly condensations of the traditional service with the addition of various prayers in English.[62] Between 1856-8, Dr. Einhorn of Baltimore issued his prayer book, *Olat Tamid*, an extreme innovation written mostly in German. It had only a small number of Hebrew prayers. Einhorn was not satisfied with condensation alone and introduced basic changes into the *siddur*. The popularity of Einhorn's prayer book is demonstrated by the fact that it went through several editions within a few years. Einhorn left no trace of prayers that speak of the renewal of sacrifices, the return to Zion, the Kingdom of David and the resurrection of the dead. Dr. Wise and Dr. Huebsch, in their respective prayer books published during these years, made radical departures from the traditional prayer book, although they were not as extreme as Einhorn's. Every one of these prayer books was unacceptable to middle-of-the-roaders like Szold and Jastrow. They awaited an opportunity to edit the prayer book according to their own ideas. The opportunity came in Szold's Baltimore congregation.

Congregation Oheb Shalom was originally Orthodox, but its ties with Tradition slowly began to weaken and the congregation began to lean toward Reform. The transition was manifest through many changes in the prayers, the invitation to Dr. Wise to preach at the dedication of its building, and in the acceptance of *Minhag America* as the prayer book for weekdays and Sabbaths. (The *Minhag America* prayer book for the holidays had not yet appeared.) When Dr. Szold came to America, he found this peculiar condition: weekdays and Sabbaths, the congregation used a Reform prayer book; but on the High Holy Days, they used the traditional prayer book. He pointed out the incongruity, but the leaders of the congregation would not listen. After a time, he convinced them of his views; but they asked him to wait until matters had become more settled in the congregation. Szold realized that, unless he acted, the congregation would become Reform. Although he was willing to overlook the transgression of many traditional principles and customs, he did not wish to see his congregation go over to the other side completely.

Szold explained to his congregation that one could not straddle the fence forever. Logic did not permit such a mixture of contradictory practices. He said that he was not willing to serve a congregation whose position was not clear. The congregation listened and appointed a committee to produce a new prayer book. This action angered Szold, who saw in it an act of religious impudence. As a result, the committee was compelled to leave the preparation of the new prayer book to Szold himself. Szold asked Henry Hochheimer, then the rabbi in Baltimore who supported Szold's views, to help him in this task.[63] Szold did not rest until he had prepared the new *siddur;* and in 1864 he completed his work, and delivered the manuscript of the prayers for the daily and festival service, entitled *Abodat Israel.*[64] It had a Hebrew text with translation in German. The congregation accepted it and, after a short time, it was used in most German-speaking congregations, especially throughout southern and western United States. The following year, Szold prepared a Hebrew-English edition.

Jastrow found in Szold's prayer book many features that he liked; but there were numerous details of which he did not approve. He prepared the second edition, and it appeared in 1871. As the number of German-speaking Jews decreased, the demand for an English prayer book increased. Jastrow adapted the text in his own English version, added some prayers, and this prayer book came to be accepted by the people under the name of *Minhag Jastrow*. The *Abodat Israel* prayer book reflects the theology of the left wing of the Historical School. We shall discuss it in a later chapter. It represented not only a collection of innovations and decorations, but a coherent viewpoint upon which Szold, Jastrow and Hochheimer insisted in their writings and sermons.

These changes brought others in their wake. The members of the left wing in the Historical School set themselves two goals: first, to recognize the obsolescence of those customs whose basic value had been lost in the countries of western Europe and America; second, the introduction of order and decorum in the service. To beautify the service they introduced an organ, had the cantor pray facing the congregation, and permitted mixed choirs. In Szold's and Jastrow's synagogues, family pews were introduced. These two rabbis made the sermon a permanent part of the service; Dr. Jastrow also introduced another custom when he came to this country: late Friday night services.[65]

One reform led to another. The time for more basic changes had come. The sale of religious honors, which had disturbed all enlightened leaders of the various factions, was quickly abolished. It was also decided to shorten the time for the Torah reading. In Szold's congregation a third of the weekly portion was read each Sabbath, so that the Torah was read completely in the course of three years. Jastrow, for his part, decided not to read the traditional portion each week; instead he selected on any Sabbath a part of the Torah that appealed to him and read it.[66]

In congregation Rodeph Shalom, most of the congregants could not even recite the blessing for the Torah, and the leaders of the congregation were therefore faced with a difficult problem. The committee that was concerned with the prayer service suggested that the custom of calling up to the Torah on the Sabbath and holidays be abolished entirely, with the exception of children who had reached the age of Bar Mitzvah. They turned to Jastrow and he wrote a responsum. He cited many facts about the development of the calling to the Torah and cited the opinion of one talmudic commentator, the "Rosh," Asher ben Yehiel: one who could not read the portion of the Torah himself should follow the public reader in an undertone. Within a short time even this requirement was abolished. Jastrow continued:

> From the above it is easy to conclude that if the state of Hebrew knowledge in a congregation is such as to make it questionable whether or no all those who are called up do really say the required benediction, and furthermore if there are persons who feel embarrassed when being called up, because they are placed in the dilemma either to refuse an honor bestowed upon him or to lend themselves to a sham; such a congregation has a right to follow analogous precedents and abolish the calling up to the Torah . . . As the Minister interested in the peace of the congregation, I take the liberty of going beyond the limits of a mere legal opinion, in offering the suggestion whether it would not be advisable to lay the question of abolishing the calling up, together with my above set forth opinion before the next General Meeting of the congregation.[67]

Still other reforms followed these changes. In Szold's congregation, Oheb Shalom, the second days of the various holidays were abolished as were all fast days except Yom Kippur, daily services and the putting on of *tefillin*. The eating of dairy meals in non-kosher restaurants was permitted. And even though both Szold and Jastrow fought for the traditional Sabbath, they traveled on the Sabbath when necessary. Similarly, Szold recited grace without a hat, although in his synagogue he did not permit the removal of hats. As for Aaron Bettelheim, who was according to Rebekah Kohut, even more liberal, he was not particularly stringent in his observance of the dietary laws, saying, "It is more important to guard that which goes out of the mouth than that which goes in."[68] These facts reveal how close in some practices the left wing of the Historical School was to Reform.

Nevertheless, on the foundations and principles of traditional practice—the Sabbath, the dietary laws and the Hebrew service—the left wing of the Historical School in America, like its teachers in Europe before them, stood on common ground with the right wing, continuing to preach the need for a basic, continuing tradition in Judaism. Therefore, a break between Wise, Jastrow and Szold was inevitable, but it did not come until several decades later. In the sixties and early seventies Szold and Jastrow, like Morais, H. Pereira Mendes, and other "rightists," ardently supported Wise and his plans for a rabbinical school which ultimately led to the founding of the Hebrew Union College. During those decades, Szold and Jastrow, like Leeser and Isaacs in the forties and fifties, tried to heal the breach in the name of unity; they always hoped to lead the Reformers to better ways.

Wise, however, who introduced his reforms slowly, continued to move toward pragmatic, but complete, Reform. He began with small changes and ended with major reforms. The abolition of the fundamental *mitzvot* was against the spirit of Szold and Jastrow; Einhorn and Hirsch were too radical for them. Jastrow considered Wise flippant. Despite their opposition to many of Wise's actions, Szold and Jastrow decided to work with him as the only way to build a unified American Jewish community. Unity without uniformity was the byword within their congregations and on the national Jewish scene. This was Szold's theme at the first graduation of the Hebrew Union College.

By the 1860s the religious picture had undergone radical changes. American Judaism was divided into three factions: extreme Reform, moderate Reform (the Wise-Lilienthal group in Reform and the Szold-Jastrow group in the Historical School), and the Orthodox (the traditionalist wing of the Historical School and the Orthodox). The voice of each of these camps was, respectively, the *Sinai,* the *Israelite,* and the *Occident*. But basic changes were beginning to be manifest. Within the next fifteen years they brought about a profound revolution in the religious life of American Jewry, a revolution which shaped twentieth-century Judaism in America.

Part II

New Alignments
(1870—1886)

Chapter One

The Growth
of Reform
Judaism

The Civil War was a needless war, a hecatomb which could have been avoided. Yet, as Allan Nevins writes, it left a lasting impression on the American character, transforming "an inchoate nation, individualistic in temper and wedded to improvisation, into a shaped and disciplined nation, increasingly aware of the importance of plan and control. . . . The resultant alteration in the national character was one of the central results of the gigantic struggle."[1] Stronger in structure and less divided within, the American people intuitively followed the advice set forth in Lincoln's last speech of April 11, 1865: simply to "begin with, and mould from disorganized and discordant elements."

The time of Reconstruction had come. The new American frontier was in the cities. Agricultural centers were flourishing but the greatest growth was in industry and manufacturing. The improving economic situation in America, which coincided with the political and social deterioration of East-European society, propelled a large number of Jews and other East-Europeans to the United States during the seventies and eighties of the century. The statistics of Jewish settlement up to 1880 reveal the sudden increase of Jewish population and the development of the Jewish community in the swelling cities of the land—all before the great mass movement from Europe to America began in earnest. The radical nature of the cultural and religious changes in American

Jewish life can more easily be understood in the light of these demographic and economic climacterics.

It is estimated that the number of Jews in the United States in 1880 had risen to approximately a quarter of a million. The great majority of them were settled in the large cities of the country. Almost half the Jewish population, more than 100,000 (about 45%), lived in eastern cities; 12,000 (about 5%) in southern cities along the Atlantic coast; 35,000 (about 15%) in the Middle West; and 20,000 (about 8%) in the cities of Texas and California.[2]

Those cities with the largest Jewish populations were: In the East: New York (with Brooklyn), 70,000; Philadelphia, 12,000; Baltimore, 10,000; in the Southeast: Richmond, 1,200; Charleston, 700; Savannah, 600; in the South: Mobile, 500; New Orleans, 5,000; Louisville, 2,500; in the Middle West: Cincinnati, 8,000; Cleveland, 3,500; Chicago, 10,000; Detroit, 2,000; St. Louis, 6,000; in the Southwest: Galveston, 1,000. There were also some Jewish settlements in Kansas, Iowa, Utah and Nevada. The largest settlement in the West was in San Francisco, 16,000.

These numbers also indicate the distribution of Jews in relation to the expanding economy. The fortunes of the native Jews rose or ebbed with the growth or decline in the regions of their respective settlement. Newcomers were naturally attracted to areas of growth. The East was caught up in a boom. New factories, businesses and mounting populations combined to double and triple the industrial production of that region. The South was stagnant. Wounded and defeated, it had to recover from the destruction of the war. The West was flourishing. The prospect of gold attracted adventurers, and small communities quickly came into existence. The Middle West was also developing swiftly. This region of America became the great competitor of the East. Cincinnati, sometimes called the "Queen of the West" and sometimes "Porkopolis" because of its meatpacking industry, now reached the peak of its development. It is no wonder that this city, the oldest Jewish community west of the Alleghenies (founded in 1817), rapidly growing in Jewish population, became a seat of authority in the spiritual life of American Jewry. But the strategic position of Cincinnati in the rapidly increasing population of the Ohio and Mississippi Valleys and the rising prosperity of the region do not wholly account for the success and influence of its Jewish community.

A new doctrine emanated from Cincinnati only after two influential and active personalities settled there—Isaac Mayer Wise and Max Lilienthal. These two dynamic leaders took advantage of a promising situation. Within a short time, Reform won over most of organized Jewish religious life. The vast majority of the builders of Judaism in America during the post-Civil War period were emigrants from Germany or descendants of such emigrants, many of whom had settled in the cities of the Middle West. Forms of religious adjustment within the context of modern nationalistic thought were being hammered out in Germany, and the Jews who came from Germany were eager to utilize that experience. In the cities of the East, they found established synagogues with customs which could not easily be changed. But in the West, where they themselves were building, it was easy to introduce new ways. Reform leadership took full advantage both of the German-American love of Fatherland and of the opportunity for making innovations offered by the new American civilization which encouraged voluntary group action. Describing the general intellectual ferment in the Midwest, Carl Wittke has pointed out that among the German immigrants of the fifties were several "enlightened" men who considered it their unequivocal mission to plant in American soil the liberal views they had brought with them from Europe. They spared no effort to eradicate the "clericalism, supernaturalism and priestcraft" rampant in American religious and cultural life. Under their influence, the entire German community in the United States experienced its "Hellenic Age."[3] Among the Jews, David Einhorn was one of the leading exponents of these views. He was extreme in his devotion to German *Kultur*.[4]

Economic success and cultural identification with the dominant German settlement in America combined to give the Reform Jews a high social status—a status many aspired to share. The ranks of Reform Judaism swelled, therefore, not only because of its principles, but because of the natural human tendency to associate with a relatively high status group. Social status and Reform, it seemed, went together, and many thought that the first was the consequence of the second. This attitude prevailed especially after the beginning of the Russian emigration, when the majority sought to emancipate itself from the cultural milieu of which traditional Judaism was an expression. A good example is congregation Beth Sholem, the Sephardi synagogue of Richmond, Virginia, which so stubbornly adhered to its Orthodox ways that in 1869 only the rabbi and cantor prayed there regularly, although the congregation had not formally abandoned Orthodoxy. But when the new Russian emigrants began coming to the state, the old German Orthodox members of the congregation joined the Reform temple as a group in order to separate themselves from their East-European brothers rather than strengthen the old congregation by receiving them within their fold.[5]

The emphatic surge of Reform Judaism was met by the counter-Reform of the Historical School. Indeed, counter-Reform was the chief characteristic of the Historical School in its early days, as well as the main reason for the growing use of the term "conservative" to describe its purpose and activities. In order to grasp the nature of this counter-Reform movement we should first see in perspective the personality and thoughts of Isaac Mayer Wise, the driving power of the Reform movement, and review the various rabbinical conferences in the late sixties and early seventies, out of which he forged a constructive program of action.

Isaac Mayer Wise

Wise, the Father of Reform Judaism, or "American Judaism," as he preferred to call it, designed and erected the three pillars upon which the Reform edifice stands today: the Union of American Hebrew Congregations, the Hebrew Union College and the Central Conference of American Rabbis. Admirer and critic alike have recognized his executive and imaginative drive. Few have succeeded in viewing him objectively. The reason for the extreme judgments which he has precipitated can be found in the contradictions of his personality and opinions.[6] But what seemed to be an unending chain of inconsistencies was actually a pattern of behavior based on his view of Judaism's role in the world. In an autobiographical statement, Wise interpreted his actions as follows:

> I was never one to storm heaven; I no more wanted to change the world than I was weary of it. The schoolteacher still resided within me; I wanted only to teach, and that in my own fashion only. To me, Reform never was an end in itself; I considered it only a necessary means to clarify the teachings of Judaism, and to transfigure, exalt, and spread these teachings. I never assumed the role of a Reformer, and never called *The Israelite* a Reform organ; it was an organ for Judaism.[7]

According to Wise, the Ten Commandments were the basis of Judaism. His slogan was "Back to Mosaism." Whoever believed in the truth of the Revelation at Sinai and observed its ethical commandments could accurately be called a Jew. The rest of the Torah Wise considered subordinate to the main principles enunciated in the Ten Commandments. "Religion," he stated, "is a set of principles and not a system of observances or a mode of belief or worship." Wise distinguished between the Torah and Israel. Ethics was the most important guide of all mankind, and all men were responsible for its observance. Wise envisaged the creation of a universal faith, and he believed that if the various sectarian customs and ceremonies were to be sacrificed in favor of this great ideal, all would accept the true religion.

> The difference between us and our opponents is simply this: We understand Judaism to be a religion, or rather, the only universal religion, while they understand it to

be a system of observances peculiar to the Jewish people. Therefore with us observances are of secondary importance, while they are of primary importance with our opponents. Only such observances and practices which might and should become universal, because they would be beneficial to all men, are with us inherent elements of Judaism, while our opponents from their standpoint look upon every Jewish custom as an essential element of their religion. We can not agree with them.[8]

Wise believed that America was the best soil in which this universal faith could grow. "Moses formed one pole and the American Revolution the other, of an axis around which revolved the political history of thirty-three centuries." The Mosaic faith had found its fulfilment in the political order of the United States, a nation based on the Declaration of Independence and the Constitution. As Bernard J. Bamberger has explained: "The American Judaism which Wise taught was not a combination of two separate elements, the American and the Jewish. Wise felt the deep inner harmony of American and Jewish ideals. At their highest and best, so he declared, Americanism and Judaism are one."[9] Such an appreciation of Americanism was uniquely appropriate to the background of an immigrant German rabbi.

What, therefore, was the mission of Israel? To propagate the future universal faith which would come into being as the religion of Israel without its traditional, national characteristics. In spite of the opposition of Christian theologians, the form of this religion would be Jewish. Wise believed that many of the Jewish customs should be incorporated into the order of universal holidays. He hoped that mankind would accept the Jewish festivals as part of its one religion: Passover as the first liberation from slavery; Shabuot as the commemoration of the giving of the Ten Commandments which are the basis of civilization; Sukkot as a holiday of thanksgiving for all mankind. Rosh Hashanah and Yom Kippur would also receive their special place in the universal holidays—Rosh Hashanah as a day of reckoning for society and the individual, and Yom Kippur as a day of forgiveness for all mankind.

The redemption of mankind, Wise taught, would come through American Israel. This idea was adumbrated as early as 1849 in a series of articles in the *Occident*. Wise named the first in the series "The Mission of Israel."[10] Again, his ambivalent statements are manifest. On one hand, in the following citation, he explained that Judaism without ceremonial is like a kernel without a shell:

> We stand before the world with the consciousness of the treasures we possess, and the duties we have to perform to the human family. . . . In order to do this, we must also preserve a number of ceremonies and observances, which are necessary to preserve the union of Israel, but appear ridiculous or at least superfluous to others, and stand in our way of progress, retarding our mission to the human family. . . . Here you stand with your grand conviction that you do possess the sublime and divine truths to redeem the human family from the miseries of centuries, but you cannot break through the shell which embraces the kernel without destroying the fruit. You cannot break asunder the bonds of observances and ceremonies, without breaking down the congregation of Israel, the very vessel, the only vessel, in which these truths have been safely kept up to date. You cannot fulfill one mission of Israel without injuring the other. . . .[11]

In another context, Wise expounded that the shell dare not conceal the kernel:

> Time changes, but our religion changes not, hence its forms must be changed, for the forms must be agreeable to the demands of the time. Forms change—this is reform; all forms are immutable—this is the principle of the orthodox, to which they do not adhere however.[12]

Since the United States was a country in which Church and State were separated, it was incumbent upon Jews to break down all divisions that separated them from the Christians, thereby clearing the road for the universal faith. Wise's opinions were directed to the entire American religious community. He strove to remove from mankind's path not only the impediment of Jewish Orthodoxy, but that also of Christian Orthodoxy. "We firmly believe," he said, in July of 1866, "that the day is not very distant when all Christians will understand the Christian story, as it originally was intended, as a legend, to convert the Heathens to the Monotheism and the Ethics of Israel."[13] With this purpose in mind, he wrote the following books: *The Origin of Christianity, and a Commentary to the Acts of the Apostles* (1868); *The Martyrdom of Jesus of Nazareth* (1874); *Judaism and Christianity, their Agreements and Disagreements* (1883); *A Defense of Judaism versus Proselytizing Christianity* (1889); and a series of articles, "Jesus Himself," that were printed in the pages of the *American Israelite*.[14]

Wise felt that with this "enlightened" ideology he would be able to capture all the wings of Reform and become their leader. He was mistaken. Those who were trained in Germany and had absorbed the theory of Reform at its source had participated in its explication and development in Europe, and did not want to leave theological interpretation to Wise.[15] Wise, moreover, was deterred by the realization that all conflicts were not theoretical ones. Some were conflicts of personality, soon to develop between the eastern and western Reform factions. These rivalries came to the fore in a series of gatherings organized in a brief span of time from 1869 to 1871. Distinctively Reform interpretation and practice in American Judaism were the outcome.

Reform Rabbinical Conferences

In 1867 and 1868, Wise began to advocate in the pages of *The Israelite* a unification of Reform forces for the sake of concerted action. It was a plea that had been heard as far back as the Cleveland Conference in 1855. Eighteen congregations agreed to participate in the proposed meeting. But meanwhile, Samuel Adler and David Einhorn went ahead on their own and convened a rabbinical gathering in 1869. Dr. Wise overlooked his own prestige for the sake of harmony and came East to participate in the meeting, held at the home of Samuel Hirsch in Philadelphia.[16]

The text of the resolutions adopted then—the first formal statement of Reform Judaism in America—bears the stamp of Einhorn's personality. In the third paragraph especially, Einhorn's unique ideas about the function of the priesthood in Judaism are clear. The other resolutions, excluding the last which in effect removes Hebrew as the language of prayer, do not effectively differ from the basic program laid down by Wise and accepted with minor changes by most Reformers.[17]

Wise's fortunes were on the decline at the Philadelphia gathering. Among the suggestions that were rejected was one calling for the reissuance of his *Minhag America* in a new edition, and its acceptance by all Reform congregations. When Wise saw himself defeated in the East, he apparently decided that, if he could not be the leading power there, he would call a session in the West, one which he could dominate. Instead of carrying out the decision which had been adopted with his consent at the Philadelphia meeting—that he convene the same group in a second session—he called a meeting in Cleveland in 1870 of all those who were interested in reissuing his *Minhag America*. Thirteen rabbis accepted his invitation. The aims of the meeting were broadened in the process; resolutions very similar to those accepted in Philadelphia were adopted, but with different headings. With the caucus organized, the rabbis with Wise at their helm decided to travel to New York and meet with the eastern group in order to gain the upper hand. In this way Wise planned to outwit Einhorn, but Einhorn proudly refused to participate. When the group returned West, the Reform camp was split.[18]

Wise announced a third gathering, this time to be convened in Cincinnati in 1871. Twenty-seven representatives appeared, most of them from the West. At this meeting, Wise revealed his plan for strengthening Reform in America. After much debate about the Sunday schools, it was decided to seek a remedy through improvement of textbooks and educational methods. A proposal was also made to appoint a number of itinerant rabbis to visit congregations lacking spiritual leadership. The prayer book, *Minhag America,* was turned over to a final examining committee. The most important suggestion, which was to give American Jews the Hebrew Union College, the Union of American Hebrew Congregations and the Sabbath School Union, was put forth by Dr. Wise and accepted unanimously by the gathering. The text of the resolution is as follows:

> The members of this Conference take upon themselves the duty to bring prominently before the congregations to advocate and support, by their influence, the following project of co-operation of the American Hebrew Congregations:
> 1. The congregations unite themselves to a Hebrew Congregational Union, with the object to preserve and advance the union of Israel; to take proper care of the development and promulgation of Judaism; to establish and support a scholastic institute, and the library appertaining thereto, for the education of rabbis, preachers and teachers of religion; to provide cheap editions of the English Bible and textbooks for the schools of religious instruction to give support to weak congregations; and to provide such other institutions which elevate, preserve and promulgate Judaism.
> RESOLVED, That whenever twenty congregations, with no less than two thousand contributing male members, shall have declared, in accordance with the preceding resolution, their resolution to enter the H.C.U. the said committee shall convoke the Synod to meet at such time and place as may be most satisfactory to the co-operating congregations.

These three gatherings—in Philadelphia, Cleveland and Cincinnati—laid the groundwork for a common platform in the future. They also introduced into American Jewry young men of great energy and imagination. One of them, Kaufmann Kohler, participated in the Philadelphia meeting a few months after his arrival in America. His notes about the gathering reveal his enthusiasm for Reform:

> The broadness of view and independence of thought, which characterized all the deliberations, formed a striking contrast to what I had heard and witnessed at the Leipzig Synod, and I thanked God for having been permitted to come to America, the land of liberty and large opportunity to help, with the power allotted to me, in the building up of American Reform Judaism, the religion of the future.[19]

Counter-Reform or Conservative Judaism

Kaufmann Kohler expressed the sentiment of Reform Jewry in general. Reform had established itself as a permanent reality in America Jewish life and, in fact, represented for most of American Jewry the "religion of the future." The concern of Kohler and his colleagues became that very issue upon which the division in American Judaism was based: how to determine the best way of accommodating Judaism to the American environment. The Reformers held that theirs was the road to the future. The Historical School sought another method. If the problem really was the definition of the Jewish tradition's relevance to American culture, then the Tradition could adapt itself in terms of its own authenticity and integrity, as it always had, to an inconstant world. The Historical group was confident that the organic development of Judaism would continue even in and through American life, if it followed its own disciplines, forms and foci of commitment. They held that Judaism was a unity and rejected the distinctions, posited by the German and American Reformers, between the particular and the universal, the practical commandments and morality, between that which was unique to the Jews and that which was common to all humanity. Through its encounter with the free and open civilization evolving in America, the Reformers saw Judaism as essentially a universal religion to be disassociated from the earlier historical forms created by the Jews. The

Historical School did not distinguish between the history
and the religion of the Jews but looked, rather, to both in
the belief that they would show the way to the "religion of
the future."

Thus the "counter-Reform" movement took shape. Although the name "Conservative Judaism" was given to the
Historical School in the late nineteenth and early twentieth
centuries, at no time in the history of the School did the name
suit it more than during the period under discussion. This
was the time, the Historical group contended, to conserve;
otherwise the winds of change would sweep away all hope of
relating American Judaism to the continuum of Jewish
tradition.

The Historical School had lost the initiative in organizing
permanent institutions. Their earlier strategy to win over
to moderation the leading personalities of the Reform
tendency had ended in failure. The internal condition of the
Historical School was also deteriorating. The leader of the
fight against Reform, Leeser, had died in 1868. Szold, Jastrow,
and Hochheimer were cooperating with the Reform group.
Morais, Isaacs and others were left to struggle as best they
could.

But the very coalescence of the Reform group created a
challenge which rallied the sagging forces. New sources of
strength were, first, the disenchantment of the "left-wing"
group with Reform Judaism; second, the arrival of like-
minded rabbinical leaders from Europe; and most important,
the mass migrations from eastern Europe which solidified
the base of traditional Judaism in America. The lines of
counter-Reform were now sharply drawn and the battle was
fought, in America as elsewhere, on the issues of the historic
Sabbath, the Hebraic character of Jewish life and learning,
and the traditional synagogue liturgical rubric.

One year before the Philadelphia meeting of 1869, when
first word of the impending gathering was heard, representatives of congregations connected with the Historical School
had convened in New York to consider the problem of Sabbath observance.[20] The very need to call such a conference

manifested the lowered religious standards of the American Jewish community. Widespread disregard of the Sabbath was a sign of Jewish group disintegration. The choice seemed to be Sabbath observance or dissolution of American Judaism:

> Our religion never was in such danger as it is today, and why? Because the day which has been kept holy by our fathers since time immemorial, which is the distinguished feature of Judaism, the only day on which we can expect to meet our brethren in the House of Worship, to address our Maker in common, and to hear from the lips of our spiritual leaders the lessons of truth, religion, and morality, is habitually disregarded, and spent as any other week day is. What avail us so many congregations? What, beautiful temples? What, fine sounding organs? What, well organized choirs? What, eloquent preachers, if people prefer to hunt up a customer to visiting the synagogue? Do you actually believe you can buy off with money the obligation to your moral self, your brethren, your family and the community? Or do you, rather, mean to have splendid coffins in which to enshrine your religion, which to you has become time-worn, antiquated, and of no more significance? Or shall these palaces be monuments to show to the coming generations that there was a time when Jews spent money for fine edifices, and that they felt a pride not to be outdone in this respect by other religious denominations . . .
>
> Remember Israelites you stand not alone . . . The world holds the Jewish nation responsible for the Jews and the nation has the right to ask of you to unite your fortune with hers. The Sabbath must be reconquered and restored or Judaism is lost for the Future . . .[21]

In 1870, the congregational leaders of the Historical School convened a second time, hoping to start a movement to retain the time-honored place of Hebrew in the *siddur*. The Reformers were slowly stripping the *siddur* of Hebrew; the Conservatives expressed their opposition, but the group dispersed and nothing permanent came of the gathering.

The times called for imaginative action on the part of the Historical School if it was not to lose its congregations to the Reform movement. Quite unexpectedly, Morais came forth with a plan which, for him, was as radical as it was bold—a unified *minhag* for all synagogues in America. The plan, worked out with the help of Samuel Isaacs, was revolutionary in approach. It was announced first in the *Jewish Record* of Philadelphia and later in Isaacs' periodical, the *Jewish Messenger*.[22] A decade earlier, it could have been prepared by Wise or Lilienthal. Obviously, Morais could not adopt the thinking of the Reformers. When he offered to relinquish the Sephardi *minhag*, on which he had been reared, in order to accept the Ashkenazi *minhag* with various modifications and changes, Morais acknowledged the compelling argument of the Reformers: the need to reckon with the desires of "young Israel of America." Because of the importance attached to this statement and all that it discloses about the prevalent mood of the Historical School, we cite a large portion of the document.

I grew in the love of the observance of Judaism, and in the fond attachment for the Sephardic Minhag, the only ritual existing in my native city. The very melodies, especially those for the New Year and the Day of Atonement had a charm which the softest of musical strains cannot surpass.... I bound myself with a written contract to follow in the wake of my predecessors and adhere to the Portuguese mode of worshipping and hold up the golden standard . . .

But here I learned how obedience to my feelings and to my pledge was surrounded with ever-increasing difficulties. A floodtide of emigration set in during the last quarter of a century. Men of all nationalities and languages came to our shores, and brought along not only the liturgies of the different countries, but local usages, around which they cast a halo of sanctity and to which they would still raise high altars.

A seething mass of Minhagim effervesced in our midst and "Reform" so called also bubbled up . . .

A quarter of a century has created changes obvious to all discerning minds. What the parents delighted in has ceased to attract their children. Let these circumstances be unwelcome or otherwise, they are palpable facts. With them we must deal, and not with abstractions. Young Israel of America ask for a code less complex in its rules; for a worship, which may prove to them more soul-stirring in its ceremonials. That portion of our household occupies my anxious thoughts; to prevent their total estrangement from us through our rejection of their request, their seeking sympathy among strangers to our faith because of our condemning of their wishes, I would sacrifice much that time and early training have engrafted on my very nature. I would work for the purpose steadfastly and to the furthest extent of my humble abilities with all sincere and understanding men; studying to discover what concessions might be made without trenching upon the essentials of our religion . . .

Portuguese and German, Polish and Hollander, in connection with the manner of worshipping Israel's God, are names that should, long ere this, have been erased from our nomenclature. They ought, at all events, to have been forgotten on reaching the shores of this land of equal freedom. The badge we all should have proudly worn is that of "American Jews"; not implying by it a severance of religious sentiments from the rest of our people beyond the sea, but signifying that the circumstances which had given origin to marked differences in the ritual had ceased to exist, and that the necessity for reconstructing another, perfectly uniform, and more conformable to our changed condition, had arrived. . . . We must work to preserve historical Judaism, though for its sake concessions for which we are unprepared may be demanded . . .

The demand is for a simpler prayer-book, and to effectually stop capricious changes, it must unavoidably be granted. Expunge, then, what relates to the ordinances followed by the ancients in the performances of sacrificial rites; strike out what belongs to Mishnic and Talmudic lore; reduce the number of Psalms now to be daily rehearsed; avoid, as far as practicable, the reiterating of a supplication, confession, or sacred song; eschew the utterance of all sorts of denunciations; compare philologically long-established Rituals; study to discover in them what is more correct in diction, select what is more chaste in style, more exalting in ideas and what is more likely to have emanated from the venerable body whose leading spirit was, our second Moses, even, Ezra the priest. Then endeavor to fill up a portion of the space made empty by the expurgatory process with compositions suited to our existing wants. The printed and inedited writings of our philosophers and poets can supply a vast deal; the learning of our modern Rabbis may also be of service in that department . . .

Whatever ritual is agreed upon for the Jews of the United States of America, must be in the language the house of Israel have ever used in communing with God: *The Hebrew Language.* That is, Mr. Editor, one of the "essentials" which I would insist upon keeping inviolable . . .

While I experience a burning wish to retain our rising generation in this country within the fold; while I am ready, for that purpose, to sacrifice individual preferences and concede much, I could never suffer my house of prayer to become a strange place to my fellow-believer hailing from another land . . .

These reflections, that is, the necessity of keeping unbroken the silvery chain that fastens our people together from one end of the earth to its uttermost end, and the importance of cultivating the language of the Bible, led me to call the retention of Hebrew in the ritual an "essential" . . .

Whatever recalls the events at Sinai, the assurances of Divine love, and our bending to "the yoke of the precepts," ought to remain a feature clearly discernible in our reconstructed ritual. I could no more agree to erase from it "Atta bechartanu," our confessions of the same import, defining the mission and duty of Israel, than to blot out the "Shemang," or declaration of the Unity of God. For, if monotheism can be said to have been the rudder which governed the course of Judaism during milennial periods, our acceptance of the status proved a safe beacon . . .

I venture further and say: the avowal of a belief in the charge entrusted to the seed of Abraham cannot be disjoined from the admission of Scriptural promises . . .

And now allow me, Mr. Editor, to sketch the manner in

which Divine Service might be acceptably conducted. The recitative method, ought, to a certain extent, displace the uniform practice of chanting; but in order to enchain the attention of the congregation, joint singing should constitute the main part of the religious exercises. . . . A judicious selection from *our* Psalter, interspersed with the best Hebrew hymns from ancient and modern poets; the rehearsing of the benedictions preceding and succeeding the "Shemang"—which, beyond all doubt, date from a period of remote antiquity; the "Shemone Esre," or "Amidah"; the perusal of the Law in a triennial cycle, if it is universally adopted by the Hebrew community in the United States, and becomes thereby a settled custom, as it was with the Palestinian Jews, in the days that Rab and Shemuel had emigrated to Babylon; together with a rightly chosen chapter from the prophetic writings, might be a formulary for each morning of Sabbath and festivals . . .

I look with disfavor upon the introduction of an organ in the synagogue. I will not be hypocritical, and allege for it reasons regarded perhaps as mere casuistical niceties. I have not the ambition of being considered the pith of orthodoxy. I, therefore, do not raise as an objection, the fact that an organ, in connection with public prayers, originated—if I am to believe history—with Catholicism; that it was never thrust into our midst till within the last half a century, and simply in imitation of the Christian Church. . . . No; I have conceived an aversion to it mainly because it has inevitably brought into the shrine of the Unity, Gentile players and Gentile choristers . . .[23]

Morais' proposal led to widespread debate. The right wing attacked him for his submissiveness, while the left wing urged him to continue his compromises.[24] He was thus opposed by both sides. Morais had offered to sacrifice the Sephardi *minhag*. But for what purpose? For more reforms? Even the members of the Historical School, with the exception of Isaacs, did not regard the proposal as practicable. Isaacs called the traditional congregations to a meeting in order to decide on Morais' proposal; but the meeting never took place. The spirit of the Historical group was low. Obviously the time to organize a movement had not yet come.

In 1873, Morais remained the only effective national leader of the School. Even his good friend and colleague, Samuel Isaacs, could not come to his assistance: his health was declining and his congregation spoke of replacing him. But almost imperceptibly a shift took place within the group. Rabbis Szold, Jastrow and Hochheimer insisted on the observance of basic principles. In spite of their earlier willingness to work with the Reformers, they began to veer away from that group. When a Reform rabbi, Dr. Mayer of Cleveland, allegedly denied (at the Cincinnati Conference of 1871) the idea of a personal God, the names of Szold and Hochheimer were on the list of those who signed a formal protest.[25]

The help that came from the outside further augmented these central groups of the Historical School. Frederick de Sola Mendes came to New York in 1873 from England to become Samuel Isaacs' assistant in congregation Shaaray Tefila and, within a year, succeeded him. Aaron Wise arrived from Hungary (in the same year). After he had assumed the spiritual leadership of congregation Beth Elohim in Brooklyn, Wise was called to one of New York's leading congregations, Rodeph Shalom, where he served until his death in 1896. In 1877, H. Pereira Mendes, the younger of the two brothers, was invited to become spiritual leader of New York's oldest congregation, Shearith Israel. These three men, although their outlooks and opinions differed, immediately identified themselves with the Historical School, bringing to it the vitality of their own personalities as well as the support of three strong congregations.

The elder Mendes (although he was later attracted to Reform) added considerable weight to the Historical School during the first years of his American career. In a memoir which he wrote half a century later, he described the state of flux in American Judaism at the time of his arrival:

> When Shaaray Tefila was called into existence, just fifty or sixty years ago, when the steeds of Reform had begun to get the bit into their teeth and had started to run away with the chariot of Jewish observance in Amer-

ica, it was the wise policy of the Orthodox leaders of those times—among whom the first minister of this congregation, Rev. S. M. Isaacs, is remembered to-day in respectful and grateful admiration—to throw all their weight backward upon the reins, to hold the runaways with might and main. . . . To check the runaways with hand and voice, to calm excited spirits, but to grip the lines relentlessly and hold them fast—this was the policy and the duty of the pulpit leaders of wise foresight fifty years ago, and though much misunderstood and censured, right valiantly did they perform it.[26]

The foundation of traditional Judaism throughout the United States was further broadened in the seventies by the great expansion of the Polish Jewish settlement. Based on various estimates in the periodical press of the day and later statistical summaries, it is generally agreed that several thousand East-European Jews arrived annually and that, within the decade, their number had risen to some 50,000.[27] With time, the group became an independent and distinct force in Jewish religious life. Until their organizational coalescence toward the end of the century, these Jews, who had not known Reform practice in Europe, were basically Orthodox in their manner of worship and created a new balance to the advantage of the Historical School. The very existence of this "mass" element gave impetus to the traditional arguments of the Historical group, although the members themselves were seeking a modern westernized adaptation of the Tradition.

These East-European immigrants were an important anti-Reform factor and aided the Historical School even before the arrival of other masses. The rabbis and leaders of the East-European congregations did not formally join the School, but they did identify with its right-wing leadership in specific areas of public activity. The first congregation of Polish and Russian Jews in New York was organized in 1852. Two congregations later developed out of it—Beth Hamidrash and Beth Hamidrash Hagadol. Congregations of the same type were also founded in other parts of the country. In Buffalo, Temple Beth El was organized in 1847 and followed the Polish ritual, while the German congregation in that city (Beth Zion) was not organized until 1850. The first Polish Jews in Chicago arrived in the 1840s and established a congregation of their own in 1849. By the mid-sixties, several *minyanim* and congregations of Polish, Lithuanian and Podolian Jews had mushroomed throughout the city. Two congregations—B'nai Jacob (founded 1862) and Beth Hamidrash Hagadol (1866)—merged in 1867. A combined synagogue became the center of Chicago's Russian-Polish Jewish community during this period. In 1873, Boston saw the founding of Beth Abraham, a congregation established by immigrants from Poland and Russia.[28]

The establishment of congregations was accompanied by the emergence of leading personalities and scholars who articulated traditional opinions. One of the most important men in this group was Rabbi Joshua Falk. After coming to America from Warsaw in 1858, he served as rabbi in Newburgh and Poughkeepsie, then became an itinerant preacher spreading his ideas throughout various centers of the East-European immigration. One of his better-known works, a commentary on the *Ethics of the Fathers,* entitled *Abne Yehoshua,* was published in 1860. It was the first rabbinic work printed in America. Rabbi Abraham Joseph Ash arrived in New York in 1852, and was the first rabbi of Russian-Polish origin to come to these shores. He was among the founders of the Beth Hamidrash Hagadol and for many years served as its spiritual leader. He wielded great influence among the eastern European immigrant community, and his reputation as a rabbinic authority extended to other parts of the country as well. A sharp opponent of Reform, Ash felt that Reform and Orthodoxy would never find a common religious meeting ground. When Kaufmann Kohler and others, in an effort at cooperation, attempted to spread their ideas by preaching in Orthodox synagogues, Ash protested vigorously. Kasriel Zvi Sarasohn, also Polish, arrived in America in 1866. He published several Yiddish religious periodicals as well as the *Ha-'Ibri,* which Rosenzweig edited.

He was also a founding member of the Hebrew literary society Shochare Sfat Ever, established in New York in 1880. That group sought to encourage the reading, speaking and study of Hebrew. Zvi Hirsch Bernstein came to the United States in 1870, and after pioneering in many Yiddish and Hebrew journalistic ventures, published the first Hebrew newspaper in this country, *Ha-Zofeh ba-Arez ha-Hadashah* (1871-1876). Such leaders contributed additional strength to the traditionalist tendency and, more important, they gave to traditional ideas the strength of sympathetic numbers.[29]

Buttressed by this new following, the core group of the Historical School took a major step forward. In 1879 its members united to create the *American Hebrew*. Historical Judaism in America at last had as a part of it a worthy instrument of expression. Frederick de Sola Mendes' subsequent inclination toward Reform does not detract from the role he played in the shaping of Conservative Judaism: since it was he who first conceived and then organized this first weekly newspaper dedicated to Historical Judaism. After participating in two brief journalistic ventures (the *Independent Hebrew* and later the *Reformer and Jewish Times*), both of which failed because of poor business management, De Sola Mendes proposed to Philip Cowen, at the time an apprentice printer, the idea of a new weekly. Cowen hesitated at first but was soon won over to the idea; his practical business sense assured the success of the undertaking. And the *American Hebrew* was launched. A board of editors, composed of rabbis and laymen who supported the Historical School, was selected. In addition to De Sola Mendes and Cowen, H. Pereira Mendes, Cyrus L. Sulzberger, Solomon Solis-Cohen (at the time still a medical student), Samuel Greenbaum, Daniel P. Hays, Max Cohen and Jacob Fonseca da Silva Solis constituted the nine members of the founding group. The names of the editors were kept secret and, in the course of thirty-three years, few succeeded in discovering their identity. Although the paper printed news of all factions in Judaism, it championed the Historical School in its editorials and news columns. Advertisements of "forbidden" food and non-kosher restaurants, for example, were not accepted. Reformers very soon realized the nature of the new journal. Samuel Hirsch called the editors of the weekly "young boys of the *American Hebrew*." In his periodical, the *American Israelite,* Isaac Mayer Wise hurled the term *kaeseblaettchen* at the *American Hebrew,* referring to the small size of the paper's pages in comparison with those of his own.[30] No one could deny, as was clear, that in the *American Hebrew* the leaders of the two wings of the Historical School joined forces, thereby creating a public counter-Reform front.

In retrospect, the two decades after the Civil War were the most difficult for the Historical School. During this period, they tried one solution after another, always hoping to achieve final stability. Their first alliances with the Reformers were the result of their own failing strength. But strategy was never confused with objective. They did not abandon their hope that American Jewry would adopt their views. In this mood, they could work with all elements of the community, making each decision in the light of an evolving, coherent program.

Chapter Two

Common
Action with
the Reformers

The guiding principle which seemed to govern the continuing interrelationship between the Reform and Historical School movements was the ancient maxim: "Even as the left hand pushes back, let the right hand draw near." Both recognized the theological and ideological gulf that separated them; but each felt that the compelling needs of the American Jewish community imposed upon them an obligation to cooperate. Both groups built national institutions which widened the breach between them; but simultaneously both sought to unite through local and noncongregational aspects of Jewish communal life. This *modus operandi* was first effected in the tense years during the seventies and eighties of the past century when the organizational split was formalized. It remained a characteristic policy of the Reform and Conservative movements into our own time.

During the period under discussion, cooperative effort took shape in such fields as education, social aid, the absorption of immigrants and the defense of Jewish rights. Serious effort was made to subdue factional interest for the sake of the entire community. However, as the leaders of the Historical School, particularly the rabbis, stepped out of the framework of the synagogue to do their part in these realms of total communal need, they did not "unfrock" themselves. They did not retreat from their legitimate place at the helm of the American Jewish community, but actively influenced the

171

extra-synagogal areas of Jewish life in accordance with Tradition. This they did by direct example and participation.

Jewish Education and Culture

The urgent need to find a way of educating American Jewish youth in their heritage remained a primary problem on the communal agenda. The members of the Historical School continued to wrestle with this basic question and formulated their educational objective in these terms:

> We mean not that education which makes a *blatt gemara* [literally "page of the Talmud," a reference to the East European concentration on talmudic studies] the Ultima Thule of educational research. This has proved itself not the best preparation for the Western World Judaism, since they are so little related, practically considered—nor do we mean the namby-pamby Jewish education which makes the mere reading of a Scriptural selection in Hebrew the "be all and end all"; but we mean a Jewish education upon a *historic* basis. The best text book for Judaism is the history of our people . . .[1]

The earnest thoughts of the Historical School were directed at the educational needs of the community. But definition of need did not necessarily bring about a coherent program of action. Each synagogue, independently chartered and motivated, organized its congregational school in accordance with its own desires. The Sunday schools remained the most popular form of Jewish education and as these schools grew in number attempts were made to conduct them jointly with the Reform group.[2] Nevertheless, the Historical group tried to pursue its pedagogy within these schools and also eliminate Reform doctrine. They wanted to adopt the methods of the International Sunday School Union; in that way the various Christian sects had succeeded in producing a unified program for all Sunday schools.[3] Kaufmann Kohler supported the unified curriculum. He went so far as to propose that in each Sunday school a distinction be made between the teaching of Jewish ethics and the *mitzvot*. Any Jewish child, whether of reform or tradition-minded parents, could then study in those schools without danger of partisan indoctrination. Naturally, the members of the Historical School opposed this proposal. It was not possible, they argued, to separate ethics from *mitzvot*, ceremonials from the moral teachings of Judaism. One must study the Tradition as a whole.[4]

The problem of available teaching time continued to perplex the maximalists in Jewish education, and the daily Jewish supplementary school seemed to be the only solution. To foster such educational institutions, the Hebrew Free School Society was founded in 1872 in New York City. Within a few years, the Society filled its classes to capacity and also created a network of supplementary schools. After attending public school, the children came to the afternoon Hebrew school and studied the laws and customs of Judaism, and Hebrew reading. The Society also established several kindergartens.[5] During this period, the Historical School did not succeed in introducing the supplementary school system into its own congregations, but its members did support its development on a communal basis. Fundamentally, the work of the Society reflected the thinking of the Historical group. For example, then as now the Hebrew language was the criterion of an intensive, as opposed to extensive, Jewish education. The leaders of the organization conducted competitive examinations among the students of the various Hebrew schools. Reformers and members of the YMHA opposed this method, but the intensivists within the ranks of the Society, supported by the *American Hebrew,* won the day.[6]

The continued deficiency of textbook material was another symptom of the still underdeveloped Jewish school system. The *American Hebrew* urged the Hebrew Free School Society to assume the additional responsibility of publishing a series of textbooks and books for children.

It is high time that the Jewish Sunday Schools gave up the practice of placing Christian books in their libraries. It is true that the officers always run their pens through the name of Jesus, but as they invariably write "God" in its place, the benefit is decidedly doubtful since it gives the children the idea that the words are synonymous.[7]

Several rabbis, who were personally concerned with this problem in their own congregations, did not limit their activity to the exhortation of others; they began to prepare educational materials. In the Historical School, the Mendes brothers were especially active in this connection. They deemed it as important to write a poem for the young as an essay for the adult. Henry P. Mendes edited a special column for the young readers of the *American Hebrew,* entitled "Stories about the Bible but not in the Bible." He also translated several well-known nursery rhymes into Hebrew so that children would become interested in "the holy tongue."[8]

The education of the poor was another communal responsibility in which the Historical School joined forces with other elements of the community. In fact, the problems in this area transcended the question of Jewish literacy. It was not enough to think through the religious education of these children. Their economic welfare and vocational training were urgent concerns. Sabato Morais, who was influenced very deeply by the work of Charles Netter, began to agitate for the establishment of trade schools. As he put it, he did not wish to see a new generation of tailors grow up from the ranks of the poor. He wanted to prepare these children for various vocations and he therefore began to advocate a change in the educational methods of the orphans' home in Philadelphia. He was a member of its board of trustees.

Industrial schools must be planted in all our institutions. The brush and the compass, the chisel and hammer must take the place of the basket and yardstick. We must foster a taste for works, in which our fathers excelled, until a cruel world compelled us to forsake them in self-protection. . . . But here, thank God, all avenues are wide open to Israel. Here industry can reach the highest step of the social ladder.[9]

As in the earlier period, some held that the educational deficiencies of textbooks and other pedagogic aids could only be solved by teacher-training institutions, for which the need was desperate. In the Middle West and in the East, two separate groups worked to found an institution of higher Jewish learning. Although some members of the Historical School, active in Maimonides College, helped with this work, the Reformers took the active lead.

In the midst of difficulties at the outset, the Hebrew Union College became firmly established after more than thirty years of struggle. Wise's dream was suddenly realized. In 1873 Wise decided that he would not be able to achieve his aim of creating a college in Cincinnati. He then agreed to leave his post and accept the invitation of congregation Anshe Chesed in New York. The leaders of his congregation made every effort to prevent him from leaving Cincinnati. They won, but on Wise's condition that they help him realize his life's aim.

Before the organizers undertook to found the college in Cincinnati, they sought to guarantee the success of the project by establishing a broader base of support. This base was the proposed Union of American Hebrew Congregations. A proclamation issued on October 10, 1872, by Moritz Loth, president of Wise's Bene Jeshurun congregation of Cincinnati invited all the congregations in the West, South and Northwest to unite. The Union's purpose was to establish a "Jewish Theological Faculty." In addition, it would publish educational books and issue a code of laws "which are not to be invaded under the plausible phrase of reform; namely that the *milah* [circumcision rite] shall never be abolished, that the Sabbath shall be observed on Saturday and never be changed to any other day, that the *Shehitah* [ritual slaughtering of animals] and the dietary laws shall not be disregarded, but commended as preserving health and prolonging life . . ." Any rabbi who did not observe these traditions "has forfeited his right to preach before a Jewish congregation," while a congregation accepting such a rabbi would not be admitted to the Union of American Hebrew Congregations. Loth concluded by urging the adoption of these provisions as a "safeguard against the so-called reform, which, if not checked, may become disastrous to our cause."[10]

Wise, for his part, did not wholly concur with these ideas, nor was he convinced of the prudence of excluding the Eastern faction from the proposed union. But he remained silent for the sake of the greater purposes which were about to be realized—the new college and the union of congregations.

Loth's position made a deep impression on synagogues connected with the Historical School. Bolstered and encouraged by a leader committed to repel the invasion of further reforms within the very citadel of Reform, many who opposed Wise's ideas agreed to come to the first session of the council held in Cleveland in 1874. Lewis N. Dembitz, the well-known lawyer and a leading spokesman for the Historical School in the Middle West was elected secretary.[11] Moritz Loth's ability to persuade the Historical School to join the Union, despite its awareness of Wise's antithetical views, exemplifies the role of individual leadership in a voluntaristic society. It has not been uncommon throughout American Jewish history for a layman of eminence and personal prestige to convince an entire group to change its policy even on fundamental issues.

With the basic structure confirmed and a foundation of congregational support laid, the financing of the college was the next step. In 1873, Henry Adler of Lawrenceburg, Indiana, had offered to contribute $10,000 towards the building of a theological seminary in Cincinnati. He stipulated that the school be organized within three years. Adler, whose brother was Rabbi Liebman Adler of Chicago, was not a wealthy man and his contribution undoubtedly represented a substantial portion of his money; but he had been deeply influenced by Wise. With this purse as a stimulus, it was resolved at the 1875 convention to raise the $60,000 necessary for the opening of the institution.[12] In the same year, Wise saw his many years of diligent and sometimes disheartening work crowned: the Hebrew Union College was founded.

Students were accepted for the preparatory and college

divisions. Lectures were held in the afternoons during week-days and on Sabbath mornings. Slowly the institution gained stability.[13] The members of the Historical School actively supported the new undertaking. The devotion and zeal of Sabato Morais, one of the right-wing members of the His-torical group, was surprising. It may be that he held the secret hope that the institution would remain traditional in character. Some evidence for this is substantiated by the fact that in a letter to Morais dated September 15, 1876, Wise wrote that, if the Philadelphia congregations would enter the Union of American Hebrew Congregations, Maimonides College would be reopened as a preparatory department to the Hebrew Union College.[14] Morais became head of its board of examiners. A report, in Morais' handwriting, of the annual examinations held in 1877 has been preserved in the archives of Dropsie College. It states that "the general results of the examination proved very satisfactory." Morais goes on to praise the progress and knowledge of the students in Bible, Talmud and Jewish history, and he advises more in-tensive study of the rabbinical commentaries. The report concludes:

> The Examining Committee perform an act of justice, in highly commending preceptors and pupils for the unwaver-ing exertions, crowned with unprecedented success in America. The College at Cincinnati may unequivocally be pronounced an object deserving the support of Israelites who wish that attachment to the ancestral faith be founded upon a knowledge of its precepts, and an extensive ac-quaintance with the national literature.

Benjamin Szold, for years a faithful supporter of Wise, was invited to speak at the first graduation exercises of the Col-lege, although at that time he opposed Wise's views on the Sabbath and *kashrut*. His words reveal the attitude of the members of the Historical School, and the reasons for their support of the college:

> Judaism in this country for a long time offered a sad spectacle to the observer when the spiritual element was

considered. I do not allude to the conflicting religious opinions which have existed among the different congregations. This, to me, never seemed a cause for regret, but rather a sign of soundness and intellectual activity of the Jewish community. A state of absolute uniformity in all religious matters always betokens indifference and stagnation which ultimately lead to the dominion of the spirit of materialism. . . . But there was still something saddening in the aspect of American Judaism—the utter want of institutions where Jewish studies might have been pursued. It appeared as if this free country were not the proper soil for their cultivation and . . . that the religious advisors who may be desired by the various congregations will have to be imported from foreign lands in the future as they have in the past. What could have been more melancholy than the fear that such a state might remain permanent . . .

Thank heaven. . . . the outlook is no longer gloomy. We have now a splendid rabbinical establishment which we owe to the enthusiasm, energy and ceaseless exertion of its worthy president and the zeal of his earnest co-laborers. And today, at its first commencement, we may with justice add that we have a successful rabbinical establishment.[15]

Efforts to launch a seminary in the East continued. It will be recalled that two such previous attempts—Maimonides College and the Emanu-El Theological Seminary—had not proved fruitful. By the early 1870's these two institutions were on the verge of closing.[16] Maimonides College closed its doors in 1875. The Emanu-El Seminary had retrenched from its originally ambitious plans; it limited itself to sponsoring American students at European seminaries and serving as a preparatory school for future rabbis who intended to continue their studies in Germany or at the Hebrew Union College. Still, in the East, all hope was not given up and in February 1876 an invitation was issued by the presidents of a number of New York congregations to other congregations in the East asking them to rally delegates for a convention to be held in May. Its purpose was the establishment of a Hebrew College. Prior to the convention, a questionnaire was sent to several scholars and ministers to obtain their reactions to the proposal and to elicit their suggestions for the scope and program of the new institution. The very form of the questionnaire shows that its proponents recognized and accepted the existence of the Hebrew Union College as a permanent institution. The new project would have to be an undertaking of a different nature. It could not duplicate or infringe upon the activities of the institution in the Midwest. But it would have to serve the needs of the Eastern community. The circular, composed by a Committee on Correspondence (consisting of Lewis May, Moritz Ellinger and Myer S. Isaacs —all of New York City), was sent to various ministers and rabbis throughout the country. It read in part as follows:

> In order to lay before the Convention of Congregations for the establishment of a college of Hebrew learning (to assemble on the 24th of May in this city) material for the information of a comprehensive plan, we would ask the assistance of all Jewish scholars who take an interest in a matter of such far reaching importance for the future development of Judaism on this continent.
>
> We desire to have your views as to the best, most practical and practicable mode of establishing such a college, and also the coordinate subsidiary branches of preparatory schools in every city, the congregations whereof shall unite in this movement. We beg to leave, therefore, to submit for your consideration a number of questions and solicit your answers thereto with such arguments, statistical statements and other considerations as you may deem best.

The questions were:

1. Is it best to establish an independent college for all the branches of knowledge, or is it preferable to found academical chairs for Hebrew science in connection with some well-known American University?

2. If you favor academical instruction in connection with a secular institution, what branches of Hebrew science are indispensable for students preparing for the Jewish ministry or for the position of Hebrew Instructors?

3. What proficiency in the Hebrew branches must a student have attained as a prerequisite to admission to the course of education at the Hebrew College?

4. What schools are required for the preparation of Jewish young men for higher education given in the college, and what steps should be taken in order to establish such schools?

5. What can and must be done in order to encourage the study of the Hebrew language and Hebrew literature, and how can the genuine foundation be laid for the pursuit and cultivation of Hebrew science?

6. Please give any additional information and suggestions that you deem of importance in connection with this subject.[17]

Answers were received from a committee of rabbis in New York—an amalgam of radical Reformers who still could not reconcile themselves to Wise's success, some moderate Reformers who were in sympathy with the Hebrew Union College but sought to resolve the problem of higher education in the East, and members of the Historical School. Thus, the signatures of Adler and Einhorn, Gottheil and Huebsch appear together with those of Samuel Isaacs, Jacobs, Lyons, De Sola Mendes and Aaron Wise. The Philadelphia list presents a similar combination of forces.

It is of considerable interest to note that the general consensus regarding the answer to the very first decisive question favored the endowment of chairs in Hebrew and cognate studies over the establishment of a second theological institution. The time was not yet ripe for the creation of another seminary. If standards of excellence were to be maintained, its academic program would have to depend on foundations laid much earlier in the students' education. Kaufmann Kohler, speaking on behalf of the Chicago group, went even further and stated that the creation of adequate preparatory schools was an essential prerequisite for a theological college and that all efforts should be concentrated in their direction. The Philadelphia committee, with the exception of Samuel Hirsch, its chairman, and consisting of Morais, Jastrow, George Jacobs and Elkin,[18] considered both propositions—the founding of a seminary as well as the endowment of academic chairs in well-known universities—as "premature."

The difference between the opinions of two such men as Kohler and Hirsch is another indication of the East-West conflict in the Reform movement. Wise, from his vantage-point in Cincinnati, quickly sensed that he had nothing to fear from this Eastern group; he wished the undertaking "success," and satisfied himself by sneering at what he called the "disunion college."[19] The convention was held as scheduled, and the founding of a Hebrew Theological Seminary Association was proposed, but the plans did not materialize.

No further attempt was made to establish a school in the East until the final break occurred between the Historical School and the Reform group. As the Hebrew Union College took on the character of an avowedly Reform institution, the traditionalists withdrew their support. On the other hand, the Reformers of the East rallied to Wise's institution, dissolving the Eastern regional alliance which had existed between them and the Historical School. The latter, left to its own resources, gradually strengthened its position and continued to seek a way to prepare a native ministry for its own congregations.

The education of the youth, the creation of a curriculum and the establishment of institutions for the education of teachers and rabbis were not the only crucial problems to be solved in Jewish education. The adult community also required serious attention. The laymen in the synagogue were abysmally ignorant of Hebrew and the teachings of Judaism. The rabbis undertook, here and there, to provide Jewish education for adults. Looking back, one can see the beginnings of institutions which are now flourishing in American Jewish life: classes for adults within the congregational system, a network of organizations which provide for both social and recreational needs (the YMHA and Jewish Center movements), and the Jewish Publication Society for the stimulation and dissemination of Jewish writings.

A concrete teaching program on the adult level was needed to insure the continued learning of Jewish values and at least the rudiments of Hebrew. This required a local and specific program. Attempts at implementing such a program

on a nation-wide basis by a national organization did not
bear fruit. Jastrow, for example, had advocated unsuccessfully
that the Board of Delegates sponsor and take full control of
adult education projects.[20] It became increasingly apparent,
therefore, that education must begin with individuals in
synagogues or with cultural clubs. The idea was first emphasized by a Reform rabbi, Henry Berkowitz of Kansas City,
a member of the first graduating class of the Hebrew Union
College. He proposed that adult educational groups be organized and instruction in Jewish subjects given by every rabbi
within his own congregation. As a result of this suggestion,
various adult groups were established, most of them in Reform temples. Rabbis of the Historical School heartily endorsed the plan whose success was making itself felt, and
proceeded to organize Hebrew, History and Bible classes in
their own congregations.[21]

The YMHA movement, in which traditionalists, Reformers
and nonreligious culturalists could come together for an
evening of lectures, discussion and sociability in a totally
Jewish environment, was a grass-roots community activity
rather than a synagogue effort. Members of the respective
religious trends met here as fellow-Jews and rabbis as teachers
of their people—a rare communal achievement. The associations were primarily educational in nature, making conscious
efforts to distinguish themselves from the purely social clubs
which flourished at that time. Classes were held in Hebrew
language and literature, and Jewish history; literary and
musical programs were presented regularly; and essay contests
were sponsored periodically. Annual lectures and concert
series, participated in by professionals, were prominently
featured and attracted many new members. Social activities
included Purim and Hanukkah pageants and balls. The
YMHAs also maintained libraries and reading rooms, audi-
toriums and recreational facilities. Everything that touched
upon the welfare of American Jewry was declared to be within
the direct scope of the YMHA program.[22]

The success of the YMHA was essentially due to the
quality of its leadership. Men of intellectual achievement

and discernment, those devoted to the spiritual and cultural content of the Jewish tradition, participated in YMHA activity. What the individual synagogues rarely achieved, the Associations accomplished. They became community centers of Jewish thought and opinion. Especially in New York and Philadelphia, the very men responsible for the national leadership of the Historical School actively engaged in these local communal enterprises. Mayer Sulzberger, for example, who was one of the remarkable figures in Jewish life on the national scene, became the first president of the Philadelphia YMHA. Jewish history and literature were taught at that institution by Sabato Morais and George Jacobs. In the New York Association, H. Pereira and Frederick de Sola Mendes conducted classes in Hebrew language and literature. A group of outstanding younger men such as Daniel P. Hays, Cyrus L. Sulzberger, Solomon Solis-Cohen, Samuel Greenbaum, Cyrus Adler, Adolph Lewisohn and Oscar S. Straus, also lent brilliance and promise to the movement.[23] An example of the important role designed for the Philadelphia YMHA in the cultural life of the city was reflected by the decision of Mayer Sulzberger and William Hackenburg, the executors of Isaac Leeser's estate, to deposit Leeser's library —in its day one of the finest Hebrew libraries in America— in the rooms of the local YMHA. As he tells us in his autobiography, Cyrus Adler, then an assistant to the librarian of the Association, undertook the challenging task of cataloguing the Leeser library. From this event Adler dates his later interest in libraries, catalogues and bibliographies.[24] That young Adler was attracted to the YMHA is further indication of the forceful place it held in the lives of the Jewishly-trained and oriented young intellectuals. Despite the attractiveness of adult classes and lectures at the YMHAs, most of the members of the community did not attend. These courses and cultural programs could be arranged only in the larger centers of Jewish residence. What of those who could not or would not come? To help them, the plan to publish books on an adult level for home study was revived.

Jastrow was ardently devoted to the idea of a society for

publishing Jewish books, and he fought for this idea at meetings of the Board of Delegates. He was appointed head of a committee to reactivate the idea of a Jewish Publication Society. The other members of this committee were George Jacobs, Isaac Mayer Wise, Samuel Myer Isaacs, and P. J. Joachimsen of New York. In 1871, the committee made public its decision that "the Jewish Publication Society of the United States be established as an independent body, commencing its operation without delay." The plan for the first year contemplated the publication of Graetz' *History of the Jews*, a portion of the Bible in English, and a translation of Geiger's *Gabirol*.[25]

The proposal was accepted and the Board of Delegates allocated a sum of $200 to begin work. Within a year, the Publication Society had 1,200 members. Individual works were published; the revived organization showed some activity. At this point, Isaac Mayer Wise put forth a new suggestion through the recently established Union of American Hebrew Congregations. He proposed the publication of the Bible in English, as a cooperative effort of the leading Jewish scholars in America. In a letter to Morais, dated November 21, 1876, Wise presented his plan, inviting Morais to participate in the project.[26] This suggestion was not acted upon, either by the Union or the Publication Society. The Society was failing. Throughout the years, Wise continued to push his idea. He proposed that each of twenty-four properly qualified scholars study a single book of the Bible and correct the existing English version, striking out misleading chapter-headings and references, on the basis of a thorough, non-biased study of the original. The members of the editorial board of the *American Hebrew* endorsed Wise's suggestion and offered their assistance. Again, the project was not realized.[27] The culturally inexperienced Jewish community could not yet cope with so vast an undertaking. It was only with the twentieth century that the Jewish Publication Society, in its third and permanent form of organization, was able to carry out the work of an authoritative English translation of the Bible.

Immigrant Absorption

From the end of the seventies, the American Jewish community became preoccupied with immigrant absorption and aid. While this problem stayed with the community until World War I and beyond, the first impact of permanent changes wrought in American Jewry as a result of this immigration was felt in the period under discussion.

Mark Wischnitzer cites two telling documents to describe the changes that occurred during the three decades of mass immigration as they affected American Jewry, which was the greatest reservoir of Russian immigrant absorption. The first reference is found in the New York *Hebrew Leader* of April 1870, where it is simply reported that "two hundred and fifty of the immigrants are already here; 500 are on the way, and 9 ships have been chartered by the Koenigsberg Frontier Committee to send over more . . ." The second document is a letter read to Congress by Representative Samuel Cox of New York and printed in 1880. This letter, dispatched by the Jews in Russia to their brethren in America, poignantly reveals the despair of the Russian Jews and the utter helplessness of their situation. "We ask you, we pray, we implore," the letter read, "we beseech you to come to our rescue, to take us out of our bondage, out of our misery; to give us a chance in your great and glorious land of liberty, whose broad and trackless acres offer an asylum and a place for weary hearts and courageous souls willing to toil and by the sweat of the brow earn their daily bread . . ."[28]

To meet this situation, the Hebrew Emigrant Aid Society of the United States was founded in 1870. This organization, the first known immigrant aid society, received financial support from the Board of Delegates of American Israelites and from the Hebrew Benevolent Society for "temporary relief to those here and soon to arrive." Upon their arrival the immigrants were provided with food, clothing and shelter, and efforts were made to find them employment and resettle them throughout the West and South.

However, recent American Jewish historiography has un-covered important data based on the primary sources of the period, which reveal the extent to which many American Jews rejected the programs of mass immigration to the United States.[29] It took some time before the existing social organizations were able to adjust themselves to the revolu-tionary psychological changes in the body politic, alterations which the new facts of world Jewry imposed upon them. They were not only unprepared to cope with the economic and social problems of immigrant absorption, they were also overwhelmed by the effect of this immigration upon the settled community.[30]

An acute symptom of this mood was the ignominy of certain "protesting rabbis" who took it upon themselves to ask the government to stop further immigration. Instead of permit-ting the wretched victims of czarist persecution to come to America, these men advocated closing the gates to refugees. Sabato Morais, speaking for most of his colleagues in the American rabbinate, expressed horror at this repugnant act:

> Shame on those renegade rabbis who dare, before the ark of God, from the pulpit of Jewish Temples, to say, that these our brothers are "too low" for us to extend the hand of sympathy and assistance. That we must send them back, prevent them at all risks from reaching these shores, lest America become Russianized![31]

Public debate and self-interested argumentation were ren-dered irrelevant by the catastrophic events of the eighties. If the years immediately preceding Czar Alexander II's as-sassination in March 1881 made the condition of the Jews in Russia pitiable, the reign of his successor, Alexander III, was even more reactionary and barbarous. An era of pogroms and savage governmental decrees was ushered in, and thou-sands of Jews who had survived the initial onslaught, but were left homeless and destitute, fled from city to city in the ultimate hope of making their way to America. Sabato Morais appealed to the American Jewish community to work hard in helping its brothers, and concluded unequivocally: "The only hope for the Jews in Russia is to become Jews out of Russia."[32]

Facing this extreme urgency, opinion could not afford to be fashioned or divided along theological or partisan lines. There was a responsibility to *Klal Yisrael*; American Jewry could only fulfill it on a united front. The original Hebrew Emigrant Aid Society was supplemented and succeeded by several other organizations, all directed toward the relief of the refugees.[33]

As part of this all-out effort, the members of the Historical School played an important individual and collective role. To Morais, for example, and to the members of the American Synagogue as a whole, the new immigrants were true martyrs to the faith whom the Almighty had spared in their hour of trial. Other members of the Historical School followed his exemplary lead, and were active in immigrant assistance. Boarding the ships as they arrived in the harbor, Morais would advise the newcomers in the business of gaining entry. Frequently he arranged their documents for them and brought them from the docks to homes he had prepared.[34]

Immediate relief was followed by plans for their individual economic settlement. Morais contacted his boyhood friend, Chevalier Emmanuel Veneziani, who succeeded in interesting Baron de Hirsch in a project to settle the Russian refugees on farms and in agricultural colonies. He explained his approach in concrete terms:

> The practical question is, how shall we who are so highly favored, perform our duty to our suffering brethren? How can we best aid them? Not by assembling mass meetings and petitioning Governments, but by furnishing the means of leaving the dominions of the Czar . . . and entering upon a new life of civilization and liberty in America . . .
>
> Help them to come to this country, and scatter them over it to till the farms of the East and the West, the North and the South—not to take up the peddler's pack or to vegetate in the small shop of the city. Say not that you have too many claims nearer home. We can take care of the home duties and still have to spare for our oppressed brethren in other lands. Their misery is our misery, their

oppression is our oppression, their freedom and their happiness will be ours. And every dollar we give to them is to Moses, to the prophets, to the sages, who gave, not dollars, but their life-blood to seal and to perpetuate the covenant.[35]

Saving lives was the first step; rebuilding lives was the objective. The immigrants came to find a home in America. To this end the Hebrew Sheltering House Association was founded in New York in 1882 (although its full title was not officially adopted until 1889). There the immigrants found temporary refuge, which lasted an average of six days, before moving on to more permanent domiciles and suitable employment. At the shelter, the residents were also provided with food and clothing, and received other services. In 1889 the Hebrew Sheltering House, or Hachnosas Orchim, was founded by East-European Jews. This agency was the immediate predecessor of HIAS (Hebrew Sheltering and Immigrant Aid Society, established in 1909). In Philadelphia, Morais, Jastrow and others participated in the work of the Alliance Israélite Universelle, which accepted responsiblity for the care of distressed immigrants. The idea of founding agricultural settlements was also included in the program of this group. For the members of the Historical School, immigrant absorption was part of a total program. Once the physical needs of the immigrants were alleviated, it was hoped that the immigrants would strengthen the forces of traditional Judaism in the United States. They were invited to the synagogues. There the dispirited and downcast were consoled. They were encouraged not to succumb to suffering and not to abandon faith in the religion for which they had suffered so deeply.

Religious and Communal Activities

The firmest bond of union between the Historical School and the Reform group was the continuing effort to secure full religious freedom. That the United States was a Christian country was still a widespread idea, and proposals to "Christianize" the Commonwealth of Pennsylvania, similar to the proposals made in previous decades, reappeared in 1873.[36] Morais and Jastrow were also engaged in this battle; they spoke out boldly and were prepared to face the barrage of misunderstanding and invective which would naturally reach them. Said Morais:

> I am taught by the religion of my fathers to "judge all men favorably," and that liberal precept shall be my guide even when my dearest interests are at stake through the designs of misdirected piety. Let me admit at once that they who desire to change the Constitution of our Commonwealth into a confession of faith may be actuated by pure motives, yet I am free to say that their zeal outruns their judgment . . .
>
> The Keystone of our Union is to be turned into the stone, beneath which the rights of my fellow-believers, the Hebrews, shall find a burial. Almost on the eve of that National celebration, to which the Israelites, above all people, look joyfully forward, because commemorative of the vindication of their manhood; in sight of the very bell which chimed the most delightful of sounds, those sounds inspiring with hope the hearts of the oppressed, promising "liberty throughout the land to *all* the inhabitants thereof"; in this city of Brotherly Love, the Jewish denizens of Pennsylvania are to be told: "Ye have no share in this State, nor inheritance in the franchises it grants."[37]

Jastrow added:

> I confess my inability to understand what a Christian country means and I defy any of those who make use of this argument to explain it satisfactorily.
>
> We speak of the Jewish country, meaning that dominion now called Palestine or Syria, at the time when it was in the possession of the Jewish nation. We speak of the French country applying the term to that portion of Europe which the French nation occupies or governs.
>
> But, is Christianity a nationality by which a country may be defined, that we should be permitted to say, "This is a Christian country"?[38]

In spite of their profound agreement on the restrictive nature of these proposals, Jastrow and Morais could not agree on the best means to resist them. Jastrow distinguished between the Fundamentalists, who adhered to a literal interpretation of the New Testament, and Christians who were influenced by modern ideas. Jastrow felt that the latter groups could be convinced of their errors. To Morais such distinctions were irrelevant. He did not wish to enter into controversy with Christian clergymen. His argument was with the civil authorities. Morais objected to confusing the question of religion with that of citizenship.[39] During the election campaign of 1885, various politicians appealed to Jewish voters as a group, proclaiming in Jewish neighborhoods their favorable feelings toward Jews. The editors of the *American Hebrew* came out sharply against such a strategy:

> The Jewish voters of this country are American citizens, and should, no doubt will cast their ballots for candidates of whose fitness they will judge according to standards of merit such as are utilized by other American citizens.[40]

To a great degree the political aspects of the Christianizing attitudes were aided by the various missionary societies which were directed at Jews. Despite failure to attract Jews to their cause, the efforts of the missionaries continued. Missionaries, trained in England, were dispatched to save souls in America, particularly those of the children of Jewish immigrants. Schools were established; their purpose was to attract children by means of gifts, and then wean them away from Judaism. To counter this insidious activity the Hebrew Free Schools movement was founded in 1872. The missionaries, although certain of their holy purpose, were not deterred by this or any other action of the Jews. They tried to reach all areas of the Jewish community. They discovered quickly enough, however, that candy was not as attractive to adults as to children.

Unsuccessful as the missionaries were with the Jews, they succeeded in the eyes of their fellow-Christians. First of all, the mere effort was equated with success. More serious was the fact that most of the Christians who read the literature of the missionaries were infected with spurious ideas about Judaism. The notions to which many had been exposed from early childhood were confirmed. De Sola Mendes devoted much of his energy to answering the charges leveled against Jews and Judaism. He had become interested in apologetics as a form of Jewish service in his student days at the Breslau Theological Seminary. This interest had been intensified when he became acquainted with a volume of Dr. Wilhelm Herzberg entitled *Jüdische Familienpapiere, Briefes eines Missionairs.*[41] De Sola Mendes tells how deeply all the students at the Breslau seminary, including Zachariah Frankel, were impressed by this work and the clarity of its ideas. Mendes immediately decided to issue the book in English. It was published by the Jewish Publication Society in 1875.[42]

De Sola Mendes published another little volume, *Defence, not Defiance, A Hebrew's Reply to the Missionaries,* which contained selections from the *Hizzuk Emunah* of Isaac Troki. He added a second part, consisting of "Biblical and Rabbinical Parallels to New Testament Principles." In the Preface, De Sola Mendes clearly announces the public service aspects of his work:

> This little book is intended, as its title signifies, not as an aggressive but as a defensive polemic. A very vast proportion of our Hebrew young men and women are utterly unable to reply to the claims put forth by Christianity upon recognition by Judaism, and in public and private intercourse frequently feel the lack of some instruction upon the matter. It is a subject unfortunately disregarded or avoided in our Sabbath-schools; consequently the average Hebrew, though firm in his own faith, can yet make no reply to the friendly, and too often, insidious assailant.
>
> Again, the reader of the abundant literature of the day is met at every turn by praises and boasts of Christian doctrine, Christian virtue, love, resignation, and so forth, and is actually led to believe that the transcendent principles of Christianity originated in the New Testament, which he is induced correspondingly to reverence.
>
> The second part of this little work gives the originals of

the chief doctrines of the new faith, from the writings of Scriptural and Rabbinical authors—men who either were of much earlier date than the founder of Christianity, or lived in countries far beyond the influence of the Hebrew of Nazareth—who possessed these principles merely in common with all his brethren of Israel.

It is hoped that Jewish readers will thus learn how much of the glory of Christianity is due to its incorporation of Hebrew principles . . .[43]

The Reformers were far more active in the production of this type of literature than were members of the Historical School. No amount of book publishing could quickly alter the teachings of centuries now firmly planted in American soil. And it was inevitable that the seeds of anti-Judaism should develop into anti-Semitism, or rather "anti-Jewism." A *cause célèbre* of antisemitic discrimination was the Hilton-Seligman Affair in 1877. The case shocked the entire Jewish community, especially those who had been lulled into accepting the equation of legal religious rights with the attitudes of some Christians. The crisis was touched off in the summer of 1877 when Henry Hilton, executor and trustee of A. T. Stewart's property and manager of Stewart's fashionable Grand Union Hotel in Saratoga, refused admission to Joseph Seligman and his family because Seligman was a Jew. Seligman, a wealthy and prominent citizen, was determined to bring the issue into the open and he retorted publicly. Newspapers throughout the country immediately seized upon the incident, featuring it for several months, inviting comments and discussion from readers and editorializing endlessly. In the wake of the event, other hotel owners began to exclude Jewish clientele. Protests did nothing to remove the objectionable signs that had been posted on the hotels. In an attempt to root out the evil from the American social scene, a group of Jews and sympathetic Christians took a determined stand by boycotting the great A. T. Stewart and Company wholesale business, which Hilton controlled, until it was ruined. When Hilton, in an effort to appease the Jews, offered to contribute $1,500 to Jewish charities, the money was returned with a note stating that the Jewish poor did not need money from those who had harmed them.[44]

This incident was not the first nor, unfortunately, the last of its kind. Two years earlier, the Jews had been publicly calumniated in the streets of Philadelphia. One man went from street to street, delivering slanderous speeches to passers-by. In these cases, shocking to the Jews who had escaped to the freedom of America, religious leaders took a firm stand. Each incident was brought into the open. The better conscience of America understood that such provocation was detrimental not only to the Jews but to the very foundations upon which the nation rested. Isaacs' *Jewish Messenger* clarified the issue:

> We must carry out to the letter the maxima of the rabbis, that "the interest of our neighbor should be as dear to us as our own." Unhindered in our efforts, encouraged in our manly aspirations, we must work for the exaltation of this land of our birth, or of our adoption. We must join all the good and true in upraising the ensign of the Republic, which proclaimed "liberty to all the inhabitants thereof."[45]

The insinuation of Christian theology into the body politic of America could be challenged forthrightly by the Jewish citizens, and the overt missionizing of Protestant organizations could be counteracted or ignored. But the new "philosophy of science" which took hold of the contemporary mind challenged all faith. The Jews of America shared the national enthusiasm for modernism, "scientism" and secularism. The advance of secularism in world thought was the most serious danger confronting the American Synagogue, since it could neither be ignored nor dispelled by theological doctrine. The rabbinate recognized that here, too, a union of constructive intellectual forces was the logical imperative.

The urgency of the problem was dramatically indicated when Felix Adler, son of the Reform rabbi, Samuel Adler, left the Reform group to found the Society for Ethical Culture.[46] Ethical Culture was one of the more effective spiritual constructs which caused the religious community anxiety because it did not fear to argue with all organized religion. It cut

across denominations and even sought out their adherents.
While yet preparing himself for the rabbinate, in Germany, Adler became convinced "that the Mosaic religion is so to speak a religious mosaic, and that there is hardly a single stone in it which can with certainty be traced to the authorship of Moses."[47] This was a decisive conclusion, which prompted his separation from Judaism. Adler felt that the ethical truths inherent in Judaism—as well as in Christianity—had to be freed from the rigid context of religion and treated freshly, without prejudice. These truths were universal, belonging to mankind as a whole, and could not be held as the property of a single "elect body." According to the Society for Ethical Culture, the highest human goal was morality, which did not depend on religious or philosophical theories. Adler believed that both Judaism and Christianity were no longer vital religions and that the contemporary situation demanded a social ethic rather than a personal religion. Although the Ethical Culture Society was essentially humanistic, individual members were permitted to belong to any religious denomination of their choice or to none.

Seen in this perspective, Jewish adherents to the Society were either actual or potential affiliates of respective Reform and Historical School congregations, whom leaders of Judaism were forced to notice.[48] One understands better, therefore, that Jewish religious leaders were bitter toward Adler, not so much for his defection as for the improper light which he shed on Judaism. De Sola Mendes was one of the most articulate opponents of the Society.[49] He submitted the doctrines of the new ethical order to careful scrutiny, comparing them with the teachings of Judaism as well as to those of Christians, Moslems and Brahmins. He indicated that the ideas propagated by Adler as his own were actually appropriated from the historical religions. Adler was not dissuaded from continuing his work. In the moral and intellectual climate of the period, the new movement flourished and remained a continuing challenge to both the Historical and Reform groups.[50]

The various denominational, social and intellectual attacks against Judaism were felt most keenly in the local communities. Consequently, religious leadership in Jewry found itself unable to unite on the national scene except under communal aegis, and found it necessary for the direct spiritual welfare of their constituencies to join forces in their own communities. Out of this need came, first, a series of *ad hoc* meetings of rabbis and, later, the formation of Boards of Rabbis in various cities. At their meetings, theological division was transcended and decisions for common undertakings made. Lectures were delivered on issues of the day and the educational problems of small-town communities were discussed. However, tension between the members of the Historical School and the Reformers was only temporarily relieved at these gatherings and more than once threatened to disrupt them.

Those who strove to maintain the cohesiveness of these local groups pleaded that fundamental good was derived from harmony within Jewish ranks as well as from the need for, in public issues, a representative rabbinic leadership which might bridge ideological divergences. The dissenters held that such forums were of no avail if basic agreement on principles was lacking among the participants. Morais, who had already suffered many disappointments stemming from disorganized cooperative efforts, held this view. In 1885, after first joining the Eastern Conference of Rabbis convened by Gustav Gottheil, he wavered, and then decided to resign. Among Morais' unpublished papers are the pleas addressed to him by Gustav Gottheil and Cyrus Sulzberger, attempts to keep him from resigning. These letters indicate the nature of the dilemma in which most members of the Conference found themselves. Gottheil wrote to Morais as follows:[51]

My dear Sir,
    Dr. Mendes showed me your letter to him which I take to be virtually a letter of resignation from the Conference. It was painful reading to me, because it sounded like a death knell to our young organization. Dr. Kohler has be-

come our adversary because we are not radical enough; you, dear Sir, will stay away because we are too radical. And as some of our more prominent members cannot attend for reasons beyond their control, we are seriously threatened with a failure which cannot but be very damaging to our position as Ministers and the cause which we have all at heart. Besides, the Baltimore Brethren have made great efforts to give us a cordial and dignified reception, ought we not all try to recognize their zeal by coming in respectable numbers? Your absence would be particularly noted, because you live so near the cause you are the leader of, the conservative side of the Conference. I will not enter now into any discussion of your reasons for staying away; I respect them, because I know them to be honestly held by you, but I would beg of you, as President of the Society and, more so, as a brother laborer with you, to let them remain in abeyance till after the next meeting. We have never come nearer each other, why? I cannot tell, but I will try to do so at Baltimore and should your objections prove insurmountable, why then we may jointly devise means, to let this, my attempt at unifying the brethren, die a decent death, so as to prevent the disgrace which would otherwise result from it for our religion. You must have felt both at New York and your own city that all members, whether agreeing with you or not, look upon you with sincere respect, are glad to meet you and to listen to you. Pray do not push us aside; do not reject the hand of fellowship held out to you in all sincerity; you can do a great deal of good to our younger members, who are scattered over the land without any salutary influence upon them by which they might be prevented from rash and injudicious steps. Make one more attempt with us and see whether your efforts must really remain so barren of results as you anticipate. Help us to avert a desecration of the Holy Name; do not our sages make the bold assertion that it would have been better for the tribe of Judah to suffer their northern brethren to serve their idols than to cause the fatal disruption of the state?

Pardon me if I ventured to advise you. I am not far from the point when age may be pleaded as an excuse and I can assure you [that] "out of the abundance of my complaint and my vexation have I spoken hitherto." Let me hear a word of cheer and comfort from you and believe me,

> With sincere regard and
> brotherly sentiment, yours,
> G. Gottheil

In a similar vein, Cyrus Sulzberger, one of the youthful editors of the *American Hebrew*, wrote Morais that his absence from such a conference of rabbis would be detrimental to the entire Historical group because it looked to him as its representative. The Historical School had previously failed to check the onrush of radical Reform precisely because it had adopted the principle of withdrawal. It was vital to maintain a line of cooperation with the Reformers and to exchange ideas on issues which concerned the entire community.

> It is no word of flattery when I say that instinctively we turn to you as our leader. I, as an individual Jew, feel that I ought to be represented in the Conference and that I will not be represented in your absence. No man like yourself stands in the American Jewish community for an intelligent, liberal, and consistently progressive Conservatism. Unless I have much misunderstood your teachings, and you do not believe that any Minhag is of divine ordination and therefore eternally fixed—consequently a fair and free discussion (and I think this conference proposes only to discuss) cannot be harmful and may be beneficent. But there can be no good influence exerted either by you in your personality or as the representative of those people for whom you would speak, if you will not confer with the others . . .[52]

The gatherings succeeded in bringing a sense of mutual respect to the ranks of the rabbinate at a time of bitter recrimination within and serious challenge from without.

In the work of education, immigrant aid, defense of Jewish rights or religious organization, the overall need for an inclusive Jewish communal agency was increasingly apparent. The Board of Delegates, at its inception, was designed to fill this need. But since the Board functioned actually in only one of these areas—namely, the defense of rights—its total scope and powers had progressively declined. The instrument which was proposed to take its place was the Union of American Hebrew Congregations. Most members of the Historical School opposed this alternative; they were well aware that their own influence would thereby diminish. And so they attempted to reorganize the Board of Delegates. Marcus Jastrow undertook to revive and broaden the activities of the Board. He published a series of articles in the *Jewish Messenger* presenting a plan of action:

1. The Board of Delegates shall annually appoint a Committee of Ministers for the examination of applicants for the ministry, the examination to enter into a scrutiny, both of the degree of knowledge, as proved by authentic certificates, and of the antecedents and character of the applicant. The Committee of Ministers shall make such recommendations to the Board of Delegates at its annual meetings, as they may deem proper for the good of the Jewish community at large, and the Board of Delegates shall act on these recommendations.
2. The Board of Delegates shall by stipends encourage Jewish talent employed in professional studies, in the *first* place, however, with the view of supplying our congregations wih ministers and teachers.
3. The Board of Delegates shall be a central organization for the exchange of views between the Jewish charities of our country.

In addition, Jastrow requested the editors of Jewish newspapers and all those interested in the matter to make suggestions for strengthening the Board.[53] Judge Mayer Sulzberger also tried to prevent the dissolution of the Board, and applied his legal and constitutional training to this problem. Sulzberger always looked for a third way, avoiding the middle. He proposed a parity relationship between the Reform and Historical School groups, so that they would recognize one another and also work with one another. The uniqueness of Sulzberger's approach lay in his decision to recognize the diversity of American Judaism and legitimize it by accepting the reality of both segments—Historical and Reform.[54]

Sulzberger's "constitution" failed to arouse much enthusiasm. The Reformers, whose views coincided with those of the Union, dominated the Board. The impetus to merge the two organizations was stronger than the drive to preserve the integrity of the Board of Delegates. Ignoring the proposals of Jastrow and Sulzberger, the Board in 1876 appointed a committee to meet with a second, corresponding group appointed by the Union. The members of the committee appointed by the Board were Leopold Bamberger, Simon Wolf and Sulzberger himself. The two groups met and after many debates decided to dissolve the Board as an independent body and merge it with the Union of American Hebrew Congregations as one of the Union's permanent committees.[55] At the 1877 meeting of the Union in Philadelphia news of the abolition of the Board of Delegates was received satisfactorily. The members of the defunct Board even promised to try to get the Eastern congregations to join the Union. Strangely, it was Mayer Sulzberger of the Historical School, whose first formula had been rejected, who became the chief architect of the merger.[56]

In 1879, the leaders of the Union came East to establish good relations with the congregations there. Representatives of all congregations were invited to meet with them. Out of an estimated 200, delegates from 118, those most important in America, participated. In a quasi-organizational sense, the Historical School was now submerged in the Union.[57] Reform was in its heyday, having won a signal victory. A rabbinical school as well as a lay organization of national constituency had been established. Everyone seemed to be swept along by the Reform current. The Historical School recognized the danger fully. But before an answer could be produced, the School had to rally strength to discover if it had the power within itself to create a program and establish institutions based on the Tradition it proclaimed.

Chapter Three

**The Struggle
for an
Independent
Religious
Movement**

The act that established the Jewish Theological Seminary
which, in turn, gave rise to the organized Conservative
Movement, was one of the consequences of the Board of Delegates' submergence in the Union of American Hebrew Congregations. Having lost the prevailing vote in the Board—
then the only all-embracing Jewish organization—the Historical School seemed to have no choice but to develop its
own institutions. The School perceived that, despite pro-
testations to the contrary, the Union would ultimately become
entirely Reform. The watershed was, then, 1878. From that
year on, until the convening session of the Seminary in January 1886, the Historical School followed an ambivalent policy
in its relationship with the Reform group. On one hand rabbis
and laymen cooperated with the Reform elements in local,
community activities and national operations. On the other
hand, they rallied their own strength within the cooperative
effort by developing an independent ideology plus the rudiments of an organizational framework.

The Synod Proposal

The ideological statement which outlined the future Conservative Movement was published in 1879, the year the
American Hebrew appeared. The statement called for recog-

nition that much of the *Shulhan Arukh* had outlived its usefulness as the decisive code of Judaism, and for a return to the condition of halakhic interpretation which had prevailed in Jewish life during the period of the Talmud.[1] To achieve this, the members of the Historical School advocated the establishment of a modern rabbinical authority through the organization of a synod. Until such a new authority could be realized, the program of the Historical School called for a fresh attempt to reconstitute traditional authority under its own leadership. The School hoped to accomplish this program by institutionalizing traditional Sabbath observance in the synagogue, strengthening *kashrut* in the home and, in general, invigorating Jewish life by emphasizing the *mitzvot*. The resettlement of Eretz Yisrael became a basic plank in the expanding program, and the Hebrew language was to be retained in its prime position in the synagogue and Jewish education. Concept and program were welded into constructive acts of organization by Alexander Kohut, who emerged as the architect of the Historical School in the eighties. The Pittsburgh Platform of 1885 was the point of no return in a division which was evident, after the Cleveland Conference in 1855, and which actively widened on both sides from 1878 on. Examining the events of the historical drama, we realize that in those decisive years, not only the Conservative Movement was being born but, simultaneously, American Judaism was taking the form we in the twentieth century know.

The case for a world Jewish synod as presented by the editors of the *American Hebrew* was an ingenious attempt to solve the problems of authority, ideology and program for the Historical School. It was a leap over divided opinion within American Jewry, an effort to engage the enlightened traditional rabbinate in the aims of the American Historical School. But at least two more factors were introduced: the need for constructive change within the framework of the *halakhah*, and the realization that American Jewry was part of the contemporary Jewish world and not a detached, independent segment across the seas. The following editorial from the *American Hebrew* eloquently presents the case for the new era, and it is interesting to note that the use of the term "conservatism" began to enter the vocabulary of argument and description during this period:

> The sad lack of harmony which has so long been felt in Jewish matters has done much to retard Judaism. Time was when a Jew from any quarter of the globe felt at home in a Jewish synagogue, but with Minhag America and Minhag Poland and Minhag Reverend This and Minhag Reverend Doctor That, we may call ourselves fortunate if we succeed in becoming familiar with the ritual and the laws prior to their being changed for some other. This is equally true of Europe and of this country, yet we doubt whether American Jews recognize their own importance as a factor in universal Judaism. Not even the most orthodox of our brethren will deny that many beneficial changes can be instituted in the rabbinical rules—provided a tribunal of acknowledged competency and authority be organized to consider and advise these changes. And did we not so sorely lack men of character, ability and disinterested conservatism among our American Rabbanim, the United States would be the place of places to assemble such a convention. New problems can here be worked out on a new field unhampered by ancient interests and the American solution would by force of example soon become world-spread. Much of the *Shulchan Aruch* has outlived its usefulness and a return to the condition prior thereto is both desirable and practicable. The only obstacle lies in the pulpit. Here is an opportunity for our American ministers to prove themselves worthy of their positions . . .[2]

The editors of the *American Hebrew* demanded action. Their suggestion was that a new body convene as the representative of congregations adhering to traditional Judaism. Week after week they agitated for the convention, each time carefully explaining what the purpose and function of the proposed European-American Jewish synod would be.

> The true want of the age is a recognized religious authority, which shall obviate all fear of head and neck change, we mean not the exaltation of a man, whose will shall be law, no Jewish Pope, far from it—but we ask for a period-

ical synod of the Jewish clergy, to consider the advance of the times and the change of thought, to decide what customs are obsolete, what innovations are desirable; to speak with a voice which shall ring through the Jewish world, because of the fact of its being the united voices of the renowned ministers of our faith in Europe and in America. No longer should our worship be fashioned after the whims and private tasks of the members of a congregation; how can they be trusted to legislate upon anything connected with Judaism when their ignorance is notorious? The brains which should think out these problems, and recommend solutions for adoption, are the brains of our ministers; it is they whose specialty consists of a study of the progress of the age, it is they alone, who know what does and does not clash with the principles of our religion, it is they alone who can, and who ought to act. But the age marches on, and Judaism is left to shape itself because shepherds are not allowed to confer, or lack cohesion, or their congregations fear that their progress may be condemned.

The dangerous sentiment gains ground, that a man can live and believe like a Unitarian and yet be considered a Jew, so long as he is *born* such—this is the danger of the hour, an over-liberal Judaism. There is no authoritative body to say this is wrong, or that is wrong—why should there not be a synod? Limit it to those ministers whose congregations are large, limit it how we will, but every thinking Jew will listen to its admonition with respect, and if it bid the orthodox to yield here a little, and the reformer yield there a little, the innate conviction of all of the advantages of a closer union would smooth any soreness . . .[3]

Morais joined the ranks of those who advocated a synod. However, he wanted to expand its field of activity to include the organization of charitable and educational agencies and to assume responsibility for the strengthening of congregational life. He contrasted the situation in America with that in France, where the Central Consistory, located in Paris and represented by Grand Rabbi Isidor, united under its authority all the Jews from the English Channel to the Pyrenees. The editor, who reported Morais' views, continued on the same theme and drew the analogy: "To this tribunal all disputes are referred: its verdict is authoritative, and as a result, Judaism in France has both unity and uniformity, and enjoys universal esteem. In America, the situation is just the reverse."[4]

Morais considered the Oral Law to be as binding as the Written Law. Nevertheless he stressed that it was possible to introduce changes in Jewish custom and law, provided such changes were made by rabbis faithful to the Tradition.[5] For this reason he advocated the synod. The problem was to define the responsibilities of such a legislative body as well as the necessary qualities of the scholar who would preside over its constituents:

> A synod in America presided over by some European of acknowledged celebrity might effect a vast deal of good. A Conference whose Chief is distinguished for profound learning, loftiness of character, and for the spirit of enlightened conservatism might restrain the rash and urge on the unprogressive. More permanently beneficial yet would be the selection by all or a majority of Hebrew Congregations, of an ecclesiastical head of a Council composed of scholarly and respectable Israelites both among the clergy and the laity . . .

The central authority, according to Morais, would set standards for rabbis and preachers and see to it that those standards were properly observed. This would help solve the problem of "self-constituted rabbis" and supply synagogue officials with the respect due them. But its most vital task would be to regulate and sanction ritual changes: "If changes are needed; if a modified ritual Code is demanded by the times, the subject would then be discussed with uniformity of purpose, and all the combined learning required would be brought to bear on the solution of a question vitally important to Judaism."[6] Morais himself was in correspondence with the leading rabbis of Italy and England, men famous for their knowledge and understanding, in the hope of establishing a synod empowered to make changes in accordance with Jewish tradition.

The editors of the *American Hebrew* gave Morais' idea wide circulation. However, the same men who, several months before, had aspired to organize a synod revolving about an exclusive traditional congregational constituency, now expanded their plan to that of uniting *all* the Jews in America. Along with the synod they had evolved a formula by which traditional rabbinical authority could not be challenged. If this same authority realistically approached the changes demanded by the times, many of the Jewish communal organizations not yet committed either to Reform or to the Historical School could perhaps be persuaded to support it. Actually this was an undisguised attempt to organize the total community under the banner of the Historical School. The voluntary character of communal organizations had long prevented a cohesive organization of the Jewish community in America. As these organizations grew in scope and number, it was felt that the time had come to include them. In such a way, the "voluntary" community might at least attain minimal powers for constructive action.

It is for the very reason that there are so many "shades of Judaism" that no extant organization or institution can dare to speak exclusively for all American Jews, and the formation of an Alliance which shall not merely represent Jews who are connected with synagogues or temples, but also the great mass of Jews, who, for various reasons, are not attached to devotional institutions . . .

Thus the editors of the *American Hebrew* moved further, beyond the organized communal organizations into the ranks of Jews who had no formal affiliation with any Jewish institution. The number of Jews in this "unorganized" category grew perceptibly in those years and began to constitute a large portion of the population. The Reform group through its synagogue movement and other agencies, such as the fraternal orders and YMHAs, had also attempted to reach many of these unaffiliated Jews. Their success was negligible because vast numbers of Jews were able to live in America and express themselves completely apart from the synagogue or other forms of Jewish life. Their Jewishness was, for most of

them, an incidental factor, to be neither repudiated nor cultivated. The "grand alliance" of organizations would be broad
enough and flexible enough to include and represent the
totality of American Jewry regardless of its present relationship or lack of relationship to the "organized" Jewish community. They continued:

> The scope of such an Alliance would simply and broadly
> be the watching and protecting of Jewish interests, the
> using of every honorable and legitimate means in securing
> for the Jew, wherever he may be, Equal Rights, in en-
> deavoring to strangle Persecution of Jews, because they are
> Jews, in a word, enforcing by every proper way, in all
> civilized countries, the grand humanitarian principle, Lib-
> erty and Equality to all.[7]

It was clear in the minds of the framers of these propositions
that this attempt to form an all-embracing union along
broadest possible lines was only the means to an end. Once
they had succeeded in attracting unaffiliated Jews, it was
their intention to move them from a program of Jewish
rights to cultural activities and finally to religious life and
observance. They were willing to go to the margins of Jewish
life in order to bring their brothers back to the center.
Throughout all these explorations into new forms of community enlargement, the Historical School hoped that the
problem of authority would be resolved and that, in questions
of Jewish religion, the voice of Tradition would prevail.

Once the synod proposal—in any of its various formulations—had been placed on the agenda of the Historical
School, it was not removed for several decades. Despite waning enthusiasm for its practicality, it remained a subject of
discussion until the end of the century and the arrival of
Solomon Schechter. It came to the surface whenever Historical School adherents actively hoped to achieve spiritual
hegemony over American Jewry. It declined whenever the
leadership recognized its weaknesses. While there was still
hope of healing the breach with Reform, the proposal was
advocated intensively by the editors of the *American Hebrew*.
These editors, on the whole, held sway over the traditional-

ists in their own School and rejected the East-European Orthodox elements as completely as they did the Reform. In an editorial of April 1884, they declared:

> Orthodoxy has learned in the past decades, that much that was held anti-Jewish thirty years ago is now to be looked upon as innocent and harmless; Reform, too, has seen the usual result of a too victorious progress, in its utter limpness and indifference to all further effort. The true procedure is in the middle; an honest confession by orthodoxy that much of its opposition to so-called "new" ideas were mistakenly based on the fact that they were new; Reform with equal ingenuousness must say, that its boasted panaceas have failed to infuse a more vigorous and lasting life into the body of Israel.[8]

Again, the *American Hebrew* editorially supported the initiative of an anonymous rabbi in the United States who had published, in the Vienna *Neuzeit,* an open letter addressed to Dr. Adolf Jellinek. The correspondent sent copies of his letter to the chief rabbis of England, Holland, France, Belgium, Denmark and Germany, requesting that a preliminary meeting be held to consider the advisability of holding a Universal Synod.

In the same year, Max Cohen, one of the founding editors of the *American Hebrew,* urged that American Jews agitate "through press and pulpit and platform, strive to educate the people so that they shall bring their representatives to convene in a Synod for the purpose of considering, amending, and adapting the laws and usages to the time and country in which we live."[9] At the same time, Marcus Jastrow published a major statement on "Judaism in Europe and America."[10] Describing the basic differences between American and European Jewries, he emphasized that the Jewish community in Europe was an internal state with a history, tradition, character and organization of its own. In America, although the Jewish community indeed consisted of uniform elements, "whoever is not in sympathy with any and all of its measures or directions, is at liberty to stay aloof, withdraw or secede, and of this liberty, as you all know ample use is made in our country, especially so among the 'sons of Jacob.' "

The Basis for Separate Action

The leap across the seas was as ineffectual as the domestic attempt to vault over the heads of the Reform group and other communal bodies. If the Historical School in America was to build an indigenous and creative Jewish community, it would have to turn its attention to the difficult, unsolved inner problems of Jewish life: the Sabbath, *kashrut,* the synagogue, Eretz Yisrael and the Hebraic core of Jewish education. The Sabbath issue was most important, and posed a problem of Jewish life which deeply concerned the laity. Each week dwindling attendance at the synagogue was a demonstration of the younger generation's indifference. The will of the youth to detach itself from traditional ways in the home and in public ceremonies frightened the elders. The elected officials of the synagogues felt it their duty, by making public prayer more attractive, to attract their children to Sabbath observance. Individual congregations seemed to find consolation, if not strength, in calling conferences. In June 1867, the Hebrew Sabbath Association was formed "to promote the more effectual observance of the Sabbath day among Israelites." The key point in the circular which it issued emphasized the desirability of securing the cooperation of Jewish businessmen who observed the Sabbath and would provide employment for members of the Jewish group. Some months before this meeting, a suggestion, novel for its time, had appeared in the *Hebrew Leader,* "to connect with the Friday evening service, hitherto sadly neglected, a religious address or discourse." In this constructive way, it was suggested to the *Hebrew Leader's* editor, Dr. Bondi, that more people might attend services and that the objects of such an association might be more quickly realized. Bondi himself expanded this suggestion in an editorial, proposing that a program for the Sabbath day be developed to involve young people in the spirit of the Sabbath and so fill their idle hours. He suggested, for example, that reading rooms be established throughout the city.[11]

This Association was one in a series of similar efforts, all of which were short-lived. A "Ritual Convention" was held in 1870 in New York. Twelve traditional congregations participated but produced no tangible results.[12] As the years passed, the need for constructive action became more and more acute. Hortatory speeches were inadequate substitutes for a new educational program among the masses. In 1880 a new Sabbath Association was formed in New York. Members of the Historical School in Baltimore and Philadelphia organized similar societies. In all of these cities the rabbis insisted that the offices be filled by laymen in order to insure adoption and implementation of a practical program. Their aim was to induce business people to observe the Sabbath publicly, to close their places of business and to organize Sabbath afternoon services for children and young adults.[13] As reported by the executive committee in charge of "a plan of proceeding," the Association would succeed only if it could elicit from its members a promise of personal commitment. "In furtherance of the Society's purpose, all its members, ipso facto, shall bind themselves *to keep the Sabbath holy* by its consecration in public and private, and membership shall imply a personal pledge of observance . . ."[14]

At first, these societies encountered considerable difficulty, but in time their influence grew. In an editorial, the *American Hebrew* suggested the appointment of committees to deal with the problems of workers. The committees would, for example, procure jobs for Jewish young men who did not want to violate the Sabbath. They would also take a stand against shopping on the Sabbath. The Association arranged Sabbath social gatherings for the benefit of those who were compelled to work on Saturday but were able to leave their jobs in the afternoon. They could then come to the synagogue for special services, sermons and study. Some congregations with Reform tendencies joined the Association in order to find ways of keeping the Sabbath day holy.[15]

The rabbis of the Historical School were much less successful in attempts at influencing their congregants, individually and in the community at large, to observe the laws of *kashrut*. Not only in the homes of most Jews but also in public places, *kashrut* was ignored. It had even become accepted custom to serve non-kosher meals at public Jewish affairs. H. Pereira Mendes worked untiringly to correct this situation. He referred to the "invariable practice of so-called Jewish societies": they offered forbidden food at their entertainments, and he suggested that a few earnest men and women should refuse to partake of any food whatever at these affairs. "It is bad enough in private celebrations, such as weddings; it is a thousand times worse to give a public entertainment, trumpet forth that it is for a Jewish society, and then outrage Jewish feelings."[16] Supervision of the sales of kosher food was another aspect of the *kashrut* question, which arose because of involvement with the New York City Board of Health. Municipal supervision was felt to be a significant step forward in giving *kashrut* observance community status. When, in 1885, the New York City Board of Health consulted with a group of rabbis about such supervision, the *American Hebrew* urged full cooperation, praising the strict sanitary laws of the board. In their great anxiety for help with *kashrut* observance, the rabbis of the Historical School confused the issues. Sanitary legislation for a public market did not necessarily imply the introduction of *kashrut* into the home. Nevertheless, the process of legislation gave them greater confidence in contentions against Reform. "What do our friends in Cincinnati who of their own sweet will declared 'Kitchen Judaism' dead, say to this evidence that it is abundantly alive and vigorous in enlightened and law-abiding communities such as New York?"[17]

Again, with the young people in mind, the Historical School turned to modifications of the prayer service and the synagogue order. The American Synagogue was an open synagogue. It was visited and studied by people of other faiths. Consequently, attention had to be given to the environment and the symbols of the environment. Moderni-

Isaac M. Wise (1819-1900), founder of Reform Judaism in America

uel Myer Isaacs (1804-1878), editor of *Jewish Messenger*

Isaac Leeser (1806-1868), organizer of American Jewry

Mikveh Israel, Seventh and Race Sts., Philadelphia, 1859-1908

Courtesy of Dropsie College

B'nai Jeshurun, Elm Street, New York City, 1826-1850

Courtesy of Maxwell Whiteman

Morris J. Raphall (1798-1868), Rabbi of B'nai Jeshurun Congregation, New York City

ernard Drachman (1861-1945), Amerian-born rabbi, active in the Historical chool until 1908

H. Pereira Mendes (1852-1937), Minister of Shearith Israel (Spanish-Portuguese Congregation of New York), co-founder of the Jewish Theological Seminary

Benjamin Szold (1829-1902), Rabbi
Oheb Shalom in Baltimore (1860-19

Alexander Kohut (1842-1894), Rabbi of
Ahavath Chesed (1885-1894), a leader of
the Historical School

Marcus Jastrow (1829-1903), Rabbi of
Rodeph Shalom in Philadelphia (1866-
1892)

zation, decorum, and the esthetic harmony of the service were an expression of inner as well as outer dignity. The Reformers had succeeded in attracting adherents precisely because they had recognized the intrinsic merit of such change. The Historical School borrowed from the Reformers. The rabbis realized that it was possible to conduct an orderly and harmonious service and at the same time stay within the forms of Tradition. They insisted, for example, that the garments of prayer be in keeping with the modern spirit. They argued that wearing a *tallit* had profound meaning for the individual worshiper.[18] They also contended that order in the synagogue did not depend on the presence or absence of a women's gallery or on the institution of family pews. It did depend on the conviction of individuals at prayer.[19]

The criticism leveled by the Historical School against many of the prevalent practices in the traditional synagogues might well have come from the Reformers. Morais, for example, said that "to make the young feel that their faith is based upon civilizing principles, was the need of the hour."[20] The editors of the *American Hebrew* called the customs and congregational habits on Simhat Torah "frivolous and irreligious."[21] They advocated that the congregations of the Historical School train their cantors to conduct services in good taste and dignity. In order to make the service meaningful to those who could not follow Hebrew, it was suggested that English translations of prayers be read on Sabbaths and holidays. Lay participation, they urged, should be invited even in the pulpit itself, and they commended the Shaare Emeth congregation of St. Louis for carrying out this idea.[22] Burial practices were also openly discussed. Aaron Bettelheim, of Baltimore, introduced a resolution before the Conference of the Jewish Ministers Association of America. It read: "*Resolved*, That the ministers in conference express their disapproval of the modern custom of lavish display at funerals, and recommend to all their colleagues to firmly discourage such and to endeavor to secure the simplest funeral rites for rich and poor alike."[23]

So far, the Historical School remained completely united.

A more serious question, that of playing the organ during services, provoked disagreement. The Reformers had introduced the organ and choirs composed of Gentile singers. The *American Hebrew* took a neutral stand on this question since many members of the Historical School, including Szold, Jastrow, Hochheimer, and De Sola Mendes had organs in their synagogues. The editorial board therefore kept silent when the opinion of Dr. Jellinek of Vienna in favor of the organ became known.[24] But the right wing of the Historical School could not be won over. Its members granted that the organ might conceivably attract a larger attendance for a while; but in the long run it would defeat its own purpose. The Jewish practice of prayer is to evoke self-expression. The organ would silence individual expression.

On this question opinion remained divided. On the problem involving the utilization of Gentile choristers in the synagogue service, a consensus soon developed. Most members of the Historical School opposed the practice. The *American Hebrew* severely criticized congregations that had Christians participate in conducting services. They also ridiculed the introduction of secular music.[25] They suggested, instead, that the congregations follow the example of H. Pereira Mendes, who had introduced into his service a choir of Jewish children. Mendes also encouraged his worshipers to participate in congregational singing. In the beginning, this custom was not generally accepted by the Ashkenazi congregations. Sephardi congregations were the first to adopt it, since their melodies were known for generations by the congregants. Slowly, other congregations followed.[26]

Sabbath and *kashrut* were ancient institutions in Judaism, basic to the very texture of Jewish life and law. Similarly the place of the Holy Land as the center of Judaism was an unquestioned tenet of the Tradition. But when the age-old prayers for the Return took the shape of contemporary ideology, as a program for the recolonization of Palestine, a cry of alarm rose from Reform Jewry. The movement of *Hovevei Zion* (Lovers of Zion), rooted in the traditional concept of *Yishub Eretz Yisrael* (the settlement of the Holy

Land), won over many religious leaders in Europe. However, it was the imperative of Russian emigration that made the traditional ideal an actuality and moved the formation of the World Zionist movement forward. Fresh voices from unexpected quarters brought the vision of a Zion rebuilt to the attention of more and more people. George Eliot, the English novelist, Lawrence Oliphant (the hero Daniel Deronda in Eliot's book who had actually taken up residence in Haifa), and Emma Lazarus, were some of the movement's eloquent spokesmen in the Western communities.[27] What was called the "dream" of George Eliot, the "wild scheme" of Mr. Oliphant and the "poetic fancy" of Miss Lazarus was one way of forcing the solution of the crises which confronted the suffering Russian Jews.

The Historical School, especially through the pages of the *American Hebrew,* supported the program and preferred to call it "The Regeneration of Palestine." Emma Lazarus' "Epistle to the Hebrews" was a passionate appeal for a return to Zion. Through this work, the Zionist idea reached most American Jews. She advocated the settlement of Jews in Eretz Yisrael as a free people. Like most supporters of the Return to Zion, she considered this plan the solution to the problem of East-European Jewry, those with no chance of emigrating westward from the lands of persecution. She wrote: "My plea for the establishment of a free Jewish State . . . has not the remotest bearing upon the position of American Jews. My sole desire is to arouse in my fellow-citizens a deeper and fuller appreciation of the fact that millions of human beings belonging to the Jewish race and faith, are despoiled of their right to justice and freedom . . ."[28]

What was self-evident to the Historical School only aroused bitter controversy in the American Jewish community. Reform had stated its position at the Philadelphia meeting of 1869: "Israel's Messianic aim is not the re-establishment of the ancient Jewish State . . . , it is the unity of all men as the children of God in the confession of the One and Sole God . . ." But the editors of the *American Hebrew,* although they were not yet aware that the acrimony over this

issue would cause great dissension in years to come, identified themselves with the developing world movement to rebuild Zion as the Third Jewish Commonwealth.[29] They
pointed with pride to the forty-nine colonization societies
organized in Rumania for the resettlement of Palestine, to
the fifty Russian students who had left the land of persecution
to become agricultural laborers, and to the settlers of the first
villages "who have commenced the arduous labors of tillage
there, happy only to get to work, so happy as to be indifferent
to scanty fare, inclement weather and even the ultimate par-
tition of the profits of their labor."[30]

When mass immigration became an unavoidable solution
to the problems raised by the persecution of Jews, the question which required immediate attention and which divided
opinion on both sides of the ocean, was the proposed direction and destination of the immigrants: America or Palestine.
The debate had manifested itself in public a decade earlier,
in 1872, with the Jewish emigration from Rumania. Benjamin Peixotto, then American consul to Bucharest, proposed to remove the Jews from Rumania and bring them
to the United States where they would be received and cared
for. This proposal met with opposition from the advocates
of the Palestine solution, and the controversy was taken up
actively by the Jewish press.[31] Through the next several
decades, as the pogroms became intensified, the need for
immediate decision continued to face entire Jewish communities in Eastern Europe.[32] In the Historical School the supporters of immigration to Eretz Yisrael were motivated in
their choice by practical and theological reasons. They maintained that Palestine could offer agricultural opportunities
to the immigrants, but on American farms there was little
possibility of absorbing the newcomers. Furthermore, once
securely settled in Palestine, the immigrants would continue
their religious life as before. In America, they would probably be cut from their religious moorings.[33]

Sabato Morais surprised his associates by taking a stand
against the views of the Historical School favoring a Jewish
commonwealth in Palestine. He distinguished between the

traditional ideas of redemption and those of practical Restoration.[34] Morais believed that in the End of Days, as the prophets had foretold, God would assemble His people from the four corners of the earth and return them to Zion. He argued, however, that it was not permissible to do so by an effort "to renationalize our people." In the first place, the time was not yet ripe for most of world Jewry to return to the Holy Land. Secondly, he claimed, the creation of a Jewish nation would jeopardize the position of Jews everywhere. Only when justice reigned throughout the world would the eyes of the Gentiles be opened, and only then would they recognize the necessity of settling Jews in their own country.

Is the Jew of today, asked Morais, ready to live in an autonomous State? "Is the Jew of to-day equal to the standing he is designed to occupy, when he will be set up famously among the family of nations?" We cannot compare ourselves to the other nations of the world, he claimed. On one hand, the leaders of the nations of the world had not yet reached an ethical level which would dictate a change in the way they treated the Jews. Most of them held the Jews in contempt as stubborn infidels. On the other hand, one could not expect the diverse and splintered Jewish people to accept a common inheritance. Morais did not believe that the various factions of world Jewry would unite for a common purpose:

> In the present condition of things, naught but a miraculous intellectual change would weld the Hebrews together, politically. The German and Russian; the Jew under the Shah, and the Bulgarian, he that hails from Turkey, and his fellow-religionist from the Barbary States (leaving aside the Frenchman, the Englishman or the Italian), constitute a heterogenous mass.

Morais considered the hoped-for "new Ezra" an illusion. It was forbidden, he said, to open the door to false messiahs. Anyone who knew Jewish history could recall the sorrow and suffering that were the result of such illusions. Morais admitted that in past generations various rabbinic authorities in the Diaspora, such as Saadia Gaon, Maimonides, Nahmanides and Abrabanel had urged Restoration movements. But these sages, he stated, "erred in their reckonings."

It was not only Morais' reading of the historical process nor his interpretation of the Tradition that kept him aloof from the advocates of an early Jewish commonwealth. He was also profoundly troubled by the secularist stand taken by many advocates of the colonization of Palestine. Emma Lazarus' views, for example, shocked him. He reproached her statements that "it is no longer necessary to preach the Unity of God" or that "Jews can mix in blood with Christians . . . and still the racial tie binds them together, even though they discard all religion."

Every attack against the Tradition, for whatever purpose, caused Morais deep anguish. How could he associate with those who denied the fundamental principles of Judaism? The combination of factors—his faith in the ultimate Divine Redemption and his belief that Zion would not be rebuilt by those whose lives did not reflect the laws of God—separated him from the majority of the Historical School. Morais believed that the Holy Land could not be established without the Divine Presence. His opposition clearly and fundamentally rested on his interpretation of the religious principles involved. While his integrity was not questioned, the practicality of his position was refuted. The great majority of the Historical School formed an important group of what later developed into the Zionist core of American Jewry.

Sabbath, *kashrut*, Synagogue and Eretz Yisrael became the basic planks of the constructive program of the emergent Conservative Movement. The problem of authority had not been solved, but the process of working together in an organization made the School conscious of its resources and potentialities. The Historical group had not yet decided to form a separate movement. But the decision was not far off.

Open Conflict

In showing the Historical School's antagonism to Reform, one must view the intensity of the struggle in the light of the anticipated future impact of Reform; the specific point at issue at any particular moment is relatively unimportant. It should be understood that within the Reform group itself there were members who were apprehensive of this future negative impact of Reform on American Judaism. For example, Bernard Felsenthal of the moderate faction, in a letter written to Osias H. Schorr, the editor of *HeHalutz*, then in Prague, summarized the Jewish spiritual conditions in America at the time: "It cannot be denied that Reform has indeed aroused a spirit which may prove very destructive within American Israel if not carefully countered."[35]

The actual decision to found a separate religious movement in American Judaism resulted from two immediate events: the shift of control within the Reform rabbinate from the moderate to the more radical Reformers as manifested in the Pittsburgh Platform; and the emergence of Alexander Kohut as the new leader of the Historical School. He transformed its program into an ideology. From the formulation of that ideology, both movements evolved into the next phase of their respective development: institutionalization.

Having examined the crystallization of opinion within the Historical School around the ideas of Sabbath, *kashrut*, Synagogue, and Eretz Yisrael, we can better understand what happened when these ideas were lined up against the opposition of the organized Reform group. The Reform practice of Sunday services was the most important single factor to disillusion even those within the Historical group who sympathized with Reform. The first experiment in conducting services on Sunday was made in Baltimore by the Hebrew Reformed Association in 1854. Although these services were intended not to supplant the traditional Sabbath worship but to serve as an added means of attracting synagogue attendance, the attempt failed in six months. After this experiment, many Reformers worked for the observance of the traditional Sabbath together with the members of the Historical School in the various Sabbath associations. But when they saw the continued decline in attendance, they again began to seek a more effective remedy. In 1874, Sunday services were introduced by David Einhorn in the Har Sinai congregation of Baltimore, by Samuel Hirsch in congregation Keneseth Israel of Philadelphia and by Kaufmann Kohler in the Sinai congregation of Chicago. The question of these supplementary services was raised at the Pittsburgh Conference in 1885, and it was resolved that the introduction of such services was not inconsistent with the Reform interpretation of Judaism. Several Reform congregations instituted them in time.[36] In this context it must be emphasized that Wise opposed this practice and vigorously attacked all those who would diminish the importance of the Sabbath day.[37]

Benjamin Szold was one of the leading forces in the Historical School to combat the Reformers on this issue. A moderate person, often in sympathy with Reform, he parted company with it. He proclaimed that desecration of the Sabbath violated one of the basic tenets of Judaism, as stated by the Talmud: "whoever denies the Sabbath is like one who denies the whole Torah." Szold did not limit his metaphors to talmudic sources. "A congregation which holds Sunday services," he wrote, "may be compared to a bigamist who still clings to his first wife and loves both his spouses. It does, in effect, what politicians call 'sitting on the fence.' "[38]

The Historical School conceded that the source of the trouble lay in the condition of American Judaism generally, but they were unable to state that the Sabbath could be saved by abandoning the seventh day. Morais stated the School's position honestly:

I do not underestimate the fearful difficulties which stand in the way of Sabbath-keeping, and to my sorrow I have nothing new to propose to bring about its observance. I cannot join those in the clergy who offer inadmissible compromises and less can I agree with such as plan out schemes which will prove murderous stabs in the heart of historical Judaism. For in Sunday services I hear dirges sung over the death of my father's religion.[39]

Kashrut was the second cause of furious arguments between the two groups. Now it was Wise who was the butt of the attack. It was he who had given currency to the epithet "kitchen Judaism," in disparagement of those who observed the dietary laws. His opinion was that only those laws contained in the Pentateuch were authoritative, and of those only the ones intended to be "eternal" rather than "temporary" should be observed. All additional regulations of the oral tradition he considered obsolete. The *kashrut* laws he placed in the category of temporary sanitary provisions. Orthodox Jews, he claimed, observed the laws of *kashrut* because they accepted rabbinic authority and not because these laws were in accordance with the laws of Moses and the prophets who knew nothing about the *mitzvot* of "the kitchen." It was time to end the uproar over the culinary problems of Judaism. Wise, who also had a gift for sharp language in debate, unleashed one diatribe after another on the "kitchen" question.

Jastrow took up the cudgels. In castigating Wise for eating non-kosher food, he added: "He (Wise) is not satisfied with this, but must prove in his lectures that the Torah never intended these laws to be binding . . ."[40] Furthermore, Jastrow charged, Wise was intentionally training his students for personal lack of observance and also for a philosophy which justified the abrogation of *kashrut*. This point was one of the main reasons that Jastrow urged his congregation to leave the Union. For that matter, he also disengaged himself from any association involving Wise. Frederick de Sola Mendes, a left-wing member of the Historical School, also broke his connection with the Reformers because of this issue. He was one of the important defenders of *kashrut*. In 1874, when the debate was just beginning, he published an article about the significance of the dietary laws in which he pointed to three basic values in their observance: physical health, spiritual edification and national survival.[41] De Sola Mendes became a fierce opponent of Wise as a result of the incident which took place at the graduation banquet of the first four graduates of the Hebrew Union College in 1883. Deliberately or not, the meal that was served included forbidden food.

Those who had hoped that Wise would not instill his students with an extreme brand of Reform, (he had promised to be more careful in such matters), were bitterly hurt and felt betrayed.[42] Many congregations of the Historical School resigned from the Union of American Hebrew Congregation in protest, among them Shaaray Tefila, of which De Sola Mendes was rabbi.[43] Wise criticized Mendes furiously, but he neither denied the fact nor felt the need to justify his about-face on this issue. On the basis of his action, Wise had destroyed the prestige his institution held in the eyes of members of the Historical School who had supported it.[44] Of all the areas of controversy between the two groups, the *kashrut* question was fought over most heatedly, and it reached the larger American community. H. Pereira Mendes and Kaufmann Kohler became involved in a sharp debate that resulted from the "Pork and Oysters" articles which Kohler published in the *New York Herald*. Pereira Mendes did not wish to hold such a debate with a Reform rabbi in the general press, and so continued his polemic in the *American Hebrew*.

The place in the prayer service that the Hebrew language should be given was the third point of bitter controversy. In his prayer book, *Olat Tamid*, Einhorn had converted the traditional *siddur* into a German book of prayers. Wise, however, had held a position closer to the views of the Historical School. In 1868, Wise had written in the preface to his book *Hymns, Psalms and Prayers*: "The Hebrew language in our public worship is the medium of our own synagogal union. Dispersed as the house of Israel is in all lands, we must have a vehicle to understand each other in the house of God, so that no brother be a stranger therein; and this vehicle is the Hebrew."

In the course of time, the argument over the importance of the Hebrew language as a factor of Jewish unity was superseded in the minds of the moderate Reformers by another, equally compelling question: "Occidentalism" versus "Orientalism." An avowed aim of Reform was to Americanize Judaism in both character and form. The utilization of English in the synagogue services was considered an indispensable means for furthering this aim. As a consequence, even Wise and the moderate Reform faction were gradually drawn to the position articulated by Kaufmann Kohler that "Judaism must drop its orientalism, and become truly American in spirit and form . . . It will not do to offer our prayers in a tongue which only a few scholars nowadays understand. We cannot afford any longer to pray for a return to Jerusalem . . ."[45] Hebrew was conceived as part of the total complex of Oriental thought and institutions. Westernization necessarily began with the gradual replacement of Hebrew by English in the service. The members of the Historical School fully understood that the issue extended far beyond the area of language *per se*. To them, as in the Tradition, Hebrew was "the Holy Tongue" with all the connotations implied by this term.

"Hebrew," said H. Pereira Mendes, "is the language in which the Torah was given, the language in which our prophets spoke and our psalmists sang. To learn Hebrew takes but a short time, and the meaning of the prayers can be easily acquired."[46] Nor was the Historical School impressed with the argument that lack of aquaintance with the language would keep Jews from attending the synagogue. The editors of the *American Hebrew* expressed the stand of the entire Historical School when they wrote:

> There is perhaps some propriety in having the *Haphtorah,* the prayer for the government and one or two hymns recited or sung in English, it is also necessary that the sermon should be delivered in that language. This is, however, all that should or may be done. More than this would destroy the Hebraic character of the service; would lead to the loss of Hebrew as a study among our youth, and would unquestionably gradually lead to the total extinction of the Jewish tone in the Jewish house of worship.
>
> It has always been an easy matter to teach boys and girls sufficient Hebrew to enable them to follow the service intelligently, and read the Bible understandingly in the original. This much Jewish education it is the duty of every Jewish parent to afford to every child. Retain the

Hebrew in the service, and this duty will be fulfilled. Discard it, and it will inevitably be neglected.[47]

If the members of the Historical School considered the abandonment of the Sabbath, kashrut and Hebrew as treason against Judaism, they considered the Reform innovations in marriage and divorce as catastrophic for the continuity of the Jewish community.[48] The Reformers had announced their extreme position in this matter at the Philadelphia meeting of 1869. They abolished the ketubah, the traditional marriage contract and the biblical injunction against a kohen marrying a divorcée and, in general, abrogated Jewish law in marriage and divorce proceedings. The inevitable result was the acceptance of mixed marriages. Despite all the protests of the Historical group, the Reformers persisted in their course.[49]

The resolute action of the Reform group created resentment and antipathy which only served to bind the members of the Historical School together more firmly. The rightists, such as Morais and H. Pereira Mendes, knew that they could now work quite closely with men such as Jastrow and De Sola Mendes, who, in turn, were determined to draw back and move to the right. The stage was set for the architect who could build a coherent structure of thought for the School. He was Alexander Kohut, a scholar and leader of Hungarian Jewry, who accepted the pulpit of congregation Ahavath Chesed in New York City in 1885. The members of the Historical School looked forward with eagerness to Kohut's arrival. In his first address from the pulpit of Ahavath Chesed, Kohut expressed the point of view of the Historical School as a cohesive doctrine. He built his ideology in a series of addresses on the frame of the Ethics of the Fathers. Kohut's premise was simple to grasp: the existence or disappearance of the Jewish community as a Jewish community depended on whether or not it was based on the authority of the Torah and the Rabbis. He developed this idea step by step:

The chain of tradition continued unbroken from Moses through Joshua, the Elders, the Prophets and the Men of the Great Synagogue, down to the latest times. On this tradition rests our faith, which Moses first received from God on Sinai. On this foundation rests Mosaic-rabbinical Judaism to-day; and on this foundation we take our stand. . .

But you may ask: Shall the fence around the garden, shall reverence be extended around everything that the past hedged in . . . ? "Remember the days of old," said Moses, *and have regard to the changes of each generation* (Deut. 32.7). The teaching of the ancients we must make our starting-point, but we must not lose sight of what is needed in every generation . . .

And as these elders did, so can—yes, so must we, the later Epigoni—do in the exigencies of our own day. If the power to make changes was granted to the Elders, is not the power given equally to us? "But they were giants," we are told, "and we, compared with them, are mere pygmies." Perhaps so; let us not forget, however, that a pygmy on a giant's shoulder can see further than the giant himself.

Let us now revert to the question raised at the outset: Is Judaism definitely closed for all time, or is it capable of and in need of continuous development? I answer both Yes and No. I answer Yes, *because Religion has been given to man*; and as it is the duty of man to grow in perfection as long as he lives, he must modify the forms which yield him religious satisfaction, in accordance with the spirit of the times. I answer No, in so far as it concerns the Word of God, which cannot be imperfect. . . . You Israelite, imperfect as you are, strive to perfect yourself in the image of your perfect God. Hold in honor His unchangeable Law and let it be your earnest task to put new life into the outward form of our religion . . .

Our religious guide is the Torah, the Law of Moses, interpreted and applied in the light of tradition. But inasmuch as individual opinion cannot be valid for the whole community, it behooves individuals and communities to appoint only recognized authorities as teachers; such men, that is to say, as acknowledge belief in authority, and who, at the same time, with comprehension and tact, are willing to consider what may be permitted in view of the exigencies

of the times, and what may be discarded, without changing the nature and character of the foundations of the
faith.[50]

In this manner Kohut differed from the Orthodox group,
which was beginning to take shape in those years, and related
himself organically to the Historical School. What had previously been said in editorials and sermons haphazardly and
only when occasion warranted it, Kohut formulated systematically, dealing with both the theoretical aspects of the
problem and with the practical consideration of re-estab-
lishing a collective rabbinic authority. Believing, as he did,
in the divine origin of the Torah and in the development of
the oral tradition out of it, he declared that the contemporary
needs of the individual Jew must necessarily be included in
the work of the synagogue, if American Judaism was to
flourish.

> A Reform which seeks to progress without the Mosaic-
> rabbinical tradition is a deformity—a skeleton without
> flesh and sinew, without spirit and heart. It is suicide; and
> suicide is not reform. We desire a Judaism full of life. We
> desire to worship the living God in forms full of life and
> beauty; Jewish, yet breathing the modern spirit. Only a
> Judaism true to itself and its past, yet receptive of the ideas
> of the present, accepting the good and the beautiful from
> whatever source it may come, can command respect and
> recognition . . .
> I do not know whether it will be my good fortune to
> have your sympathy in my religious attitude—that of
> Mosaic-rabbinical Judaism, freshened with the spirit of
> progress, a Judaism of the healthy golden mean. I hope I
> shall . . .[51]

The Historical School responded to Kohut's question by
rallying to his banner of leadership. But the Reform group
was ready for the challenge. Its spokesman was Kaufmann
Kohler, who answered Kohut's presentation with an equally
well-balanced and organized analysis of the role of Judaism
in a series of addresses entitled "Backward or Forward."[52]
This was a call for Reform Judaism to formalize its commit-

ment to "progress." Kohler asked whether American Judaism, after a thirty-five-year struggle to reform and advance Judaism in this country, ought to retreat or stand firmly on the basis of the universal prophetic-messianic ideal. The answer was implicit in the question. Reform, he argued, had come to bring Judaism out of the darkness of the Middle Ages into the light of modern progress.[53] The "Kohut-Kohler Controversy" filled the columns of the *American Hebrew* and continued to excite the public throughout the summer of 1885. Unlike the prevailing tone of other Reform-Historical School polemics of the period, such as the dispute between H. Pereira Mendes and Kohler, in which personal animosity played a major role, Kohler and Kohut fought out their battle in orderly fashion and avoided invective.[54] But the breach was widened and deepened. Both the *American Hebrew* and *American Israelite* printed letters, comments and editorials while the debate endured, and for months afterward services at the contenders' respective synagogues, Ahavath Chesed and Beth El, attracted large attendances as the public followed the controversy.

Thus, by a peculiar combination of circumstances, the newly-arrived Alexander Kohut became the immediate cause for the crystallization of "classical Reform" in the United States. He who disliked the expression "American Judaism" because it implied a separation from other Jews in the world, he who dreamed of a universal Jewish community, was to help bring about the coalescence of Reform as a "uniquely American" faith. The Pittsburgh Conference was called to give the Historical School and its spokesman, Alexander Kohut, an "official" answer. Whoever stood for Reform and for "progress" was invited to come to the meeting at Pittsburgh. Nineteen rabbis appeared, and Isaac M. Wise was elected chairman. Kohler was the moving spirit of all the meetings, and he had prepared a platform of ten paragraphs as the basis for a united Reform movement. In this platform he revealed his belief that Reform would fulfill all the spiritual needs of American Jewry.

The Conference adopted an ideological statement which came to be known as the Pittsburgh Platform:

First—We recognize in every religion an attempt to grasp the Infinite, and in every mode, source, or book or revelation held sacred in any religious system, the consciousness of the indwelling of God in man. We hold that Judaism presents the highest conception of the God idea as taught in our holy Scriptures and developed and spiritualized by the Jewish teachers, in accordance with the moral and philosophical progress of their respective ages. We maintain that Judaism preserved and defended, midst continual struggles and trials and under enforced isolation, this God idea as the central religious truth for the human race.

Second—We recognize in the Bible the record of the consecration of the Jewish people to its mission as priest of the one God, and value it as the most potent instrument of religious and moral instruction. We hold that the modern discoveries of scientific researches in the domains of nature and history are not antagonistic to the doctrines of Judaism, the Bible reflecting the primitive ideas of its own age, and at times clothing its conception of Divine Providence and justice, dealing with man in miraculous narratives.

Third—We recognize in the Mosaic legislation a system of training the Jewish people for its mission during its national life in Palestine, and to-day we accept as binding only the moral laws, and maintain only such ceremonies as elevate and sanctify our lives, but reject all such as are not adapted to the views and habits of modern civilization.

Fourth—We hold that all such Mosaic and rabbinical laws as regulate diet, priestly purity, and dress, originated in ages and under the influence of ideas altogether foreign to our present mental and spiritual state. They fail to impress the modern Jew with a spirit of priestly holiness; their observance in our days is apt rather to obstruct than to further modern spiritual elevation.

Fifth—We recognize, in the modern era of universal culture of heart and intellect, the approaching of the realization of Israel's great Messianic hope for the establishment of the kingdom of truth, justice, and peace among all men.

We consider ourselves no longer a nation, but a religious community, and therefore expect neither a return to Palestine, nor a sacrificial worship under the sons of Aaron, nor the restoration of any of the laws concerning the Jewish state.

Sixth—We recognize in Judaism a progressive religion, ever striving to be in accord with the postulates of reason. We are convinced of the utmost necessity of preserving the historical identity with our great past. Christianity and Islam being daughter religions of Judaism, we appreciate their providential mission to aid in the spreading of monotheistic and moral truth. We acknowledge that the spirit of broad humanity of our age is our ally in the fulfillment of our mission, and therefore, we extend the hand of fellowship to all who operate with us in the establishment of the reign of truth and righteousness among men.

Seventh—We reassert the doctrine of Judaism, that the soul of man is immortal, grounding this belief on the divine nature of the human spirit, which forever finds bliss in righteousness and misery in wickedness. We reject as ideas not rooted in Judaism the beliefs both in bodily resurrection and in Gehenna and Eden (Hell and Paradise) as abodes for everlasting punishment or reward.

Eighth—In full accordance with the spirit of Mosaic legislation, which strives to regulate the relation between rich and poor, we deem it our duty to participate in the great task of modern times, to solve on the basis of justice and righteousness, the problems presented by the contrasts and evils of the present organization of society.[55]

With these eight tightly-worded paragraphs, the Conference produced one of the basic documents in American Jewish history, the one which guided the Reform movement for almost half a century. It consolidated the opposition who fought, laughed and jeered at the Reform "I-do-not-believe." Professor Elbogen, writing nearly a half-century after the event, described the platform: "It was not a *Confessio Judaica* but an homage to the latest European school of thought in science, in history of religion and particularly of the religious evolution in Israel."[56]

The Pittsburgh Platform, as it stood, was approved *de facto* by the Central Conference of American Rabbis, the Reform Rabbinical organization, founded in July 1889.[57] Many Reform rabbis, like Gustav Gottheil, could not accept its formulation. On the other hand, Kaufmann Kohler called the document the Jewish Declaration of Independence. His opponents asked, "Independence from what?" and answered, "Independence from Judaism."[58]

The bitterness engendered by the Pittsburgh Platform finally severed all relationships between the two groups. Sometimes the conflict was heard even at funerals, rabbis polemicizing in eulogies while the dead still lay unburied. Congregational realignment was inevitable. Benjamin Szold pleaded with his congregation to leave the Union of American Hebrew Congregations, and although he did not succeed, he never ceased to oppose the Union publicly, even when faced with his congregation's adherence to it. He particularly criticized the use of the term "God idea" in the Platform. Jastrow proclaimed that there was no need for a platform: Jews had only one law—the Torah. Jastrow objected in particular to the Reformers' denial of the *mitzvot*. Without hesitation, they called them antiquated, obsolete rites.[59]

Morais, an expert polemicist, knew that words were of little avail. He felt that as long as rabbis with such destructive ideas were the teachers of Jewish youth, there would be no hope for the survival of traditional Judaism. He therefore turned to congregation Shearith Israel in New York and asked it to be first in beginning the organization of a new rabbinical institution around which it would be possible to organize all anti-Reform forces. Morais' proposal was accepted as timely. It was received with full agreement; for behind his suggestion lay years of discussion, thought and preparatory work. It was a time to build. The conflict with Reform created a rabbinical institution which became the fountainhead of an assembly of rabbis and congregations later to become the Conservative Movement in American Judaism.

Part III

Organizing The Historical School (1886—1902)

Chapter One

Program
of Action

Already in the eighties of the past century the emergent
Conservative Movement, according to the editors of the
American Hebrew, consisted of two main elements: those
who desired to perpetuate the Tradition but could not
themselves observe the details of Jewish practice as codified
in the *Shulhan Arukh*; and those who accepted and desired
to observe Judaism as prescribed and codified by the *Shulhan
Arukh.* Common to both of these groups was the recognition
that the Bible and the Talmud had always been the bases
of Judaism.[1]

The editors' statement did more than establish the sociological and contemporary composition of the Historical
School. It emphasized that both the right and left wings
wished to reckon realistically with the situation. When Szold
and Jastrow repudiated the Reformers and joined in a common program with the right wing of the Historical School,
neither side gave up any of its basic convictions. They joined
each other to unify the anti-Reform forces. Furthermore, in
spite of the differences of opinion between both groups in
the Historical School, they affirmed the singular obligation
of keeping the *mitzvot* and the authority of the Talmud.

As late as a year before the official organization of the
Conservative Movement, its establishment could not have
been predicted. In June of 1884, a reader wrote a letter to the
American Hebrew proposing to organize the forces of the

Historical School; the editors replied that such organization would come about in due time, that for the moment it was premature because the number of traditional rabbis in the country was too small to carry out the program.[2]

The extent to which "counter-Reform" motivated the advocates of the Historical School can be measured by the polemical articles of Solomon Solis-Cohen. In a piece directed against Gottheil, Solis-Cohen proposed to declare Reform a schismatic Jewish sect. His colleagues on the editorial board of the *American Hebrew* rejected the idea on the grounds that it was "opposed in spirit to Historical Judaism, to the enlightened conservatism" which they were anxious to uphold. To them, Reform could be a legitimate party within Jewry and should not be isolated into a sect. Certainly the Historical School should not alienate the Reform group from the totality of the Jewish people: "If we must use different prayer books and catechisms, let us at least leave the way open for allowing our bones to be placed in the same resting place. Let us continue to marry and give in marriage, to heal the sick, protect the orphan and help the needy in union, whether we believe in the coming of the Messiah or not."[3]

Solis-Cohen defended his position. He rejected the Reformers' claims of loyal adherence to Judaism. He asserted that they were inconsistent and disloyal to the principles of Judaism. Solis-Cohen could conceive of the existence of "a dignified, independent movement within the Hebrew Church" whose followers would consider themselves "moral descendants" of the Hebrew thinkers and whose elevated moral ideals might contribute only good to the world. But Reform as practiced and preached in Cincinnati did not measure up to these standards:

> While everyone has a perfect right to believe or disbelieve, obey and disobey, in accordance with the dictates of his reason and his conscience, no one has the right, and no truth-seeking man would attempt, to teach as Judaism that which contravenes Judaism; and we have proved that the practices and tendencies of Cincinnati and its champions are anti-Jewish. The question of the truth or error of

Cincinnati teachings in themselves does not here come into consideration. They are true only if Judaism is untrue. . .

He therefore pleaded for a revival of "true Judaism" and for unity within the ranks of American Jewry.[4]

Despite the polemics, new attempts were made to win back into the tradition men of learning and leadership, men who had enlisted in the Reform movement. Kaufmann Kohler was such an outstanding example; although often more extreme in his views than Wise, Kohler was respected and admired. Jastrow once told Wise that it was impossible to criticize Kohler as Wise was criticized because Kohler at least was consistent. Morais tried to influence Kohler, who was largely responsible for the Pittsburgh program, to return to traditional habits and thoughts. He corresponded with Kohler frequently:

> Believe me, brother, the burning question of the hour is not the retention of the *Chalitzah*, as you suggest, nor the acceptance of the work of Caro and Isserles in its entirety, nor even the restoration of a Hebrew nationality at the advent of the Messiah. What concerns us all now most deeply is the rearing of a generation, reverent, thoughtful, and ready to lend its aid to the moral elevation of millions among our co-religionists who do need refining influences and a soul-inspiring example. Change your championship of a pseudo "reform" for that of a veritable reformation, and you will have labored with the Lord and in the interest of humanity.[5]

Morais' appeal to Kohler reflects the conviction of the Historical School that its members could not and should not build their movement merely as a counter-Reform organization. Although this was an immediate reason and had brought the dissonant elements together, it was the constructive program of Historical Judaism alone which could sustain them. Morais' letter also reveals the quality of his leadership. It was hopeless to try to change Kohler's views.[6] Nevertheless Morais placed the program of the School in proper focus by seeking the reformation of Jews rather than the reform of Judaism.

With the reasons for the organization of the new movement declared and with the principles of its program defined, the members of the Historical School were prepared to take the next step. This was the establishment of an institution through which they would be able to expound and develop their views of Judaism. At first, the existence of the Hebrew Union College prevented such an undertaking because the Historical group did not wish to endanger the resources of that institution. They came to realize that they would have to establish their own organization. As they saw it, the Hebrew Union College had enabled the Reform group to educate teachers and rabbis who would eventually undermine the Historical School. Eight Reform rabbis had already been graduated and thirty-five were studying under Wise. Originally, the Historical School thought it could remove Wise from the presidency, thus changing the Hebrew Union College from a school teaching Reform principles to a seminary where all Jewish groups might send their students. Unwilling to destroy the institution they had helped to create, individual members of the Historical School proposed Dr. Moses Mielziner as temporary successor to Wise until an acceptable replacement could be found in Europe.[7] In order not to further estrange those traditional rabbis who supported the institution, some members of the Hebrew Union College board publicly maintained that the students studied "from the sources" and that the teachers taught "only from the opinions of our rabbis of blessed memory, reserving their own opinions and keeping the minds of the students free from bias and untrammeled by the various dogmas now extant."[8] But by 1886 the Historical School knew that its original design had been frustrated, and it resolved to establish a second institution.

The Historical School needed a leader to direct the financing, organize the new school and plan an effective educational program. Alexander Kohut, who had welded the disparate elements of the Historical School into a cohesive group by formulating a unifying ideological program, was unable to give practical direction to the group. He was a newcomer to America and had very little experience in local communal affairs. Moreover, Kohut was fully immersed in his scholarly work. The mantle of leadership fell naturally upon Morais' shoulders. At an age when most people expect to enjoy the rewards of leisure after a life's work, Morais assumed the responsibility of building an institution for conservatism in Judaism.[9]

The Jewish Theological Seminary Association

Cyrus Adler tells us that Morais loved to call the Seminary "his Benjamin—the child of his old age."[10] Every aspect of the young school concerned him deeply—curriculum, staff, classroom teaching, the library, as well as administration, finances and public relations. Morais studied the contemporary theological schools and planned to make the Seminary the model of them all.

It was Alexander Kohut, however, who determined the fundamental character of the Seminary. He stood beside Morais and supported him in every way. For Kohut, the rabbinical seminary in Breslau, the institution that had trained most of the rabbis of the Historical School, was the archetype. Morais had other intentions. When, for example, the question of the name of the new institution arose, Morais suggested that it be called "The Orthodox Seminary." But Kohut influenced him to call it "The Jewish Theological Seminary." Kohut's idea, simply expressed, was to give a universal character to American Judaism:

> Judaism is a consistent whole. The Mosaic, prophetic, talmudic-rabbinic Judaism is an organic totality. . . . The Judaism of history is a unity, an organic development. May Moses be its head, the prophets its heart, the Rabbis its links, one without the other is a halfness, a wanton mutilation. . . . Reform, Conservatism, and Orthodoxy—these are the watchwords under which the verbal battle is fought, and the result is that the pure faith cannot obtain its due acknowledgment. Therefore, we imperiously need a semi-

nary, which will have no other ambition, no other title than that it be purely and truly Jewish. We do not desire it to be destined for a sect, whether reform, conservative, or orthodox . . .[11]

Kohut's view was generally accepted. He not only formulated policy but worked with Morais on the details of implementation. Morais would visit New York every week, meeting with Kohut. Together they raised the small sum needed to start the work of the institution. It was not an easy task. They recognized, as Kohut later wrote in a letter to Felsenthal, that "the Seminary is a stepchild of the New York Jews. It does not excite them . . ."[12] Morais and Kohut spoke widely on behalf of the Seminary, and Kohut's congregation, its women especially, contributed a substantial sum.[13]

Other important colleagues were H. Pereira Mendes, Joseph Blumenthal, Frederick de Sola Mendes, Marcus Jastrow, Solomon Solis-Cohen and Cyrus Adler. Morais had always felt that congregation Shearith Israel should assume the major responsibility for the Seminary. Pereira Mendes, the *hazzan* of the congregation, shared this view. He made an unusual offer, indicating both his respect for Morais and his concern for the new Seminary. Mendes sought to have Morais reside in New York, and he proposed that Morais be the chief *hazzan* of the synagogue and that he himself serve as his assistant. If the congregation decided it could not support two *hazzanim*, he was prepared to exchange his post with Morais. Morais declared that he would not leave his own congregation because of deep personal ties to it, and decided to undertake to commute weekly to New York. Mendes then prevailed upon his synagogue to be host to the new Seminary in the building of Shearith Israel.

Joseph Blumenthal (called "honest Joe" by his political associates), was a public servant in New York who devoted the last years of his life to the Seminary, as president of its Association. Blumenthal was of German Jewish descent, but had joined the Sephardi synagogue. He worked unstintingly. Through the constant exchange of letters between him and Morais, Blumenthal's strong devotion to the nascent institution was reflected.[14]

When De Sola Mendes and Jastrow succeeded in influencing their congregations to join the board of the Seminary, they at once weakened the Union of American Hebrew Congregations while strengthening the new institution.[15] They brought into the ranks of the Historical Movement many of those who had been wavering between the two camps.

Dr. Cyrus Adler and Dr. Solomon Solis-Cohen were the only American-born leaders of the Historical School. Solis-Cohen often defended the Seminary against criticism from the Reform group, writing some of his finest essays to explain the Historical viewpoint.[16] Cyrus Adler's career in the Seminary began after this period. But, even in these early years, while he was at the Smithsonian Institution in Washington, he was active in the affairs of the young Seminary and was drawn particularly by the presence of his teacher, Sabato Morais, the Seminary's founding president.[17]

Two other men who played secondary but distinctive roles in the early years of the Seminary were Bernard Drachman and Jacob Schiff. Drachman later became an adversary of the institution which he helped to build. Nevertheless, until Schechter's coming, Drachman was a forceful personality on the faculty and was appointed its dean.[18] Jacob Schiff understood the practical importance of supporting academic endeavors. His chief importance to the Seminary was realized later. When he heard about the founding of the library of the Seminary, Schiff wrote that he wished to participate because it was an opportunity to aid the development of Hebrew scholarship. He also requested to be included from the very beginning in all such undertakings.[19]

The willingness of these men to help build a new institution impelled the numerous congregations in the Historical School of thought to join in establishing the Jewish Theological Seminary.

Twelve representatives gathered in the Trustee Room of Shearith Israel synagogue on Sunday, January 31, 1886, and announced the founding of a rabbinical seminary "in conservative Jewish principles." Present at that gathering were, as reported by the *American Hebrew,* "the Rev. A. P. Mendes of Newport, R.I., the Reverend ministers Morais and Chumaceiro of Philadelphia, Rev. Dr. Schneeberger of Baltimore, Rev. Dr. Drachman of Newark, and of New York, Rev. Drs. Weil, Davidson and Meyer." Following a resolution offered by A. P. Mendes, it was voted to found a seminary to train teachers and leaders for the coming generation "in sympathy with the spirit of Conservative Judaism." The institution was to be called the Jewish Theological Seminary of New York. The resolution was unanimously adopted.[20] This gathering issued a public announcement of its constitution and by-laws in which the object of the Association was declared to be "the preservation in America of the knowledge and practice of historical Judaism."[21]

When the administration of the Union of American Hebrew Congregations recognized the existence of the Seminary Association, it issued a statement, hoping to avert the opening of classes.

> The Executive Board requests as a simple act of justice that the Union be held responsible only for its own acts as shown by the doings of its Councils and Executive Board, and not for the acts, opinions and utterances of any man or body of men, unless the same be officially endorsed by said Council or the Executive Board.[22]

This rationalization was repudiated even when it had come from individual members of the Union. The members of the Historical School refused to distinguish between the organization and its president.

Preparations for the opening exercises of the Jewish Theological Seminary moved ahead rapidly. In March of that year delegates from sixty congregations assembled at Shearith Israel to complete the organization of the Association. De Sola Mendes, chairman of the committee for the creation of the constitution, introduced the chief resolution on behalf of the congregations, and so the Seminary received a congregational constituency in the most important American cities of Jewish settlement.[23]

The next step was to find students. Through the newspapers the Association announced entrance examinations. Seven candidates appeared. What pleased the founders was not only the scholastic achievements of the applicants but the fact that most of them were American-born. Clearly, potential students were available, as had been hoped.[24] On the basis of this registration, it was possible to open the institution officially. Opening exercises were held in New York City's Lyric Hall on January 2, 1887. Addresses were given by Sabato Morais, president of the faculty, Alexander Kohut, professor of Talmud, and Joseph Blumenthal, chairman of the board of trustees.[25] Kohut explained the purpose of the institution:

> The hope is based upon the assumption that in the new Seminary a different spirit will prevail, different impulses will pervade its teachings and animate its teachers. This spirit shall be that of *Conservative Judaism,* the *conserving* Jewish impulse which will create in the pupils of the Seminary the tendency to recognize the dual nature of Judaism and the Law; which unites theory and practice, identifies body and the soul, realizes the importance of both matter and spirit, and acknowledges the necessity of observing the Law as well as of studying it.[26]

The same week a brief and simple item appeared in the press; it marked the conclusion of one phase of Historical Judaism in America and the commencement of a new and different chapter:

> The Seminary has been in regular operation during the week. The Preparatory Class was formed on Monday afternoon at the Nineteenth St. Synagogue. Eight bright, intelligent students constitute the class, their names being: William Kurtz, Israel Cohn, Joseph H. Hertz, Emanuel Hertz, Solomon Bernstein, Samuel Seiniger, Hyman Simson and Raymond Rubenstein.[27]

The number of students soon increased, and a senior division was organized. An account of the way in which the first Seminary class originated is contained in the weekly reports of Bernard Drachman.[28] It was soon necessary to expand the faculty. Benjamin Szold was invited, but he could not leave Baltimore.[29] The Seminary outgrew the rooms provided by congregation Shearith Israel and was moved to Cooper Union.

We have described the broad objectives of the Seminary as stated in the constitution and by-laws, as well as the basis of the program as defined by Kohut. How were these goals implemented in the classroom? The curriculum of the Seminary indicates the way in which the faculty wanted to interpret the Tradition for their generation. Every paragraph restated the basic ideas of the Historical School (in the following we have italicized certain phrases for emphasis):

Course of Study—The course of study in the Seminary will embrace a Preparatory Course, a Junior Course and a Senior Course. Advanced pupils will be admitted to the grade for which they are qualified.

Not alone will thoroughness of scholarship be assured, but long association with men of dignified life and sincere purpose cannot fail to impress the pupil's character with similar qualities.

The principal text book in the Seminary will be the Bible. It will be studied from the original, and made the basis of such grammatical studies as may be deemed necessary.

A thorough familiarity with the Hebrew text will thus be acquired gradually and in the natural method.

The books as read will be expounded with impartial critical accuracy but at the same time with an endeavor to inspire the students with love for the living instruction therein contained.

The Talmud—Selected portions of the Talmud will form a part of each year's instruction; the *Mishna* only, during the preparatory course; the *Gemara* will be added during the first year of the Junior course, beginning with Treatise *Berachoth. In Talmudical as in Biblical teaching, truth will be the object ever in view; and the practical application of the wisdom of the sages to the conditions of Jewish life will be a prominent feature of the teaching.*

Jewish History—Jewish History, Biblical and Post Biblical will be taught throughout the course, not as a mere collection of names and dates, but in *its bearing upon the history of the world, and the practical lessons it contains for the life of today . . .*

Secular Education—The Trustees and Faculty of the

Seminary will exercise supervision over the secular studies of the students and will secure for the pupils every advantage possible at Columbia College or at the University of the City of New York. *All graduates will be required to have a secular collegiate education.*

Faculty—The following chairs will be established, two or more being combined if necessary, according to the funds at the disposal of the Trustees: (1) A chair of Bible (2) A chair of Talmud (3) A chair of History (4) A chair of Homiletics (5) A chair of Philosophy. *In the selection of Professors to fill the various chairs, the Trustees will endeavor to secure men of eminent ability and of acknowledged repute as upholders of Historic Judaism.*

Permanent Fund—In order to secure the permanency of the Seminary it is desired to establish a permanent fund of One Hundred Thousand Dollars. *In a cause that appeals to every Jew who desires the perpetuation of true Judaism as a system of right living based upon the Revealed will of of God this amount should be readily secured . . .*

Joseph Blumenthal,　　　Newman Cowen,
　President　　　　　　　Treasurer
Dr. A. Friedenwald,　　　Joseph E. Newburger,
　Vice President　　　　　Secretary.[30]

The statement was prepared by Morais. For the heading of the proclamation he chose a quotation from the prayers which Isaac Leeser before him had selected for Maimonides College and which had become the seal of Historical Judaism in the nineteenth century: "To learn and to teach, to heed and to do." The words "to heed and to do" were printed in large letters.

Education and Study

The efforts of the members of the Historical School to establish the Seminary did not diminish their activities on behalf of Jewish elementary and adult education, or for that matter, any of their other efforts to preserve Judaism in America. They hoped that the success of the Seminary would bring about renewed interest and vigor in American Judaism. Now the leaders of the Movement could turn to the vital questions confronting the community: the problems of Jewish education and learning, immigrant absorption and social aid, Zionism and civil equality. Although the basic approach to these problems remained constant, various proposals were made to meet changing conditions.

Foremost on the agenda during the period of 1886-1902, as in earlier periods, was the question of Jewish education. In an editorial, "And Once Again," the *American Hebrew* expressed the prevailing mood: "It is not at all pleasant to be persistent but we have entered upon the crusade for a Jewish education for every Jewish child with the firm determination to conduct it to an issue. It cannot be too often agitated, discussed and disseminated."[31] The leaders of the Historical School were aware of the disastrous implications for American Jewry, if Jewish illiteracy continued. They accepted and even published the criticisms leveled against them. As one Hebrew writer from the Orthodox ranks charged: "If these worthy gentlemen heed the rabbinic exhortation to be 'circumspect with the children of the poor for the Torah may come forth from them,' why do they not also heed the scriptural commandment 'And thou shalt teach thy children.' "[32]

Such criticism touched the Historical School deeply. It knew that education could not be transmitted vicariously, and that the future of its synagogues depended upon proper schools. Congregations which had only Sunday schools and even those that had added one other day of studies, were reminded by the editors of the *American Hebrew* that the congregation was the result of the school, and not the reverse. The school was "the cradle of the congregation."[33] The existing Sunday schools, they contended, had no *raison d'être*. It is true that they were replacing the old-fashioned *melammed* and *heder* type of instruction, but they were as yet not much more than new, empty forms. Instead of daily instruction, the Sunday schools were restricted to two hours per week devoted to securing order, transferring the children from one

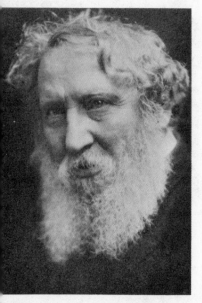

Solomon Schechter (1850-1915), President of the Jewish Theological Seminary of America, 1902-1915

Sabato Morais (1823-1897), Minister of Mikveh Israel, Philadelphia, and first President of the Jewish Theological Seminary of America (1886-1897)

Mayer Sulzberger (1834-1923), American jurist, scholar and foremost lay leader of the Historical School

Cyrus Adler (1863-1940), President of Dr sie College (1908-1940) and of the Jew Theological Seminary of America (1! 1940)

Solomon Solis-Cohen (1857-1948), physician, poet and Hebrew scholar

Joseph Blumenthal (1834-1901), a founder and President of the Board of the Jewish Theological Seminary (1881-1901)

Vestry room of the Mound Street Temple, Cincinnati, Ohio, where classes of Hebrew Union College first met

Professor Joshua A. Joffe and his pupil friends at the Jewish Theological Seminary, 1897

first row: Leon H. Elmaleh, David Levine, Joshua Joffe, Herman Abramovitz, Charles H. Kauva
second row: Elias L. Solomon, Mordecai M. Kaplan, Alter Abelson, Morris Mandel, Nathan Wol
third row: Menahem M. Eichler, Michael Fried, Bernard Ehrenreich, Bernard Kaplan, Juliu
    Greenstone

room to another and reading from the prayer book and the English "hymns." And the *American Hebrew* reported that parents were not interested in the Jewish education of the children. They sent them to Sunday school to get the children out of the way. The children were ill-mannered and even impudent. A unified educational program with a definite aim was completely lacking.[34] Could self-criticism be sharper or more revealing? Unfortunately, the countenance of despair could not alone improve education. The members of the Historical School continued in their old unproductive ways. It is possible that because the administrators of these schools were rabbis, not trained educators, a solution was not forthcoming.[35] The trend seemed to be backward, to the acceptance of the system of voluntary teaching in the Sunday schools. The rabbis' lofty words about education, which undoubtedly came from their disturbed consciences, were not put into practice the way they were in the founding of the Seminary.

Although the synagogues of the Historical School could not yet alter the form of the Sunday school, they did try to change the content of the studies as followed in the Reform curriculum. Two questions arose which underscored the division between the Historical School and their Reform colleagues. The first question concerned the curriculum proposed by Kohler for the Sunday schools. In an article devoted to the topic, he suggested that the Sunday schools emphasize the character of the Jew and not the facts of Judaism; second, that they reconcile the conflict between natural science and the study of Scripture; and third, that they offer the study of all of Jewish history, not only the biblical period (all this in a two-hour session on Sunday).[36]

Cyrus Adler replied to Kohler's suggestion. Kohler's aim was mistaken, Adler argued, and his means for achieving that aim were erroneous as well. The basic emphasis in teaching, he contended, should not be on emotional training but on education. The first mistake was to believe that Jewish education could be achieved with a minimum of time allotted for instruction. After five years of attendance, a child should "understand historical Hebrew at sight. Hebrew instruction needs all the Reform (with a big R) you can give it." Adler then proceeded to answer Kohler point by point. When ethics are taught to children abstractly, children become casuists. It is only possible to teach children good conduct by example so that experienced knowledge of ethical precepts will stimulate right conduct. To fulfill this objective, time and textual study are required. Concerning the study of Scripture, Adler reminded Kohler that the Bible and its language was part of the very structure of world literature, speech and culture. Its phrases and expressions should be familiar to every educated person and must be learned in childhood. Regarding the expansion of the study of Jewish history, Adler heartily concurred with Kohler.[37]

All solutions appeared to revolve around the question of time. Since the Sunday school structure seemed inviolate and teaching days could not be added during the week, the only alternative was to add years to the teaching schedule. Here the "maximalists" came up against the problem of Confirmation. The Confirmation ceremony, which was widely accepted throughout the country, was usually the terminus of the student's Jewish schooling. In the Reform group it was Kaufmann Kohler who first suggested that the ceremony be delayed until the sixteenth or seventeenth year. The editors of the *American Hebrew* earnestly supported this suggestion and gave it wide publicity. They had always advocated separating the traditional individual Bar Mitzvah ceremony from the group Confirmation. For them Confirmation was no more than an important educational venture which prolonged the years of study in the congregational schools. In the Historical School, Frederick de Sola Mendes wrote a long essay on the development of the custom of Confirmation and its aim. He particularly stressed the need for increasing the number of years available in Hebrew training. This supported the suggestion to postpone the Confirmation ceremony.[38]

The rabbis of the Historical School were confronted by an educational dilemma. What their constituency wanted was totally inadequate. Yet if they should not give in, their charges would be denied any Jewish education whatever. They chose the former course. At the beginning of the twentieth century, Bernard Drachman suggested a comprehensive proposal to improve the situation. Drachman's summary of the failures in American Jewish education reflects the failures of the century. He outlined a plan in accord with the historical approach, but went far beyond the will of the Historical School of the time.

Drachman raised the basic question, "What constitutes an adequate religious training for a Jewish child?" And he answered:

An adequate Jewish religious training is one which fits the Jew or Jewess to lead a consistent religious life, which makes him or her perfectly at home in the synagogue, and able to participate in all the ceremonies and observances open to those not of the ministry, which enables him or her to perform all the duties, to think the thoughts and to feel the emotions which are the historical heritage of those of the household of Israel, and which inspires him or her with the desire to do so. This means that the Jewish child shall understand the Hebrew language sufficiently well to follow with ease the prayer-ritual and the Scriptural readings of the whole year, shall be familiar with Jewish history, both Biblical and post-Biblical, shall know the doctrines of Judaism, and the duties, ethical and ceremonial which it inculcates, and shall, in addition, be well acquainted with the stirring and touching chants and melodies in which so much of the spiritual life of our people is stored up, and that all this shall be communicated in a pleasant and attractive manner, which makes the child content and even happy to be a Jew . . .

Drachman suggested that there were four ways of achieving this goal:

Our congregational schools might be increased in size, in number and in efficiency, and made absolutely free to all comers, so as to offer to all Jewish children the opportunity for proper religious schooling. But it is safe to say that the problem will never be solved in this manner. This plan would require the union and unification of all Jewish congregational schools under one plan and method of instruction, the broadening and increasing of the facilities they possess to a degree beyond the powers of many congregations, and the opening of the schools to the Jewish public without restriction, an argument incompatible with the internal conditions of many congregations . . .

A second plan would be to introduce religious instruction into the public schools, that is to say, to grant the use of the public school to the various denominations for an hour or two daily which they would devote to the religious instruction of the children attending the school who are members of their communion. This plan possesses so many advantages that, considered in itself, it is no doubt the ideal one. It would reach substantially all the children, for the number who would refuse to receive religious instructions on the ground of avowed unbelief or disinclination to be identified with any denomination, would be so small that it might be safely left out of consideration; it would reach them during ten or twelve years of their lives steadily and continuously, and great results might be attained by such a long and steadily maintained course of systematic instruction; it would reach them at a time of the day when their minds are fresh and unwearied, and better able on that account to assimilate the ideas communicated by their instructors. But this plan has as little chance of realization as the first named, perhaps less. It is similar to the Catholic standpoint, and that is fatal. It would be looked upon as conflicting with the American doctrine of the separation of Church and State, and with the alleged non-sectarian or secular character of the public schools, a character more apparent than real, and which does not prevent the insidious exercise of Protestant Christian influence in many forms, but which would nevertheless be utilized as an efficient engine with which to prevent the adoption of this plan. I, for my part, do not share these objections. I do not think the State becomes a religious institution when it simply recognizes the fact of the existence of religion among its citizens and permits the various bodies to utilize its facilities for the sake of lightening their internal burdens. The State should be non-religious, it need not be anti-religious. I think, furthermore, that the common instruction of all citizens in secular matters, with a free and frank recognition of their religious differences, is the best way to teach mutual tolerance and forbearance, better far than to suppress all acknowledgement of the existence of religion in the public school, or rather to force all to submit to the tacit sway of one creed, which is frequently not even the creed of the majority. But I realize that these views are not those of the majority. I do not anticipate that the majority will ever be converted to the really liberal views which prevail on this subject in England, in many respects the freest country in the world, and we may therefore leave this method out of consideration as a feasible way out of our Jewish educational difficulties.

A third method is to maintain Jewish schools, in which both secular and religious training will be given. This is identical with the Catholic system of parochial schools, and was recently advocated by Rabbi David Wilowsky, of Slutzk, during his visit to this country. This method, though a few such schools may be established, will probably never become general, and may, therefore, be dismissed from consideration.

There remains, therefore, only one method which is practicable and which, if our Jewish community has the requisite earnestness and generosity, can become a reality. It is to establish a great system of Jewish public schools housed in their own buildings and equipped with all pedagogical requirements, to supplement the general public school system.

In every district of, let us say, a thousand Jewish families, such a Jewish public school should stand. It should be cheerful, commodious, light and well ventilated. It should have at least five sessions weekly of two to three hours each; its methods should be thoroughly modern and up-to-date, but its matter should be the ancient subject of Jewish instruction, the Hebrew language, grammatically and thoroughly taught, Bible, prayer book, the ethical and religious duties of the Jew and Jewess. Special attention should be paid to the teaching of Hebrew hymns and chants, both in order to preserve the knowledge of our traditional melodies, and to prepare the next generation for that great and devoutly to be wished for consummation, congregational singing. The teachers should be graduates of Jewish normal schools, thoroughly familiar with their subjects, masters of a pure English, and refined and cultivated in their manners, and above all, inspired with a reverent spirit in order to be able to instill it into their pupils. They should, of course, use one harmonious system of text book and instruction. For those pupils who desire to go further, Jewish High Schools should exist, in which Mishnah and Gemarah and selected works from the vast sea of post Biblical literature would be studied. The whole system would naturally be capped by the Jewish Seminary in which the rabbis and masters of Hebrew lore in America would obtain their training.

This plan, while not perfect nor all comprehensive, would do away with most of our difficulties, and would rear up a generation adequately acquainted with the religion and literature of their people. I do not think this plan chimerical. Our noble-hearted and most generous philanthropists are beginning to realize the necessity of educational institutions among those devoted to the alleviation of physical ills. Twenty years ago the gift of nearly a million dollars for an academy of rabbinical learning would have been inconceivable. Twice the amount would build and maintain twenty excellent Hebrew schools in our metropolis, and I believe the day will come when our community, realizing the wrongfulness and even danger of the inadequate and slip-shod methods of Jewish religious instruction at present pursued, will grapple energetically with the problem and will solve it substantially on the basis outlined above.[39]

Had Drachman's plan been put into practice, the Jewish community of the twentieth century probably would have been more deeply rooted in Jewish values. But the Historical School was not sufficiently mature, as a movement, to implement this plan, either in its own synagogues or the community at large. It seemed easier for the members of the Historical School to organize their forces around one central institution such as the Seminary or a school for the training of teachers.

The basic and continuing discussion of Jewish educational needs revealed the urgent need to train Hebrew teachers as well as rabbis. The establishment of the Hebrew Union College and the Seminary had not solved this deficiency; and the few qualified teachers from Europe did not understand American children. The demand for American-trained teachers increased. Some in the Historical School, among them Alexander Kohut, felt it was more urgent to train teachers than rabbis.[40] At the very beginning, when he heard Sabato Morais' proposal to establish the Seminary, Kohut thought that it should train teachers first. He preached accordingly to his congregation and his proposal received the support of the members of the Hebrew Free School Association in New York. They were ready to undertake a program.[41] But the idea was postponed in favor of a rabbinical seminary; it was hoped that in time the Jewish Theological Seminary would train teachers as well as rabbis.

What the Seminary builders rejected, a distinguished member of the Philadelphia Jewish community forced them to reconsider. In 1893, a fund was bequeathed to congregation Mikveh Israel in Philadelphia by Hyman Gratz, the brother of Rebecca Gratz, who had been active in commercial, professional and religious activities. A bachelor, Gratz had willed all his property to his nieces and nephews in 1857, under the explicit condition that, if they should die childless, the property would go to congregation Mikveh Israel "in trust for the establishment and support of a college for the education of Jews residing in the city and county of Philadelphia for which purpose the rents and income only of the said Trust Estate shall be used and applied from time to time and to and for no other use, intent or purpose whatsoever."[42] The last descendant, Horace Moses, died in 1893. All the properties, valued at almost $150,000, went to the congregation.

The Board of Adjunta of Mikveh Israel appointed a committee of seven members, including Solomon Solis-Cohen as chairman, Cyrus Adler, Sabato Morais, Gratz Mordecai, and Mayer Sulzberger.[43] The annual income was about $6,000. Gratz Mordecai, one of the leading members of the board, undertook to correspond with presidents Seth Low of Columbia College, Charles W. Eliot of Harvard, J. G. Schurman of Cornell and other university heads, to learn their opinion about the possible establishment of a Jewish university in America. In his letter, Mordecai stated the general proposition as follows: "One plan which has occurred to us is the establishment of a postgraduate college for education in ancient and modern languages and literature, manners and philosophy (combining possibly a small seminary of Jewish theology) . . ." He then placed several specific questions to these authorities. "If we can collect in the United States" twenty-five students would it be financially feasible? After completing their education, would these students be accepted as teachers, writers, editors? Would such a university have as much chance as a music school? What influence would it have on non-Jews? The answers of the presidents were almost unanimously opposed. To the first two questions, they answered, no; to the third, they replied that they did not wish to forecast the future; to the fourth, that it would make a negative impression. Gratz Mordecai tried another tack. In a second letter to Seth Low, Mordecai asked his opinion of the possibility of establishing a Hebrew division in a general university. The president of Columbia, having previously consulted with Richard Gottheil, answered this question in the negative also and suggested that, at the most, one course in Judaism should be established at a university.[44] Thus the plan to establish a Jewish university in America failed.

Sabato Morais, who was a member of the special committee as the *hazzan* of the congregation, was very much disturbed by the approach which Mordecai had taken. He wanted a school exclusively for the teaching of Judaism, not a Jewish university. In a letter to his student Solomon Solis-Cohen, the chairman of the committee, he affirmed that the trust was intended to establish a college for Jewish education, and that it would be therefore unwise to combine the plan with a general university which had no Judaic characteristics. Moreover, to contemplate the establishment of "a chair, or even a college as a separate department, would prove of little use to the Jews of Philadelphia, on whose behalf the Will was executed." It would not produce rabbis or Hebrew teachers. If the Jewish Theological Seminary were not in existence, Morais argued, then this would be the time to revive Maimonides College. But since such a step was unwarranted, the proper course to follow was the creation of a Jewish high school in the city of Philadelphia. That school could serve as a preparatory school for the Seminary.[45]

Morais' views won out because they answered a basic need and were more practical than those of Gratz Mordecai. After weighing all the factors, the committee decided, following Morais' proposal, to use the funds to establish a college for the study of Jewish history, the Hebrew language, Jewish literature, and the Jewish religion. It was understood that the curriculum should be especially designed for teachers. Thus Gratz College, was created. It was the first Jewish teachers college in the United States.

Regular instruction began in 1898.[46] Rabbi Henry M. Speaker was appointed principal, Arthur A. Dembitz, instructor in Jewish history, Isaac Husik, instructor in Hebrew and Bible. Moses A. Dropsie was president of the board of trustees from the beginning. The greatest number from the first group of students were adults who came to improve their Jewish education. As the student body increased, most of them began to prepare for certification as teachers. According to the proposal of Morais, preparatory classes for the Jewish Theological Seminary of America were organized.

A teachers' training school meant that Jewish education was to become a career and a profession. This idea was opposed to the quasi-voluntary system then prevailing. The establishment of Gratz College dramatically raised a fundamental problem in Jewish education, that of insufficient salaries for teachers. Solis-Cohen, chairman of the Mikveh Israel Committee for the Gratz fund and one who had been interested all his life in Jewish education, began to concern himself with the question of salaries. He was also among the first members of the Historical School to discuss publicly Jewish teaching as a profession. He tried hard to make the leaders of the various congregations face the shameful conditions, and asked: "How can we ask young men and women to enter this college and undertake a time-consuming course of study in order to fit themselves for the profession of teaching our history and faith to the young, unless we seriously intend that such profession shall at least provide its followers with bread and butter?"[47]

Solis-Cohen and his colleagues were lonely voices in those days. For these men the training of rabbis and teachers was the indispensable means to the achievement of their ultimate purpose of raising a new type of laity. In a brilliant and penetrating analysis of the character of the American Jewish community, Mayer Sulzberger had pointed out as early as 1868:

> Few realize how profound is the ignorance amongst most men on the subject of religion and its duties. Vague notions, instilled into the mind in early youth, of the professions and practices of their fathers, indistinct recollections of morning and evening prayers, of grace said and blessings spoken, float through their minds and remind them, after a lapse of years, of the creed in which they have been reared; but so far as concerns a genuine appreciation of the grave truths and important teachings which religion should promulgate, there is a lamentable deficiency . . .

> At the present time, in this country especially, the whole subject of religious change is in the hands of laymen, who, to a great extent are unlearned in theology. We are not content with the fact that those having spiritual charge of the communities are able men; for it is not a healthy state in which one man is the exclusive thinker for a thousand. The greatest genius may err, and in such case his blind followers imitate his defects. All should be properly informed on the questions that arise, so far, at least, as to enable them to act intelligently . . .[48]

Another way to help create a learned laity, the members of the Historical School determined, was to develop new methods for popular adult education. The first step was to organize a publishing house. They joined the leaders of the Reform group to support another attempt to establish the Jewish Publication Society permanently. This time they succeeded.

The initiative to found the third Jewish Publication Society came in 1887 from Joseph Krauskopf, the Reform rabbi of Keneseth Israel in Philadelphia. In a sermon to his congregation he deplored the fact that while Christians were active in the dissemination of religious literature, Jewish efforts to propagate Jewish literature were nonexistent.

> Go down your business streets, read signs: "The Episcopalian Publication Society," "The Methodist Book Concern," "The Presbyterian Tract Society," "The Baptist Bible Society," and then look for the name of "The Hebrew Publication Society," and when you have sought for it in vain, think how true to our mission we are . . .[49]

The sermon was effective. Meetings were held in Philadelphia in the spring of 1888 to define the program of the proposed society. On April 13, Krauskopf and Solomon Solis-Cohen issued an invitation addressed "To Jews, Jewish Congregations, Jewish Orders, YMHA, and Kindred Associations."

The object of the proposed American Jewish Publication Society was declared to be: "To familiarize American Jews with, 1st the ethics of Judaism; 2nd the history of the Jewish people; 3rd the writings of Jewish masters; by the publication of works, essays and such other writings as may from time to time be deemed advisable, of such a tendency as shall command the support of all parties among Jews." The signers emphasized the necessity and importance of the Society not only for the benefit of Jews who resided in the cities of America where they could affiliate with synagogues, but especially for those who "in smaller places are cut off from congregational influence and associations."[50]

The actual founding meeting of the Society took place in Philadelphia on June 3, 1888, and was attended by representatives of all factions. The aims, as stated in the Constitution were the following: "(1) To publish works on the religion, literature and history of the Jews; (2) to foster original work by American scholars in those subjects."

Cyrus Adler, Solomon Solis-Cohen and Alexander Kohut agreed to be the unofficial representatives of the Historical School, and the entire group, through its periodical, earnestly supported the venture. The editors of the *American Hebrew* agreed that the time had come to establish the Society for reasons which they stated clearly and frankly:

> Let us have at least one national organization which can with propriety appeal for support, moral and financial, to every Israelite and to every Jewish organization in the country; which shall enlist the sympathy of all, even the most rigidly orthodox, and even the most wildly radical; which shall form a meeting point of intellectual kinship to those who, on religious and doctrinal grounds, are most widely and bitterly dissevered; which shall demonstrate that Judaism is a religion large enough and broad enough to grasp within its fold all the discordant elements that, contest as they may for things they hold dear or estimate cheaply, still retain a scholarly respect for that which is noble and elevating in Jewish literature.
>
> Is it necessary to dwell upon the need of such an organization as the American Jewish Publication Society? Surely not. It is simply disgraceful to acknowledge before the Gentile world how lacking we are in Jewish books in the English language. We have no history that is worthy of the name except of fragmentary periods; we have but few biographies; we have but little of the doctrinal or religious writings. In a word, if our young men or women ask us for some works that enable them, for themselves, to discover from some authoritative source what Judaism is, what it has achieved, and to what it has been the inspiration; what the Jews have done, have been and have suffered— we must needs bid them study German.[51]

It was time, the editors of the *American Hebrew* concluded, for young people to be provided with a body of Jewish literature written in an English style that would not "move them to mirth." American Jewry had the money and the talent to provide such texts.

One of the voices that contested this nonpartisan stand was that of Sabato Morais. He protested in a sermon that despite promises to the contrary the proposed Society would be an instrument of Reform. He based his opposition on the statements issued by the president of Rabbi Krauskopf's congregation that "Sunday services was parent to the proposed Publication Society." And so he vowed: "A Sunday ritual to be published next fall, is the first fruit, and I am requested to aid such an undertaking; sooner my right hand wither and my tongue cleave to my mouth, than that I should raise my voice in behalf of a work with such unholy and profane an origin."[52]

Alexander Kohut had another vision of the Society's role and future. He predicted glorious benefits because "Israel's history is the history of its literature and so it is with American Israel." Beyond the need to support and nurture Jewish writers, Kohut felt that the Society could influence the Americanization of the immigrants, that its total effect would be to give the American Jewish community "a moral and mental support."[53]

During its early years, the Society encouraged the publication of basic studies by writers in America and abroad. The whole sweep of Jewish life, history and thought was encompassed in its program of publications. A unique catalog, *Of Making Many Books*, by Joshua Bloch, "an annotated list of the books issued by the Jewish Publication Society of America, 1890-1952"—the first summary bibliography of some 250 volumes that were published—tells the story of the Society. It also reveals that the Society thought in breadth as well as in depth, and began to implement its vision immediately. Thus a more comprehensive, yet equally accurate subtitle to Dr. Bloch's compendium could have been—the creation of an Anglo-Jewish literature in the United States.

An excellent example of the Society's conception of its function is the *American Jewish Year Book* which appeared in 1899. The *Year Book* was designed to fill the absence of works in contemporary Jewish historiography and more specifically in the history of American Jewry. The project was suggested and carried out by Cyrus Adler, who conceived it as a mirror reflecting the life of the Jewish community. Adler saw the need for accurate documentation on matters which concerned Jews, such as exact Jewish population counts in various countries and the contribution of the Jews to the culture of these countries. "The experience of the past years has demonstrated," Adler wrote in his preface to the fifth volume, "that if Jews are to grapple successfully with the large problems of the Jewish situation, the facts of Jewish life must be discovered."[54] Moreover, Adler hoped that the *Year Book* would serve as a link between the American Jewish community and Jewish communities throughout the world. And so, the first volume reported events that had occurred not only in America but elsewhere in the world; and in subsequent issues articles on Jewish communities and institutions overseas were included. The sixty-three volumes which have appeared since 1899 follow the general form laid down by Adler.[55]

If the members of the Historical School achieved a measure of success in the spheres of teaching and adult education, their effort to foster Jewish scholars and scholarship was, with very few exceptions, less effective. The rabbis were not active in the nineteenth-century European movement of Wissenschaft des Judentums, despite the fact that some of them, graduates of the Rabbinical Seminary in Breslau, wanted to model the Jewish Theological Seminary after the Breslau seminary. A few, like Marcus Jastrow and Alexander Kohut, produced works of serious scholarship (most of Kohut's activity was not in the United States). From time to time, Benjamin Szold printed articles on Scriptural interpretation; he also published a commentary on Job, but most of his work remained in manuscript form. Most other members of the Historical School were translators and interpreters, in the sense of the ancient *meturgemanim*, and did not compose any original scholarly works.

It is not difficult to understand this. These men were rabbis who were concerned with practical affairs. The rabbi was the spiritual leader of his community: he was immersed in Jewish communal affairs, in the school, in the charity groups, and in the general community as spokesman and interpreter of the Jewish faith and experience. In those days the American rabbi was primarily a preacher and a public teacher, not a scholar of Jewish tradition and law. The rabbis of the Historical School were, in the main, builders of synagogues and institutions. Others would come, as they did, to give these institutions the learning and creative scholarship which was their aim.

Another aspect of the problem was that Jewish academic learning of the time was divorced from the questions that troubled the generation. Jewish scholarship regarded the end of the eighteenth century as the conclusion of its legitimate interest. Of all the younger men associated with the Historical School, Cyrus Adler, above all, grasped the nature of the problem and dedicated himself to finding a solution. Born and trained in America, he devoted his life to the correlation of scholarship with Jewish communal concerns. "Everything must have a beginning, and the beginning is necessarily imperfect," Adler declared in the preface to the first volume of the *American Jewish Year Book*.[56] Adler sought to establish a Jewish Academy of America through which he planned to raise men of learning who, by their very training, would relate their learning to the life around them. He made a concrete proposal upon his return from England in 1894. Adler did not hedge; he went to the heart of the matter: "We in America are poverty stricken," he argued. "At present we have no libraries, no publications, and no independent scholars." There were manuscripts to be found at Columbia College, the Library in Philadelphia, the Library of the Hebrew Union College, the Cohen Library in Baltimore and the Adolph Sutro Library in California. But all these combined, Adler emphasized, did not equal the value of one of the better libraries in England, Germany, Italy or Austria. Those equipped for scholarly work were busy men—rabbis, lawyers, teachers in colleges, physicians, or men occupied "in engrossing administrative work." On Adler's list the only two exceptions to this rule were Bernard Felsenthal and Marcus Jastrow. "For the rest, scientific work is done by stealth, or when they should be sleeping or taking a walk." His suggestion was, therefore, to organize an academy of Jewish research in America. This institute was to build a library, to print the results of scholarly research, to convene gatherings of scholars and, above all, to invite and support individuals who wanted to devote their full time and energy to the advancement of Jewish learning in America. As a beginning, at least half a million dollars would have to be collected for this purpose.[57] In a later period such an institution, the Dropsie College for Hebrew and Cognate Learning was founded for this purpose.

As indicated, the participation of the Historical School in Jewish scholarship was essentially cast in the mold of translation and interpretation, rather than original research. Hence the failure of the School, with exceptions, to participate in the effort to create an indigenous Hebrew literature in America may be explained. No wonder that Bernard Drachman subtitled his essay on the neo-Hebraic literature in America "a hitherto unnoticed side of the intellectual activity of the Jewish people."[58]

By the turn of the century, seven weeklies and eight monthlies appeared in the country. In a very short time all of them had disappeared from the literary scene. The small sums needed to pay printer and publisher could not be found. S. B. Shwartzberg, editor of the *Ner Hamaarabi* (Western Light), describes the attitude of the Jewish community toward Hebrew Literature and the consequent unfortunate situation of the writer: "We show no love for our language, we do not have a spark of mercy for those who sacrifice themselves for our literature. . . . We look on calmly as our authors and scholars die prematurely of hunger and poverty . . ."[59]

Only Morais' name is mentioned favorably in Shwartzberg's memoir which he called *Tikatev Zot le-Dor Aharon* (Let This be Recorded for Future Generations). Indeed, Morais did encourage every kind of Hebrew literary effort.

He also wrote poetry and prose in the modern Hebrew idiom; but most of those writings remained unpublished. Nevertheless, Morais was not the only member of the Historical School who loved Hebrew. Jastrow, Kohut and Szold all wrote and published in Hebrew.[60] The latter, particularly, wrote essays and published a commentary on Job. Szold was also active on behalf of Hebrew culture. He and his daughter Henrietta helped to form the Baltimore branch of the Lovers of the Hebrew Language. The regular meetings of the society in Baltimore reached European readers through the pages of *Hamelitz*, the Hebrew periodical which began to appear as a daily in St. Petersburg in 1886. The American correspondent of the *Hamelitz* was especially gratified to report that a society of "Friends of Hebrew Rhetoric" was formed by Dr. Szold, and that young people gathered once a week to study the Bible in the original.[61]

A new branch of scholarly endeavor that progressed with the help of the members of the Historical School was the writing and study of American Jewish history. The idea of organizing all those interested in the history of Jews in America into a society originated in 1886 with Abram Samuel Isaacs, editor of the *Jewish Messenger*, after the death of his father. Dr. Isaacs wished to see the publication of a work in commemoration of the 400th anniversary of the discovery of America.[62] Cyrus Adler replied to Isaacs that the idea was a good one, but that it would first of all be necessary to gather the source materials which had been abandoned and scattered before they disappeared completely. After these works were collected, it would be possible to approach such a work.[63] The suggestion was picked up again in the *Menorah* by Leo N. Levi, an official of the B'nai B'rith fraternal lodge of Galveston, Texas.

The Anglo-Jewish exhibition, organized in 1887, inspired many of those who saw it and diverted interest from the proposed collective work to the project of founding a society for research in American Jewish history. This was the objective Bernard Felsenthal had in mind when he wrote privately to Adler and urged him to undertake the responsibility of forming such a society. Felsenthal proposed that basic documentation be extracted and digested from the national and state archives, where it was buried along with congregational records. If interpreted by men trained in scientific method and *objectiv Geschichtsschreibung*, future historians would be able to write a history of American Jewry. Adler shrank from "the thankless task of organizing yet another society."[64] Meanwhile Marcus Jastrow joined those who urged Adler to accept the obligation; Adler finally agreed.

In 1892, when he returned from his trip to the Orient, which he had taken in order to secure exhibits for the Chicago Fair, Adler drew up the proclamation in which he expressed the purpose of the new society:

> The Anglo-Jewish Exhibition held in London in 1887, the publication of its results, and the impetus it gave to the special historical research, brought to light many facts, before unknown, of interest to the Jews of the British Empire and of importance for the general history of England. There is good ground for the belief that an organized attempt at collecting, preserving and publishing data having reference to the settlement, and history of Jews on the American continent may prove of at least equal importance. To this end it is proposed that an American Jewish Historical Society be formed.[65]

One hundred and fifty copies of the circular were sent out and fourteen answers were received promptly. The first meeting was held in New York in the building of the Jewish Theological Seminary on June 7, 1892. Oscar Straus was elected president. The composition of the Society, largely due to geographical factors, was, in the beginning, "of the eastern conservative group, though leading reform advocates cooperated."[66]

A sentence from the report in *Hamelitz*, published in Hebrew in Europe, aptly summarizes the significance of the birth of the Society to American Jewry. "The 'native' American Jews are rooting themselves like strong cedars and they are growing in strength materially and spiritually."[67] The foreign correspondent caught the historical significance in the decision made by American Jewry to write its own history.

The Impact of Russian Immigration

By the end of the century, the inflow of East-European immigration was so great that the German character of the Jewish settlement in America was beginning to change, despite the fact that institutions still remained in the hands of German, Ashkenazi, leaders. As was indicated earlier, the shattering events in Russia during the eighties and nineties confronted the American Jewish community with sudden stark reality: the need to absorb within two decades more than half a million immigrants, a population of newcomers which far exceeded the resident Jewish population of 1880 and which was about twice the number of Jews that had come to the shores of America over a period of two centuries.[68]

About this phase there have come to light many inglorious episodes of callousness, economic exploitation and other suffering, which time alone redeemed.[69] Within the Historical School, the *Jewish Messenger,* for example, played a disheartening role. Representative of the "uptown" Jews and the conservative employer class, it criticized, jeered and preached at the new immigrants and their social and religious ways of life. However, most of the members of the Historical School, like their colleagues in the other factions, tried to identify the older community with the plight of the new immigrants. For example, in Boston Solomon Schindler frequently attacked the immigrants in press articles and public statements. Wolf Schur, the editor of the Hebrew weekly *Hapisgah,* vigorously fought these views. On one occasion he appealed "to the German Rabbis in America," including Kohut, Jastrow and Szold, to defend the immigrants against Schindler's attacks, and published their answers in his paper.[70] Grievous and petty errors notwithstanding, it became increasingly clear to American Jewish leadership, and to religious groups particularly, that the problem of absorbing the new immigrants, who were streaming to America by the tens of thousands from all directions, was twofold: first, to help them adjust to their new environment and, second, to save them for Judaism.

There was an additional factor which caused the Historical School to work so emphatically for the absorption and Americanization of the new immigrants. Members of the School recognized the weight that could be given to traditional Jewish elements in American Jewry by the additional learning and tradition of East-European Judaism.[71] To use Israel Friedlaender's phrase, the story of Russian Jewry was the story of coal, or concentrated sunlight.

It is the story of primeval forests, filled with luxurious ferns, which for years out of number had been drinking in the rays of the sun, but, having been buried beneath the ground and excluded from the reviving touch of light and air, were gradually turned into coal—black, rugged, shapeless, yet retaining all its pristine energy which, when released, provides us with light and heat.[72]

The prevailing attitude within the Historical School of personal, communal and spiritual responsibility for the immigrants as brothers-in-need, whose children would contribute to the future American Jewish community, was reflected by the acts of individual members of the School as well as by their corporate coordinated effort. Among the members of the Historical School who gave of themselves unstintingly, acting on the talmudic precept that "whoever saves one life is like one who saves the whole world," were Jastrow, H. P. Mendes, Morais, Szold and Sulzberger. Each gave in his own way. Jastrow and Morais, whose acts of generosity were an inspiration to their congregants, collaborated on one occasion in 1890 to help settle a strike called by immigrant Jewish shirtmakers against their fellow-Jewish employers. The issue came to a climax on Yom Kippur eve. In the *Kol Nidre* sermon, which he customarily devoted to a discussion of charitable institutions, Morais directed biting and clear words to those worshipers in his synagogue who owned manufacturing establishments. He cited the prophetic reading for the Yom Kippur day, from the book of Isaiah, chapter 58, and emphasized verses six and seven:

> Is not this the fast which I have chosen, to let the debt-burdened go free . . . to break thy bread with the hungry; to bring the evicted into thy house; when thou seest the naked to clothe him; and that thou hide not thyself from thine own flesh?

According to Morais, the principles enunciated in the corn fields and in the vineyards of the Holy Land applied to human relationships in the markets and factories of contemporary America. He exhorted his congregants: "Prayer and oppression go not together. Amendment must prove the reality of repentance. Cease your vain words. Leave the synagogue. Go to the squalid homes of your work-people; look upon their wretchedness and their suffering, and there make your atonement."[73]

Szold, too, thoroughly identified himself with the plight of the newcomers. Speaking in the cadences of biblical thought, whose language and insight always guided him, Szold affirmed his faith in the ultimate redemption of the Jews from the yoke of the czar and simultaneously demanded responsibility from American Jewry, for its own sake as well as for the sake of its brethren, not to rest until that redemption had come.

> From Russia comes the horrible news of millions of people suffering the pangs of hunger. You fancy that because we in America are free, we can repose in peace. I say that so long as a single Jew, in any corner of the earth, can with impunity be insulted on account of his faith, thus long not one Jew anywhere is free. The Russian people will not always continue to be a dumb beast of burden. The time will come when it will, like Balaam's ass, open its mouth and speak. It will demand that its human right be respected. Then it will remember also those who bore neither malice nor hatred, and its hour of redemption will also be ours. Above all, remember that

here are men and women perishing and holding out their hands to us for bread.[74]

Szold practiced what he preached. He, his family and his congregation regularly visited the Baltimore docks to greet new arrivals, and then helped them find jobs in Baltimore or establish contacts among friends in other cities.[75]

H. P. Mendes insisted that succor and economic aid were but the first steps. He attempted to improve the religious and spiritual condition of the immigrants by suggesting that American-born English-speaking rabbis move into the over-crowded sections of the cities and live with the immigrants to serve them. He urged the establishment of a synagogue for young people among the immigrants and he wanted to see new experiments in neighborhood work. The immigrant should not be lost because of lack of counsel and interest.[76]

In their effort to strengthen the immigrant, these rabbis first opened their own hearts and homes to the newcomers; then they utilized the vast human resources available in their congregations. The ladies' committees and sisterhoods were most helpful. The rabbis sensed that the women would respond instantaneously to the need for acts of *hesed,* of lovingkindness. Indeed, the ladies' groups in the congregations of the Historical School and others, extended individual help to immigrants, promoted religious and vocational schools, dormitories, settlement houses, kindergartens, parks, employment offices, shops for the learning of trades, afternoon and evening classes for children, and evening lectures to young immigrant women who were busy during the day. Delinquent and abandoned children were helped by them in the same way.

As a group, the members of the Historical School combined to seek long-range solutions for the new immigrants outside the domain of synagogue institutions. In some projects, such as agricultural colonies, they worked together with other communal agencies. In others, such as the Jewish Alliance, lay members of the School took the initiative.

An intriguing chapter in American Jewish history is the attempt to establish a group of Jewish agricultural colonies in the state of New Jersey. It is a complicated story involving among others the Baron de Hirsch Fund and the Alliance Israélite Universelle, ideological back-to-the-land movements originating in Europe as well as American Jewish communal groups who sought to diversify the methods of immigrant absorption. An important contemporary source-book is the little volume *Migdal Zophim* (The Watch Tower) by Moses Klein. In this book published with illustrations of the homesteads, the streets, the schools and the synagogues in the three colonies—Alliance, Carmel and Rosenhayn which were situated in the triangular district of southern New Jersey of which the towns of Vineland, Millville and Bridgeton formed the corners—the author presents his interpretation of "The Jewish Problem and Agriculture as its Solution."[77]

While the members of the Historical School did not associate themselves with the ideological implications of this view, they did nevertheless actively help to make the entire enterprise a success within the concentric circles of economic, social and religio-cultural aid. Sabato Morais and Mayer Sulzberger were trustees of the Baron de Hirsch Fund, the forerunner in the United States of the Jewish Colonization Association. In this capacity, among other duties, they were instrumental in aiding the farmers of the Carmel colony to establish and maintain themselves on the land. In 1888 the hard-pressed farmers appealed to the Baron for help. Morais wrote to his childhood friend, Chevalier Emmanuel Veneziani, the almoner of the Baron, and a sum of $5,000 was sent. Frederick de Sola Mendes was secretary of the Alliance Land Trust, the organization which succeeded the Hebrew Emigrant Aid Society in supporting the colony of Alliance. Moses A. Dropsie was president of the Philadelphia branch of the Alliance Israélite Universelle, which supported the colonies and fostered agricultural schools. Cyrus Adler, too, was a member of the Philadelphia committee which visited the Alliance settlement in 1884 and reported on the conditions and accomplishments of the colony in the Philadelphia *Jewish Ledger*.[78]

Whether these men and their colleagues supervised the distribution of funds, helped rebuild homes razed by fire, provided food to the needy in a colony, or dedicated a Torah at a humble synagogue inauguration—what defined their activity was a sense of responsibility to the human needs as well as the specifically Jewish needs of the immigrants.[79] It was not so much a dedication to the agricultural form of rehabilitation which motivated these men; more important was the imperative to absorb the immigrant into the total economy. Above all, it was urgent to avoid squalid congestion in the immigrant neighborhoods of a few cities on the eastern seaboard. Toward this end, the Jewish Alliance of America came into being; many of the lay members of the Historical School were active members, foremost among them Solomon Solis-Cohen and Mayer Sulzberger. A meeting was called in 1891 and representatives of nineteen cities assembled. The "plan of action" adopted by the Central Executive Committee stated the problem and indicated a solution:

> . . . Not merely money, but brain and muscle are essential for the building up of a community, and although few of the victims of Russia's monstrous tyranny succeed in passing her frontiers without being robbed of practically all their property, yet their stout hearts and willing hands are sufficient capital to warrant them a welcome in this country. They are prepared to do all kinds of work, and experience, wherever they have been established, proves that they make good factory hands, tailors, seamstresses, carpenters, etc.
>
> It is, however, manifest that the assimilation of these immigrants is retarded through their concentration in the larger communities, and particularly in the seaboard cities. . . .
>
> The immediate purpose to be kept in view is the settlement of small Jewish communities in the towns and villages of the interior throughout the country. It is manifest that if two or three families could be settled anywhere under self-supporting conditions, they would soon become the nucleus of further growth through the accession of relatives and friends, for whom the first comers would have made more or less adequate provision.[80]

The key to this "plan of action" was the principle of preventive rather than curative measures. These measures would go into action as soon as the immigrants landed in the United States. But there were those who argued that prevention should start much earlier, at the point of origin. As George M. Price (the author of a contemporary volume *The Russian Jew in America* published in St. Petersburg in 1893) described the problem: "Something must be done at the first halting point where their (the immigrants') miseries begin. These halting points are the Prussian and Austrian border towns through which the Russian Jewish immigrants are passing." Price published his plan in the *American Hebrew*. He called for an official centralized body to be set up in Europe. Its purpose would be to select from among the immigrants bound for America those best suited, and to reject the others. This, he argued, would prevent disappointment, poverty and hardships afterwards. The work of this bureau, he envisaged to be as follows:

(1) to disseminate information about America; (2) to advise those desiring to emigrate and prevent those unsuited for emigration; (3) to protect emigrants from being deceived; (4) to regulate immigration through procuring information from the United States and to direct the emigrants only to those places where they can find employment and where the local Jews can help them; (5) to organize and send from Europe those best-fitted for colonization.[81]

But no amount of planning, wisdom and foresight could anticipate the developments in Europe. The propulsion of immigration to America was so swift and immense that it excluded all attempts at organization. American Jewry could only resign itself to *ad hoc* activities in this sphere—to ameliorate the condition of individual families to the best of its ability, and let time and new events create a better basis for profound solutions. This truth slowly dawned upon those who were devoted to the immigrants; it was underscored by the fact that Jewish immigration in those decades was only a fraction of the general mass streaming to the shores of "the promised land," America. For the Historical School, as for the rest of the settled American Jewish community, history determined that Russian Jewish immigration could not be absorbed into the existing communities; the existing settlement would be absorbed by the new and emergent community.

The Role of Zionism

Zionism was an integral part of the program of thought and action which the Historical School developed in the closing decades of the past century and which it transmitted to the Conservative Movement. Conservative Judaism and Zionism developed separately, but their interaction was constant. As a result, both were stimulated conceptually and organizationally.

More than anything else, the persecutions in Europe educated Jews to the need for a national Homeland. Social and economic necessity gave a new meaning and impetus to the historical longing for a return to Eretz Yisrael. Zionism became a dominant ideology in world Jewry. In America, most of the members of the Historical School were deeply committed to Zionism, particularly Louis N. Dembitz, Marcus Jastrow, H. Pereira Mendes, Benjamin Szold and Solomon Solis-Cohen. The popular base of Zionism was built on the East-European immigrants who carried with them the living traditions and ideologies of Jewish life, both religious and secular.[82] Thus, Zionism in America was another force welding the West-European religious leadership of the Historical School to the East-European Jewish settlement in America. For example: the Hebras Zion or Zionist Association of Baltimore—probably the first Zionist society in the United States, organized in 1893 by Hebraists and East-European immigrants—was encouraged by such members of the Historical School community as Harry Friedenwald, Benjamin Szold, and his daughter, Henrietta. Sabato Morais associated himself with the Hovevei Zion organization in Philadelphia. His appearances and lectures before its members were reported not only in the local American Jewish press but in the European Hebrew press as well.[83]

In the beginning, the Hovevei Zion (the Lovers of Zion) was not a political movement, but emphasized the progressive colonization of Eretz Yisrael. The editors of the *American Hebrew* supported any such undertaking. When a new agricultural settlement was founded they welcomed the event in the editorial columns. The editors praised the organization of the Dorshei Zion, whose plan of aid was based on the formation of cooperative building and loan associations. They lauded the petition which the Christian clergyman William Blackstone submitted to President Benjamin Harrison and Secretary of State James G. Blaine—"to use their good offices to the end that an international conference may be held to consider the condition of the Israelites and their claims to Palestine as their ancient home."[84] They recognized that such a conference could adopt one of two alternative courses: to attempt to secure for Palestine a form of local government which would guarantee the prosperity of its citizens; or to work for the most radical plan "to invest Palestine with territorial independence." Without eliminating the second possibility, the Historical School concentrated its efforts on the first.

When, in 1896, Herzl published his *Judenstaat,* followed by the First Zionist Congress, convening at Basle a year later, the alternatives were joined. Wide differences of opinion resulted. Practical help to the residents in Zion was one thing; to rally around the cause of a Jewish State was quite another. Under the direction of Wise, the Reform group generally denounced Herzl's views. They recalled Gustav Poznanski's utterance of 1841: "America is our Zion and Washington our Jerusalem." The Central Conference of American Rabbis repudiated "any attempt for the establishment of a Jewish State." Emil Hirsch proclaimed that American Jews had no intention of returning to Jerusalem to establish an altar for sacrifices like the slaughter houses in Chicago. Kaufmann Kohler used a more moderate epithet when he called Zionism a "fraud." There were a few individuals among the Reformers who opposed these views completely: Gustav Gottheil, Bernard Felsenthal and the young Stephen S. Wise. The Reform movement remained officially anti-Zionist for many decades, until the Columbus Platform was adopted in 1937.

Most of the members of the Historical School were enthusiastic supporters of the new cause, and were among its main spokesmen. Their names were inscribed on the rolls of the first Zionist organization, the Federation of American Zionists, organized in 1897. It must be emphasized, however, that many had their doubts about Zionism and expressed those doubts. They feared that Zionism might become too concerned with material as opposed to spiritual values, that the spirit of politics would supplant the spirit of the Torah. Frederick de Sola Mendes, who later moved into the Reform camp, was most outspoken against the official Zionist program. Recognizing Zionism's accomplishment in bringing back "certain stray sheep of ours to the parental flock," and fully aware of the "doughty championship" of Herzl and Max Nordau, De Sola Mendes nevertheless argued that world Jewry was not ready for the Herzlian doctrine of statehood. "The loudest leaders, or the liveliest, are not always the wisest," he warned.

De Sola Mendes also raised a more serious question: "the hard, solid fact of the sanctity attached, wrongfully or rightfully to the many 'holy places' of Christianity and Islam in Palestine." He pointed out that Palestine was a "thrice Holy Land." Would it be possible to settle the Jews in a country that was also holy to Moslems and Christians? What would the Moslems do if the Jews took away their Mosque, which stood on the site of the Temple of Solomon? Would the Jews permit worship in the Church of the Holy Sepulchre? The most important thing, advised De Sola Mendes, was to "colonize the land, if you can; help and guide the colonists, if you will, but we did not need exactly the new blue flag of Zionism for that. . . . As for political Zionism, with its absurd 'Jewish State' and 'Jewish independence,' its prospects are as blue as its flag . . ."[85]

Sabato Morais' opposition to the Herzlian program was based neither on tactical nor political grounds. He fully accepted the promise of the ultimate restoration of the Jews to the Holy Land. He believed that the entire world would come to recognize Palestine as the center of spiritual truth and that the Jews would return to Zion and spread "words of peace and truth" to all corners of the earth. But a prerequisite condition of that Return was a religious revival of the Jewish people. Political action could not lead to spiritual redemption. Settlement aid, cultural work and religious commitment could pave the way.

Thus, in their acts and words, De Sola Mendes and Morais, in spite of their opposition to the idea of the Jewish State, always supported any effort to build the new country.[86] It is true that even the anti-Zionist Reform rabbis, particularly Isaac Mayer Wise, contributed periodically to specific undertakings on behalf of Palestine. But there was a marked difference, as we shall see, between the resistance of De Sola Mendes and Morais to the idea of a Jewish State on one hand, and of Wise and his group on the other. The Reformers saw in Zionism a basic contradiction to their ideology; they were against it unqualifiedly. Moreover, as Selig Adler and Thomas Connolly point out, Reform Judaism "badly underestimated the new European anti-Semitism that, since 1870, had assumed the complexion of persecution on the basis of race rather than religion." They also feared Zionism because "it seemed to negate the almost religious love that these men had for their adopted land."[87] Consequently the Reformers, in their attitude to Palestinian settlement, distinguished between humanitarian endeavor and the building of a State. Opposition in the Historical School, however, affirmed that the return to Zion was a fulfilment of Judaism; but it felt that to organize the Zionist movement on the basis of political nationalism was premature.

Most other members of the Historical School participated enthusiastically in Zionist affairs. Marcus Jastrow took a very deep interest in the Zionist movement and was elected vice-president of the Federation of American Zionists.[88] Benjamin

Szold's active participation in Zionist societies is documented in the American and Hebrew press of the nineties. Even before the organization of the Hebras Zion, or Zionist Association of Baltimore, he helped in 1892 to form a branch of the Shavei Zion in Baltimore.[89]

Thus the creation of the Zionist movement brought in its wake profound new issues of disagreement between the Historical School and the Reform movement. These were publicly debated. The question of dual loyalty was the subject of one of the most important such debates. In an exchange between Kaufmann Kohler and Solomon Solis-Cohen, who represented the two schools of thought on this issue, Kohler interpreted the classic Reform position that "to advocate the creation of a separate nation in Palestine was an act of disloyalty to the Government, whose loyal citizens the Jewish people are. . . . Zionism was not a cause but an aggravation of anti-Semitism . . ." Solis-Cohen refuted this notion, emphasizing the hope for the restoration of a "Judean State" as not incompatible with the strictest loyalty to the government of the United States on the part of its Jewish citizens. "The fact that individuals might or might not favor the creation of a Jewish state gave them no right to interfere in any way with their fellowmen, who had the right to do as they pleased in the matter." Solis-Cohen concluded therefore that the attitude of the anti-Zionist was an indefensible one.[90]

Solis-Cohen conceived of Zionism as a prelude to the universal redemption of the Jewish people and of mankind in general. This was his dream of Zionism:

> If in God's providence there shall come about the establishment of a Jewish State in Palestine, it must repent of the sins for which our ancient kingdom was destroyed—the sins of social injustice so scathingly denounced by Amos and Isaiah and their successors. It must be a model state, wherein there are neither rich nor poor, wherein every man dwells under his vine and fig tree with none to vex him or make him afraid, loving for his neighbor and for the stranger the freedom and the opportunity of full de-

velopment of all their powers and God given faculties of body, mind and soul, that he loves for himself.[91]

Zionism, as the spiritual evolution of the Jewish people, found its most eloquent spokesman in H. P. Mendes. The idea of restoration, he repeatedly stressed, meant more than the physical possession of Palestine. It meant making Palestine for the world at large what Rome was for the Catholic world—its spiritual center. And all this would bring mankind to a new stage of development. Writing on Palestine as "the spiritual impulse of the world," Mendes formulated the views of most members of the Historical School:

> When we speak of "Palestine" we mean the ideals it stands for in prophetic vision.
> By the restoration of Palestine to the Hebrews, we mean the establishment of a spiritual center for the world, and ultimately the establishment of the Kingdom of God on earth.
> The realization of the prophetic ideals for the benefit and blessing of the world at large, and not for us Hebrews only, constitutes what is called "Prophetic Zionism," or "Bible-Zionism," or "Spiritual Zionism." These ideals are:
> 1) The establishment of a central spiritual influence for the world at large, for all mankind . . .
> 2) A House of Prayer for all nations, and consequent gradual world-recognition of the Universal Fatherhood of God and the Universal Brotherhood of Man . . .
> 3) Universal Knowledge of the Lord, with a center World-University for inspiration, help and guidance thereto . . .
> 4) Universal Peace, secured by the establishment of a World's Court of International Arbitration, to whose decisions all nations will pledge their loyalty and honor.
> Said court shall include representatives of Religion, Law and Science as prescribed by the Bible for the Highest Court of Appeal . . .
> We Hebrews humbly believe that God selected Abraham in order that through his descendants "all the families of the earth should be blessed"; that at Sinai He constituted

us a nation of priests to lead all mankind to Him; that although our ancestors were expelled from their land and have for centuries been persecuted, slain, imprisoned or exiled, nevertheless they cherished, as we cherish today, the hope that the prophetic ideals associated with Palestine will be one day realized for mankind's happiness, that earth's wrongs shall be righted and the world at last be at rest . . .[92]

Mendes believed so deeply in Zionism as the solution to mankind's problems that he composed a letter to the editors of the daily press during the Spanish-American War. In it he promised that, if the Jews succeeded in obtaining Palestine, they might "arbitrate for the nations and thus settle the Spanish Cuban-American imbroglio."[93]

Inspired by such rabbinic and lay direction, it was not to be doubted that these ideas of Zionism-Judaism would strongly influence both faculty and students of the young Seminary. Bernard Drachman and Gustave Lieberman, respectively dean and Talmud instructor at the Seminary, had been associated even earlier with the Hovevei Zion movement.[94] The students followed their example. The first intercollegiate Zionist society, the Young American Zionists, was initiated in 1896 by Seminary students. This society, which included young men and women, was organized with the help of undergraduates of the College of the City of New York. Two years later it became an exclusive Zionist fraternity, the first Jewish fraternity in the United States to call itself ZBT, three Hebrew letters based on the phrase in Isaiah I.27, *Ziyyon be-mishpat tipadeh* (Zion shall be redeemed with justice). The purpose of the fraternity was to further the Zionist movement, and thus "to benefit the welfare of the Jews in general." By fashioning a body of Zionists who were educated university men, the organization hoped to bring "the respect of the world to the Zionist movement."[95] The name and original purpose of the *Ziyyon be-mishpat tipadeh* society reflect the teachings and hopes which the Historical School as a whole placed in Zionism.

Religious Questions: Sabbath Observance and the Synod

The religious problems that agitated the members of the Historical School in the period of 1886-1902 were similar to those which concerned them in earlier years. Fundamentally, these problems stemmed from the "prevailing irreligion" among youths and adults alike. The phrase "prevailing irreligion" was coined by a principal Reform rabbi, Kaufmann Kohler, but, in this regard, he spoke for the Historical School as well. "It is a sad but indisputable fact," he wrote, "that young men do not want to hear Judaism and its history expounded. They unreservedly disown God and religion . . ."[96]

Although there was general agreement on the essential problem, the Historical School and the Reform movement continued to debate methods of solution. The intensive ideological and theological argument with Reform did not lapse even while both groups struggled to find their separate, individual organizational forms. Beyond this continuing battle, the Historical School, after it had established the Jewish Theological Seminary, concentrated its efforts on the Sabbath question which threatened to disrupt the historical continuity of the Jewish group. Also, the suggestion to create a synod appealed to many, and this crucial issue would have to be resolved within the School.

One of the most forthright voices in the Historical School was that of Solomon Solis-Cohen. Always urbane, unswervingly determined, Solis-Cohen fought Reform as the enemy of American Judaism. During the debate with Reform, he created a philosophy of historical Judaism in America, which he built on the three pillars of God, Revelation and the selection of Israel. In the development of his views Solis-Cohen conceded that some of the ceremonial laws had passed "into desuetude" and that men of "historical conscience" should meet with those imbued with the scientific spirit of the times and "calmly, carefully and deliberately, prepare a substitute for the *Shulhan Arukh;* being extremely cautious to avoid again making the error of giving a permanent character to temporary things, and a divine character to purely human desires." But once having recognized the rigidity of some of the traditionalists, Solis-Cohen turned to those "teachers of rebellion" against the Tradition, or as he called their school of thought, "Cincinnatism," and urged them to see that their teachings could only serve to destroy the "idea of communal life, communal law, communal responsibility" —the life-blood of Judaism. Whatever the personal attitude of individuals to the basic tenets of Judaism might be, Solis-Cohen argued, "the community of Israel" cannot exist without the historical Sabbath, the dietary laws, circumcision, and the avoidance of "strange marriages."[97]

Obviously Solis-Cohen was not speaking in historical terms only. His words were directed to the contemporary situation and to the very heart of the disagreement with Reform. The most vexing problem of all seemed to be that of Sabbath observance—how to counter the Reform attempt to transfer the seventh-day Sabbath to the Sunday Sabbath. The Reformers, of course, adhered to the "idea" of the Sabbath. But since the pattern of American life made it very difficult to observe the day of rest on Saturday, Sunday was suggested and adopted in most Reform congregations, as the day of Sabbath worship.

The controversy raged for many years. One can find virtually all the points of view expressed on this issue throughout the country concentrated in Stuart Rosenberg's essay on "*The Jewish Tidings* and the Sunday Services Question."[98] *The Jewish Tidings* appeared in Rochester, New York from 1887–1894. In 1888 the paper advocated Sunday services "as a matter of necessity." Representative members of the Historical School participated in the discussion which followed in the pages of the *Tidings*. Moses A. Dropsie and Cyrus Adler were among the members. The *Jewish Exponent* of Philadelphia, a paper then largely under the influence of the Historical School, was the first to condemn the argument citing convenience as a motive power in religion. Dropsie argued both historically and constructively. He suggested that anyone who was unable to attend services on Saturday could easily attend Friday evening services. It was Cyrus Adler, however, who counterattacked forcefully:

> The movement is largely one to satisfy the vanity of our preachers. The members of the congregation are to them not worshippers but an audience. I have heard the term used by more than one minister. The entire new movement is coldly intellectual, led by men who are quite satisfied of their ability to reason their way up and down the universe. The entire object of public worship is the delivery of what passes for information, done up with a greater or lesser degree of rhetorical skill. I believe that if our ministers, editors and public men had devoted more attention towards turning the synagogue into a place of worship, and less towards making it a lyceum, we would never have been confronted with the problem of scandalously forsaking our honored customs and traditions . . .

> We have now entered upon citizenship in the world, and the impulse of many has been to yield the religious tie. This is the unconscious philosophy of Reform Judaism of which the Sunday service is the latest phase. It is to my mind a fatal mistake. Let us by all means enter upon the larger life which the world has accorded us, but let us keep up our old association, not in race (social) clubs, not even exculsively in the philanthropic society, but by an adherence to our useful customs and traditions, by the sacred gathering in the home on the Sabbath evening, and by meeting, not to have our aesthetic senses appeased by concerts and orations, but for worship, not once a week, but often, to emphasize that we are the people of a common idea which is worth preserving.[99]

Debate, in and of itself, did not fill empty seats in the synagogue on the Sabbath day.[100] Naturally, new organizational methods were tried. In 1896 a new society for Sabbath observance was organized in New York. Most of its members were of the Orthodox group, but H. Pereira Mendes was vice-president and Bernard Drachman a member of the board. At a special meeting held in New York, rabbis concerned about Sabbath observance discussed the possibility of making the Sabbath into an official state holiday. Perhaps in this way the sanctity of the day could be restored.

Another proposal was to call a meeting of congregational leaders, Reform as well as Historical School and Orthodox, for the sake of united action in communal affairs. This time, it was suggested by the editorial board of the *American Hebrew*.

> We care not what its doctrines or principles or religious standpoint may be; nor what its membership or social influence is, that congregation which is wrapped up in itself is not performing its full functions. More urgent than our duty to a congregation, is our duty to Israel. No congregation has any authority except such as it receives from Judaism. No congregation has a right to be a religion and a law unto itself.
>
> We have repeatedly called attention to at least three spheres of activity eminently adapted to congregations united for these and other purposes. Such a union could be instrumental in creating a movement for the more widespread observance of the Sabbath. Such a union could secure more adequate and more appropriate facilities for divine worship on the great holidays than are now offered by the *Chebras* and *Minyanim*. Such a union could provide opportunities for religious instruction for the thousands of children particularly in the upper portion of the city, who now are utterly without such regular tuition.[101]

Little enough came of all this talk. The Sabbath was not being observed and historical Judaism was honored in the breach. Whatever the reason—despair or anxiety—the synod proposal once again appeared on the agenda of American Jewish religious life as a way to stir interest where apathy reigned.

This time it was the Reformers, led by Kaufmann Kohler, who advanced the proposal. In the eighties the *American Hebrew* initiated the idea of an American-European synod, in that way hoping to give traditional authority to American Judaism.[102] Kohler desired an *American* synod which would introduce measures in the spirit of Reform. He felt that most

American Jews were Reform and, if matters came to a popular vote, that all questions could be settled in the favor of Reform. Lewis Dembitz granted some of the premises of Kohler. He, too, faced facts: many Jews had dropped the observances enjoined by biblical and rabbinic laws; and many of the innovations of the Reformers were genuinely inspired by love and concern for Judaism. Nevertheless, he asserted that it was unthinkable to consider summoning an "American synod," in which the leading authorities of the faith would not be present. Further, Dembitz stated, the only proper place for such an "Oecumenical Council" was the Holy Land. Only then could it represent all Israel, within and without its borders.[103]

Mayer Sulzberger, in a fashion consistent with his character, attempted to bring the divided house together. He demanded full recognition that in America there were two religious groups, each one uniquely interpreting Jewish Law to its adherents. Sulzberger, who wanted peace, understood both Reformers and traditionalists, and again sought a third path. He knew that the Reformers and the Historical School would not join in a synod. He put hope in a new kind of division—lay and clerical. Such an assembly, consisting of representatives from congregations who were prepared to agree on a program involving changes, might establish the basis for a future synod.

The views of various scholars on the possibility of a synod were solicited, but most of them responded from the point of view of their own groups. Solomon Schechter, in London, was also consulted. He replied:

> On the whole, I think, Synods, unless confined to purely administrative affairs, are useless and even harmful. Religion is one of *dvarim ha-mesurim la-lev* (matters of the heart), which are vulgarized by every public discussion. Besides that, I think no man is capable of representing other men in matters spiritual. Synods have also a tendency to create among us a certain sacerdotalism which is quite foreign to the Jewish spirit . . .[104]

A sharp and analytical article directed against the synod was written by a young woman, Henrietta Szold. It was entitled "Catholic Israel." It examined the ideological structure that had been built by the Historical School, and anticipated the approach taken by the Conservative Movement in the twentieth century—to avoid a programmatic consolidation until such time as the greatest number of American Jews should come to believe and to live in accordance with the precepts of the Tradition. An extensive quotation from Henrietta Szold's basic statement reveals the immediate problems of the Historical School and indicates the way it prepared, as a movement, to meet the future:

> In characterizing what he calls the historical school of Judaism, at present in the ascendant, Dr. Schechter uses the term "Catholic Israel" to designate the "living body" which it constitutes the final authority for the interpretation of the Scriptures and the fixing of custom . . .
>
> I shall speak . . . of our relations and obligations towards this broad, universal, Catholic Israel; Israel at once a race, a nation, a religious brotherhood; Israel past and present; Israel scattered from East to West; whose subtle, yet none the less real, standard is explicitly laid down in no one book, expressed with finality in no one age, illustrated completely in no one synagogue, monopolized by no one community. The Chassidim of Galicia and the Bene Israel community of Bombay alike may contribute to the spirit informing Catholic Israel. On the other hand, the American Jew, liberal and cosmopolitan, may fail to grasp it in its breadth . . .

Henrietta Szold voiced her objections to a synod on the grounds that, in an age when the Jews were dispersed and subjected to the regulation of multiple authorities, such a body could not adequately exercise the necessary control on the Jewish people. The Sanhedrin in Jerusalem had had such power because it functioned at a time when "religious life and civil life were co-terminous." But in contemporary times the main dilemma of Jewry is involved with the observance of the Sabbath, "the kernel of the whole modern question":

What, now, can a Synod do about it? Invent a legal fic-
tion which shall prove that it is all a mistake about the Sabbath we have been celebrating these three thousand
years . . . ?

Far be it from me to dismiss the Sabbath difficulty
lightly. . . . But I do maintain that Judaism is powerless
in the matter. To abrogate a practice that is the vital fluid
of Judaism is a crime; moreover, a useless crime. So long as
injustice is not perpetrated, a cause that will outlast and
benefit generations, must be set above individuals. An
eternal statute is abolished that it may cease to be true that,
as Judge Sulzberger said, "the weak point in the whole
structure is the teaching that Saturday is the only Sabbath
of the Lord with the uniform and continuous avowal by
act that it is not." I ask, are the defenses strengthened by
the declaration that the Sabbath of men is the Sabbath of
the Lord? Concessions are made for the sake of those who
either will not or cannot, in any event, do not observe the
Sabbath, and are therefore elapsing into irreligion. Will
concessions save them from their fate? We emasculate a
religion in their behalf; we shear it of its essential elements
of stability and eternity; is what remains a religion or a
cracked reed? . . .

At this point Catholic Israel becomes definite and practical, though not very startling in its suggestions. It pro-
poses a solution, a conversion to which there is no royal
road—education it was formerly called, intellectualism it
is now nicknamed. The remedy has at least the quality of
universal applicability to recommend it. It may be adopted
by Zionists, and need not be scorned by the Synod partisans . . .

If we persist in our demand for pastors we must inevitably take the retrograde step from rabbi—that is, teacher-
hood, to priesthood. The doom can be averted, I maintain,
not by beginning at the top, with the training of rabbis, but
by educating the people. With the people truly educated
even the Synod idea is robbed of some of its terrors.

The remedy is efficacious and universal, but not easy.
Discussion helps little, enthusiasm alone is abortive. Every
man and woman of us must stop talking and buckle down
to steady work. It again resolves itself into the impressive

home-thrust: "Thou art the man." Upon thee everything depends. Thou canst create a world, thou canst destroy it. The alternatives are set before thee: in the Ghetto of American Judaism, death and evil; in open-hearted, intelligent communion with Israel, past and present, life and good. Choose thou life everlasting.[106]

The method of achieving the concept, *Klal Yisrael*, as presented by Henrietta Szold in the spirit of the entire Historical School, was inherent in the concept's very definition. The confirmed view of the Historical School, as it reckoned with the low level of Jewish literacy and lack of religious observance, was that as one studies the sources of the Tradition and the history of the Jewish People, he was naturally brought nearer the Tradition's answers to perplexing problems of the times. Despite the expansive nature of this appeal—and the critics were quick to seize upon it—study, or Talmud Torah, as understood both in the Tradition and by the Historical School, was the core of its ideology.

Chapter Two

Interpretation of
the Jewish
Faith

"Theology is not religion," the late Louis Ginzberg taught his classes at the Seminary, "and yet whoever has any religious experience must have some form of theology. Theology is the articulation of religion."[1] Characteristic of the Historical School in the past century, as of the Conservative Movement in the twentieth, was its comprehension of several theological approaches within itself, instead of one binding system. A variety of theologies characterizes American religion generally, to the extent that European scholars of religion consider the very term "American theology" self-contradictory.[2] Self-contradictory or not from a purely theological point of view, the acceptance of the legitimacy of theological diversity was a cohesive force for the Historical School, and led to increasingly effective organization. Thus, while deferral of unified theological thought was not an unmixed blessing, many potentially divisive arguments were dispelled in advance, and possible differences were turned into programmatic agreements. But the compatibility of different theological trends within the Historical School, as a Jewish religious movement in America, is in itself one of the major characteristics which the nineteenth-century pre-Conservative group bequeathed to its successor.

In the abundance of books, articles and essays on the Jewish religion produced by the Historical School, there is little theological writing. In the first place, the Jews, (with notable exceptions) did not historically concentrate on systematic

283

theological thought in their literature. Traditionally, Jewish ideas had been derived from the study of the classic texts and were expressed through commentaries and super-commentaries on these texts. In modern times Jewish scholarship became highly developed, but (again with notable exceptions) this scholarship is primarily the study of the past. Because of these and other factors, some of which stemmed from the specific American Jewish experience, systematic theological writing was a limited form in American Jewish literature. Such work was not demanded by the American religious tradition, nor did it spring naturally out of the Jewish intellectual past.

This is not to say there was no intellectual tradition or theological thought in American Judaism. One must simply seek it among many other sources. For example, to construct the theologies of the Historical School one must consult prayer books, articles, sermons, prefaces to books, poems and even schoolbooks for children. One must also study specific situations which were evaluated—public events, founding meetings, communal decisions.

As we have seen, the three trends of the Historical School-traditionalist, developmental, and progressive—found a unifying ideology in the concept of *Klal Yisrael*, in their devotion to the practice of the *mitzvot*, and in their common opposition to Reform. Nevertheless, their ideological agreement should not be equated with theological unity. All three developed theological positions which served as the underlying bases for their respective points of view as they were expressed in immediate situations.

It is revealing to note the contradictions of ideology and theology, even within the respective subgroups of the School, which resulted from the succession of crises that confronted them plus the urgent need to meet those crises in words as well as action. Thus we attempt to indicate the differing reaction of the three trends in the School to these crises. To best understand the respective interpretations of the faith, we shall forgo the method of periodization utilized up until now to present the development of the School. In this area it is more useful to take the entire half-century as a conceptual whole and analyze the views of its people against the background of the theological problems which disturbed their generation and, as a consequence, concerned them as religious leaders: belief in God; Torah and *mitzvot*; the messianic ideal and the mission of Israel. Although this review will span the entire history of the School, the emphasis will be placed on the last decades of the century, when the respective views crystallized.

Belief in God

In one sentence, Sabato Morais expressed that faith in God and His revealed Word which all members of the Historical School shared: "I believe in the omnipotence of God, hence, in His power to manifest His will to the human mind by super human means."[3]

This article of faith in God as Creator of the Universe was proclaimed by the Historical School whether it addressed itself to the fully committed, to the skeptics in the congregations, to intellectuals who were attracted by current scientific thought, or to the American Christian communities. Time and again the spokesmen for religion were called upon to deal with those who challenged Faith in terms of the growing rationalism of the times. Most often they would fall back upon the formulations of the medieval Jewish philosophers, particularly Maimonides and Joseph Albo, each one selecting the construct of ideas most congenial to his own way of thought. The response, whatever its form, was always based on the underlying belief in the existence of God as the Supreme Being whose existence did not depend on any other being.

When asked by those who doubted the literal truth of the Bible, for example, whether God spoke with a voice, Leeser answered unequivocally: "Let it be clearly understood that our religion is true, not because other systems are false, but because it is based upon divine revelation, which to a believer is the only source of truth."[4] Morais, speaking on the theme of Revelation and describing the Patriarch Abraham, adopted another view of the Tradition, saying that he could not "pretend to decide whether a verbal communication came from on high, or whether the soul of the Patriarch communed with the Great Soul of the Universe. . . . [However] it was a veritable inspiration that guided him . . ."[5] H. Pereira Mendes, when he was called upon to explain the postulates of the "Jewish Church" at the World's Parliament of Religions, which was held as part of the World's Columbian Exposition in Chicago, declared that "religiously the attitude of Historical Judaism is expressed in the creeds formulated by Maimonides . . ."[6] Alexander Kohut, in a symposium called "What is it to be a Jew," adopted Joseph Albo's three basic principles to explain the "practical working of Judaism": belief in the unity of God, in Revelation and compensation in a hereafter. To be a Jew, he concluded, is to put into practice these three principles.[7] Benjamin Szold, in his *Outlines of the System of Judaism*, taught in categorical terms that all events in nature or in the life of man are ordained by Providence. There is no chance in Nature. "God governs all the phenomena in Nature and all the events in history according to his plan."[8] Frederick de Sola Mendes, debating with the partisans of evolution, polemicized on the issue which was raised by "half-taught, pseudo-science":

> True scholarship, which looks out from a high standpoint and surveys with keen and searching gaze the facts of nature beside the mere observations of one phase, like Herbert Spencer and John Fiske, acknowledge that there is some Higher Power operative in nature than is discoverable by the microscope or by chemical analysis. Narrowminded shallowness, deluded by some natural phenomenon, such as the evolution of one form of animal life from another, jumps at the conclusion that matter possesses within itself the power to create other forms of matter, and that therefore no creative mind was ever needed.[9]

Although many of the statements were prepared for public forum, the belief itself, of course, could not be advanced or disputed by argument, clever or learned as it might be. Religion for the Historical School was the faith in a personal

God, and all the skepticism in the world could not shape the believer's position. Thus Solomon Solis-Cohen wrote in a poem he published in the *Century:*

> "Yea, I know!" cried the true man of old, and
>   whosoever wills it may know.
> "My Redeemer existeth!" I seek for a sign of
>   his presence, and lo,
> As he spoke to the light, and it was—so he
>   speaks to my soul, and I know![10]

Little appears in the writings of the School on the traditional belief in the after-life, the resurrection of the dead and the doctrine of reward and punishment. But what does come through is marked by the differing interpretations of the respective trends. Leeser wrote: "We . . . say, that to deny the resurrection is denying a principle laid down by the prophets . . ."[11] In the preface to his English translation of the Bible he states that we cannot depend on the King James translation because life "in this world and in the world to come" depends on the correct interpretation of the Scriptures.[12]

Morris Raphall propounded two questions in his public debate in Albany in 1850 with Gustav Poznanski. They were: "Do you believe in the coming of the Messiah?" and "Do you believe in the resurrection of the dead?" Raphall wished, with these questions to define the basis of the theological dispute with Reform.[13] At this same debate, Isaac M. Wise's denial of these doctrines caused Raphall to publish a ban against him.[14] Sabato Morais, H. Pereira Mendes and Alexander Kohut also wrote about their belief in the world to come, the resurrection of the dead, and reward and punishment. They all affirmed the traditional faith. Morais used the arguments of natural science to demonstrate the indestructibility and independent existence of the soul. An example of his approach may be found in his argument about the immortality of the soul: the existence of matter cannot be denied and if it has its existence contained in it from its creation and can never be lost, how can it be imagined that the soul, which is much loftier and purer than matter, should be vulnerable to destruction?[15] He found it necessary, however, to state that "the Almighty does not put off the recompense due to our virtues till we be dead."[16]

Szold reinterpreted the traditional view of reward and punishment. Man can destroy his happiness here and here-after, he wrote. Sin is always followed by punishment, by the torments of a disturbed conscience in one's lifetime, and by the most severe and complete punishment received "beyond the grave before the tribunal of God."[17] However, consider-ing the doctrine of the resurrection of the dead, Szold and Jastrow did not stop at reinterpretation; they substituted for it the idea of the immortality of the soul. They composed their prayer on immortality to read: "And this conviction of immortality which the Creator of the universe has placed in our minds ... *is the surest* evidence of the immortality of the soul ..." The Reform critic, Bernard Felsenthal, attacked this compromise in which, he felt, the prayer book blessing for the resurrection of the dead might be uttered without conviction.[18] Dr. Felsenthal's criticism was justified, for if we compare unqualified statements by Leeser and Morais with those of Szold and Jastrow (and at the same time with the ideas of Wise and the more extreme position of Einhorn), we see quite clearly just how far the authors of the *Abodat Israel* prayer book departed from the traditional view.[19]

In analyzing the statements on the major concepts of faith: belief in God, creation and immortality—studying carefully not only the statements themselves but the incidental phrases, nuances of language and discourses as well—one realizes the manifest influence philosophical and scientific ideas of the day had on the Historical School generally. All factions of the School, traditionalists included, recognized that simply to state a belief, even the belief in God, was not necessarily to gain widespread acceptance for it. The skeptical and anti-religious convictions of the time were creating a powerful antireligious faith. Therefore, those involved entered into the battle, utilizing contemporary ideas and vocabulary. Whether they accepted, modified or rejected these ideas, they could not avoid being influenced by them in the encounter. Most often, the first impulse was to seek the source for current ideas in the Tradition. Szold found biblical verses ready to expound his idea of the compatibility of the Tradition with human reason and change: *For this commandment.... is not in heaven, that thou shouldst say, who shall go up for us to heaven, and bring it unto us, and cause us to hear it, that we may do it.... But the word is very nigh unto thee, in thy mouth, and in thy heart that thou mayest do it.* (Deut. 30.11-14.)[20]

Leeser, it is known, did not veer from his deep conviction of the ancient Tradition's relevance to contemporary life. Yet, he did not escape from reason into mystic faith when he tried to explain—as few in the Historical School attempted— the most vexing problem which faces the man of religion, the problem of Evil. He argued that evil was part of good.

> ... Whatever evil is discoverable in any part of our investigation is a part of goodness which necessarily enters into the arrangement of those things where we ourselves can discover the beneficence of the Creator. ... Evil then is a means of correction or progress rather, which helps things from a state of inferior felicity to one of a higher degree, and is constantly accomplishing whatever has been from the first in the mind of Almighty Power as his object to effect in the universe . . .[21]

The doubts of the "thinking young men and young women of the congregation" also impelled Sabato Morais to deal with fundamental questions raised in the general American environment. In a course of lectures about God, immortality and revelation, he promised to examine all philosophical opinion, both old and new, and demonstrate that each and every argument could be answered.[22]

Alexander Kohut attempted to explain the eternal significance of Judaism in the light of the new science. Religion without science is not a growing and dynamic religion.

> Ought we to maintain two kinds of logic, one for theology and the other for science? I believe decidedly, no! The indubitable results of science can and must agree with

the truths of religion, for a religion which cannot bear the light of science or must first soften the light through all kinds of lenses is to be classed with the dead. Such a religion could vegetate among the lower classes, lead a sad existence, become sometimes dangerous by fanaticism, but could not exercise a decisive influence upon the development of mankind.

Fortunately, the Mosaic religion does not belong to religions that fear the light. . . . There never existed a time or party or sect which required, recommended, or even asserted as admissible, to neglect the use of reasoning . . .[23]

Kohut demonstrated his thesis with three examples: creation, revelation and *kashrut*. His analysis reveals the fundamental difference between the approach of the Historical School and the Orthodox.

The Bible does not teach a theory of revolution or evolution as a popular book; it does not contain philosophical principles; but it is not in contradiction with the results of honest, thorough science. Let us read, without bias, the first four verses of the Biblical account of the creation: "In the beginning God created the heaven and the earth." Enough. How sublime are these words! Each of them outweighs hundreds of philosophical systems. At first there was a beginning. Is it less comprehensible to speak of a beginning of the world than of an eternity of the world? "He created," He brought into being, by mere commanding. Is this more difficult to understand than an established Hylo, a perpetual matter existing for all eternity? A God created and established a beginning. Is it less rational than a nothing, a blind accident? The creation comprised the heaven and the earth, i.e., the universe. The Bible does not give a description of the heaven; it merely treats about the earth; for "the heavens are the heavens of God; the earth He gave the children of men." The created earth was "void and chaotic" darkness covered the depths, and the spirit of God moved over the waters.

How long lasted the chaos—how long continued the process of development—the Bible does not consider; it refers us to geology. We may consider these theories proved, or reject them; it does not affect the Bible. It is only concerned in the fact that the world had a beginning, produced by God, and is unbiased to report that for a time chaos existed.[24]

In reference to the doctrine of the immortality and resurrection of the dead, a comparison of two select prayers in the Szold-Jastrow prayer book and the traditional *siddur* indicates the major theological changes introduced by the former:[25]

1. In the morning prayer, *Elohai, neshamah she-natatah bi:*

The Siddur

O my God, the soul which thou gavest me is pure; thou didst create it, thou didst form it, thou didst breathe it into me; thou preservest it within me; *and thou wilt take it from me, but wilt restore it unto me hereafter.* So long as the soul is within me, I will give thanks unto thee, O Lord my God and God of my fathers, Sovereign of all works, Lord of all souls! *Blessed art thou, O Lord, who restorest souls unto dead bodies.*

The Abodat Israel Prayer Book

My God, the soul which thou hast placed in my body is pure, for it is a portion of thy Holy Spirit, an emanation from thee, who art the fountain of purity. Thou hast created it and formed it. Thou hast breathed it into me, and dost carefully guard it within me. *When thou seest fit, thou wilt take it from me, but wilt restore it in the eternal happiness of the future world.* Whilst this soul shall continue within me will I adore thee, O Lord my God, and God of my fathers. Blessed be thou, O Lord, Author of all works, Source of all souls.

2. In the burial service:

The Siddur

The Rock, his work is perfect, for all his ways are judgment . . . *he killeth and maketh alive: he bringeth*

The Abodat Israel Prayer Book

". . . Fear not! there is a reward for thy work; there is a hope for thy future which cannot fail!"

*down to the grave and bring-
eth up again* . . . Just art
thou, O Lord, in killing and
in making alive, in whose
hand is the charge of all
spirits . . . Blessed be the
Lord our God, King of the
universe, who formed you in
judgment, who brought death
on you in judgment, who
knoweth the number of you
all in judgment, and *will
hereafter restore you to life
in judgment. Blessed art thou,
O Lord, who quickenest the
dead.*

And this conviction of immortality which the Creator
of the universe has placed in
our minds . . . *is the surest
evidence of the immortality
of the soul.* . . . This struggle,
this striving on earth, must
find a reward, a reward not
of an earthly nature, as the
struggle and strife are not of
this earth. This flame that
turneth upwards, must eventually reach the great Source
of light . . . Ye, our beloved,
whose affection made us
happy, . . . ye stand this moment before our mental gaze.
Death has not rent asunder
the ties which life had wo-
ven . . .

To summarize, the Historical School, as a unit, believed
and taught the traditional doctrine of divine revelation. But
when it came to the belief in immortality, reward and punishment, there were internal differences. The traditionalists and
the developmentalists accepted the fundamentals of the Tradition and argued their views in the manner of the medieval
Jewish philosophers; the progressivists accepted modern
thought and presented it as a legitimate interpretation of
historical Judaism. None was afraid to face the challenge of
science and analytic inquiry. To them, the belief in God
meant the affirmation of truth.

Torah and Mitzvot

*And this is the Torah which Moses set before the children
of Israel, according to the commandment of the Lord by the
hand of Moses.* (Deut. 4.44; Nu. 4.37). From their interpretation of these verses of Scripture recited in the prayers before

returning the Torah to the Ark, one can relate the views of the respective factions in the Historical School as they responded to the issues of Sinaitic Revelation, biblical criticism and the authority of the Talmud and *Shulhan Arukh*. The traditionalists accepted this prayer literally; the developmentalists permitted themselves to qualify its rabbinic exposition; the progressivists omitted the phrase *by the hand of Moses* from their prayer book.

In his writings, Leeser stressed that the Jews have no profession of faith and that they hold the "whole word of God to be alike fundamental." Referring to the sanctity of the Bible, he quoted the Rabbis as saying there is no difference between the verses *I am the Lord thy God* (Ex. 20.2), and *And the sons of Dan: Hushim* (Gen. 46.23).[26] Leeser proudly proclaimed his faith in every miracle just as it was recorded. When he had to contend with criticism leveled against divine miracles in the Bible, or the attestation of other faiths to what they believed to be miracles, he argued that miracles are the instruments God uses to convince people of truths already existing "or to effect certain purposes which He deems of sufficient importance for Him to subvert for a time or permanently the laws of Nature." No miraculous abstraction can alter in the least any religious or moral truth, or do away with any precept of the Bible. Thus, in Leeser's view, when miracles substantiate the truth of Judaism, they are to be believed; otherwise, they are not.[27]

Leeser did not distinguish, as others in the School did, between the Pentateuch and the rest of the Scriptures. "The translator," he wrote in the preface to his English version of the Bible, ". . . believes in the Scriptures as they have been handed down to us, as also in the truth and authenticity of prophecies and their literal fulfilment." Leeser's position was supported by his contemporaries and his successors in the traditionalist segment of the Historical School. Morris Raphall, for example, did not even deem it worth while to debate with those "rationalists" who denied the possibility of prophecy.[28]

It might have been expected that Morais would stand foursquare with the traditionalists. Yet in his statements on the Bible, which are not always explicit, he cites evidence primarily from the Torah and is careful to emphasize the "ordinances of Horeb," the commandments given on Sinai.[29] It is most interesting to note, regarding the article of faith formulated by Maimonides, "all the words of the prophets are true," that not only Szold and Jastrow but even Kohut and Solis-Cohen did not accept the belief that every word of the prophets was divinely inspired. Solis-Cohen said that folk-stories and tales are mixed with the truthful accounts. Against this stand truths which have been revealed to mankind in the course of generations. But those truths are not necessarily included in the Bible. To these questions the differences of approach within the School were brought out by the currents of criticism directed against the Bible both from within and outside of Judaism. The statements are often confused because of the conflict between belief and scholarship. In attempts to comprehend inner contradictions, one discovers the rationalizations which were evoked and caused the mind to write what the heart really believed. One also finds evidence in some of the writings that the authors were actually writing to themselves to dispel some of their own doubts emphasized or originally raised by the critics. An excellent example of the difficulties experienced by members of the Historical School who did not summarily reject critical biblical scholarship is afforded in the series of lectures Morais gave to the Seminary students on "Bible and Bible study." Morais, in many respects, followed the method of the Italian Jewish scholar, Samuel David Luzzatto.[30]

In his teaching, Morais always stressed that the Bible was a guide to life. He kept in touch with Christian as well as modern Jewish Bible interpreters.[31] To discredit the influence of the "higher critics" among those Jews who tended to accept these "scientific" views was Morais' personal mission. "I read my Bible without the spectacles of Wellhausen," he wrote.[32] In his lectures Morais did not say that the text of the Bible was perfect. He explained that the books comprising it, having passed through the hands of many scribes and copyists, contained a considerable number of textual errors. Similarly, he discussed the chronological differences in the books of Kings and Chronicles. Furthermore, he stated that the inclusion of *kre* and *ktiv* (traditional distinction between pronunciation and spelling) demonstrates that the compilers of the Bible were aware of the problems in the text. The Rabbis also realized that Ezra existed in a number of manuscript versions. However, as indicated, Morais differentiated between the Five Books of Moses and the rest of the Scriptures. It was not possible, he believed, to apply the same measure of analysis to both. Whoever undertook the criticism of the Pentateuch, would touch the basis of Judaism.[33] Precisely because the Scriptures were a target of constant criticism, he felt it crucial to prepare traditionally-trained Jewish scholars. They would be taught how to examine the Bible. Anyone who wanted to conduct original research would have to use the Greek and Aramaic translations and, above all, Bible critics would have to learn Semitic languages and Near-Eastern archaeology.[34]

Szold, Jastrow and De Sola Mendes, although they agreed with the basic approach of modern Bible criticism, recognized the latent anti-Judaism that motivated many Bible scholars, particularly in Germany. They, like Morais, recognized the scholars' attempts to shed light on the Scriptures on their own terms rather than on the basis of objective materials. Kohut's opinions were similar, except for his introduction of a new element of thought concerning the correlative position of critical research in the Talmud. Kohut's views on the teaching of Bible and Talmud at the Seminary serve both as a statement of method in Bible instruction adopted by the Seminary faculty, and a prognosis of the central role which the teaching and research of the Talmud was to play in the curriculum of the reorganized Seminary after the coming of Solomon Schechter. With regard to the teaching of the Bible, Kohut straddled the questions raised by critical research. He said that he was not disinclined to have the Seminary students familiarize themselves with the results of the so-called higher criticism of the Bible, if they clearly understood that such researches were in truth anti-biblical studies, as he called them. The real purpose of studying the Bible was to tap its inner wealth and, possessing a comprehensive view of circumstances contemporaneous with the Bible, to inquire into the time of its composition and examine the influences under which the sacred text originated. To achieve this purpose, it is not necessary "to lean on the brittle seed of our hypercritics." Kohut reiterates the view of Morais and the others who were responsible for the method of Bible study at the Seminary—to teach the Bible critically, with the exception of the Torah, the Five Books of Moses. "To us the Pentateuch is a *noli me tangere!* Hands off! We disclaim all honor of handling the sharp knife which cuts the Bible into a thousand pieces."[35]

The Talmud, Kohut claimed, is another matter altogether. Here keen criticism is not to be abhorred, but is an essential desideratum. "Talmudic archaeology, since some indefatigable pathfinders, like Rapoport, Zunz, Frankel, Geiger, Graetz, Zuckermann and others have paved the way into its deep mines, yielded many a find to earnest workers, but the ore-containing regions are so deep and widely stretched that their thorough exploration necessitates a well-organized band of co-operating unselfish laborers."[36]

Whereas the respective positions within the School on Torah were clear and unequivocal, ambiguities did develop in the practice of *mitzvot*. These ambiguities were due essentially to divided opinion on the authoritative character of the *Shulhan Arukh* as the decisive code of Jewish practice. The traditionalists accepted the regimen of Jewish life and practice incorporated in the *Shulhan Arukh* and its commentaries. Sabato Morais, reared on the Italian rites and practices of the Sephardi tradition, was the only member of the traditionalist group who doubted the definitive quality of the *Shulhan Arukh,* although privately and as rabbi of Mikveh Israel congregation he was careful to observe the law in all its details as defined in the code. The developmentalists and the progressives in the School rejected the traditionalist position. While they proclaimed the indispensability of the *mitzvot* in the structure of Jewish life, they based their interpretation of Jewish Law on the Torah and Talmud. Unlike Morais, in their own practice they deviated from the *Shulhan Arukh* and were prepared to make decisions according to their own reading of the Law and in accordance with the interpretations of various talmudic authorities.

Isaac Leeser, Morris Raphall and Samuel M. Isaacs, among the rightists, were uncompromising on the question of observance. Their firm position was based on the divine purpose of the *mitzvot* to unite the Jewish People and remind the Jews of the Belief and duties of their Faith. The ceremonies of Judaism, Leeser explained, are an indissoluble part of Jewish history, binding "the recollection of these mighty deeds to the observance of many ceremonials and festive occasions, which by their constant recurrence, should constantly remind the people of the causes why they are ordained."[37] When Gustav Poznanski introduced an organ into his synagogue, thereby sanctioning instrumental music on the grounds that the synagogue was the legitimate successor to the Temple, Leeser declared unequivocally that instrumental music was not permitted in the synagogue service. The synagogue had always been "a place for prayer, proclaiming of the law and prophets and public instruction in the manner of religion."[38] The Reformers, attempting to embarrass Leeser about those Jewish practices which seemed obsolescent as a part of American life, received a forthright answer: the neglect of an observance by any particular generation does not mean that it is either wrong or absurd.[39] Therefore, no deviation was to be permitted unless the possibility of such variance had been expressly built into the Jewish law.

Raphall, for his part, prepared a series of popular texts and materials to propagate these same views. In his work *The Festivals of the Lord,* Raphall examined the traditional holidays and explained them in the spirit of the Talmud and the *Shulhan Arukh.*[40] Writing about the history and meaning of Jewish prayer, he explained his objections to any change in the form of prayer as set down by the rabbis.

This prayer book, may it never be expelled from our public and private worship; may it never be superseded in our
synagogues or our houses; may it never be forced to yield
to the would-be improvements of innovators, whose pro-
ductions, however good in intention, however approved of
by any particular congregations, would nevertheless destroy
that bond of union and of brotherhood among Israelites,
which the Hebrew prayer book now is, has so long been
and always will remain.[41]

The maximum "reforms" permitted by Samuel M. Isaacs
were abolition of the sale of honors in the synagogue and a
move to make services more decorous. He opposed any other
changes in Law or custom, declaring that they endangered
the essence of the religion and the continuity of the Jewish
people. He was deeply attached to the old London ritual of
the Hebrew service. Occasionally, he accepted the decision
of European rabbis concerning some minor changes in the
Sabbath and holiday services. But he taught that Judaism
was a religion based on law and, if it had to be changed, the
change must come slowly and with the authority of generations, not by a majority vote of some congregational meeting, most of whose participants knew almost nothing about
Jewish Law. Towards the end of his career, however, he did
support Morais' approach to revisions in the service. By that
time, it was too late to gain a consensus in the Historical
School. Each trend had gone its own way and produced its
own prayer book.[42]

Strangely, it was Morais who became the ideologist for the
developmentalists and progressivists of the School in their
approach to the *Shulhan Arukh*. While he did not agree to
alter any of the traditional *mitzvot*, he also did not agree
with Leeser and Raphall on the *Shulhan Arukh*. "Not every
custom to which your unsophisticated fathers adhered, flowed
from a high source," he wrote to Kaufmann Kohler. "Those
who are conservative, because they recognize in 'orthodoxy'
the depository of eternal principles, do not claim for each
Jewish practice a Divine origin and immutability; but neither
do they cast aside olden ritualism without the certainty that

its absence can be supplied by what exceeds it in fitness and sterling worth."[43]

Morais denied the final authority of the *Shulhan Arukh* and proposed a more modern code in which the rules, followed by American Jews throughout life, would be set down clearly and unequivocally, with proper regard for changed conditions. The Jews, Morais explained in his essay on "The Ritual Question," know very well that the Talmud was the depository of laws adhered to by the disciples of Moses, "though not plainly set forth in the code he was inspired to write." Although some practices were derived from the Torah and introduced in talmudic times, he felt that these facts should also be candidly admitted and acted upon. Moreover, occasionally the personal habits or utterances of an ancient rabbi brought about the introduction of customs which time gradually endeared to posterity. Frequently, circumstances and surroundings gave rise to observances hallowed by the Jews in subsequent ages simply because of their antiquity. Morais, as an individual, did not object to any of those ancient practices. He admitted that they had contributed to the unity of the people in past ages, through all the political and social changes which the Jews had undergone since the close of the Talmud.

They may be regarded simply as fences; still I would not dare to raise my feeble hand to help in casting down what has, in a degree, prevented the devastation of the "vineyard of the Lord of hosts." But I would unscrupulously tear and uproot every excrescence raising a barrier among the children of my own people . . .

Among these barriers, Morais objected to two "illogical" yet prevalent facts in contemporary Jewish life: first, the differences between interpretations of Jewish Law made by the Sephardi and Ashkenazi communities; and second, the different modes of worship practiced by the Jews in various geographic centers of residence.

Whatever is permitted to the Jew whose predecessors happened to be born in the west of Europe, should on no account be prohibited to his brother in faith whose progenitors first saw the light of day in the northern part of that continent. This anomaly has been suffered to continue too long. It must cease to exist in America . . .

It has happened, however, that many stringent rules by which men of the Ashkenaz rite chose to be bound, were, at times, accepted, from pious motives, no doubt, by their co-religionists of the Sephardic Minhag. And, again, in cases where Germans were not urged to be so exact, they would borrow from the Portuguese usages of rigorous character. Thus has a state of confusion been created . . .

Nay, the reputed digest of Rabbinical laws called "Shulchan Aruch," is, in its present, or even in its primitive form, anything but that which the name denotes, namely, a table spread out, where all has been arranged methodically and distinctly. Clashing opinions may be met there blended together and obscurely brought forth. I do not intend to disparage the arduous labor of Joseph Caro. As an abridgement of this extensive comment "Beth Yoseph," serving as a hand-book, so to say, both for teachers and scholars it possesses merits, and it may have proved of use. That the Rabbi designed hereby to familiarize all with the decisions of olden sages, we gather from a preface he wrote, but I lament that in doing so he introduced objectionable features, not alone in the system adopted, but in the selection of several of the rules laid down . . .

I repeat it: The Talmud, as the archives of early traditions, and the receptacle of the wisdom of our forefathers, challenges our deepest veneration; but the Talmud as the source whence ideas unfit to be reproduced—and never commanded to be reproduced—have been with extreme care collated and codified, is, to use a mild term, utterly valueless. At any event, we of the present century absolutely need a code where the rules which an American Israelite has ritually to follow on all occasions through life, are laid down unequivocally, with clearness and brevity, and likewise with due regard to our changed condition . . .[44]

The distinction in Jewish practice between what Morais proposed, on one hand and what was proposed by the developmentalists and progressives, on the other hand, becomes clear if we consider the congregations in which they served. In addition to Morais' own proclivities, the very situation in Mikveh Israel demanded that he be punctilious in his rulings on observance. The congregations of Kohut, Szold, Jastrow and De Sola Mendes, however, preferred Reform practice. A key, then, to an understanding of the ambiguity in as well as the disparity between forms of observance within the Historical School—and later in the Conservative Movement—is the distinction between the real views and goals of religious leadership and the temporary measures those leaders took because of their congregations' Reform tendencies.

The questions, dilemmas and direction of the developmentalists and progressives in the area of observance were, on the whole, similar. Their approaches can be described as one. Whatever differences existed among them were precipitated by the immediate local situation. The fact is that in time, the centrist and progressive trends in the Historical School became dominant. Therefore, it is of paramount importance to understand the way that they coped with their congregations' Reform mood. They accepted temporary retreats in ritual observances while holding on securely to the fundamentals of *Shabbat, kashrut* and Hebrew; in this way they intended to bring the people closer and closer to Tradition. To this extent, Kohut, Szold and Jastrow serve as examples of the predicament of the School and as examples of learned and beloved rabbis who were caught between their wishes and reality. Although their congregations did not observe the second days of festivals, the rabbis had never approved this change. Kohut struggled with his congregation, Ahavath Chesed, to introduce the Hanukkah and Purim holidays, but in spite of the affection they felt toward him, the leaders of the synagogue forbade this compromise with "Orthodoxy." Many of the innovations accepted or initiated by the Historical School had their origin in the pressures exerted by the congregations, and had not been preconceived by the religious leaders. Kohut was prepared to permit family pews if it would increase synagogue attendance. For the same reason, he agreed to shorten the order of the service.[45]

As a result of these pressures, the change in the mode of Jewish practice in their congregations, and their desire not to be separated from their people's way of life, the centrist and left-wing religious leaders personally adopted many of the habits of the congregation. They did not conduct themselves like their traditionalist colleagues in the details of religious life, digressing from certain ritual practices. These subtle influences then entered into their writings and their explanation of the Tradition. An example of the modified form of American Jewish practice, as it influenced interpretations of the past, can be seen in Benjamin Szold's explanation of the fast-days, particularly the fast of the Ninth of Ab. In his *Outlines of the System of Judaism,* Benjamin Szold makes obligatory the putting on of *tefillin,* the observance of *kashrut,* the placing of the *mezuzah* on the doorpost, the wearing of the *tallit,* observing the second day of festivals, grace after meals, etc.[46] Then, in the part of the book dealing with the *mitzvot,* he departs from traditional practice in one matter only: fast days.

> There are also some days during the year formerly observed as fast days, in commemoration of some sad events in our past history in connection with the fall of Jerusalem. The most important of these days is the Ninth of Ab, the day of the destruction of Jerusalem and the Temple. On this day we should reflect upon the causes of the fall of Jerusalem, and pray to God for the restitution of Israel to its *spiritual* glory. The fasting on these days is, as the Prophets say, only a custom but no religious requirement.[47]

Although we have emphasized the differences between the traditionalists and the other segments of the Historical School in interpreting the *mitzvot,* these differences should not be exaggerated. In perspective, the area of disagreement was very small compared with the area of agreement between them. The very commitment to *mitzvot,* to the binding authority of Torah, however broadly interpreted, and to the transmission of this commitment to American Jews, was the foundation and keystone of the unity within the Historical

School. Solomon Solis-Cohen, a layman, summarized this unity of understanding:

> Judaism has never taught that the salvation of souls depends upon formal professions of faith or upon adherence to certain forms. It has taught and does teach, however, that the salvation—the physical preservation of the Jew—in this world does depend upon adherence. Without the protection of his guardian code his absorption into heathendom would have been a matter of very short time. . . . Not by numbers but by the devotion of her children does Zion count her strength.[48]

The Messianic Idea and the Mission of Israel

In nineteenth century theology the great debate between religions revolved around the question of which one exclusively possessed the *truth*. The teachers and ministers of Christianity explained to their adherents that Judaism was a prologue to Christianity, and that the Jewish mission in history had been completed. This debate became one of the prime problems and concerns of organized Jewish religion, Reform, Historical School and Orthodox. Compelled to combat these teachings, Jewish religious leadership determined to impress upon its adherents that the mission of Judaism was to demonstrate, through the living people of Israel, the historical superiority of Judaism over the other religions, especially Christianity.

In this light, one can readily understand the vast amount of polemical writing and preaching devoted to the explanation of the Mission of Israel. The divergences within the Historical School were greatest on this subject. Traditionalists and developmentalists claimed that the Jews were ordained to be the Chosen People. The progressives, while concurring with the messianic imperative of the Jewish people, radically altered the traditional belief. They spoke of the coming of the Messianic Era, but not of the Messiah, the son of David.

Specifically, the traditionalists believed in the coming of the Messiah, the son of David, and in the Return of the people of God to the Holy Land. As foretold by the prophets, Israel was the elected of God, and He would fulfill His promise to gather together its remnants out of exile. Leeser explained the messianic idea in contemporary language and with reference to current thought.

The Messiah whom we expect is not to be a god, nor a part of the godhead, nor a son of god in any sense of the word; but a man simply eminently endowed, like Moses and the prophets in the days of the Bible, to work out the will of God on earth in all that the prophets have predicted of him. His coming, we believe, will be the signal for universal peace, universal freedom, universal knowledge, universal worship of the One Eternal. . . . In the days of this august ruler the law which was at first given as "an inheritance of the congregation of Jacob" will become the only standard of righteousness, of salvation for all mankind, when will be fulfilled to its fullest extent the blessings conferred upon Abraham, Isaac, and Jacob, that "in their seed all the families of the earth should be blessed." We believe farther, that the time of this great event is hidden from our knowledge, and is only known to the Creator, who in his own good time will regenerate the earth, remove the worship of idols, banish all erroneous beliefs, and establish his kingdom firmly and immovably over the hearts of all sons of man, when all will invoke Him in Truth, and call Him God, King, Redeemer, the One who was, is, and will be, for ever and ever. We believe that the time may be distant, thousands of years removed; but we confidently look forward to its coming, in the full confidence that He who has so miraculously preserved his people among so many trials and dangers, is able and willing to fulfil all He has promised, and that his power will surely accomplish what his goodness has foretold; and that He will not rest in the fulfillment of his word, till all the world shall acknowledge his power.[49]

Sabato Morais defined the messianic belief in similar language, directing himself at the same time to the believing Jew, to the Christian attack on this doctrine and to Reform's misuse of biblical prophecy to explain its own views. "The Jewish idea," Morais said, "was of a personal Messiah who could lead back into Palestine a reconstructed nation." That idea rested upon the prophecies of Moses and Isaiah. The Reformers, he added, deserved praise for their "constant labors against the propagandists," but they should not refer to prophecies in figurative terms.[50]

Catechisms, not theological tracts, offer clues to the theology of the authors. In the catechism of Leeser a whole chapter is devoted to the appearance of the Messiah, his reign and his accomplishments, according to Jewish tradition. In the catechism of Szold the people of Israel is declared chosen "to be the covenant of peoples and the light of nations. Israel is the Messiah of mankind . . ."[51]

In the Szold-Jastrow prayer book, the traditional passages are deleted, and in their place new ideas appear. The reformulation of the prayer "Thou hast chosen us" is a good example. The traditional prayer in the *siddur* reads:

> Thou hast chosen us from all peoples; Thou hast loved us and taken pleasure in us, and hast exalted us above all tongues; Thou hast sanctified us by Thy commandments, and brought us near unto thy service . . .

The Szold-Jastrow prayer reads:

> Thou hast chosen us from among all nations, and in thy love *hast assigned unto us the priestly mission of spreading the knowledge of thy Holy Name,* so that we may not alone perform thy commandments, but consecrate ourselves to thy service . . .[52]

The language Szold and Jastrow used in their prayer book carries the overtones of the Reform theology of the period. But it would be a misreading of their views to say that this was their intention. The universal aspect of historic Judaism is strikingly brought out by Szold and Jastrow when they write on the concepts of the Messiah, the doctrines of election, the mission of Israel and the redemption of mankind. Unlike the Reformers, Szold and Jastrow did not anticipate the disappearance of the national aspirations of the Jewish people, nor the leveling of its unique role among the nations of the world, nor the demolition of Judaism's *mitzvot* structure. They taught that Israel must maintain its own "peculiar laws" by which it will be able to perform the "national task" assigned to it. Quite the contrary, they argued, accepting the religious challenge of the time: uniqueness is not exclusiveness. "Israel," Jastrow wrote, "is only one of the chosen people of the earth, selected to become the exponent and standard-bearer of religious truth."

Jastrow devoted a series of articles to explain this view of Israel's uniqueness, statements which became, finally, the consensus in the Historical School: it stemmed from the Tradition although it did not represent the traditionalists. It had the strong advantage of being an answer which reckoned with and directed itself to the changed conditions and ideas in nineteenth-century America.

> We have spoken of Israel's mission of spreading the truths of religion, and the question is often asked, "Is the religion of Israel an universal one? Do we wish all people to recognize our truths?" The answer that undoubtedly arises is an emphatic yes. The Unity of God, the brotherhood of mankind, the acknowledgement of one sole Creator of the universe, who rules it in justice and righteousness, these are universal truths which we hope will grow and spread among the nations. And yet if we reflect and ask, "Is it altogether universal, have we no special laws for our own peculiar existence?" we cannot deny that this is true. Israel's religion contains universal truths upheld and supported by national laws and institutions.
>
> There are those among us now, however, who wish to tear down these national supports, to remove all barriers which separate us from the rest of the world. "There are thousands," they say, "who fully agree with the cardinal truths of our religion, and yet are not identified with us. Let us now perform our mission, let us sweep away all distinctions, that the many who already think with us may find easy access and a warm welcome. The power of Trinitarianism is waning." We might, in the first place, question the last assertion. When, at the command of this power,

cruel, unjust and partial Sunday laws can be enacted, when the Jew has yet only the choice of two days' rest or none, and the Jewish workman is forbidden under penalty of arrest and punishment, to work even his sewing-machine on the first day of the week, to supply the necessaries of life for himself and family, he is rash who can boldly assert that this power is on the decline.

But even to those who can no longer believe in the mysteries of Trinitarianism, is it our barriers alone which separate them from us? If all the distinctive and peculiar Israelitish laws were abolished, are they willing to enter our fold and cast their lot with us? Few, very few indeed, have the courage of their convictions, are strong enough to overleap the barriers which they themselves have created, the barriers of prejudice, of pride, of social ostracism and practical necessities.

Can we ourselves then preserve our truths best by giving up our peculiar laws? . . .[53]

The issues of nationalism and universalism, uniqueness and exclusive selection, were reflected in other, more internal aspects of Jewish theological discussions, such as the prayers for the restoration of the sacrifices and the Hebraic character of the service. The question of the restoration of sacrifices, in particular, led to stormy debate, not only between the respective groups in American Judaism but within the Historical School itself. In traditional thought, the rebuilding of the Temple is considered of an importance beyond the building of the Land. Judaism does not observe a fast day to commemorate the destruction of the Jewish state; the fast day is for the destruction of the Temple. Jews ask God, in their prayers, to help them "prepare before thee the offerings that are obligatory for us." This idea was, of course, accepted completely by the rightists of the School. Leeser looked forward to the return of the divine service to Jerusalem. He hoped, too, that it would be carried out as prescribed.

Once again Morais surprised his colleagues when he expressed his views in a letter to Kaufmann Kohler. Unlike Leeser, H. P. Mendes and the others in the traditionalist faction, he wondered whether the ancient belief in the restoration of sacrifices in the divine service would indeed come to pass "in the distant future." Moreover, he clearly stated that his own feelings were repelled by such a thought, and admitted that perhaps modern training had brought about the "abhorrence for that which the ancients regarded with reverence." Given independence in their ancient Land, it is conceivable, Morais continued, "that those conditions may assume a different form from that which they had anciently, it is not impious to conceive. God, who unfolds and shapes events, will direct the redeemed of a long and bitter oppression, how best to show evidence of filial gratitude."[54]

To Szold and Jastrow and the progressives generally, the idea of the reestablishment of the sacrifices was something that the human mind could not tolerate. This is demonstrated by the omission of all such references in their prayer book.[55]

Whatever the differences of other theological discussions on the selection and uniqueness of Israel, unanimity of view prevailed with regard to "the holy tongue." Hebrew must be preserved as sacred and as a symbol of Jewish uniqueness. Leeser feared that if the Reformers succeeded in their plan to remove Hebrew from the prayer book, the Jewish people would cease being one people with one language and become divided and confused.[56] S. M. Isaacs recognized the inseparable bonds between Hebrew prayer and the Land of Israel. It is not enough to read Hebrew, he said; it is important that it be understood. Isaacs asked:

> Should the Hebrew language be disregarded, reflecting as we must, that in that language God promulgated His laws, and which once was the vernacular in that land on which our hearts are fixed and where we hope to return . . . ? It is to be deplored that, in the present age of novelty, our language so sedulously cultivated by aliens to our faith is by us considered as unsuited for God's house. Thus is the only remnant of our departed greatness become forsaken . . .[57]

The Historical School's united opinion of the unique role of Hebrew is indicated by the fact that even De Sola Mendes came out against the Reform prayer book *solely* because of its diminished Hebrew content.

> We do love our Hebrew prayers; no editing committee can afford to forget that fact. We love it, too, quite regardless of the extent to which it is grammatically understood by our worshipers, who cling to its majesty and venerate its sonorous mystery even when they only vaguely grasp its meaning. For similar reasons the Catholic church to this day retains its Latin rituals. Why not accept this characteristic of our common humanity and avoid wounding or dissatisfying people by the omission of their treasured passages.[58]

As we review the efforts expressed by the Historical School to interpret Judaism to its fellow-Jews and to the general American community, we can see that it did not think philosophically or theologically, but practically. It did attempt to formulate an intellectual position which would help to assure the continuity of the Jewish people as a People living by the Tradition. The survival of the People despite continually changing conditions was central to its thought. When the traditionalists held fast even to obsolete custom, it was because they believed such was the best way to maintain Jewish continuity. Similarly, when the developmentalists adopted modifications of the Law, or when the progressives introduced innovations, they, too, held the needs of the living People uppermost in their minds. Sabato Morais was the man who spoke for the entire School when he said that the first law in fulfilling the Jewish "mission of Israel" to the world was to live and create as a Jewish group. Any diminution of the Jews' own unique natural gifts and responsibility to that mission would render their contribution less effective. For the sake of humanity the Jews as a people must survive and nurture their own endowments.[59] In this instance Marcus Jastrow also spoke for the entire Historical School when he differentiated between the synagogue as a religious *body* rather than as a religious *center*. As one is born into a country, a state, a nation and into one's respective rights and duties, so a Jew is born into a *congregation*—the congregation of

Israel. The role of the synagogue is to sustain and invigorate the "religious body" of the Jews, which is the "congregation of Jacob" in its true sense, as the "Jewish community as an ideal religious body, the carrier of a mission, the embodiment of a complex of ideas."[60] It was at this goal that the several theological approaches within the Historical School were directed.

Chapter Three

The Turn of the Century: from Historical School to Conservative Movement

Toward the end of the century, Jewish religious life in America was characterized by a diminution of the debate among the several religious groups as each concentrated on its own development. The Reform group had made great strides. It had an organized lay constituency in the Union of American Hebrew Congregations and a rabbinical training center in its Hebrew Union College. In 1889, with the formation of the Central Conference of American Rabbis as the collective rabbinic authority of Reform Judaism, the tri-pillared organizational structure, through which the Reform movement continued to function in the twentieth century, was completed. Intensification and propagation of its views was the order of the day as Reform surged to the dominant position among the Jewish religious groups.

Orthodoxy, although in those days it was very far indeed from a secure basis of organization, gave promise of a great future. One word explains the source of its hope: immigration. And with the increasing numbers which strengthened Orthodoxy day by day came the *yeshivot* to prepare rabbis in its spirit, a growing network of supplementary schools to build its future laity, and overfilled synagogues to guarantee wide popular support. A rare statistical table establishes the vast demographic changes which were taking place in those decades, and which inevitably brought about the unusually swift rise of Orthodoxy to a place of central importance in

American Judaism. The United States census of 1890 accepted for the first and only time the existence of two bodies within the "Jewish Church," the Orthodox and the Reform, and collected data from each. Philip Cowen, the publisher of the *American Hebrew*, who had been assigned to this task was commended highly by the government for his work, reported 533 Jewish religious organizations, an increase of 344 organizations or 182% since the census of 1870. The Orthodox group was listed as having 316 or 59.3% of the recorded congregations, while the Reform body registered 217 or 40.7%. In actual membership count, the Reform group dominated, with 54.9% of the total reported Jewish membership. But to understand the meaning of these individual figures, one must take into account that the Orthodox synagogues had few annual members and that they sustained their synagogues through the sale of "seats" for the High Holy Days. Nor did they keep careful records, as did most of the Reform synagogues.[1] Therefore, as early as 1890 the adherents of Orthodox synagogues probably outnumbered the respective Reform and Historical memberships.

These statistics do more than explain the numerical power of Orthodoxy. They also explain the peculiar status of the Historical School at the time, and indicate its sudden change of direction. Most of the congregations which were affiliated with the Jewish Theological Seminary Association were classified in the census as Orthodox, despite the fact that in 1890 the Orthodox group technically had not yet organized into a formal national religious body. However, neither had the Historical School become an organized religious body. While it had a rabbinic training school and some thirty congregations devoted to its program, particularly the Seminary, it had neither the mass base of the Orthodox nor a formal lay organization such as the Union of American Hebrew Congregations. What better course was there than to follow the lead of H. P. Mendes, who proposed to intertwine the Historical School with the natural constituency available in the East-European Orthodox synagogues? The last years of the century were marked by the quest of the Seminary leaders to found a lay synagogal body. The easiest way to do this, it seemed at first, was to amalgamate with the rising Orthodox element.

Reasons of internal weakness accelerated this decision. The vital ideological leadership of Alexander Kohut was lost to the School with his death in 1894. Sabato Morais passed away in 1897. Szold and Jastrow were aging and were pressed hard by their own congregational problems. Without enthusiastic rabbinic leadership, the laymen of the School were not encouraged to remain firmly banded together. The young Adler, who was later to play a pivotal role in the reorganization of the Seminary, lived in Washington; Solomon Solis-Cohen was busy with medicine and Judge Sulzberger with the law. There was a need for new rabbinic and lay initiative. But it was not yet forthcoming. Nor was the Seminary itself developing into the kind of rabbinical school which the founders had originally designed. The number of students was very small. It was a critical time for the Seminary.

The active heads of the Seminary, Mendes and Drachman, had always leaned toward Orthodoxy. The two thought that they could save the institution and exert more influence within American Judaism through a union with Orthodoxy and a conversion of the Seminary into the official institution for the training of its rabbis. Mendes convinced most of the Seminary's trustees that such a step was destined to bring many blessings. The decisive argument was that by uniting the religious forces of both East- and West-European Jews, an institution could be created which would completely nullify the effectiveness of the Reform movement. Thus began an interesting and unanticipated chapter in the history of American Judaism—the advancement of American Orthodoxy under the initiative and prodding of the Historical School. The Orthodox willingly accepted the leadership of such known traditionalists as Mendes and Drachman, and they were impressed when eminent lay leaders like Max Cohen and Lewis Dembitz placed themselves in the forefront of this effort. Organizationally, Orthodoxy had everything to gain, and ideologically it had nothing to fear.

To understand the logic of Mendes' proposal and the agreement of many Orthodox leaders to work with him hand in
hand, it should be recalled that the roots of Orthodoxy in
America ran back to the earliest period of the American Jewish settlement and that, by the end of the century, it consisted
of three main segments: the indigenous Sephardi element
(for example, Mendes' own congregation, Shearith Israel);
the West-European Orthodox which, even in the mid-century
decades, refused to associate with the Historical School leadership (for example, Abraham Rice of Baltimore); and the
East-European Orthodox which transplanted entire communities from their native lands to sections of American cities,
longing to re-establish in their adopted land the religious way
of life they had followed in "the old country." The first segment, by and large, was part of the traditionalist sector of
the Historical School, and it was this group Mendes wanted
most to sustain. As for the second group, Mendes could now
argue that they need have no religious concerns about a movement which was to have East-European Orthodoxy as its base.
To the third segment, particularly those in it who sought
to integrate with the new environment, Mendes offered the
open hand of the settled and "Americanized" community. In
addition to this line of argumentation, Mendes recalled the
sad record of Orthodox attempts to organize in the past
(which Mendes himself had supported as early as 1879), all
of which had ended in failure.[2]

The new constellation of leadership forces, lay constituency
and ideological emphasis, seemed to spell success. The first
proclamation to convene the Orthodox congregations was
issued in Hebrew and English and addressed to the rabbis,
presidents and "all sincere friends of the historical faith of
Israel," who "have long lamented the sad state of Judaism in
this country." The aims of the conference were fourfold: to
define the permanent principles of the conference; Sabbath
observance; Zionism; Orthodox congregational union. Signed
by H. Pereira Mendes, as provisional chairman, and Max
Cohen, Secretary of the Jewish Theological Seminary, the
address of the circular is marked as 736 Lexington Ave., the

home of the Seminary. Of the thirteen members of the provisional committee, all but two were active members of the Seminary and the Historical School: H. P. Mendes, B. Drachman, M. de Sola, S. Schaffer, H. Schneeberger, M. Friedman, Joseph Hertz, J. Blumenthal, D. Sulzberger, C. Adler, S. Solis-Cohen, M. A. Dropsie, and J. D. Eisenstein.[3]

The convention of Orthodox congregations met in the vestry room of Shearith Israel. About a hundred delegates participated, representing congregations associated with the Historical School. The official languages of the convention were English and Hebrew. H. Pereira Mendes was elected president. In the month of Sivan, in the Jewish calendar year 5658 (June, 1898), the Orthodox Jewish Congregational Union of America was formally declared in existence "to promote the religious interests of the Jews in America and to further the welfare of the Orthodox Congregations in America."

Two questions which were raised early in the proceedings of the convention reveal the character of the assembly. The first issue related to the variety of religious practices throughout the congregations. The chairman was "informed" that some of the delegates came from congregations "where organ and pews were in vogue." Mendes replied that the acceptance of an invitation by any congregation entitled them to representation. The second issue dealt with the very name "orthodox" in the proposed statement of principles. Lewis Dembitz objected to the use of the term; he argued that it did not sufficiently indicate the purpose of the new organization. "Persons who did not live a Jewish life," he said, "but read the olden prayers were, according to the generally accepted view, orthodox." He preferred a name like *Shomrei Hadath* (Observers of the Law). When Drachman, Meldola de Sola of Shearith Israel, Montreal, and H. W. Schneeberger of Chizuk Amunah, Baltimore, argued for the name "orthodox," it was Mendes who protested its use. The majority of the delegates, however, ruled against the president.

The principles the convention adopted read as follows:

This Conference of delegates from Jewish congregations in the United States and the Dominion of Canada is convened to advance the interests of positive Biblical Rabbinical and Historical Judaism.

We are assembled not as a synod, and, therefore, we have no legislative authority to amend religious questions, but as a representative body, which by organization and cooperation will endeavor to advance the interests of Judaism in America.

We favor the convening of a Jewish Synod specifically authorized by congregations to meet, to be composed of men who must be certified Rabbis, and

   a. Elders in official position (cf. Numbers XI:16);
   b. Men of wisdom and understanding, and known amongst us (cf. Deut. I:13);
   c. Able men, God-fearing men, men of truth, hating profit (cf. Exodus XVIII:21).

We believe in the Divine revelation of the Bible, and we declare that the prophets in no way discountenanced ceremonial duty, but only condemned the personal life of those who observed ceremonial law, but disregarded the moral. Ceremonial law is not optative; it is obligatory.

We affirm our adherence to the acknowledged codes of our Rabbis and the thirteen principles of Maimonides.

We believe that in our dispersion we are to be united with our brethren of alien faith in all that devolves upon men as citizens; but that religiously in rites, ceremonies, ideals and doctrines, we are separate, and must remain separate in accordance with the Divine declaration: 'I have separated you from the nations to be Mine.' (Lev. XX:26.)

And further, to prevent misunderstanding concerning Judaism, we reaffirm our belief in the coming of a personal Messiah and we protest against the admission of proselytes into the fold of Judaism without *millah* (circumcision) and *tebilah* (immersion).

We protest against intermarriage between Jew and Gentile; we protest against the idea that we are merely a religious sect, and maintain that we are a nation, though temporarily without a national home, and

Furthermore, that the restoration to Zion is the legitimate aspiration of scattered Israel, in no way conflicting with our loyalty to the land in which we dwell or may dwell at any time.[4]

As events unfolded, it turned out that in the United States the Historical School had indeed stimulated the creation of the second organized Jewish lay religious body after that of Reform. But the Orthodox Union was not destined to serve the purpose intended for it by the leaders of the School. The Orthodox Jewish Congregational Union of America became what its name said it was, an Orthodox union. Moving slowly at first, then more decisively, it turned from the synagogues of the Historical School and entered the orbit of the East-European congregations. To their chagrin, the leaders of the Historical School soon recognized that this trend would become the actuality. Nevertheless, in their dilemma, they continued to work within the new Congregational Union for the fulfilment of its objectives. Meanwhile, they began to look for a successor to Sabato Morais, someone other than H. P. Mendes. They sought a scholar to be the natural leader of the entire Historical School, a man who would unite all its factions rather than embrace its traditionalist side.

Mendes did not budge from his committed position. He remained at the helm of the Union for several terms of office. When the organization met for the second time, in December 1900, he was able to give a comprehensive account of its many, different activities.[5] Nevertheless, the negative aspects of the admixture of backgrounds and interests in the Orthodox Union were felt. The meeting itself was not held in Shearith Israel, but downtown at the Eldridge Street Synagogue. Ninety-six congregations were represented, yet the national character of the first meeting was lost because many of the out-of-town congregations elected proxies living in New York City. Mendes, who spoke in English was barely understood. For him, Yiddish was a foreign language, as was English to most of the representatives. Meldola de Sola, Orthodox in ideology but Sephardi in background and representing his Canadian congregation, had similar difficulties as he rose to express his views.

The man who captured the hearts of the delegates was Rabbi Jacob David Wilowsky, known as the "Slutsker Rav." He was on a visit to the United States to introduce his commentary of the Jerusalem Talmud. Rabbi Wilowsky spoke in Yiddish. Not only his language but his content found favor. After appealing for consideration for Chief Rabbi Jacob Joseph of New York, who had been stricken ill and seemed deserted by the congregations which had brought him to the United States, the "Slutsker Rav," speaking "in the regulation rabbinical style to the delight of some and the consternation of those who did not understand him," took the occasion to announce publicly that anyone who emigrated to America was a sinner, since, in America, the Oral Law is trodden under foot. It was not only home that the Jews left behind in Europe, he said, it was their Torah, their Talmud, their *yeshivot*—in a word, their *Yiddishkeit,* their entire Jewish way of life.

At a convention where Rabbi Wilowsky could make such a proclamation to the resigned noddings of most of the delegates, and the best response that could be made on behalf of the Historical School viewpoint was that of Dr. Drachman, in German, it was apparent that other problems would develop. The dissatisfaction of the Orthodox with the conduct of the congregations of the Historical School came into the open. Criticism was especially directed against the Jewish Theological Seminary—the very institution which Mendes and Drachman had hoped to save through the Union. The issue was crystallized around the question of its support. It was declared more urgent to support the Yeshibah Etz Chayim, a day school (founded in 1886) which combined elementary general education with its Jewish studies program. For the sake of public peace, a compromise omnibus resolution was passed which offered support both for the Seminary and the Yeshibah Etz Chayim.

This second convention, of December 1900, served to reduce the interest of the Historical School in the Orthodox Union. By the third convention, in 1902, that interest virtually disappeared. Even though various leading laymen, rabbis

and their congregations continued their activity in the Orthodox Union, it was clear to those who wanted to build a lay
constituency for the Historical School that West-European
Jews, even though Orthodox in belief and practice, could not
capture the leadership of American Orthodoxy.

When the practical aspects of the Historical School's move
toward Orthodoxy had been originally contemplated, it was
recognized that the gap between the two groups was social
and cultural as well as ideological, and that these social and
cultural differences would be more divisive than those of
ideology. The reasons, then, for the failure of this experiment
ran much deeper than those which appeared on the surface
of the conventions or were reported in the press. The first
reason was esthetics—a factor which in the American milieu
was not to be taken lightly. Throughout the nineteenth century constant emphasis had been put on decorum and the
beautification of the synagogue service. This was the chief
"reform" of the traditionalist group in the Historical School;
and they were prepared to conceive the organization of a
synod in order to abolish the sale of "honors" in the synagogue.

A second reason for the separation was administrative,
caused by differences in countries of origin. The Jews who
settled in America came from many places. It was not always
possible to keep the members of one German congregation
together; it was extremely difficult to get them to join and
work in congregations made up primarily of Russian and
Polish Jews. The social disdain of the Sephardim even for the
German immigrants was an old problem. What could they
find in common with the most recent immigrants?

The attitude of the extreme Orthodox toward the environment and the manner of Christian life which prevailed in
America was a third reason for division. The Orthodox were
isolationists by choice and by experience; they had managed
in the past to maintain their religious group individuality and
solidarity by the practice of segregation. In Europe, this
segregation was imposed mainly by circumstance and decree;
in America it was voluntary, but segregation nonetheless. The

Conservative-Orthodox within the Historical School, trained in western Europe and as citizens anxious to be organically involved in the American way of life, were alert to the dangers facing Judaism as a result of such involvement. But they would not forgo the challenge of freedom. Consequently, segregation never entered their minds as an answer to the danger to Jewish group survival faced in the form of emancipation. Free interchange in school and society was an opportunity for the advancement of Judaism in America, they claimed, and not "a kiss of death" as the East-European religious leadership of the time contended.

The use of the vernacular both in the home and in public, in the synagogue and in communal Jewish life, was a fourth cause of actual separation between the two elements. Yiddish was the language of the Orthodox immigrants, by decision as well as training. It embodied the values and the way of life which were enjoined upon them by the past. Without it, they felt that they would dissolve as a solid entity. For the Conservative-Orthodox the use of the English language was fundamental. They wanted to be part of America, not a separate community. This attitude is summarized in a statement by Lewis N. Dembitz, one of those lay leaders of the Historical School, who actively fought for alliance with the Orthodox and became an officer of the Orthodox Union. Writing on the subject "The Rabbis from Eastern Europe," Dembitz recognized the great worth of these rabbis and their role "toward preserving in this country the faith of our fathers." He understood their shock that higher critical ideas of the Bible were taught at the Seminary. Nevertheless, he continued, they must be blamed for "their selfish and short-sighted fight against the use of the English language by and for English-speaking Jews in preaching and teaching." Dembitz went on to castigate them because they concentrated on the ritual backslidings of their charges when, in fact, they should be concentrating on communicating the moral aspects of Jewish religion to their congregants.[6]

These specific social and cultural factors explain in large measure the principal reasons why the western-trained

Orthodox chose to remain identified with the Historical School rather than join their Orthodox Russian-Polish brothers, with whom they shared theological beliefs. Unwilling to foster little enclaves of East-European Jewish life in America, when the test came they severed their affiliation from the Orthodox Union because they recognized the inevitability of the occidentalization of the Jew, seeing in the culture of the enlightenment and in modern citizenship affirmative values for Jews and Judaism.[7]

The retreat from Orthodoxy did not in itself solve the problems of the Seminary or those of the Historical School in general. Now the School was the only religious group in American Judaism without a central organization of member congregations. Moreover, the attempts to solve the problem of the Seminary by finding a common basis with the Orthodox only succeeded in awakening a powerful opposition. With a surging Reform movement on one side and a massive Orthodox movement looming on the other, the Historical School and the Seminary seemed doomed to be crushed.

In desperation other solutions were advanced, but despite the abject state of affairs, they were rejected by those in charge of the Seminary. When Wise died, in 1900, it was proposed to unite the Seminary and the Hebrew Union College under one president.[8] This administrative suggestion, while prompted by good will, was not seriously considered. Nor was that of Dr. Isaac Singer, editor of *The Jewish Encyclopedia,* who put forth a more extreme proposal: to abolish the two institutions and incorporate them in a "Jewish University of Theology, History and Literature." He prepared a complete and detailed plan. But the founders of the existing institutions did not want to erect a new seminary on the ruins of their previous work.[9]

Meanwhile, the fortunes of the Jewish Theological Seminary continued to decline. In 1901, Joseph Blumenthal, the president of the Seminary board of trustees, died. The institution was left with its one building on Lexington Avenue. It was being supported from loans against the building and small contributions. It seemed that there was no hope for the institution, the symbol of the achievement and future of the Historical School. Suddenly, a change of fortune took place. Cyrus Adler and Jacob Schiff were invited to the home of Isidor Straus. The conversation turned to Jewish education in America. Adler remarked that it would be a disgrace for New York Jewry, which was destined to be the largest Jewish community in the world, if the Seminary closed its doors. He described the precarious state of the Seminary, the only institution of higher Jewish learning in the city. Schiff listened, agreed, and took the initiative. Within several weeks, they met with Leonard Lewisohn, Mayer Sulzberger, and Daniel and Simon Guggenheim. This small group of half a dozen persons, with the very effective assistance of Louis Marshall, decided to reorganize the institution and collect a fund of half a million dollars in order to realize an earlier plan to invite Solomon Schechter from England to America to head a new faculty.[10] Hence, a small group of wealthy men, who were members of the most distinguished Reform congregation in New York—Temple Emanu-El—worked together with lay members of the Historical School to establish the Seminary on permanent foundations as the center of Conservative Judaism.

The main reason for this support was clearly stated. These laymen, who had chosen the path of Reform Judaism for themselves and for the training of their children, felt that there was no hope for Reform to influence the new East-European immigrants. They wanted these immigrants to become "Americanized," to learn English quickly and give their children a good general education. They believed that only the graduates of the Seminary, whose rabbis would be close to the immigrants and who also would be given a general modern education, could help "Americanize" the newcomers. Consequently, they hoped that what could not be accomplished organizationally by a merger of the Historical School and the Orthodox Union, would be accomplished in the course of time by the graduates of the Seminary, through the slower process of education. This was another way of uniting the Orthodox and Conservative factions so that there would be only two Jewish religious groups: Reform and Conservative.

It is important to stress, however, that these men were not "theoretical" reformers. They respected the Tradition and respected observant Jews. They also respected the learned lay leaders of the Historical School, who differed from them— such men as Solomon Solis-Cohen, Mayer Sulzberger, Harry Friedenwald, and Cyrus Adler. In these men they placed their trust to carry forward the plan of creating a great school of learning based on the historical tradition. Thus it came about in Conservative Judaism, though not in the other two movements which were created during the nineteenth century, that the rabbinical seminary became "the fountainhead" of the Movement. In Reform and Orthodoxy, it was the lay body of congregations which gave birth and strength to their respective rabbinic schools. In Conservative Judaism, it was the scholars, rabbis and laity, organized around the Seminary, who later brought into being the United Synagogue of America. The significance of this sequence of institutional development within the Historical School was deep and far-reaching, as was demonstrated in the twentieth century evolution of the Conservative Movement. But, even at the time, the reorganization of the Seminary saved the Historical School, which had lost its moorings, from being submerged into one group, or another. Also, with the association of this new group of leaders, the School regained its distinguishing characteristic of including all elements of Jewish life and learning. The new Seminary board, like the older Seminary Association built by the Historical School, was representative of the traditionalist, developmental, and progressive trends in the School. From this viewpoint, the decade of crisis was, in fact, a blessing, for it helped the School reappraise its basic position in American Jewry. It was strengthened by the regrouping of some of its leaders and congregations; they had left the School to join the Reform or Orthodox branches. It solidified the Seminary as the institution for the training of its future rabbinic and lay leaders. It made possible the coming of Solomon Schechter to guide its destiny in the decades ahead. It helped Conservative Judaism maintain the principle of diversity of thought and practice as one of its most distinctive qualities.

The new supporters demanded fundamental changes in the organization and program of the Seminary. They did not want to contribute large sums destined to be controlled by a board of trustees whose composition and character was changed bi-annually through elections. They desired continuity of purpose, which could be accomplished only by founding a society with a "charter." A precondition for all action was the invitation sent to Solomon Schechter asking him to become president of the faculty, and the appointment of Cyrus Adler as the head of the reorganized board of trustees. Dr. Adler, who was working in Washington, agreed to come to New York three days a week. The trustees, in order of appearance at the "act of incorporation," were: Jacob A. Schiff, Leonard Lewisohn, Daniel Guggenheim, Mayer Sulzberger, Cyrus Adler, Simon Guggenheim, Adolphus S. Solomons, Felix M. Warburg, Philip S. Henry and Louis Marshall. These men, their associates and successors, were constituted as

> a body corporate by the name of the Jewish Theological Seminary of America, in perpetuity, to be located in the City of New York, for the purpose of establishing and maintaining a theological seminary for the perpetuation of the tenets of the Jewish religion; the cultivation of Hebrew literature; the pursuit of biblical and archaelogical research; the advancement of Jewish scholarship; the establishment of a library, and for the education and training of Jewish rabbis and teachers . . .[11]

With a secure budget in view, plans to implement the reorganization moved rapidly. Jacob Schiff also agreed to erect a new building for the institution in the neighborhood of Columbia University, and to preserve there the enormous private collection of manuscripts as well as the rare literary documents of Mayer Sulzberger. Requirements for the admission of students were changed. Only students who had finished their college work and received the B.A. degree were accepted in the Seminary. With the B.A. behind them, they would be able to devote all their time and energy to Hebrew studies. The last class of the old administration completed its course in June of 1902, at which time eight rabbis were ordained, bringing the number of Seminary graduates during the lifetime of the Association to seventeen.[12] At that time, the new program went into effect. Recalling the new Seminary leaders' vision of the institution, Sol M. Stroock, one of the twentieth-century builders of the Seminary and chairman of its board of directors after Louis Marshall, wrote that these men realized "that the Seminary must be national in character, that no 'pent-up Ithaca' should restrict its powers, and that the whole broad continent must be inspired through its influence."[13]

The document which summarizes the role of the Historical School as it transmitted its chief creation to the emergent Conservative Movement, is the "Agreement of Merger," entered into on the 14th day of April, 1902, between the Jewish Theological Seminary Association and the Jewish Theological Seminary of America.[14] Duly signed by the respective presidents of the old and new corporations, A. S. Solomons and Cyrus Adler, and attested to by Louis Marshall, secretary *pro tem,* authority was indeed changed and responsibilities were transferred, but the purpose of the Association remained unchanged.

> . . . being the preservation in America of the knowledge and practice of historical Judaism, as contained in the Laws of Moses and expounded by the Prophets and Sages of Israel in Biblical and Talmudical writings . . .[15]

The merger was an act of consolidation and continuity, through which the work of the nineteenth-century Historical School established the basis for the Conservative Movement in the twentieth century. The reorganized Seminary became the dynamic center of the Movement. Out of this center grew the Conservative rabbinate, constituting the Rabbinical Assembly of America and the association of Conservative synagogues, which was called the United Synagogue of America. Within seven decades, a school of thought composed of individuals and synagogues with similar views, concerns and objectives, had coalesced, and the principal institutions of the present-day Conservative Movement were created.

A distinguishing aspect of the Conservative Movement continued to be its ability to unite the diverse elements within itself. When America became a center of world Jewry, and the Conservative group developed into a leading force in American Jewish life, the words of Sabato Morais were good counsel to those who had to grapple with unprecedented situations: "We must work to preserve historical Judaism, though for its sake concessions for which we are unprepared may be demanded."

Fundamentally, however, it was more than a dedication to unity which guided the destiny of the Movement. Unity was based on the organic pattern of ideas which the Historical School bequeathed to the Conservative Movement. These principles, although not formulated in any creed or doctrine but rather in a construct of values and objectives, were the centrality of Torah and learning; the Hebraic character of Judaism; the continuity of Jewish Law; the discipline of the *mitzvot;* the positive influence of the American environment on Jewish group life; and the indissoluble relationship of American Jewry to *Klal Yisrael.*

The legacy that the Historical School gave to the Conservative Movement was explained by Solomon Schechter in his Inaugural Address delivered in November 1902. He called his speech "The Charter of the Seminary."[16] "Divine, however, as the work may be—and it could certainly not be accomplished without support from heaven—it is not entirely superhuman . . ." Accepting the charge of his contemporaries, Schechter recorded the creation of his predecessors. The reorganized Seminary, the chief architect of the Conservative Movement declared, "is not a *Creatio ex nihilo*. The foundations are laid and the materials are given."

APPENDICES
A: *Biographical Sketches*
B: *Supplementary Documents*

ABBREVIATIONS

NOTES

BIBLIOGRAPHY

INDEX

Biographical
Sketches

AARON (ALBERT SIEGFRIED) BETTELHEIM

Although most of Aaron Bettelheim's contribution to the
Historical School has remained unrecorded, it was substantial.
Ideologically, he belonged to the progressive element of the
School. The lifelong friend of Benjamin Szold and the father-
in-law of Alexander Kohut, he was one of the first rabbis of
the Historical School to serve on the West Coast.

Aaron Bettelheim was born in Galgóc, Hungary, on April
4, 1830. The tradition which had existed in his family for several generations was that the oldest son become a rabbi, a
physician, or both. Young Aaron was determined to embrace
both professions. At the age of eleven, he entered the Pressburg Seminary, then pursued his studies at Leipnik, Moravia
and Prague. In Prague he studied under Judah Loeb Rapoport. Bettelheim was ordained at the age of eighteen. After
serving briefly as rabbi in a small town, he returned to Prague
to complete his secular studies, obtaining his Ph.D. from the
University in 1848. His literary abilities soon became evident
and he acted as correspondent on matters relating to Jewish
communal life for several periodicals, both in Europe and
America. For a number of years, Bettelheim wrote on Austrian affairs for London newspapers. He returned to Hungary
to become director of a network of Hebrew schools as well as
editor of a political weekly, *Elore* (Forward). In 1856 he was
appointed official translator of Oriental languages and censor
of Hebrew books in Czernowitz, the first Jew to hold such a
position in that city. In 1858 he married Henrietta Wein-
straub, the first Jewish woman schoolteacher in Hungary.

While serving at Kaschau, he edited a political weekly which, through its progressive ideas, elicited the disfavor of his congregation. His congregants' threat to impeach him prompted his emigration to America in 1867, where he was received by his friend Benjamin Szold. Called at first to a pulpit in Philadelphia, Bettelheim served also on the faculty of Maimonides College. He then moved on to Richmond, Va., where he was graduated from the Virginia Medical College, and became editor of a new German weekly, *Der Patriot.* In addition to his numerous activities, Bettelheim found time to do research in the field of medicine, but his articles were not published. When he completed his medical studies, Bettelheim was tempted to pursue his career as a physician. In the end, however, he was swayed by the entreaties of his congregation, Beth Ahabah, to remain in the rabbinate. In 1875 he received a call from congregation Ohabai Shalom to come to San Francisco.

On the West Coast, Bettelheim organized a Society for the Study of Hebrew for Christian clergymen, and became active in community work. His daughter, Rebekah Kohut, who herself contributed extensively to civic activities, reported that her father became interested in social reform after visiting a Jewish prisoner in San Quentin. He was appalled by the primitive conditions which existed in the prisons, becoming so incensed that he traveled from one community to another in California urging a revision of the penal code. In the end he met with some success.

Bettelheim was also director of the Society for the Suppression of Vice. While in San Francisco, he co-edited a weekly the *Jewish Times,* from 1880-6, which supported the Historical School.

In 1887, he returned East to assume the pulpit of the First Baltimore Hebrew Congregation. When asked by his congregation to state his religious position, he affirmed unequivocally: "When anyone with rude iconoclastic hand makes an attack upon this historical continued Judaism, I say to you, my friend, 'Stand back; you are on holy ground'" (*AH,* XXVIII [Aug. 27, 1886], 37).

As he grew older and weaker, Bettelheim availed himself of the health spas in various European resorts; he died at sea returning from one such visit on June 21, 1890. Two Catholic priests, with whom he had become acquainted on the ship, read the Jewish burial service and recited the *kaddish* as his body was lowered into the waters.

Bettelheim's writings are scattered in the general and Jewish press in America and Europe. They include articles on art, belles-lettres as well as medicine and various other subjects—including a revised edition of the Bible. In addition, many of his notes and suggestions were incorporated in the last two volumes of Kohut's *Arukh Completum.* Yet he left no complete, unified scholarly work.

To perpetuate his memory, his daughter Rebekah Kohut created the A. S. Bettelheim Foundation in Vienna as an aid to scholars in various fields of endeavor.

JOSEPH BLUMENTHAL

Joseph Blumenthal, one of the lay founders of the Jewish Theological Seminary, was born in Munich on December 1, 1834. At the age of five he emigrated with his parents to America. After completing his formal education, he went to California where he engaged in business for five years, returning East in 1859. He spent the remainder of his life in New York.

For a number of years, Blumenthal belonged to the Third Regiment of Cavalry of the New York State National Guard. However, he had a natural bent for politics and civic affairs, and he soon engaged in public life as a member of the famous Committee of Seventy responsible for the downfall of the notorious Tweed Ring. From 1873 to 1874, and again from 1888 to 1891, he served as a New York State assemblyman; and from 1893 to 1895 he was Commissioner of Taxes and Assessments in New York City.

Blumenthal participated untiringly in Jewish communal endeavors. He was trustee and president of congregation Shearith Israel; president and member of the board of directors of the Young Men's Hebrew Associations and occupied important posts in B'nai B'rith. The Jewish community knew it could depend on him to fill positions that demanded responsibility and integrity, and it did not hesitate to call on him when the need arose.

Basic to Blumenthal's Jewish communal concern was the

Seminary. He was the first president of the board of trustees of the Jewish Theological Seminary Association, a position he held from the inception of the Association in 1886 until his death, on March 2, 1901.

In his last printed report to the Association at its Seventh Biennial Convention, March 25, 1900, Blumenthal not only looked forward "to the promise of things to be accomplished," but also "backward to the assurance of things already achieved." He noted that the Seminary had already succeeded in demonstrating "that there still is vitality left to historical, traditional Judaism; that our people have not yet entirely surrendered to Radicalism and Agnosticism, and that our ancestral faith can be made to flourish if those who expound it shall be endowed with the gifts of modern culture as well as the treasures of our own literature" (*Proceedings of the Seventh Annual Report of the Jewish Theological Seminary Association* [New York, 1900], pp. 12-3).

Recognizing the creative role which Blumenthal as a layman played in the early formation of the Seminary, the student body honored his memory by associating him permanently with Sabato Morais. They named their student organization, The Morais-Blumenthal Society of The Jewish Theological Seminary.

JONAS BONDI

Jonas Bondi edited and published the weekly *Hebrew Leader* during the period (1865-74) when it became the principal literary vehicle of the Historical school of thought, the *Occident* having ceased publication in 1868 and the *American Hebrew* not coming into existence until 1879. Thus he contributed significantly to the evolving Historical School in an early phase of its development.

Bondi was born in Dresden, Saxony, on July 9, 1804. His mother was a descendant of the famed Rabbi Jonathan Eybeschütz. His father, a wealthy banker, provided his son with an excellent education, both Hebrew and secular, sending him to Prague, to the yeshiva and to the University of that city. After his studies, Bondi returned to Dresden to succeed his father in the banking business. He also became president of the congregation in his native city. Bondi was not successful in his business ventures, and in 1859, decided to emigrate to America.

Shortly after his arrival in the United States he was elected rabbi of the Anshe Chesed congregation in New York. He left the pulpit after one year, but his active concern for the spiritual development of Jewish life in the United States remained. In 1865 he purchased and assumed the editorship of the *Jewish Record*. Bondi changed the name of the periodical to the *Hebrew Leader* and modified its form. He introduced a German section in order to represent and cater to the views of the influential element of German Jews in America. Furthermore, he declared the editorial views of the *Hebrew Leader* to be those of the Historical School, despite the bitter criticism leveled at him from all sides. "We find ourselves in the very unpleasant though to us indifferent situation," he wrote in an editorial, "to be held forth as orthodox—a very false use of the term—by one party and a heterodox or reformer by the other, and this only for the reason, because the scientific system of the golden middle way . . . is hated on both sides . . ." (*HL*, VIII [June 29, 1866], 4). Bondi was determined to follow this middle path and to publish a paper which would deal fairly and objectively with both sides. He constantly emphasized his commitment to "positive historical Judaism, which we shall never give up; it contains all the ideas of the development of Judaism . . ." (*HL*, IX [Feb. 8, 1867], 4).

Bondi died in New York on March 11, 1874 after twenty-five years of service to the cause of historical Judaism in America as editor and spiritual leader.

LEWIS N. DEMBITZ

Lewis Naphtali Dembitz, distinguished American lawyer and scholar, was born in Zirke, in the province of Posen, Prussia, on February 3, 1833. He obtained the major part of his education in Europe, but came to the United States in 1849 and completed his law studies at Cincinnati. Dembitz settled in Louisville, Kentucky, practicing law there until his death in 1907. Dembitz was marked at the age of sixteen, as a young man "born for distinction." His nephew, Louis D. Brandeis, who changed his middle name from David to Dembitz out of admiration for him, described Dembitz's influence on his contemporaries as follows: "To those of my generation, he was a 'living university'" (Alpheus Thomas Mason, *Brandeis: A Free Man's Life* [New York, 1946] pp. 20, 27).

Early in his career, Dembitz was drawn into politics and was elected on the Republican platform to several important offices. An antislavery agitator, he was chosen a delegate to the Republican National Convention of 1860 which nominated Lincoln to the Presidency of the United States. Dembitz drafted the first Australian-ballot or closed-ballot to be adopted by the United States voting system, in 1888. Many of his articles on jurisprudence were printed in the general press. Some of his major legal works include: *Kentucky Jurisprudence* (1890); *Law Language for Shorthand Writers* (1892); *Law Titles in the United States* (1896); *The Question of Silver Coinage* (1896).

Although he worked with the Reform group at first, Dembitz cast his lot with the Historical School. He supported the plan of the Union of American Hebrew Congregations to establish the Hebrew Union College, and was a member of the commission on the plan of study for the college. But after the institution openly espoused the cause of Reform, and especially after the Pittsburgh Platform, he set himself wholeheartedly to the task of helping to found the Jewish Theological Seminary. In 1898 he joined H. P. Mendes in his effort to bring together the Historical School and Orthodox communities at a convention of the Union of Orthodox Jewish Congregations, in order to further solidify the position of the Seminary.

Dembitz contributed several articles, mainly on talmudic jurisprudence and on liturgy to *The Jewish Encyclopedia*. It was he who prepared the translation of the books of Exodus and Leviticus which were incorporated into the revised English Bible of the Jewish Publication Society. He also wrote for the *American Hebrew*. His volume on *Jewish Services in Synagogue and Home* was published in 1898.

When he was awarded an honorary doctoral degree by the Jewish Theological Seminary, the following editorial appeared in the *American Hebrew*:

> The Jewish Theological Seminary in conferring the degree of Doctor of Hebrew Literature upon Mr. Lewis N. Dembitz

has indeed honored itself . . . Dr. Dembitz, as we may now greet him, has been a powerful force in Conservative Judaism. Himself living up to his religious convictions, observant of much of the minutiae of rabbinical law, which some, claiming to be enlightened consider a mark of a belated civilization, Dr. Dembitz has never sought to read out of the camp those who have gone even far afield in seeking for freedom from religious restraint (*AH*, LXXV [June 10, 1904], 101).

BERNARD DRACHMAN

Bernard Drachman, the only rabbinic member of the Historical School reared in America, was born in New York on June 21, 1861. Descended from a family of rabbis, he pursued his general studies in the American school system, attending high school in Jersey City and later Columbia College. After completing his undergraduate courses at Columbia in 1882, Drachman continued his education in Germany. He studied at the University of Breslau, and received high graduation honors from the University of Heidelberg where he obtained his Ph.D. His rabbinical training was acquired at the Breslau Seminary and he was ordained by Rabbi Manuel Joel in 1885. That year he began his rabbinic career at congregation Oheb Sholom in Newark (from 1885 to 1887). During the following years he was rabbi of Beth Israel Bikkur Cholim (1887-9), Zichron Ephraim (1880-1909) and Oheb Zedek (1909-22), all in New York.

Drachman was one of the founders of the Jewish Theological Seminary and made a marked contribution to its development in the formative years as administrator and instructor. From 1887 to 1902, he taught biblical exegesis, Hebrew grammar and composition, as well as Jewish philosophy; from 1889 to 1901 he served as dean of the faculty. After Solomon Schechter's arrival, he continued as Assistant Reader in Codes from 1902 to 1908.

He published various works in English, German and Hebrew; among them: *Die Stellung und Bedeutung des Jehudah Hayyug in der Geschichte der Hebräischen Grammatik* (Breslau, 1885); a survey, "Neo-Hebraic Literature in America" (1900); and the translation into English of Samson Raphael Hirsch's *Nineteen Letters of Ben Uziel* (1899).

Active in the overall development of the Jewish community, particularly along traditional lines, Drachman was a founder of the Jewish Endeavor Society and of the Jewish Sabbath Alliance, the presidency of which he held for a number of years. He remained consistent in his traditional views during his long and effective career. From the outset his association within the Historical School was with the right wing, as he hoped always to direct the Seminary into an alliance with the group that later became the Orthodox movement in American Jewry. He devoted himself to the translation of Hirsch's *Nineteen Letters* during his incumbency as dean of the Seminary. Writing about Hirsch in his introductory biographical sketch, but at the same time speaking his own mind and ambition, Drachman said:

> He covered orthodox Judaism with glory by demonstrating that the old synagogue ritual, so bitterly attacked and decried, not only best expressed the true spirit of Judaism, but could be carried out in a highly dignified, impressive, and aesthetic manner. He has been accused by advocates of the so-called Radical Judaism of making the synagogue service an antiquarian show. This accusation, is however, utterly superficial. Whatever of the antique his synagogue service presented was due, not to his inception, but to the laws which, as a true Israelite, he was bound to hold sacred and to obey. The service in radical temples is undoubtedly not at all antiquarian. It is modern, but because it is a purely modern conventional arrangement, with very much of the nineteenth century in it, but very little of Judaism and its sacred heritage of inviolable law. The credit of having boldly taken his standpoint within, not without, Judaism, and having elevated and glorified it by demonstrating its intrinsic beauty and merit, and its own native adequacy for every spiritual want of humanity, will forever belong to Samson Raphael Hirsch . . . (pp. XXXIII-XXXIV. For a statement on Drachman's theological position, see *AH*, XXXII [August 26, 1887], 41).

Drachman severed his connection with the Jewish Theological Seminary in 1908, transferring to the Orthodox movement in which he was active for the rest of his life. He died on March 12, 1945. His autobiography, *The Unfailing Light,* appeared posthumously. It furnishes us with a vivid portrait of the American Jewry of the last few generations, especially of the Orthodox movement.

MOSES AARON DROPSIE

In bequeathing the Dropsie College for Hebrew and Cognate Learning to the American Jewish community for the advancement of modern Jewish scholarship, Moses A. Dropsie formulated his testament of faith "that the meridian sun of the golden age of Spanish-Jewish literature may again shine in the United States, where every avenue to learning and every path to distinction and honor are open to all, regardless of condition, sex or color." (*On Deform in Judaism ...*" p. 7). Influenced by the spirit of his teachers and associates in the Historical School, but primarily guided by his own deepest convictions, Dropsie gave his estate to found an institution— later to be called after his name by decision of the trustees— for instruction in Hebrew and cognate languages and their respective literatures as well as "Rabbinical learnings and literature."

Moses Dropsie was born on March 9, 1821 in Philadelphia, the child of a Jewish father and a Christian mother. His parents, who had come from Holland, allowed the children to choose their own religion. Moses studied at a private Christian academy, but when fourteen years old formally embraced Judaism. His knowledge of Hebrew subjects was taught him by Isaac Leeser. The extent of Leeser's influence upon him and Dropsie's respect and esteem for his teacher are expressed in the "Panegyric on the Life of Isaac Leeser," which he later wrote. Dropsie engaged himself in the jewelry business, but at the age of twenty-seven began to study law. He joined the office of Benjamin Harris Brewster, one of Philadelphia's renowned lawyers and later attorney-general of the United States. In 1851, Dropsie was admitted to the Bar in Philadelphia, and in 1856 he was qualified for practice before the U.S. Supreme Court. Within a short time he became a successful lawyer, scholar of the law and civic figure.

Dropsie helped develop the street railway system in Philadelphia and was president of two of its companies. In 1870 he was elected chairman of a commission to build a bridge across the Schuylkill River. He also took an active interest in political affairs, and in 1852 was a candidate of the Whig Party for mayor of the Northern Liberties District of Philadelphia.

He was a founder in 1856 of the Republican Party in the State of Pennsylvania and remained one of its staunchest supporters and a vigorous opponent of slavery.

Dropsie translated and edited Ferdinand Mackeldey's Handbook of the Roman Law in 1883. In 1890, he published *The Life of Jesus From and Including the Accusation until the Alleged Resurrection,* analyzing the trial from a legal position and showing his command of both Jewish and Roman Law. He also published a work on *The Roman Law of Testaments, Codicils and Gifts in the Event of Death (Mortis Causa Donationes),* and began a study on the *History of Religious Liberty.*

Always involved in Jewish life, Dropsie was a member of the Board of Adjunta of Mikveh Israel and a contributor to the various charities. He was president of the Philadelphia branch of the Alliance Israélite Universelle from 1883, for the needs of the Russian immigrants concerned him deeply. His major interest, however, was Jewish education. Dropsie devoted himself to the Hebrew Education Society for more than forty years, being one of its founders and serving in the diverse capacities of secretary, vice-president and president. In 1894 he was elected an Honorary Director for Life. He was president of the board of trustees of Maimonides College from its inception in 1867 to its closing in 1873, and of that of Gratz College from 1893 until his death on July 8, 1905. According to Cyrus Adler, the final impetus for creating the Dropsie College was given him as a result of the convention of the Central Conference of American Rabbis held in Rochester in the summer of 1895, where it was resolved that all post-biblical Jewish literature had no binding authority. Dropsie was moved to write an essay *On Deform in Judaism and on the Study of Hebrew* in which he deplored the ignorance of spiritual leaders of the community and their irreverence for Jewish tradition which could lead to such extreme positions. (In Dropsie's use of the term "deform" as applied to Reform, Leeser's influence is seen.) He deemed the need to preserve and develop Jewish learning imperative and the creation of the Dropsie College resulted—a lasting memorial not only to his name, but to the understanding and commitment of Moses A. Dropsie to Judaism in America.

HENRY HOCHHEIMER

Henry Hochheimer, one of the rabbinic "forty-eighters," emigrated to America in 1849 and settled in Baltimore. He allied himself to the progressive wing of the Historical School, collaborating with Szold and Jastrow in 1871 in the revision and second editing of the *Abodat Israel* prayer book in the German translation.

Hochheimer was born in Ansbach, Middle Franconia, on October 3, 1818. His father, Rabbi Isaac Hochheimer, destined him for a rabbinical career. In 1835, Henry entered the *gymnasium* at Augsburg, and in 1844 received his doctorate from the University of Munich. His early Hebrew training was given to him by his father and grandfather, and he later studied under Rabbis Guggenheimer and Aub. From 1844 to 1849 he served as his father's assistant in Ichenhausen. He participated in the Revolution of 1848 both as soldier and writer of political essays. Several of his articles aroused the disfavor of the authorities and he was forced to leave the country.

After emigrating to America in 1849, he was offered the pulpit of Nidche Israel (Baltimore Hebrew Congregation), the oldest congregation in Baltimore. In this post he succeeded Rabbi Abraham Rice, who had led the congregation according to Orthodox rules. Hochheimer immediately identified himself with the ideological position of Benjamin Szold and Marcus Jastrow in their struggles with Orthodoxy and radical Reform. Nevertheless, he maintained close contact with the Reform group, even joining some Reform rabbis on one occasion during the Civil War in a public protest against the Board of Delegates, claiming that the Board did not represent all Jews.

In his congregation, Hochheimer attempted to introduce several innovations into the service, among them Confirmation for boys and girls. Most of the members of the congregation agreed to his proposed changes, but a strong, organized minority was opposed to them and even threatened to bring the rabbi to court. Hochheimer left the congregation and in 1859 became rabbi of the Fell's Point Hebrew Friendship congregation where he served until 1892. Later he was made rabbi emeritus of the congregation.

Hochheimer was known for his learning and for his mastery of classical German. He made frequent contributions to the Jewish press, especially to the *Allgemeine Zeitung Das Judentums,* and to *Die Deborah* of Isaac Wise. Several of his sermons appeared both in pamphlet form and in anthologies. He was also the author of a journalistic essay, "Die Napolieniden in Amerika." Hochheimer died on January 25, 1912.

SAMUEL MYER ISAACS

Samuel Myer Isaacs filled a major role in the early years of the Historical School. He was not a pathfinder in the manner of Leeser and Morais, but he was their firm associate. Interpreting their ideals and plans in New York City in a national publication, the *Jewish Messenger,* Isaacs supported Leeser in all his endeavors; and after Leeser's death he worked closely with Morais.

Isaacs was born in Leeuwarden, Holland, on January 4, 1804, one of five brothers of whom three others also chose rabbinical careers. All received their early training from their father, who was originally a banker but had entered the rabbinate when the family removed to England after the Napoleonic invasions of 1813-4. Beyond this home education, Isaacs was self-taught, neither attending nor graduating from any insitution of learning, Jewish or general. His intellectual curiosity and diligence and the vast and diversified knowledge he acquired won him respect and recognition. Appointed principal of a charitable and educational institution, Neve Tsedek, in West Norwood, London, Isaacs remained in that position until 1839, when he accepted the call of the trustees of congregation B'nai Jeshurun to come to New York. In this Ashkenazi congregation, he assumed the double function of Preacher and Reader, or *hazzan.* Isaacs was the first rabbi to be invited to preach regularly in English in a synagogue in America. An eloquent and practiced speaker, his sermons attracted large crowds to the synagogue, including many interested Christians.

For several years, B'nai Jeshurun had been torn by internal dissensions. In 1845, one of many disputes in the congregation gave rise to a rift which prompted some of the members to found a new house of worship, Shaaray Tefila. Isaacs was chosen to serve as its spiritual leader, a post he retained from 1846 until his death.

Throughout his career, Isaacs remained committed to the traditional interpretation of Judaism, and to the penetration of that view into the rank and file of American Jewry. He stated his program clearly and succinctly:

> In order that I may be properly understood, I will first define my position . . . My object is . . . to prove, from facts, that our system of worship, apart from its *temporalities,* is the best of all systems; and to adduce evidence that adding or diminishing, abrogating or altering our form of prayers, handed down to us from the Men of the Great Synod, *Anshe Knesset ha-Gedolah,* and other saints of a later date, at the will or caprice of men, who, however well-intentioned, are yet tinctured with the spirit of the age, and not capable of judging correctly or dispassionately—that reforms so instituted—will lead to inevitable ruin on our polity, and tend to unfetter the chain by which we have ever been riveted in union and in love . . . (*Occ,* II [Sept., 1844], 284).

This thought Isaacs expressed again and again in articles, addresses, sermons, and in action. He was a regular contributor to the press, notably to the *Asmonean,* edited by Robert Lyons, and to Leeser's *Occident.* In 1857, together with his sons, he founded the *Jewish Messenger,* which became a platform aiding particularly the right wing of the Historical School while staunchly opposing Reform. All the proceedings of this venture were donated to Jewish charitable organizations.

Isaacs' manifold activities on behalf of the American Jewish community covered a wide range of accomplishments. He was a pioneer in the establishment of Mount Sinai Hospital (1852), the Jewish Theological Seminary and Scientific Institute (1852), the Hebrew Free School Association (1864), Maimonides College (1867), the United Hebrew Charities (1873), and other local and national institutions. The urgent needs of Jews in other countries and Palestine were also his concern. He was one of the founders of the Board of Delegates of American Israelites (1859), and in 1853 had played a key role in the organization of the North American Relief Society for Indigent Jews in Jerusalem and Palestine. He continued to collect money and to work closely with Moses Montefiore on Palestine projects. His sons, especially the eldest, Myer Samuel Isaacs, collaborated in many of these activities.

Deeply involved in civic and social affairs of the total American community, Isaacs was strongly opposed to slavery and befriended and supported the Abolitionists. His congregation, however, insisted that he refrain from using his pulpit to express political views. When Lincoln's body was carried to New York, Isaacs was chosen as one of the two ministers to participate in the funeral services. He was also a close friend of Ulysses S. Grant.

As he grew older and therefore unable to carry on all his duties, his congregation urged him to engage an assistant. Wary lest such help might bring about ideological deviation from the stand of the Historical group, Isaacs at first opposed these wishes, but ultimately had to comply. His fears proved true. In 1874, an invitation was extended to Frederick de Sola Mendes to come from England to accept the post. Shaaray Tefila remained within the confines of the Historical School throughout Isaacs' lifetime, and during part of Mendes' spiritual leadership, but it later turned toward Reform. Isaacs retired in 1877; he died on May 19, 1878.

MARCUS JASTROW

Among the rabbinic members of the Historical School, few combined so felicitously the qualities of scholar, teacher and preacher as Marcus Jastrow. He exemplified for mid-nineteenth-century American Jewry the dignity of Jewish learning and the responsibility of rabbinic leadership. In the words of Solomon Schechter, Jastrow was a *komah shelemah*, a harmonious personality.

Born in Rogasen, Posen, Prussian Poland, on June 5, 1829, Jastrow received an excellent formal Jewish and general education: he studied at the *gymnasium* in his native city and in Posen, graduating as valedictorian. He then attended the Universities of Berlin and Halle, earning his doctorate from the latter institution in 1855. His Jewish studies were undertaken under Rabbi Moses Feilchenfeld—by whom he was ordained in 1853—and under other rabbis in Berlin, among them Michael Sachs, who deeply influenced him. His ordination was confirmed in 1857 by Rabbi Wolf Landau of Dresden.

Jastrow taught briefly at Michael Sachs' school in Berlin, and in 1858 Dr. Heinrich Graetz helped him get an appointment as preacher at the German congregation of Warsaw. When, in 1861, Poland arose in insurrections against the Russian authorities, Jastrow joined in the demonstrations and delivered patriotic addresses from the pulpit. As a result, he was seized in 1862 and imprisoned for three months. Only his German citizenship saved him from certain exile to Siberia and he was deported to Germany. He stayed in Manheim until the edict against him was lifted and he could return to Warsaw. In 1864 he served in Worms where he composed a series of historical lectures, *Vier Jahrhunderte aus der Geschichte der Juden* (Heidelberg, 1865).

In 1865, congregation Rodeph Shalom of Philadelphia invited him to come to America as its rabbi at the then considerable annual salary of $4,000. He arrived the following year, and was received with acclaim.

Jastrow's thirty-seven years in America were replete with fruitful activity in numerous areas—communal, religious and scholarly. Three years after his arrival he was invited to open the session of the House of Representatives in Washington, D.C. In Philadelphia, he took a prominent part in the founding of the United Hebrew Charities and the Jewish Foster Home. He helped organize the local Young Men's Hebrew Association and was on the central board of the Alliance Israélite Universelle. In 1890, appalled by the cruelties perpetrated by the Russian government and remembering the sufferings of his own youth, he was moved to write a letter to the czar asking him to abolish the punishment of exile to Siberia.

His work in his congregation was filled with difficulties. Rodeph Shalom had originally been Orthodox but, under the impact of changing conditions and membership, began to veer toward Reform. When Jastrow assumed leadership he conceived as his main task to prevent the congregation from becoming entirely Reform and to hold it within the confines of historical Judaism. While he was more permissive than other rabbis in the Historical School, Jastrow taught that the seeds of historic Judaism had to be planted from within and that apathy could be countered only by a constructive program. He devoted his time and energies to education within the congregation. However, he was not successful in stemming the Reform tide. His early concessions in the modification of ritual and practice were a source of anguish to him in his later years. In 1892 a Reform rabbi, William Berkowitz, who had graduated from the Hebrew Union College, was appointed in his stead and Jastrow was made rabbi emeritus. In his farewell sermon, Jastrow was moved to reveal his bitterness and disappointment at the congregation, rebuking the people for their laxity, indifference and commercialism in matters of religion. (See "Farewell Sermon," *A Warning Voice* [Philadelphia, Nov. 27, 1892].)

In his scholarly works, Jastrow met with far more gratification. He was on the teaching staff of Maimonides College, serving as professor of Talmud, Hebrew philosophy and Jewish history, and as provost after Leeser's death. He headed the committee organized in 1871 to re-establish the first Jewish Publication Society under the auspices of the Board of Delegates. From 1895 until his death in 1903 he was editor-in-chief of the English version of the Bible projected by the third Jewish Publication Society and he translated the book of Job. In 1900 he became editor of the Department of Talmud of *The Jewish Encyclopedia*. He took part in the founding of the Jewish Theological Seminary and served on its advisory board in charge of examining applicants for admission. His chief work, which had demanded of him twenty-five years of labor was the monumental compendium, *A Dictionary of the Targumim, the Talmud Babli and Yerushalmi, and the Midrashic Literature* (London and New York, 1903), an indispensable tool in the study of rabbinical literature. Solomon Schechter called it a most thankless task, "for dictionaries belong to that class of literature which is mostly studied but rarely quoted."

One of Jastrow's last acts before his death, on October 13, 1903, was to come to New York to participate in the dedication exercises of the new building of the Jewish Theological Seminary.

ALEXANDER KOHUT

In the course of the decade Alexander Kohut lived in America, he made a lasting contribution to American Judaism. By the power of his erudition, conviction, vision and persuasiveness, he joined together the traditionalist and progressive elements in the Historical School, emerging as their leader and ideologist in the establishment of the Jewish Theological Seminary.

Born on April 22, 1842, in Felegyhaze, Hungary, to a learned but poor father, Alexander Kohut was not taught to read and write until his ninth year. The family then moved to the town of Kecskemet where he received his first instruction, at the local Grammar school. His Jewish studies were taught him by Rabbi Fishman and Prof. Heinrich Deutsch, the principal of the school, who was later associated with the Seminary at Budapest. Kohut studied Talmud with Rabbi Gershon Lovinger. Despite his late start, Alexander's brilliance and diligence both in Hebrew and secular studies advanced him to the third year of the *gymnasium* by the time he was thirteen.

The idea for the *Arukh Completum* came to him in that very thirteenth year when he could not find certain talmudic terms in the *Arukh* compiled by Moses Landau. Kohut then vowed that he would some day write a complete lexicon. The tale of this decision is told by Kohut in a most interesting autobiographical document, "A Chapter from My Life— The Origin of the Arukh Completum" (*AH*, LII [Dec. 2, 1892], 147-8). When he was nineteen, Kohut went to Breslau to attend the Seminary and was ordained in 1867. He had obtained his doctorate in Oriental languages from the University of Leipsig in 1864.

In his last year at the Breslau Seminary, Kohut began to preach during the holidays at Tarnowitz. Shortly before graduation he was appointed to the pulpit in Stuhlweissenburg, Hungary. While there he was named county superintendent of schools by Baron Joseph von Eötvös, becoming the first Jew thus honored. He also served as Secretary of the Congress of Jewish Notables in 1863. In 1872 he was called to be chief rabbi of Fünfkirchen where he remained for eight years. There he began to compile his lexicon in German. He accepted a post in Grosswardein, all the while continuing his scholarly work. Four volumes of his *Arukh* were published during his four years there. The Hungarian prime minister, Koloman von Tisza was so impressed by Kohut that he had him elected to the Hungarian Parliament as representative of the Jews. Kohut never took his seat because he was called to America.

Kohut's reputation as rabbi, author, scholar and educator had preceded him to America, where he had been invited on several occasions. Upon his arrival in the United States in May, 1885, he was given an enthusiastic welcome by the Jewish community, and greeted as a "new light in Israel." Light was precisely what was most needed in those days, for as Alexander Kohut wrote, "it was a period of white heat" in the controversy between the traditionalists and Reform. Kohut became involved in this struggle even before he could settle down in America and learn the specific problems of his congregation. The Kohut-Kohler debates became the ideological battleground. Out of this debate came Kohut's volume on *The Ethics of the Fathers* (New York, 1885), in which he established the position of the Historical School.

To his congregation, Kohut brought the example of a rabbi who was eloquent in the pulpit but even more eloquent in his scholarship and in his emphasis on the daily pursuit of Jewish study. "If our congregations could only form a Union and our Rabbis did not devote themselves exclusively to preaching sermons, these Institutions could increase their usefulness" (p. 100). Through his teaching Kohut tried to face the difficult task of leading his congregation back to more traditional practices which it had given up under the guidance of his predecessor, Dr. Adolf Huebsch.

Kohut remained primarily the scholar and teacher. He finished the *Arukh Completum* in the United States in 1889, which Schechter later described as "the greatest and finest specimen of Hebrew learning ever produced by a Jew on this continent." Until the very last years of his life, when sickness overtook him, he continued to teach his classes at the Seminary as professor of Midrash and Talmudic methodology. Even as he suffered in his final illness, his students came for instruction at his bedside.

Kohut always carried with him some of the earth of Eretz Yisrael. It was his wish to end his days in Eretz Yisrael as his father and father's father had done before him, but this wish was denied him. He died on May 25, 1894. In his will he requested that on the anniversary of his death his children should perform some good deed, and that some poor rabbinical student should be helped, thus fulfilling the teaching that "the memory of the righteous should be for a blessing." This testament was carried out literally by his wife Rebekah Kohut and his children.

ISAAC LEESER

Pioneer rabbi, teacher, and author, organizer of American Jewry, Isaac Leeser was the model of the new type of spiritual leader who emerged on the American scene. He was born in Neuenkirchen, Westphalia, Germany, on December 12, 1806. When he was eight years old, his mother died and his father moved to Dulmen, near Münster, where the child was reared by his grandmother. There he began his schooling and showed great promise. His first teacher was Rabbi Benjamin Cohen, a native of Amsterdam and himself a student of the famed Rabbi Ezekiel Landau of Prague. At the age of fourteen, Leeser was orphaned of his father and he then came under the influence of his second teacher, Abraham Sutro, the chief rabbi of Münster and Mark, who had proven himself an opponent of Reform in his polemical work, *Milhamot Adonai*. Leeser's secular education was obtained at the *gymnasium* of Münster. He came in intimate contact with Christians, for despite the political conditions in the German provinces which made life difficult for Jews, the college was relatively free of anti-Semitism.

In 1824, his uncle Zalma Rehiné invited him to come to America, to live and work with him in Richmond, Virginia. While engaged in his uncle's business, Leeser found time to study English and to assist the Reverend Isaac B. Seixas teach religion to the younger members of the Richmond congregation. In 1825, an article defamatory to the Jews appeared in the *London Quarterly* and was reprinted in a New York newspaper. Leeser's rebuttal was printed in the Richmond *Whig* and incorporated in 1834 in his first original published work, *The Jews and the Mosaic Law*. These defensive articles attracted wide public notice. In 1829, the Sephardi congregation, Mikveh Israel of Philadelphia, elected him its *hazzan*.

His incumbency marked the start of the period of intensive activity which characterized his entire life. Leeser was the first to introduce the regular English sermon into the synagogue service, considering the sermon as a positive instrument of education. At first this practice met with opposition, and he only preached occasionally and after the service so as to allow those who wished to leave to do so. After a number of years, the members of the Adjunta were won over and sanctioned him to preach every Sabbath. Gradually the custom spread in congregations throughout the land.

Desiring to extend his thoughts beyond the sphere of the congregation, Leeser founded the *Occident and Jewish Advocate* in 1843. During the twenty-five years of it existence, the pages of the *Occident* were replete with articles on religion, Jewish history and secular subjects, translations from the German and Hebrew, discourses and sermons, and news items describing the activities of congregations and societies all over the United States. Leeser acted as editor, chief contributor, publicity agent, bookkeeper and often as Hebrew typesetter since there were no setters capable of reading Hebrew.

Experience taught Leeser what difficulties lay in the path of every author who wished to publish his own work. He therefore founded the first Jewish publication society in America. As translator, editor and publisher, Leeser brought important works to the attention of the American Jewish community. In 1837 he translated the Sephardi prayer book and in 1848, when the influx of German immigrants warranted it, he did the same for the Ashkenazi rite. In 1850 he translated Rabbi Joseph Schwartz's *Descriptive Geography of Palestine*. His crowning achievement, however, was the translation of the Bible. Seventeen years of diligent labor were spent on this. The Bible was published in 1845 and became the accepted English version among American Jews for more than half a century.

Despite Leeser's pre-eminence in American Jewish life, his relations with his congregation became strained, and in 1850 he severed his relations with Mikveh Israel. For seven years Leeser devoted himself wholly to his literary work, then yielded to the entreaties of his friends who had formed the congregation Beth El Emeth to become their *hazzan*, a position he retained until his death.

Leeser was a bachelor and lived a lonely life. His salary was a meager one; the proceeds from the *Occident* and from his other writings never covered even the publishing costs. Leeser died on February 1, 1868. His death was a serious loss to American Jewry. The opening of Maimonides College, which he headed, some very few months before his death, caused him unbounded joy. It was the fulfilment of a lifelong aspiration. Leeser's works in virtually every area of Jewish cultural life established him as one of the master builders of American Judaism.

FREDERICK DE SOLA MENDES

Frederick de Sola Mendes served as spiritual leader of congregation Shaaray Tefila for a period of forty-six years, from 1874 until 1920, when he was appointed rabbi emeritus. During these years, he moved the congregation gradually from its position at the right of the Historical School (under Samuel M. Isaacs' leadership) to identification with Reform.

Until the turn of the century, both rabbi and congregation remained committed to historical Judaism, lending their strength and prestige to the evolving Conservative Movement. De Sola Mendes had been influential in the decision to withdraw the Historical group from the Hebrew Union College. Yet, with the passing years, younger men joined the congregation and demanded changes in the ritual and relaxation of the *mitzvot*. De Sola Mendes, who from the start had allied himself with the left wing of the Historical School, modified his own viewpoint even further. Like his younger brother, Henry Pereira Mendes, Frederick severed his connection with the Historical group after Schechter's arrival. Whereas his brother joined the Orthodox group, he turned to Reform.

A key to De Sola Mendes' seeming ambivalence is his concept of "Conservative Reform." He led his congregation by this standard—that is to say, by the view that in matters of Jewish Law and ritual, "it is only experience that can decide —not the experience of a bygone generation, but of the one that is present to be legislated for" (*AH*, LVII [June 21, 1895], 161-2). Therefore, even when he was identified personally and congregationally with the Historical School, De Sola Mendes always sought the association of the Reform element. Significantly, the rabbi-scholar whom De Sola Mendes preferred to speak at the 25th anniversary of his ministry in 1902—the year Schechter arrived at the Seminary —was Kaufmann Kohler.

Frederick de Sola Mendes was born on July 8, 1850, in Montego Bay, Jamaica, British West Indies. His father, Abraham Pereira Mendes, a descendant of David Pereira Mendes who had fled the Inquisition, was *hazzan* of the Sephardi congregation. On his mother's side, De Sola Mendes traced his ancestry to Isaiah Meldola of thirteenth-century Toledo. When Frederick was a year old, his family moved to Birmingham, England. There they remained until 1858 before going on to settle in London. He studied at the Northwick College for Jewish Studies founded by his father, and received a B.A. degree in 1869 from London University. He then attended the Univeversity of Breslau and obtained his Ph.D. from the University of Jena in 1871. In 1873 he was graduated from the Jewish Theological Seminary at Breslau. Upon his return to England, the Sephardi chief rabbi, Benjamin Artom, licensed him to preach, and he began his ministry at the New Synagogue, Great St. Helen's, London. During that year, he was invited by congregation Shaaray Tefila of New York to come serve as Isaacs' assistant and assumed his new office in January 1874. When Isaacs withdrew from the ministry because of ill health, De Sola Mendes succeeded him.

De Sola Mendes' contribution to American Jewry did not confine itself to congregational leadership. His work in the field of literature and journalism was of equal importance. In 1876 he founded the *Independent Hebrew*. This venture was short-lived, and he then inspired the founding of the *American Hebrew* in 1879, the Historical School's principal organ, serving as its leading editor during the first six years of its existence and contributing to it regularly. He belonged to the Editorial Committee for the new English version of the Bible of the Jewish Publication Society and he himself translated the book of Deuteronomy. In 1901 and 1902 he was editor of the *Menorah Monthly*. From 1900 to 1902 he served on the staff of *The Jewish Encyclopedia* as revising editor and chief of its translation department. Likewise he contributed to *Johnson's Encyclopedia* and to *The Encyclopedia Americana*.

His published volumes include *Defence, not Defiance: a Hebrew's Reply to the Missionaries* (1876); *The Child's First Bible* (first edition, 1877); *Outlines of Bible History* (1886); *Synagogue and School: Hymns, Songs & Religious Memoranda for Jewish Congregations* (1887) and several translations from the German.

De Sola Mendes was active in social and community work. He was one of the founders of the agricultural colony of Vineland, N.J., for Russian immigrants. He was on the Executive Board of the Jewish Ministers' Association of the Atlantic Coast, the forerunner of the Central Conference of American Rabbis. He died on October 26, 1927, terminating a career of almost fifty-four years of rabbinic, educational and literary labors for the Jews of America.

HENRY PEREIRA MENDES

In the forefront of the leaders of the Historical School for some thirty years, and a co-founder of the Jewish Theological Seminary, Henry Pereira Mendes was Acting President of the Seminary from the death of Sabato Morais in 1897 until the appointment of Solomon Schechter in 1902. Mendes then severed his ties with the School and fully associated himself with the Union of Orthodox Jewish Congregations whose formation he had promoted in 1898. In this shift, Mendes, like Bernard Drachman, was consistent, for even as a leader of the Historical School, he had been the foremost spokesman for its traditional sector.

H. Pereira Mendes was born on April 13, 1852, in Birmingham, England. The younger brother of Frederick de Sola, Henry also was deeply influenced by the religious atmosphere of their home. At his Bar Mitzvah ceremony, Henry solemnly dedicated himself to the service of God and the Jewish people. After completing his studies at Northwick College he went on to University College in London, while pursuing his Hebrew studies under his father and the Reverend H. L. Harris.

In 1874 when the Sephardi chief rabbi, Benjamin Artom, offered him the choice of serving as rabbi in St. Thomas, Danish West Indies, or in the new Sephardi congregation in Manchester, his choice fell upon the latter. He served in Manchester until 1877, when congregation Shearith Israel of

New York invited him to act as assistant to its rabbi, Jacques Judah Lyons. When Lyons, who had headed the congregation for approximately forty years, died some months later, Mendes became head of the congregation.

In those decades of the nineteenth century, Reform was making prodigious strides and even the Sephardi synagogues were gradually attracted to it. Some members of Shearith Israel tried to prevail upon Mendes to introduce changes in the liturgy and ritual, but they found their rabbi adamant in his stand to preserve traditional Judaism. During this period of struggle, thinking that he might perhaps be compelled to leave the rabbinate because of his unwillingness to compromise, Mendes took up the study of medicine, graduating from the medical school of New York University in 1884. His fears were without foundation for Shearith Israel remained bound to its traditions as formerly.

Mendes was an excellent teacher. Soon after his arrival he began to open classes in which he himself taught Hebrew, Jewish history and literature. He supervised the Polonies Talmud Torah attached to the congregation. The education of children especially interested him and he composed many volumes of poetry and stories for them. In the *American Hebrew*, which he had helped to found, he maintained a special column entitled "Stories about the Bible but not in the Bible." In addition, he translated well-known nursery rhymes into easy Hebrew verse.

His interest in education prompted him to be among the founding group of the Jewish Theological Seminary. The preparatory meetings were held in the rooms of his own synagogue. There, the Seminary was formally opened in 1887, and classes were held for a whole year. Mendes served as president of the Seminary's advisory board and as professor of Jewish history. In 1904 the Seminary awarded him the honorary degree of Doctor of Divinity.

Mendes was constantly engaged in humanitarian and social-welfare activities. Among his accomplishments may be noted the Montefiore Home for Chronic Invalids (later the Montefiore Hospital), which was founded at his initiative in 1884 as a concrete means to celebrate Moses Montefiore's approaching centenary; the Horeb Home and School for Jewish Deaf-Mutes, which he expanded in 1908 to the Jewish Institution for the Improved Instruction of Deaf-Mutes; the Jewish branch of the Guild for Crippled Children founded in 1901 and many other projects.

In the religious domain, Mendes was the spokesman of the Sephardi Jews in the United States and he encouraged them to be proud of their heritage. In 1881, the historic congregation of Newport, R.I.,—closed since 1791—began to reorganize, and both Mendes and his congregation offered their help, lending Torah scrolls and other ceremonial objects to the synagogue to make possible the conduct of regular religious services. A year later, Mendes' father, Abraham Pereira Mendes, was called from England to assume the pulpit of the new house of worship.

Pereira Mendes established relations with synagogues in Central and South America. In 1925, he went to St. Thomas, to the congregation whose ministry he had been offered forty-eight years before, to revive the Sephardi community of the island. He established regular services, organized a religious school and adult study groups, and sent sermons for every holiday. His influence was also felt in Cuba, when he intervened before the United States government to allow the Jewish community of Havana to purchase a cemetery. Mendes was one of the founders of the New York Board of Ministers, serving first as its secretary and then as its president.

He was an ardent champion of Jewish rights, and in 1878 he was elected to the Executive Committee of the Board of Delegates of American Israelites. A dedicated Zionist, and among the first in America, he served as vice-president of the Federation of American Zionists and as a member of the Actions Committee of the World Zionist Organization at the second and third Zionist Congresses, held in Vienna and Basel in 1898 and 1899 respectively.

A prolific writer, Mendes' works include articles, textbooks, liturgical works, children's books, poems, sermons, plays and commentaries. In 1895 the Jewish Publication Society invited him to prepare the translation of the book of Amos for its projected English Bible. He also served as consulting editor of *The Jewish Encyclopedia* and was a frequent contributor of essays to the American Jewish Historical Society.

After he became rabbi emeritus of the congregation in 1920, and until his death, on October 20, 1937, Mendes continued to initiate projects in Jewish religious life in various parts of the Western hemisphere with the same dynamic spirit and zeal which had always characterized his jubilee of years and consecration to the congregation and to the wider traditional community in America.

SABATO MORAIS

Sabato Morais, Italian-born and trained rabbi, was an unflagging champion of historical Judaism in America, becoming the founding president of the Jewish Theological Seminary. Thus he successfully united the forces of counter-Reform in this country and led in the establishment of the central institution of American Conservative Judaism.

Morais was born in Livorno (Leghorn), Italy, on April 13, 1823, the third of nine children. His grandfather and father had been patriots of Italian independence and unification and belonged to the Order of Freemasons. Sabato inherited his passion for freedom and justice from his father and his love for Jewish learning from his mother, who always entertained the pious hope that he would become a rabbi. His early Hebrew education was given him by teachers in his community: Rabbis Furano and Curiat. He studied Talmud under *Haham* Abraham Baruch Piperno together with other young men destined to achieve important careers, such as Emmanuel Felice Veneziani, who subsequently became a Chevalier of the Crown of Italy and almoner of Baron de Hirsch, and Israel Costa, who was to become chief rabbi of Leghorn. When Morais was twenty-two he applied for the post of assistant *hazzan* at the Spanish-Portuguese congregation in London. Because of his inadequate knowledge of English he was not accepted, but in 1846 the same congregation did call him to direct its orphans' school.

The five years Morais spent in England were a practical and spiritual prelude to the long and distinguished service he was to give to American Jewry. His London period acquainted him with the character of a Jewish community in the Anglo-Saxon environment; during this time also he was befriended by Mazzini, the great Italian patriot who had found refuge in England; and he began a long relationship with Moses Montefiore by becoming a tutor to the family's children.

Morais arrived in America on March 17, 1851, and on April 13th he was elected *hazzan* of the Mikveh Israel congregation in Philadelphia, succeeding Issac Leeser, and remaining in this capacity until his death, forty-seven years later. During his ministry the services in the synagogue were greatly enriched by his love and knowledge of liturgical music. He would always say with pride "I am not a rabbi, I am a hazzan." Despite the honor and respect bestowed upon him, Morais' relations with his congregation were at times strained. His predecessor had left the congregation because of the tensions between the Sephardi and Ashkenazi factions. Morais, too, had to reckon with this problem and he finally prevailed upon the older, more settled Sephardi members to relinquish some of their control in favor of the others.

Morais' influence did not limit itself to the synagogue. He made his home, too, the meeting-place for young inquisitive minds. Such future leaders of American Jewry as Solomon Solis-Cohen, Mayer Sulzberger and Cyrus Adler grew under his influence. In the field of Jewish learning, Morais had the advantage of being the only ranking student in America to render the writings of Italian scholars into English. (These writings were collected by Julius H. Greenstone in his edition of Morais' *Italian-Hebrew Literature*.) He greatly admired S. D. Luzzatto, translating his *Prolegomena to a Grammar of the Hebrew Language*. Morais constantly urged the revival of Hebrew and became the accepted supporter of all literary attempts in Hebrew by Americans. He wrote several pieces himself both in prose and poetry, and enjoyed corresponding in Hebrew with students and colleagues. His contribution to biblical scholarship manifested itself in the brief work he wrote on the book of Esther and the translation of the book of Jeremiah which he completed for the Jewish Publication Society shortly before his death. He was a frequent contributor and polemicist in virtually all the leading Jewish periodicals of the day. Morais was recognized for his varied achievements in every sphere of endeavor in the Jewish and civic community when in 1887 the University of Pennsylvania conferred upon him an honorary degree of Doctor of Laws, as the first Jew to receive this distinction from that University.

Morais died on November 11, 1897. He left instructions not to eulogize him at his funeral and not to hold any memorial service in his honor. But the spontaneity of human love and feeling was not to be restrained. Among those who thronged to his funeral—citizens of Philadelphia, congregants and students—were the Russian Jews for whom he had done so much, and who served as "a guard of honor which kings might envy."

MORRIS RAPHALL

Morris Jacob Raphall came to the United States in 1849 and immediately associated himself with Isaac Leeser and S. M. Isaacs in the traditional group of the Historical School. His reputation and activity in England as orator and interpreter of Judaism to the general community placed him in the forefront of Jewish leadership. From the pulpit of the influential congregation B'nai Jeshurun in New York City, he inveighed against Reform and engaged in religious debates with its spokesmen, and his learned discourses attracted wide audiences.

Raphall was born in Stockholm, Sweden, on October 3, 1798. When he was five, both he and his brother fell gravely ill. Their father vowed that if one son were to be spared, he would dedicate him to the service of God. Morris recovered and his Jewish education began. In 1807 he was sent to Copenhagen to pursue both religious and secular studies. He later attended the Universities of Giessen and Erlangen, earning his doctorate at the latter institution. Raphall traveled to England, France, Germany and Belgium to broaden his knowledge of foreign languages and cultures, finally returning to England in 1825 to settle there for nearly a quarter of a century.

At the time that Leeser was fighting the detractors of Judaism in America, Raphall was similarly engaged in England. Not only did he fiercely combat the Society for Promoting Christianity among the Jews, but he also directed his efforts toward the enlightened Christians to bring about their better understanding of Judaism. He delivered several lectures on Hebrew poetry and on post-biblical history which achieved great success among the general population. Yet he was primarily concerned with the Jews and their own lack of knowledge of their heritage. In 1834 he published a weekly, *Gil'ad* (the Hebrew Review and Magazine of Rabbinical Literature), the first Jewish periodical in England. It contained translations of Hebrew rabbinical works from the period of the Talmud and the Middle Ages as well as the philosophical works of Maimonides and others. The magazine ceased publication in 1836, after the appearance of seventy-eight issues. In 1843, collaborating with David Aaron de Sola, he published *Eighteen Treatises from the Mishna,* the first English translation of the Mishna. He also began working on a translation of the Bible.

Raphall began to serve as honorary secretary to the chief rabbi of the Ashkenazi congregations of England, Samuel Herschell in 1840. He prepared the formal refutation in four languages to the Damascus blood libel. The following year, he was appointed rabbi and preacher of the Birmingham Hebrew congregation and director of the local Hebrew school of the community. His reputation spread throughout England. Raphall was considered the unofficial spokesman of British Jewry and the leading exponent of Judaism to the Christian world. His efforts on behalf of political rights for Jews were untiring, and he earned numerous friends and admirers in the community. His departure for America was deeply regretted.

From Raphall's incumbency in 1849, B'nai Jeshurun enjoyed the largest attendance of any synagogue in New York City. As in England previously, large numbers of Christians flocked to hear him speak. He was invited to deliver lectures on Hebrew poetry and post-biblical history before distinguished audiences of Christians and Jews in all parts of the country. In 1860 Raphall was asked to pronounce the invocation at the opening session of the House of Representatives in Washington, D.C. This was the first time such an honor had been conferred on a rabbi.

During fund-raising campaigns on behalf of the needy, in which he was always actively engaged, Raphall's words were always most effective. He was in direct contact with Moses Montefiore concerning the raising of money for the destitute Palestinian Jewish community, and the friendship formed between them yet in England became strengthened.

As a writer, Raphall was no less prolific. In 1852 he published a volume, *Ruhama, Devotional Exercises for the Use of the Daughters of Israel.* In 1856, two volumes composing a weighty *History of Post-Biblical Literature,* encompassing the period from about 420 B.C.E. until 70 C.E., were printed. In 1859, he wrote *The Path to Immortality.*

Raphall's relations with his congregation were mutually satisfactory and remained so during his whole career, except for a small incident which occurred in 1860. He had written a letter to the *Jewish Messenger* stating that he endorsed a certain candidate for political office. The trustees of B'nai Jeshurun asked him to refrain from intervening in politics as such action was not in keeping with his rabbinical duties and might even prove detrimental to the interests of Jews in general. Raphall complied with their wishes, at least until he delivered the addresses in which he explained the biblical view of slavery. The shocked responses throughout the country elicited by these addresses were a serious blow to his reputation.

In 1865 a series of personal and family difficulties, compounded by the criticism heaped upon him for his virtual espousal of slavery, left him aged and weakened. The congregation decided to ease his burden by naming in his stead Dr. Henry Vidaver, without, however, curtailing his salary. Thus a distinguished rabbinical career came to an end. The impression which Morris Raphall made on American Jewry was essentially a personal one. He died on June 23, 1868.

SOLOMON SOLIS-COHEN

Physician, communal leader, poet and translator, descendant of an American family of Sephardi lineage, Solomon da Silva Solis-Cohen was born in Philadelphia on September 1, 1857. He attended and in 1872 was graduated from Central High School, Philadelphia, and received his M.A. from the same institution five years later. While serving as teacher in the School of the Hebrew Education Society, he pursued his medical studies at the Jefferson Medical College in Philadelphia, obtaining the degree of M.D. in 1883. One year later he was appointed chief clinical assistant to the Medical Department at his alma mater.

During the next few years, he was rapidly promoted to several important positions within the college, until he became professor of Clinical Medicine in 1904. His professional attainments earned him distinguished posts in other institutions as well, such as Physician to the Philadelphia General Hospital and to the Jewish Hospital of Philadelphia (both during the period from 1887 to 1927); at Rush Hospital for Consumptives (1890-1920); trustee of the United States Pharmaceutical Convention and chairman for the decade 1910 to 1920 of its Committee on Scope, and many others. Such recognition was awarded him for his work on the treatment of typhus and of allergies, and for his discoveries in the field of endocrinology. He edited the medical journal, *Philadelphia Polyclinic,* from 1894 to 1899 and also served on the editorial board of *American Medicine* from 1901 to 1905.

Solis-Cohen was equally dedicated to the cause of Judaism. For him, there was no conflict between science and religion. He was able to serve both and achieve inner harmony. Among the original founding group of the Jewish Theological Seminary and of the *American Hebrew,* Solis-Cohen was founder and president of the Philadelphia Young Men's Hebrew Association, head of the Board of Overseers of Gratz College, and a co-founder of the third Jewish Publication Society of America. Together with Joseph Krauskopf, he called the convening session of the new Society in 1888. For sixty years he remained loyal to this undertaking, serving on its Publication and Classics committees.

One of the earliest Zionists in America, he was a delegate to the Third Zionist Congress in Basel in 1899. Even after he withdrew from the Federation of American Zionists when he disagreed with its policies and warned of the dangers of Jewish political nationalism, the needs of Eretz Yisrael did not cease to occupy his heart and thoughts. In 1929 he joined the Jewish Agency for Palestine as one of its non-Zionist members.

Despite his many taxing professional duties, Solis-Cohen found time to contribute to the general press, to medical and scientific journals and to encyclopedias. For Jewish periodicals he wrote poems, stories and critical essays. He not only wrote original poems (which were collected into a volume, *When Love Passed By and Other Verses* [New York, 1929], while others were incorporated into anthologies of American verse), but he also translated into English the works of Hebrew poets of the Middle Ages, notably of Moses Ibn Ezra, as well as portions of Spanish-Judaic literature connected with medicine.

His life was animated by love of traditional Judaism. Having studied under Sabato Morais, he was deeply influenced by him. Solis-Cohen was attached to the Sephardi ritual. He belonged to congregation Mikveh Israel, of which he also held the presidency for a number of years.

Solis-Cohen, ever conscious of his role as a kohen in the family of Jews, often spoke of the verse in which the entire people is enjoined to be "a kingdom of priests and a consecrated nation." He taught, too, that in Judaism there is no distinction between the clergy and laity, and that responsibility for Jewish knowledge fell equally upon rabbi and layman. These standards he maintained for himself and demanded of the rest of the community.

In 1939, paralysis set in and forced him to retire from active work. His mind, however, was unimpaired and as sharp as ever. Solomon Solis-Cohen, the last standard-bearer of the original Historical group, died in his ninetieth year on July 12, 1948.

BENJAMIN SZOLD

In the course of almost a half century of spiritual leadership in America, Benjamin Szold strove equally against Reform and Orthodoxy. He taught that Judaism is a way of life, not only a faith or creed, and that the development of Jewish Law is an imperative to its proper functioning. He was a motivating figure of the progressive wing of the Historical School.

Benjamin Szold was born in Nemiskert, Hungary, on November 15, 1829. His parents, the only Jews in the town, were landowners, an occupation held by the family since the days of Joseph II. Young Szold was educated under Rabbi Jacob Fischer of Shalgaw, and under Rabbi Wolf Kollin, director of the yeshiva of Werbau. At the age of fourteen, he was given the title of *morenu* by Rabbi Benjamin Wolf, his teacher at the Pressburg Seminary. Vienna, the great metropolis, then attracted him, and he pursued his higher studies there until 1848 when the authorities expelled him from the city for joining in the Revolution. From 1849 until 1855 he acted as tutor in private families, later marrying one of his students, Sophie Schaar. At the age of twenty-five, he began to study philosophy and languages at the University of Breslau, remaining until 1858. There he came under the influence of Zachariah Frankel, Heinrich Graetz and Jacob Bernays and decided to enter the service of Judaism.

In 1858, Szold applied for the vacant rabbinical post at Stockholm and he was asked to officiate in the congregation during the High Holy Days and Sukkot as a test of his candidacy. Another contender, Dr. Ludwig Lewysohn of Worms was selected. Lewysohn had also been invited to America by congregation Oheb Shalom of Baltimore but he preferred to remain in Europe and he persuaded Szold to go to America in his place.

Oheb Shalom was not disappointed in its new rabbi. Szold immediately attracted friends and sympathizers and the congregation began to enjoy a new era of influence and prosperity, growing in numbers and stature until it was one of the largest and most important in the United States. When Szold assumed the pulpit in 1859, Oheb Shalom was on the verge of becoming Reform. (Before Lewysohn, an invitation had been extended to Abraham Geiger, who refused to transfer his activities from Germany to America.) Szold was determined to lead the congregation away from Reform to a moderate, middle-of-the-way Judaism which allowed for changes and innovations in ritual practice but not in basic tenets. Szold was one of the first to understand the value of the regular sermon as a means of instruction, and from 1861 on he spoke every Sabbath in a synagogue filled to capacity.

The order and decorum of the service, as well as the form of prayers, concerned him deeply. The congregation had been using two prayer books, Wise's *Minhag America* and the traditional *siddur*. In 1863, Szold introduced his own prayer book, *Abodat Israel*, which appeared with German translation, and which saw several printings (including the English translation). It was widely adopted by congregations throughout the country. In 1871 Szold revised it in collaboration with Jastrow and Hochheimer.

Szold's sense of responsibility and leadership were felt outside of the congregation, in civic, humanitarian, as well as

Jewish communal, relief and scholarly affairs. His European liberalism found fertile ground in America. During the Civil War he strongly supported the Union and worked actively on behalf of Negro emancipation, a daring act for a rabbi in the Southern city of Baltimore. He took part in the founding of many local charitable institutions. When the refugees from Russia began to stream into Baltimore, his own home was open and material and spiritual aid were always forthcoming. He was in full sympathy with the Jewish nationalist movement and spoke on its behalf before the Zion Society of Baltimore as early as 1893.

Szold was an advocate of Hebrew education, a member of the Society of Hovevei Sfat Ever (Lovers of the Hebrew Language). Together with his daughter Henrietta, he organized a biblical poetry study group and a library for the immigrants. He contributed scholarly articles on the poetry of the Bible. His commentary on the book of Job (1886) won special acclaim for its Hebrew style and scholarship. Several of his manuscripts on the Bible were left unpublished. For his studies on the Bible, Szold was commended when the degree of Doctor *honoris causa* was conferred upon him by the Hebrew Union College. Szold died on July 31, 1902, having fulfilled to the end of his days the description given to him even in Europe in his youth: "one of nature's noblemen."

MAYER SULZBERGER

Judge in American law and scholar in the history of Judaism, Mayer Sulzberger was the foremost lay leader of the Historical School. He was called the "father of Jewish libraries in America," and his Judaica collection formed the nucleus of what was to become the Library of the Jewish Theological Seminary. Sulzberger was involved in virtually every major national cultural and religious development in American Jewish life for almost sixty years until his death on April 20, 1923. The nature of his contribution to the American Jewish community in general and to the Historical School-Conservative Movement in particular is epitomized by Louis Ginzberg's description of him as "the outstanding Jew produced in America."

Sulzberger was born in Heidelsheim, Baden, Germany, on

June 22, 1843. His mother belonged to the Einstein family from which Albert Einstein also descended. His father, Abraham Sulzberger, had been a teacher and minister of the congregation of his native town and the home atmosphere was imbued with the richness of Jewish tradition and Hebrew language. Following the revolution of 1848, the family came to settle in Philadelphia. Mayer studied in the public schools and received his B.A. in 1859 from the Central High School in Philadelphia. His Hebrew education was given him first by his father, later by Isaac Leeser and Sabato Morais. From the latter two, he drew his great love for the Bible and Hebrew, and he became their friend and devoted student. Leeser was anxious that Mayer turn to a rabbinical career, but Abraham Sulzberger guided his son to the study of law. Since Mayer finished High School at a very early age, he was advised by Moses A. Dropsie to gain practical business experience before commencing his formal studies in law. After two years, Sulzberger returned to study under Dropsie's guidance, remaining in his office for 13 years.

Sulzberger was admitted to the Bar in 1864 and quickly attained eminence in his profession. In 1895 he was elected a judge of the Court of Common Pleas No. 2 of Philadelphia County on the Republican ticket—the first Jew to hold judicial office in Philadelphia—and in 1904 he was candidate of both parties. In 1902 he became the Court's President Judge. Later, President William Howard Taft offered him the post of ambassador to Turkey but he declined the honor because he did not want to give up his judicial duties and leave Philadelphia. Sulzberger belonged to several learned societies, such as the American Philosophical Society, the American Oriental Society, the Union League, etc. In 1915 he declined reelection to the Bench in order to devote himself fully to his scholarly and public pursuits. He did accede in 1920 to Pennsylvania's Governor William Sproul's request that he be on a commission to revise the state constitution.

While yet studying for the Bar, Sulzberger taught at the Hebrew Educational Society school. At the age of twenty-four he inherited a difficult task from his master Isaac Leeser. He had to promise him that he would continue the publication of the *Occident* at least another year after Leeser's death.

Sulzberger was the founder and president of the first YMHA to be established in Philadelphia, in 1888. When the Jewish Publication Society was reorganized, he agreed to be the editor of its Publication committee. The Philadelphia *Jewish Exponent* was founded on his initiative and received his earnest support. Sulzberger was also associated with the American Jewish Historical Society. He was a founder of four institutions of higher Jewish learning: Maimonides College; the Jewish Theological Seminary, of which he was a life director; Gratz College and the Dropsie College for Hebrew and Cognate Learning.

Sulzberger was equally active in charitable organizations, giving freely of his services to the Hebrew Aid Society, a branch of the United Hebrew Charities. He was a trustee of the Baron de Hirsch Fund which established the agricultural colony in Carmel, N.J. In 1880 he became vice-president of the Jewish Hospital of Philadelphia.

Sulzberger championed the views of the Historical School. He was opposed to the Reformers but understood the factors which had brought about their rise. He criticized them often, yet he never allowed himself to repudiate them as did many of Reform's other opponents. Sulzberger deplored the apathy and ignorance of the Jewish community towards religion which had led to a confusion of values and an abdication of its rights and responsibilities, placing the whole burden of decisions upon the rabbis, who themselves were not always qualified. He summed up the situation in these words ("A Synod," Dropsie College Archives [n.d.]):

> As to American Judaism the case stands thus: Traditional Judaism in the sense in which it was understood a hundred years ago, has practically yielded . . . In short the reverence for the ancient establishment has departed.
>
> In place of this reverence there has been substituted a *sentiment* in favor of certain or uncertain theoretical and essential principles which are supposed to underlie the ancient customs. What those principles are, every clergyman assumes to decide for himself and his congregation, and the variety and confusion of their opinions lead with fatal directness to an entire indifference in the lay mind; to a despairing disbelief in the possibility of fixing any certain principles for religion in general or Judaism in particular. Catchwords are substituted for principles. Morality is said to be identical with religion and men

are told to be sober, honest and charitable and their religious duty is done. The general improvement in certain features of morality during the last century tends to obscure the mischief of such teachings. Morality after all is but a rule of conduct, a refined and purified police regulation. Religion is a rule of thought and of feeling. Individuals are worthy who act well, but mankind halts unless men think well and aspire high . . .

The primary need of American Judaism therefore is the re-establishment of reverence for the Jewish religion, for Jewish law and for Jewish institutions.

Sulzberger did not leave much material behind in writing. Most of his influence was felt directly by his gen-eration through the strong impact of his personality. How-ever, the twenty-sixth volume of the *Occident* (the last volume, which he edited), contains many editorials, learned articles and translations by him which give an adequate reflection of his vast intellectual knowledge, even at his very early age. In addition he wrote four books dealing with unexplored legal areas of ancient Jewish history: *Am-Ha-Aretz. The Ancient Hebrew Parliament* (1909), *The Polity of the Ancient Hebrews* (1912), *The Ancient Hebrew Law of Homicide* (1915) and *The Status of Labor in Ancient Israel* (1923).

AARON WISE

Aaron Wise came to America in 1873, a time when the Historical School was in crucial need of rabbinic leadership to strengthen the congregations. As the rabbi of Rodeph Shalom congregation in New York City, he fortified the builders of the School, was among the founders of the Jewish Theological Seminary, and actively advanced the cause of historical Judaism during the last decade of the past century.

Wise stemmed from a rabbinical family of several genera-tions. He was born in Erlau, Hungary, on May 2, 1844. (He took pride in the fact that his son Stephen S. also followed the rabbinical family tradition.) His father, Rabbi Joseph Hirsch Wise, chief rabbi of one of the wealthier provinces of the Austro-Hungarian empire, began to prepare Aaron for the rabbinate at a very tender age. Young Wise studied at the Pressburg yeshiva and received his rabbinical degree from the Jewish Seminary of Eisenstadt, where he had studied under Rabbi Israel Hildesheimer. He pursued his secular studies at Berlin, Leipzig and Halle, obtaining his Ph.D in 1869. He then returned to Erlau to assume the post of director of the public schools, in which task he achieved distinction and which he left to accept the position of rabbi of the important congregation of Febony. In addition to his many duties, Wise found time to edit a Yiddish-German newspaper. However, he soon felt the need for a broader field of activity and decided to come to America.

Upon his arrival in the United States, he accepted the pulpit of Beth Elohim in Brooklyn, New York, where he remained for two years. In 1875, Wise was asked by Rodeph Shalom, one of New York's influential congregations, to speak at its rededication service, and was immediately elected rabbi of the congregation, a post he held until his death. Stephen Wise described the Rodeph Shalom congregation of that time as "the last of the reform-conservative synagogues in this country." By that he meant that, while the policy was in the direction of Reform, in practice Conservatism prevailed.

In Hungary, Wise had been a staunch leader of Orthodoxy. In the United States, identifying with the Historical School, Wise attempted to bring his congregation back to the traditional fold, while yet retaining some of the Reform innovations. He reinstituted the religious school of the congregation and gave the study of Hebrew a central place in the curriculum. In 1891, Wise edited a new prayer book for the congregation, entitled *The Temple Service,* and in order to draw a larger attendance to the synagogue, he prepared special prayers for late Friday night services. Wise was an eloquent preacher. His warm personality won him numerous friends and adherents, and through his efforts, his congregation achieved special prominence.

Wise did not limit his work to congregational activities. When the leaders of the Historical School began to envisage the creation of a theological institution, he was among the first to join in the undertaking. In 1884 he began to edit a new periodical, the *Jewish Herald.* Wise also prepared a text to be used in Hebrew Schools, *Beth Ahron,* and a book of meditiations, *Mateh Ahron,* read regularly by his congregation. He devoted considerable time and energy to a volume which he did not manage to finish, *Reflections on Prophecy and the Prophets.* Rabbi Wise died on March 30, 1896.

Supplementary
Documents

PLAN OF A JEWISH PUBLICATION SOCIETY*

1. This society shall be known as the American Jewish Publication Society.

2. Its object shall be to reprint, in a cheap and convenient form, such books already in existence, as may from time to time be approved of by the publication committee; and to aid Jewish authors or gentiles writing works of interest to Israelites, to bring their respective books before the people without any risk of loss on their part, and, if possible, to grant them such compensation, according to the respective merits of their works, as the funds of the society may admit of.

3. The annual contribution to the society's funds shall be one dollar; but donations will be received, especially in the commencement, for the purpose of establishing a fund with which to commence operations. Members are likewise at liberty to give a larger annual contribution than one dollar.

4. The above annual subscription will entitle every person to the benefits resulting from the distribution of the publications hereafter to be provided for; but no one except a male Israelite of the age of twenty-one years shall be allowed to vote at any meeting of the society, or to hold any office.

5. The society shall consist of a parent society, to hold, for the present, its meetings in Philadelphia, until otherwise ordered, and such auxiliary societies as may from time to time be formed in the different cities of America.

* *Occ*, II (Feb., 1845), 525-7. (See text: Part I, Chapter 2, Note 29.)

6. The officers of the parent society shall consist of a president, vice-president, treasurer, recording-secretary, corresponding-secretary, and three managers.

7. The board shall elect three persons as a publication committee, either from themselves or the society at large.

8. Auxiliary societies are to elect each a president, treasurer, and secretary.

9. A member of any auxiliary society shall have the right to vote at a meeting of the parent society.

10. Whenever the benefit of the society can be promoted by the change, some one of the auxiliary societies shall assume the functions of the parent society, provided the change is made with the concurrence of the majority of the societies constituting the society at large.

11. All moneys obtained from subscriptions, donations, and sales of books are to be placed in the hands of the treasurer of the parent society, to be drawn out by the order of the president, as is usual in all societies.

12. The publication committee is to print nothing without having it carefully revised beforehand, and to see that nothing objectionable shall appear in the publications of the society.

13. They are to publish as often as the funds of the society will admit such works as have been approved of.

14. Members contributing one dollar per annum are to receive at least one copy of all the publications of the society, and in the same ratio for larger contributions.

15. One tenth of all the publications is to be set aside for gratuitous distribution among the poor; the remainder to be sold as above, and the proceeds to be added to the general fund.

16. Should any author obtain compensation for his works, the copyright thereof becomes the property of the society.

17. There shall be appointed three trustees, in whose names all the funds not required for the current expenses, investments, and copyrights, are to be placed; these trustees are to be removable by the society, for any misconduct in the discharge of their duties.

18. Should hereafter the society obtain a charter of incorporation, all the property vested in the trustees is to be conveyed by them to the society.

The above is a mere outline, which will, doubtlessly, require a good deal of amendment before it can be put in practical operation; still, imperfect as it is, and thrown off merely on our own responsibility, we see nothing in it to make us doubt of its being able to be carried into effect in its main features . . . We are always sufficiently ready to give charity to relieve the bodily wants of the poor; let us then once do something to relieve the spiritual wants of both poor and rich.

UNION FOR THE SAKE OF JUDAISM*

PREAMBLE

The Israelites of Philadelphia, in common with their brethren in other places of America, have long since been alive to the many evils under which they labour in the great downfall of religious observance, and the want of proper religious education among them. But deeming it their duty to leave no means untried to counteract the deplorable state of want of proper observance, and to promote a due knowledge of the blessed religion they have received from their fathers, they have resolved to propose a union of all Israelites residing in America, to effect by a common and unified effort, that which would evidently be beyond the power of accomplishing by any one of the small congregations in which the Israelites of this country are divided; they therefore offer the following suggestions, which they hope will forward greatly the desired result; in, first, establishing a competent ecclesiastical authority, agreeably to the injunction of the law in Deut. xvi. 18: "Judges and officers shalt thou appoint for thyself in all thy gates, which the Lord thy God giveth thee throughout thy tribes"; secondly, by establishing schools for general and religious education under Jewish superintendence, as commanded in Deut. vi. 7: "And thou shalt teach them diligently to thy children"; and thirdly, by promoting harmony and a concert of action among all their brethren scattered over the western hemisphere, in accordance with the lofty aspiration of the Psalmist, who says (cxxxiii. 1): "Behold how good and how pleasant it is for brethren to dwell together in unity." With these views the committee recommend the adoption of the following rules and regulations for the government and action of the Israelites in America.

* *Occ*, III (July, 1845), 176; (August), 222-7. (See text: Part I, Chapter 2, Note 32.)

Article I

The Ecclesiastical Authority

Section 1. The delegates of the different congregations, as hereinafter described, or of as many as may come into the measure, shall elect at their first meeting, or as soon after as practicable, three gentlemen of undoubted moral and religious character, who are duly learned in the written and oral law, who shall have the authority conferred upon them by their election, to act in, and decide on all cases of religious inquiry, and to determine all questions laid before them, according to the law, and the approved rabbinical authorities: the members of this Central Religious Council not to be at any time subject to any authority abroad, nor under the control of any congregation, except in cases of misdemeanour, and wilful false decisions, in which cases, one or all of such offending parties, are to be removed by the delegates of the Union as above; and a majority of the delegates present shall be required for a vote of suspension for a period of from three to twelve months, and a majority of two-thirds for a suspension for a longer period, or expulsion from office.

Sect. 2. Whenever any case for adjudication comes before any one of the Board hereby constituted, he may decide for himself only, if the emergency will not permit him to consult his colleagues; but if otherwise he is bound to consult them, either in person or in writing, before he gives any answer; in order to insure that the laws of God be properly expounded, and strictly obeyed, as far as lies in the power of the Board herewith proposed.

Sect. 3. In case a decision is made by one member in the absence of his colleagues in any emergency, the said decision must be transmitted without delay to the President of this Union, for the approbation of the other members of the Central Religious Council, and a copy of all decisions is to be forwarded to the recording secretary, as hereinafter described.

Sect. 4. The Hazanim of all the congregations of this Union, are to be ex officio associates of the Board, provided always.

that nothing is to prevent the delegates from electing a Hazan to be a member of the Central Religious Council, if he be duly qualified for the office in character and capacity.

Sect. 5. In a place where no one of the members of the Central Religious Council resides, the Hazan, or Hazanim, or other persons in whom the community have confidence, may decide in any emergency, but the decision must also at once be transmitted to the Central Religious Council for their approbation.

Sect. 6. Any party deeming himself aggrieved by the decision of any one member of the Board, or any other person acting under an emergency, may appeal to the whole Central Religious Council, whose decision by a majority shall be final.

Sect. 7. The associates as above provided, shall merely have power to speak at a meeting of the members of the Central Religious Council, but not to vote.

Sect. 8. One of the three members as above shall be the President of the Board, and shall be specially elected for this purpose by the delegates. He shall have the power to convene the Board, whenever he may deem the public good requires it, and have a general supervision of strictly ecclesiastical matters in this Union.

Sect. 9. As the authority herewith delegated is merely advisory, the Central Religious Council shall never exercise the power of excommunicating any one, for any offence whatever; nor to possess the right of summoning any individual who, in their opinion, might be guilty of any transgression of the Mosaic Law; but shall merely designate the offences which of right deprive any offender from the usual Jewish rights and privileges.

Sect. 10. The privilege of performing the marriage ceremony being the right of each congregation, the customary authority heretofore exercised by the Hazanim remains inviolate; nevertheless the party to be married has the option of selecting the Hazan or any member of the Central Religious Council to perform said ceremony.

Sect. 11. The Congregations belonging to this Union shall not elect any Shochet, who has not been examined as to qualifications by one or more members of the Central Religious Council; and it shall be the duty of the respective

Shochetim belonging to this Union, to be examined once at least in three years by one or more of the Central Religious Council, for which examination no fee whatever is to be required.

Sect. 12. No Shochet is to be suspended for frivolous reasons; and if any member of the Central Religious Council should find it his duty to exercise this prerogative, he must state the reason for so doing in writing to the person so suspended.

Sect. 13. It is expected that the Central Religious Council will watch over the state of religion, and use every proper occasion to exhort the people in sermons or lectures; and whenever any member of the Central Religious Council wishes to address any congregation, he shall have the privilege so to do, upon giving notice to the Parnass of said congregation.

Sect. 14. Whenever a new Hazan is to be elected, he must be examined as to his qualifications by one or more members of the Central Religious Council, so as to prevent any incompetent person being forced upon the respective congregations; and if any congregation should elect a Hazan who has not obtained a certificate of the Board, or who has been rejected by them, such Hazan shall not be admitted an associate of the Central Religious Council.

Sect. 15. The superintendence of the schools is herewith vested in the Central Religious Council and the above associates, and it is made their duty to report any delinquency in the teachers to the Board of Control, as hereinafter mentioned.

Article II

The Schools

Section 1. As soon as practicable, schools for both sexes are to be established in every town where Israelites reside, and the teachers are to be paid out of a common local fund, and on no account to receive any pay or fee whatever from the parents.

Sect. 2. Whatever rates for education it may be necessary to charge, are to be paid to the local treasurer of this Union, who is to pay the amount of salary which may be agreed upon, to the teachers, upon warrant of the local president.

Sect. 3. The system of education is to be strictly Jewish, and is to embrace, *a.* Hebrew reading, grammar, translation, catechism, Biblical commentaries, and at least an introduction to the Jewish Oral Law, and if possible, an elementary knowledge of the Talmud.

b. English grammar, composition, elocution, arithmetic, writing, singing, geography, universal history, history of the Jews, history of England, and history of the United States.

c. For the higher classes, in addition to the above, Hebrew composition, Talmud, general Jewish literature, Latin, Greek, French, German, Spanish, mathematics, natural history, natural philosophy, moral philosophy, political economy, and chemistry.

d. Any other useful matters to be added as occasion may require.

Sect. 4. The government of the schools is to be moral throughout, and on no account can any cruel punishment be permitted.

Sect. 5. A High School for education in the higher branches, is to be established in some central point whenever practicable, in which the branches enumerated under *c* are to be taught; and where young men are to be educated in such a manner, that they may be fit for the office of Hazan, lecturer, and teacher; and young women be educated for the high calling of female instructors; and all persons educated in our schools, are to have the preference if any vacancy occurs, for any office in the gift of this Union.

Sect. 6. No teacher to be appointed, whether Jew or gentile, who has not been examined, by one or more members of the Central Religious Council in the first instance, and afterwards by the local president, treasurer, secretary, and Hazan, as to capacity and moral worth: Provided, That the distance from one of the members of the Central Religious Council be not above 300 miles, in which latter case, the local authorities may temporarily appoint a teacher or teachers, till one of the members of the Central Religious Council visits the place, when the teacher or teachers must be examined by him; and if an Israelite, he is to be examined also as regards religious knowledge and conformity.

Sect. 7. Though it may be found requisite to charge for

education to those able to pay—yet no person, who brings evidence of his inability to pay, shall have his children or wards refused admission into our schools, provided he or she sign a pledge to send them regularly to school at least three months in the spring, and four months in the winter.

Sect. 8. Whatever regards books to be used and other regulations, is to be left to the Central Religious Council and to the Central Board of Control for their action and advisement.

Article III

The Union

Section 1. It is recommended that all regularly organized congregations in America do elect delegates to meet at Philadelphia on the 7th day of November, 1841, for the purpose of carrying the above recommendations into effect.

Sect. 2. The ratio of representation to be as follows: Every congregation numbering fifty male seat-holders or under, to send one delegate; from fifty to one hundred and fifty, two delegates; from one hundred and fifty to three hundred, three delegates; and one additional for every two hundred additional seat-holders.

Sect. 3. All votes of delegates shall be decided by the majority, under the usual parliamentary restrictions and regulations.

Sect. 4. The delegates shall be empowered to elect, in the first instance, the members of the Central Religious Council, and to fill all vacancies therein from time to time, provided always that the persons to be elected be duly qualified.

Sect. 5. They shall assemble, after the first organization, every two years, on the 4th Sunday after the first day of the Passover, and remain in session, by daily adjournments, till all the business before them be duly transacted, or postponed to another meeting.

Sect. 6. An extra meeting may be called whenever the majority of delegates, or a sufficient number of congregations entitled to send a majority of all the delegates, shall require it; in which case they are to notify the President of the Central Board of Control, who is then to issue general notices, and summon the delegation, by giving them at least *sixty* days' notice.

Sect. 7. The delegates shall be appointed by the respective congregations in the manner they may themselves direct.

Sect. 8. The delegates shall elect a President to preside over them, and a Secretary to keep the minutes, whose offices are to continue till the next general meeting.

Sect. 9. In addition to the above officers, they shall elect, at every biennial meeting,

One Vice-President,
One Corresponding Secretary,
One Treasurer,
Four Councillors,

Who, together with the President and Recording Secretary, shall constitute a Board of Control to direct the affairs of the Union in the vacation of the assembly.

Sect. 10. In addition to the above Central Board, each town shall elect a President, Treasurer, and Secretary, to take charge of all local matters and moneys for local school purposes, but it shall be their duty to report every six months in full to the Central Board of Control.

Sect. 11. The biennial meetings shall be held alternately, unless otherwise ordered; first at Philadelphia, next at New York, and lastly at Baltimore.

Sect. 12. The Central Board shall sit in Philadelphia unless otherwise ordered; and if the President of the delegation should not be a resident of the place where the Central Board meets, then the Vice-President shall act for him, unless the President happen to be present, when he has the precedence as a matter of course; the same rule applies to the Recording Secretary, whose place, in his absence for the above or any other reason, shall be supplied by one of the Councillors.

Sect. 13. The records shall always be open to every Israelite belonging to this Union who desires to inspect them, but they are never to be taken out of the possession of the Recording Secretary or his substitute; and any Israelite, as aforesaid, is to be at liberty to procure a copy of any of the records.

Sect. 14. The delegates in general assembly shall have power to deliberate on all subjects, which may tend to the general welfare of the Israelites, with the exception of matters properly belonging to legal points of the Mosaic law, which shall be left, as is reasonable, with the Central Religious Council.

Sect. 15. They shall devise ways and means to defray the expenses attending the execution of this plan, and to fix salaries and other outlays properly coming under the object of the Union.

Sect. 16. They shall not interfere directly or indirectly in the internal affairs of the congregations, except to offer their advice when any thing should be undertaken in opposition to the law and the commandment, and to judge between contending parties, if such should unfortunately arise in our congregations.

MAIMONIDES COLLEGE*

BOARD OF DELEGATES OF AMERICAN ISRAELITES, OFFICE OF THE EXECUTIVE COMMITTEE

New York, July 1st, 5627, 1867

The Board of Delegates of American Israelites have, in conjunction with the Hebrew Education Society of Philadelphia, established a college in that city, styled MAIMONIDES COLLEGE, under the charter granted to that Society by the Legislature of Pennsylvania.

The College will for the present be under the charge of seven Trustees.

Faculty

The faculty of the College, so far as appointed, consists of the following professors:

REV. ISAAC LEESER, Professor of Homiletics, Belles Lettres and Comparative Theology.

REV. S. MORAIS, Professor of the Bible and Biblical Literature.

REV. DR. M. JASTROW, Professor of Talmud, Hebrew Philosophy and Jewish History and Literature.

REV. DR. BETTELHEIM, Professor of Mishnah with commentaries, Shulchan 'Aruch and Yad ha-Chazakah.

REV. L. BUTTENWIESER, Professor of the Hebrew and Chaldaic languages and of the Talmud.

The vacant professorships will be filled before the opening of the College.

Collegiate Course.

The usual collegiate course will be pursued in addition to the Hebrew course. Students have the option of pursuing simply the Hebrew course.

The full course will embrace a period of five years, at the expiration of which the graduates who shall pass a satisfactory

* *Occ,* XXV (Aug., 1867), 228-30. (See text: Part I, Chapter 2, Note 55.)

examination and be otherwise qualified, will receive the usual degrees. Candidates for the ministry, having the proper theological knowledge, will receive the degrees of Bachelor and Doctor of Divinity.

The branches of instruction are as follows: Greek, Latin, German, French, Hebrew, Chaldaic and their literatures, the Natural Sciences, History, Mathematics and Astronomy, Moral and Intellectual Philosophy, Constitutional History and Laws of the United States, Belles Lettres, Homiletics, Comparative Theology, the Bible with its commentaries, the Mishnah with its commentaries, the Shulchan 'Aruch, Yad ha-Chazakah, Jewish History and Literature, Hebrew Philosophy and the Talmud with its commentaries.

Competent instructors in *Chazanuth* and *Shechitah* will be provided for those desiring to become Chazanim.

Admission of Students.

Candidates for admission must be able to translate with facility the historical portions of the Bible. The requisite qualifications in the other branches will be determined hereafter by the faculty.

Those not qualified to enter the College will be received in the preparatory school of the Hebrew Education Society, on the usual terms of that institution.

Tuition Fees.

Tuition fees will be one hundred dollars per annum. Board and lodging will be furnished to students for two hundred dollars additional, yearly.

Scholarships.

There are two classes of scholarships provided for students, the resident scholarship of three hundred dollars per annum, which includes board, lodging and tuition, and the regular scholarship of one hundred dollars per annum for tuition only.

Any congregation or individual contributing the sum of $300, or $100 annually, shall be entitled to nominate a student (qualified as to character and capacity) to fill a resident or regular scholarship respectively, such student to be entitled to all privileges; and any such society, individual or congregation contributing $1500 shall be entitled to a permanent regular scholarship.

Opening of the College.

The College session for the first year will commence on the fourth Monday of October 5628 (1867).

Applications for admission to the College, and offers by individuals, societies or congregations to avail themselves of the terms above laid down in regard to scholarships, should be addressed at as early a date as possible, to either of the Trustees:

MR. ABRAHAM HART, President, 430 Library Street, Philadelphia.

MR. MOSES A. DROPSIE, 29 South Sixth Street, Philadelphia.

MR. I. BINSWANGER, 241 Chestnut Street, Philadelphia.

MR. HENRY JOSEPHI, 58 Nassau Street, New York.

MR. ALEXANDER S. SARONI, 5 Barclay Street, New York.

MR. MYER S. ISAACS, 243 Broadway, New York.

MR. MAYER SULZBERGER, Secretary Board of Trustees, 29 South Sixth Street, Philadelphia.

Donations to the College Fund and Annual Subscriptions will also be received and acknowledged by either of the Trustees.

ABRAHAM HART, President,
Board of Delegates of American Israelites.

MYER S. ISAACS, Secretary,
243 *Broadway, New York.*

THE BOARD OF DELEGATES[*]

Sketch of what its Constitution ought to be.
by Mayer Sulzberger

The Israelites of the Western Continent, desiring to form a more perfect religious union, to promote uniformity in liturgy and observances, to advance religious education, and to aid the cause of Judaism generally, have adopted the following

CONSTITUTION.

Article I. — Name

Sec. 1. The union hereby formed shall be called "The Board of Delegates of American Israelites."

Article II. — Organization

Sec. 1. The Board shall be divided into two houses; the one house to be called the Rabbinical Delegates, and the other the Lay Delegates.

Sec. 2. Each house shall be further subdivided for the purposes hereinafter named, into a Committee on the Conservative Liturgy and a Committee on the Reformed Liturgy.

Sec. 3. Each religious congregation of Israelites may send one rabbinical and two lay members to the Board, and for each one hundred members and seat-holders above the first hundred, it may send an additional lay member.

Sec. 4. Each incorporated educational or charitable society may send one lay member to the Board, and for each one thousand members in addition to the first thousand, it may send an additional lay member.

[*] *J Rec,* I (Sept. 3, 1875), 5. (See text: PART II, Chapter 2, Note 54.)

Sec. 5. All the delegates from conservative congregations shall be members of the Committee on Conservative Liturgy, and all delegates from Reformed Congregations shall be members of the Committee on Reformed Liturgy in each house. They shall be placed on the rolls of such committees respectively by the Secretary of the Board. He shall be guided in so placing them only by their written credentials, which shall plainly express to which Committee they are to be assigned.

Sec. 6. Delegates hold their seats for the stated meetings to which they have been elected, and for all the special meetings intervening between such stated meeting and the next stated meeting thereafter. If delegates are elected for a special meeting, their terms expire before the stated meeting thereafter.

Sec. 7. Only recognized Rabbis shall be eligible as Rabbinical Delegates, and they shall be ineligible as lay delegates. Readers and others having inferior ecclesiastical functions, may become Lay Delegates.

Article III. — Meetings

Sec. 1. There shall be a meeting of the Board on the last Sunday in Iyar, in the year 1876, and in every third year thereafter, in such places as shall be determined by the Board; and, in case there shall be an epidemic, disease, or any other overpowering reason to render it necessary to alter the place fixed on for any such meeting of the Board, the President thereof shall have it in his power to appoint another convenient place (as near as may be to the place so fixed on) for the holding of such meeting.

Sec. 2. Special meetings of the Board may be called at other times by the President, on the request of the majority of the Rabbinical or Lay Delegates, expressed in writing. The place of holding any special meeting shall be that fixed on at the preceding stated meeting, except in case of an epidemic, disease, or some equally strong ground, in which case the President may appoint another place as near as may be to the place originally appointed.

Sec. 3. Ten Rabbinical Delegates and twenty Lay Delegates shall form a quorum of the two houses to transact business, but any smaller number may adjourn.

Article IV. — Powers

Sec. 1. The Rabbinical Delegates have the exclusive right to originate and propose, for the concurrence of the Lay Delegates, acts on the subject of liturgy and ritual observances.

Sec. 2. All such acts, when proposed by the Rabbinical Delegates, must first be put to a vote of the Committees on Conservative and Reformed Liturgies, respectively, and if two thirds of each present decide that the subject is general, and approve the same, it shall be certified as such by the Clerk to the Lay Delegates, who shall consider the same in full house. If two thirds of the number present approve the same, it shall be solemnly and formally published as binding to all congregations.

Sec. 3. If two-thirds of each of the said Committees do not decide that the subject is general, then if two-thirds of one committee decide that they will take cognizance of it, they may consider the same, and if two-thirds approve it, the Clerk of the Rabbinical Delegates shall certify the same to the Lay Delegates as approved by the particular Committee. The President of the Lay Delegates shall immediately refer the same, without action, to the Committee corresponding to that from which it has been certified, and if two thirds of the members present of that Committee approve the same, it shall be solemnly and formally published by the Board as binding on all congregations represented in the Committee approving the same.

Sec. 4. All business other than that relating to Liturgy and observances can originate only in the Lay Delegates, and no motion of ordinance shall be adopted except with the consent of a majority of those present in each house.

Sec. 5. The Board shall, as soon as practicable, devise and carry out a comprehensive and rational plan for the primary religious education of the Israelites of this continent.

Sec. 6. The Board shall, as soon as practicable, devise and carry out a comprehensive and rational plan for the advanced religious education of the Israelites of this continent.

Sec. 7. The Board shall, as soon as practicable, devise and carry out a just and liberal method of supervising persons who are, or may be, desirous of becoming Jewish ministers, to the end that only such as are competent intellectually, morally, and religiously, may be recognized as such.

Sec. 8. The Board shall, by systematic and accurate inquiries, ascertain and collect all possible statistical information respecting the Israelites of the Western Continent, and have the same properly arranged and published from time to time. It shall also keep up communication with central Jewish bodies throughout the world.

Sec. 9. The Board shall publish such of its proceedings as may be deemed advisable, and also such matter, literary or religious, as may tend to promote the objects of its organization.

Sec. 10. The Board shall appoint an Executive Committee, composed of the President, Secretary, the Clerks of the two houses, five Rabbinical Delegates, and ten Lay Delegates, who shall attend to all routine business that may be necessary to be transacted during the recess of the Board.

Article V. — Amendments

This Constitution shall be unalterable except at a stated meeting of the Board, and all alterations shall be first proposed at a stated meeting, and made known to the several bodies represented in the Board, before they shall be finally agreed to in the ensuing stated meeting of the Board. Two thirds of the Delegates in each house must assent to carry such an amendment.

Article VI. — Officers

Sec. 1. The officers of the Board shall be:—

1st. A President, who shall be a Rabbi, and shall preside over the Rabbinical Delegates.

2nd. A Vice-President, who shall not be a Rabbi, and shall preside over the Lay Delegates.

3rd. A Secretary, who shall be a Rabbi, and shall act as Clerk of the Rabbinical Delegates.

4th. A Clerk, who shall not be a Rabbi, and shall act as Clerk of the Lay Delegates.

5th. A Treasurer, who shall receive and disburse all moneys.

Sec. 2. In the event of disability of the President during a recess, the Vice President shall act, but at the next meeting the vacancy shall be duly filled.

Sec. 3. All offices are held until the next stated meeting, or until a successor is appointed.

Article VII. — Revenue

Sec. 1. Each body represented in the Board shall pay for each representative the sum of ————dollars.

Sec. 2. For the special purposes of the Board special funds may be raised from time to time, in such manner as may be deemed advisable.

CERTIFICATE OF INCORPORATION
OF THE
"JEWISH THEOLOGICAL SEMINARY ASSOCIATION"*

WE, JOSEPH BLUMENTHAL, JOSEPH E. NEW-BURGER, NEWMAN COWEN, SENDER JARMALOW-SKI, ISAAC ROSENTHAL, ISAAC FLES, NATHAN LEVIN, Citizens of the United States of America, and of the State of New York, and residents of the City of New York, County of New York and State aforesaid being each over Twenty one years of age, and desirous of associating ourselves, with such persons as may hereafter be as member for literary and scientific purposes in conformity with and under the provisions of an act of the State of New York entitled "An act for the incorporation of benevolent, charitable, scientific and Missionary societies" passed April 12th 1848, an act amendatory thereto passed March 8th 1870, do certify that we have associated, and hereby do associate ourselves into a society to be known and distinguished in Law or otherwise by the name of the "Jewish Theological Seminary Association," that the particular business, purpose and object of such association and society will be imparting religious and moral instruction to the children of the Jewish persuasion and the training of Rabbis and Teachers for the Jewish Congregations in North America, conformably to their law, ancient doctrines and traditions confided to them by the sages of Israel, English Grammar and Literature, Moral Philosophy, Hebrew in all its branches, Biblical Lectures, the Talmud comprising the Mishna and Gemara and Jewish History and Antiquities and in the discretion of the Trustees the following languages: Latin, Greek, Spanish, French, Italian, and German; and such other languages and branches as they deem proper; and that the said Institution will be under the management and control of Fifteen Trustees; that Joseph Blumenthal, Joseph E. Newburger, Newman Cowen, Joseph M. Emanuel, Isaac

* Files of the State of New York, Albany. (See text: Part III, Chapter 1, Note 21.)

386

Fles, J. Edgard Philips, Dr. S. Solis-Cohen, Samuel Morais Hyneman, Dr. Aaron Friedenwald, Tucker David, S. Jarmalowski, Nathan Levin, David M. Piza, Isaac Rosenthal, and Samuel Jacoby shall be the Trustees of such Institution or Society for the first year of its existence; and that said Joseph Blumenthal, shall be the President; the said Dr. Aaron Friedenwald, Vice-president; the said Joseph E. Newburger, Secretary; and the said Newman Cowen, Treasurer of the said Institution for the first year; and that the place of business of the said society and Institution will be in the City, County and State of New York.

IN WITNESS WHEREOF WE have hereunto set our hands and seal the 23rd day of February 1887.

> Joseph Blumenthal
> Joseph E. Newburger
> Isaac Fles
> N. Cowen
> S. Jarmalowski
> I. Rosenthal
> Nathan Levin

PLAN OF ACTION ADOPTED BY THE CENTRAL EXECUTIVE COMMITTEE OF THE JEWISH ALLIANCE OF AMERICA WITH REGARD TO RUSSIAN-JEWISH IMMIGRATION*

It may be stated beyond question that if the annual influx of the many thousands of immigrants could by some effective system be quickly distributed through the vast interior of the Union, they would prove a desirable acquisition to the respective localities in which they settle, and also speedily better their own condition.

A careful analysis of the whole subject of immigration, as elucidated by both American and European economists, has shown that each new-comer positively adds a more or less definite amount to the wealth of the general community, and hence no intelligent person can regard the coming of these immigrants otherwise than with satisfaction. Not merely money, but brain and muscle are essential for the building up of a community; and although few of the victims of Russia's monstrous tyranny succeed in passing her frontiers without being robbed of practically all their property, yet their stout hearts and willing hands are sufficient capital to warrant them a welcome in this country. They are prepared to do all kinds of work, and experience, wherever they have been established, proves that they make good factory hands, tailors, seamstresses, carpenters, etc.

It is, however, manifest that the assimilation of these immigrants is retarded through their concentration in the larger communities, and particularly in the seaboard cities. If some outlet into the more thinly settled interior districts could be opened, if some system could be devised by which the numerous places throughout the country, particularly in the Southern and Western States, which are soliciting new settlers, could have their demands supplied from the overcrowded cities, then a great desideratum would be accomplished and the most beneficent result obtained. The material condition of the new-comers would be benefited, their introduction into

* From the author's private papers. (See text: Part III, Chapter 1, Note 80.)

388

varied branches of industry would be simplified, their education in the rights and duties of American citizenship would be facilitated, and their complete assimilation into our American commonalty would follow as of course. To compass such ends for the refugees from Russian barbarism, the Jewish Alliance of America has been organized, and the movement has now become sufficiently extended to permit practical work in this direction being undertaken.

United efforts by Jews in all quarters of the Union will be potent in doing what is required. Wherever Jews dwell they can assist in placing a few of the new-comers. Their wants are not unreasonable; all they need is a chance to work, in order to earn a livelihood. A little interest displayed in their cause by those who are better off will solve the question. It has always been the custom of Jews to allow no man to go unrelieved, and it is now especially a duty to apply this principle to these afflicted refugees. Let every member of the community give a little time and effort to guide them where they can settle and make a living, and it will be found that in one place a few families may be provided for, in another place opportunities can be given to still more, and so on. If Jews at all places where they are settled will look through their neighborhood for the purpose, they will be able to furnish the Alliance with enough information to enable us to direct the immigrants where they should go. Pecuniary help will come from the members of the Alliance, from the Baron de Hirsch Trust, and from the liberality of our community.

The immediate purpose to be kept in view is the settlement of small Jewish communities in the towns and villages of the interior throughout the country. It is manifest that if two or three families could be settled anywhere under self-supporting conditions, they would soon become the nucleus of further growth through the accession of relatives and friends, for whom the first comers would have made more or less adequate provision. Such has been the history of many well-established communities of Jews in the smaller towns of the country, and the process by which these have become settled can be repeated to any reasonable extent through the Union. Any one who has witnessed the process of establishment in this country of the German-Jewish immigrants who came in such considerable numbers during the past two or three decades, and whose influx has, within a comparatively recent period, totally ceased through the amelioration of their condition at home, will have observed how many thriving communities have grown up out of the settlement of one or two families in a locality. The only reason why the present immigrants cannot well be left to their own devices, as were their predecessors, is that the immigration of the latter was a normal process, while that of the Russian Jews is abnormal, through their forced expatriation and consequent poverty and helplessness.

With these facts in view, it is now proposed that the establishment of small Jewish communities be furthered by the Jewish Alliance of America through the medium of its branch organizations. The plan, in general, is as follows:

PLAN OF DISTRIBUTION

Section I.

The entire country shall be divided into districts whose boundaries and number may be varied from time to time as occasion may prove to be expedient.

Section II.

Each district shall be directly controlled by the branch organization in the principal city of the district, all other branches in the same district to co-operate under the direction of the principal branch. All measures of general policy are to remain subject to the revision and control of the Central Executive Committee of the Alliance.

Section III.

The board of officers of each of the branches of the Alliance shall appoint a number of their members whose duty it shall be to find locations where one or more families may be settled under circumstances affording them a reasonable subsistence. The officers of the local branch shall endeavor to locate in the places thus determined such persons or families as have applied to them for the purpose, and in the absence of such applicants they shall report the occasion to the Central Executive Committee, who shall thereupon take such action as may best promote the end in view.

Section IV.

If the local board of officers find it expedient to further this work through one or more paid agents, they shall communicate that fact to the Central Executive Committee, together with the name or names of such persons as they shall deem competent for the position.

Section V.

The local agent shall be paid a regular monthly salary, to be determined by the Central Executive Committee, by and with the advice of the local board, which salary shall be paid from the general treasury of the Alliance upon orders from the president and secretary of the local branch, countersigned by the president and secretary of the Central Committee.

Section VI.

For the furtherance of the general plan of local establishments, the new settlers may be aided by the local branch, through the officers and agents, with transportation, tools or subsistence, as may be found expedient, the expenses of such aid to be paid out of the general treasury of the Alliance upon authorization by the Central Executive Committee.

Section VII.

On the basis of this general plan, one great aim of the Alliance can be realized. The work can be carried forward to whatever extent, more or less, that the actual means of the organization may permit, and can be gradually expanded with the growth of membership and increasing income of the Alliance.

Section VIII.

It is especially recommended that congregations, clubs, lodges, the various Jewish orders and other Jewish organizations, be urged by their members to take an interest in this matter. There is no cause which better deserves their attention, or by the furtherance of which so much good can follow.

This plan, which was originally projected by Mr. Louis E. Levy, has been approved by the Central Executive Committee, after incorporation of amendments proposed by Dr. Solomon Solis-Cohen and Secretary Bernard Harris, together with a supplement by Mayer Sulzberger, Esq., a trustee of the Baron de Hirsch Fund.

CENTRAL OFFICE
632 Chestnut Street,
Philadelphia, Pa., July 14, 1891.

THE JEWISH THEOLOGICAL
SEMINARY OF AMERICA*

Agreement of Merger.

Agreement entered into this 14th day of April, 1902, between the Jewish Theological Seminary Association, hereinafter termed the Association, as party of the first part, and the Jewish Theological Seminary of America, hereinafter termed the Seminary, as party of the second part:

WITNESSETH: Whereas, The Association is a corporation organized and incorporated under the provisions of Chapter 271 of the Laws of 1888, and Chapter 674 of the Laws of 1892 of the Legislature of the State of New York, for the purposes and with the powers therein enumerated, and for the objects specified in Article II of its constitution in the terms following, to wit:

The purposes of this Association being the preservation in America of the knowledge and practice of historical Judaism, as contained in the Laws of Moses and expounded by the Prophets and Sages of Israel in Biblical and Talmudical writings, it purposes in furtherance of its general aim the following specific objects:

I. The establishment and maintenance of a Jewish Theological Seminary for the training of rabbis and teachers.

II. The attainment of such cognate purposes as may upon occasion be deemed appropriate; and

Whereas, The Seminary has been incorporated by and under the provisions of Chapter 56 of the Laws of 1902 of the Legislature of the State of New York, for similar objects and purposes which are specified in said act; and

Whereas, The Association desires to enter into a merger with the Seminary, and to transfer to said Seminary all of its property and trusts, and the biennial convention of the Association, held in conformity with its constitution and by-laws, at the City of New York, on the 30th day of March, 1902, unanimously authorized such merger and transfer, and

* *The Jewish Theological Seminary of America, Documents, Charter and By-Laws* (New York, 1903), pp. 12-4. (See text: Part III, Chapter 3, Note 14.)

the Association and the Seminary have agreed to consolidate with each other pursuant to the provisions of Chapter 56 of the Laws of 1902 aforesaid;

Now, therefore, in consideration of the premises and of the mutual covenants herein, and under the authority of the action of the aforesaid biennial convention of the Association, the unanimous action of the incorporators of the Seminary and of the affirmative vote of more than two-thirds of the Trustees of the Association and of the Directors of the Seminary respectively, the parties hereto have agreed as follows:

I. They hereby consolidate into one corporation, under the name of the Jewish Theological Seminary of America, with all of the powers for the objects, and under the terms set forth in Chapter 56 of the Laws of 1902 aforesaid.

II. The Association is hereby merged into the Seminary, and hereby conveys, transfers and assigns unto the Seminary all of its property of every name and nature, both real and personal, wheresoever the same may be situated, and agrees to execute and deliver to the Seminary such instruments of further assurance that may be deemed necessary or useful to carry out the interest and purpose of this instrument.

III. The Seminary hereby consents to the aforesaid merger and accepts the conveyance, transfer and assignment aforesaid, subject to all existing obligations and incumbrances of the Association with respect to such property and subject likewise to all trusts vested in and imposed upon the Association on account thereof.

IV. The Seminary adopts the provisions of Article II of the constitution of the Association as hereinbefore set forth.

In Witness whereof, the parties hereto have hereunto affixed their respective corporate names and seals, and have caused this instrument to be subscribed and executed by their respective trustees and directors the day and year first above written.

THE JEWISH THEOLOGICAL
  SEMINARY ASSOCIATION,
[SEAL]   By A. S. SOLOMONS, President.
THE JEWISH THEOLOGICAL
  SEMINARY OF AMERICA,
           By CYRUS ADLER, President.

Attest:

    LOUIS MARSHALL, Secretary pro tem.

In the presence of
    NATHAN BREUER.

                    A. S. Solomons,
                    Percival S. Menken,
                    Newman Cowen,
                    Moses Ottinger,
                    A. R. Altmayer,
                    Simon M. Roeder,
                    Samuel W. Korn,
                    Daniel P. Hays,
                    Samuel Josephs,
                    L. Napoleon Levy,
                    Nathan Hirsch,
                    Max Cohen,
                    Jonas Weil,

In the presence of as to
    (Solomon Solis-Cohen,   Solomon Solis-Cohen,
    (Samuel M. Hyneman,   Samuel M. Hyneman,
    (Edward L. Rothschild and   Edward L. Rothschild,
    (Jacob Singer.   Jacob Singer,
      ISRAEL HECHT.

In the presence of as to
    (The Directors of the   Daniel Guggenheim,
    (Jewish Theological   Jacob H. Schiff,
    (Seminary of America.   Mayer Sulzberger,
      MORRIS LOEB.   Simon Guggenheim,
                        Cyrus Adler,
                        Philip S. Henry,
                        Felix M. Warburg,

In the presence of as to
    (Louis Marshall and   Louis Marshall,
    (A. S. Solomons.   A. S. Solomons.
      A. J. DITTMAR.

AH—American Hebrew
AI—(American) Israelite
AJA—American Jewish Archives
AJYB—American Jewish Year Book
Asm—Asmonean
HL—Hebrew Leader
JEn—Jewish Encyclopedia
JEx—Jewish Exponent
JMes—Jewish Messenger
JRec—Jewish Record
JT—Jewish Times
MMo—Menorah (Monthly)
Occ—Occident
PJTSA—Proceedings of the Jewish Theological Seminary Association
PAJHS—Publication of the American Jewish Historical Society
Yearbook CCAR—Yearbook of the Central Conference of America Rabbis
YIVO Annual—YIVO Annual of Jewish Social Science

INTRODUCTION

1. From the Phillips Bradley trans. (New York, 1948), I, 308.
2. James Ward Smith and A. Leland Jamison, *The Shaping of American Religion* ("Religion in American Life Series," vol. I), Princeton, 1961, p. 4.
3. *Ibid.,* pp. 4-5.
4. See H. P. Mendes, "Historical Judaism," *AH,* LVI (February 1, 1895), 373-5; also *The Jewish Theological Seminary Semi-Centennial Volume,* ed. Cyrus Adler (New York, 1939), pp. 37-8, where Mendes recounts his first conversations with Morais about the proposed name for the Seminary.
5. For the Kohut statement, see *AH,* XXV (February 5, 1886), 194-5; and the editorial, *ibid.,* XXIX (January 14, 1887), 146. These statements are consistent with the position defined by Leeser as early as 1867 in the *Occident* which, it is interesting to note, was quoted at the beginning of Cyrus Adler's "Semi-Centennial Address" on the Seminary in the *JTSA Semi-Centennial Volume,* p. 4. The citation is as follows:

   Some may object to the movement, that it is not pledged to either reform or orthodoxy. These hateful words are always at hand when anything is to be done, from the election of a secretary to a society, to printing a book or establishing a college. The illiberal always ask: To what party does he or it belong? For our part, strange as it may sound, we belong to no party. We commenced life with certain convictions and have not swerved from them. We know only Judaism; and if you call it "orthodox," you do so—not we.

PART I: CHAPTER ONE

1. See Vernon L. Parrington, *Main Currents in American Thought* (New York, 1927, 1930), II, 141-52.
2. Arthur M. Schlesinger, Jr., *The Age of Jackson* (Boston, 1945), pp. 8-17. Between 1820 and 1840, the number of people involved in manufacturing increased 127%, while agricultural workers increased only 79%. These statistics explain the rapid rise of city dwellers and the curtailment of the rural population. In 1820, less than a twentieth of the nation lived in communities of 8,000 or over; in 1840, the proportions had so radically changed that more than a twelfth lived in such communities and more than a ninth in towns larger than 2,000.
3. For a study treating the social history of New York in this period, with emphasis on the adaptation of the immigrant to American life, see Robert Ernst, *Immigrant Life in New York City 1825-1863* (New York, 1949).
4. Parrington, *op. cit.*, vol. II, chap. II, especially pp. 193-202.
5. Edwin Wolf, 2nd, and Maxwell Whiteman, *The History of the Jews of Philadelphia from Colonial Times to the Age of Jackson* (Philadelphia, 1957), pp. 267 ff.
6. Israel Goldstein, *A Century of Judaism in New York* (New York, 1930), pp. 51-3 and ff.
7. Because of the scarcity of basic records, there are variations among the scholars of Colonial Jewish history as to the number of synagogues founded as well as to the dates of their establishment:
   Joshua Trachtenberg has compiled the following list (*Consider the Years* [Easton, Pa., 1944], p. 317, note 1):
   "Sheerith Israel, New York, 1655; Jeshuat Israel, Newport, R.I., 1658; Mickve Israel, Savannah, Ga., 1733; Mickveh Israel, Philadelphia, 1740; Beth Elohim, Charleston, S.C., 1750; Beth Shalom, Richmond, Va., 1790; Rodef Sholom, Philadelphia, 1802."
   Rudolf Glanz in "Di 25 Eltste Yidishe Kehilot in di Fareinikte Shtaten" (The 25 Oldest Congregations in the United States), *YIVO Bleter*, XXVI (September-October, 1945), 42-5, differs with regard to: Mikveh Israel,

Philadelphia (1745); Beth Elohim, Charleston (1749).
He adds a congregation in Reading, Pa. (1761).

Jacob Rader Marcus dates the origins of several of these
congregations as follows: Beth Elohim Unveh Shallom,
Charlestown (1749); Beth Shalome, Richmond, Va., 1789.
For congregation Jeshuat Israel, Newport, R.I., he states
that "the cornerstones . . . were laid in 1759; and the
synagogue was finally consecrated in 1763." (*Early
American Jewry* [Philadelphia, 1951, 1953], I, 121; II, 6,
223, 232-3).

Authors of local histories establish the following for the
congregations in the communities they studied:

Morris Gutstein (*The Story of the Jews of Newport:
1658-1908* [New York, 1936], p. 30) writes: ". . . fifteen
Jewish families arrived in 1658 . . . they organized a
Kahal-Kadosh—Holy Congregation. . . ." On pp. 81-2:
"By 1759 . . . the Congregation Yeshuat Israel was ready
to lay the foundations of its synagogue . . ."

Edwin Wolf, 2nd, and Maxwell Whiteman (*op. cit.*, p.
389, note 38; pp. 225-6) cite Hyman P. Rosenbach as
saying that the synagogue began "as early as 1747,"
whereas Mikveh Israel sets its founding at 1740. As for
Rodeph Shalom, by 1795 there were enough Jews who
wanted to say their prayers in Ashkenazi fashion to form
their own congregation. The official dedication of Rodeph
Shalom was in 1802.

Charles Reznikoff and Uriah Z. Engelman, *The Jews of
Charleston* (Philadelphia, 1950), p. 17, set the founding
of Beth Elohim Unveh Shalom in 1749.

8. The board not only fixed the hours of the services, the
arrangement of the prayers and the distribution of honors, but it also had the right to allow or deny the *hazzan*
permission to officiate at weddings. This ruling exists in
certain Sephardi congregations even today, and was prevalent in many of the Ashkenazi congregations in the nineteenth century. Dr. Morris Raphall, rabbi of B'nai
Jeshurun, was compelled in 1854, in accordance with the
congregation's ruling, to request from the president permission to officiate at the wedding of his own daughter.
Goldstein, *op. cit.*, p. 132.

9. Alexander M. Dushkin, *Jewish Education in New York*

City (New York, 1918), pp. 39-45. See also Hyman B. Grinstein, "Studies in the History of Jewish Education in New York City (1728-1860)," *The Jewish Review,* II (April, 1944), 41-58; (July-Oct.), 187-201.

10. Jacob Rader Marcus, *Early American Jewry* (2 volumes, Philadelphia, 1951, 1953), II, 48 ff.; Wolf and Whiteman, *op. cit.,* pp. 136-7.

11. Israel Goldstein, *op. cit.,* pp. 48-50.

12. Jacob Rader Marcus, *op. cit.,* II, 512.

13.

B'nai Israel, Cincinnati, O.	
B'nai Jeshurun, New York, N. Y.	1825
Anshe Chesed, New York, N. Y.	1828
Shaaray Chesed, New Orleans, La.	1837
United Hebrew, St. Louis, Mo.	1838
Beth El, Albany, N. Y.	1838
Achduth Israel, St. Louis, Mo.	1839
Shaaray Zedokoh, New York, N. Y.	1839
B'rith Sholom, Easton, Pa.	1839
Beth Israel, Philadelphia, Pa.	1839
B'nai Yeshurun, Cincinnati, O.	1840
Shaaray Shomayim, New York, N. Y.	1840

Joseph Krauskopf, "Fifty Years of Judaism in America," *American Jews' Annual,* IV (Cincinnati, 1888), 70; Glanz, *loc. cit.,* and the list of Jewish institutions, synagogues and societies given by Jacques J. Lyons and Abraham De Sola, *A Jewish Calendar for Fifty Years* (Montreal, 1854), 148-73. See also Grinstein, *Rise of the Jewish Community of New York* (Philadelphia, 1945), pp. 472-4.

14. From the earliest days there were already Jews from Germany and Poland, such as the famous families of Haym Salomon, Jonas Phillips, Gratz, Simon, Levy, Hart, Simson, Moses, etc. Certain Jews, like Jacob Franks, were thought to have come from England but they really stemmed from Germany. See Max J. Kohler "The German-Jewish Migration to America," *PAJHS,* 9 (1901), 88. See also Cecil Roth's study on the diverse origins of the Jews who fought in the Revolutionary War, "Some Jewish Loyalists in the War of American Independence," *PAJHS,* XXXVIII (Dec., 1948), 82-3. Likewise, the first

Ashkenazi synagogue in Philadelphia was established as early as 1795. For the social factors involved, see Wolf and Whiteman, *op. cit.,* p. 7.

15. For a comparison of the rules of three Sephardi congregations (Bevis Marks, London, Beth Elohim, Charleston, and Shearith Israel, New York), for the purpose of restraining the development of other congregations, see Jacob Neusner, "The Role of English Jews in the Development of American Jewish Life, 1775-1850," *YIVO Annual,* XII (New York, 1958/1959), 147-8. For a further description of the Charleston congregation, see Reznikoff and Engelmann, *op. cit.,* p. 118.

16. See Goldstein, *op. cit.,* p. 54; Grinstein, *The Rise of the Jewish Community* . . . , pp. 40-9.

17. David and Tamar de Sola Pool, *An Old Faith in the New World* (New York, 1955), p. 275; also pp. 436-9.

18. For a comprehensive description of the changes in the synagogues of New York, see Grinstein, *The Rise of the Jewish Community. . . .* See especially his description of the *kahal* and the congregation, pp. 33-6.

19. Reznikoff and Engelman, *op. cit.,* pp. 123-36.

20. *MMo,* I (Aug., 1886), 66.

PART I: CHAPTER TWO

1. Quoted in Henry Englander, "Isaac Leeser, 1806-1868," *Yearbook CCAR,* XXVIII (1918), 221.

2. Quoted in D. W. Amram, *Address on the Tenth Anniversary of the Death of the Rev. Dr. Marcus Jastrow* (Philadelphia, 1913), p. 9.

3. Shabbat, 119b.

4. "The difference between orthodoxy and reform," Jastrow wrote, "is unimportant in the face of the indifference of our young people to both. Young Israel is suffering, while allopathic orthodox physicians and homeopathic reformers are wrangling over their *materia medica.* They have both diagnosed the disease and they should know that neither of them has medicines that will avail. The young patient needs a good substantial, national diet that will avail." D. W. Amram, *op. cit.,* p. 8.

5. Leeser, "Jewish Children under Gentile Teachers," *Occ,* I (Dec., 1843), 413.

6. For a history of the school, see Alexander M. Dushkin, *Jewish Education in New York City* (New York, 1918), pp. 40 ff., 449 ff.; Hyman B. Grinstein "Studies in the History of Jewish Education in New York City (1728-1860)," *The Jewish Review*, II (April, 1944), 41-2. See also *PAJHS*, XXI (1913), 14.

7. Grinstein, *The Rise of the Jewish Community . . .* , pp. 234-7.

8. Leeser's article mentioned above, *Occ*, I (Dec., 1843), 408, 411-3.

   What is the remedy? Diffusion of religious knowledge in the full sense of the words; it would be best to establish Jewish elementary schools in every district where there are sufficient children to occupy the time of a teacher, who should be both religiously and scientifically qualified to instruct his charges in the way they ought to walk, and in the things it behooves them to know . . . (p. 413).

9. About two hundred students in that neighborhood steadily attended the various churches and some of them were baptized. See Dushkin, *op. cit.*, pp. 53-8.

10. For a biography of Lilienthal and a selection of his writings, see David Philipson, ed., *Max Lilienthal, American Rabbi* (New York, 1915).

11. The curriculum of the school is described in a letter of M. M. Noah in *Occ*, VIII (Nov., 1850), 424-6. Judge Noah also proposed the formation of a boarding school in 1843 and carefully formulated its purpose and scope in *Occ*, I (Sept., 1843), 303-7.

    From the examination given the students of Dr. Lilienthal's boarding school in 1851, a picture can be gained of the limited place of Hebrew studies. The examination was divided as follows (*Occ*, IX [May, 1851], 104-5): Religion and Hebrew; Arithmetic; Book-keeping; Mechanical Problems; Piano; English Recitation, German ditto; History of the United States; Geography; Piano; English Recitation, French ditto; German Language; Commercial Letters in German, French and English; Violin; French; French Recitation, German ditto; Violin; English Grammar, Parsing, and Writing.

12. For an endorsement and support of the school conducted by the Misses Palache by the *Hebrew Leader*, see VIII

(June 15, 1866), 76; by Isaac Leeser, *Occ,* I (May, 1843), 104-5; (July), 200-1; II (July, 1844), 209-10.

13. *Occ,* X (Nov., 1852), 412.

14. *Ibid.,* XI (July, 1853), 232.

15. Quoted in Solomon Solis-Cohen, "The Hebrew Sunday School" in *Judaism and Science, with Other Addresses and Papers* (Philadelphia, 1940), p. 8.

16. *Ibid.,* p. 6. Rosa Mordecai, the great-niece of Rebecca Gratz, published a memoir of the school, tracing its history up to 1877, in the *Hebrew Watchword,* Philadelphia, February-April, 1897. The memoir was republished with an introduction and explanatory notes by Joshua Bloch in *PAJHS,* XLII (1952-53), 397-406.

17. The offer was made by the junta of Mikveh Israel and was refused by Miss Gratz, for reasons which are not clear. See Joseph R. Rosenbloom, "Rebecca Gratz and the Jewish Sunday School Movement in Philadelphia," *PAJHS,* XLVIII (Dec., 1958), 74 and sources cited in notes 16, 17 and 18.

It should be pointed out that although Leeser was the moving force in this undertaking of Miss Gratz, she, in turn, aided him in his work all his life. Leeser recognized her efforts and thanked her publicly. He dedicated to her his first educational textbook, the *Catechism for Jewish Children,* in 1839, with the following words:

To Miss Rebecca Gratz, Superintendent of the Sunday School for religious instruction of Israelites in Philadelphia.

Esteemed Friend:

I have long wished for an opportunity to acknowledge my indebtedness to you for the approval you have kindly bestowed on my youthful labours, and the frequent marks of friendship I received from you since my lot was cast in this place. As this little book has been undertaken to assist your efforts, which have so far been crowned with signal success, to form an institution whence the waters of life might flow alike to the rich and to the poor; permit me to inscribe it to you, that your respected name may contribute to its introduction into the houses and schools of our people who dwell in this land.

18. See "Sunday-School for Religious Instruction of Israelites

of Philadelphia," *Occ*, I (April, 1843), 38-40; II (May, 1844), 83-7; (June), 147-50. See also Maxwell Whiteman, "Isaac Leeser and the Jews of Philadelphia," *PAJHS*, XLVIII (June, 1959), 229, note 129.

19. For a biographical background on Abraham Rice, see the author's *Yahadut Amerikah be-Hitpathutah* (The Shaping of American Judaism, New York, 1951), pp. 333-4; Isidore Blum, *The History of the Jews of Baltimore* (Baltimore, 1910), pp. 11, 13.

20. Edgar B. Wesley, *NEA: The First Hundred Years. The Building of the Teaching Profession* (New York, 1957), p. 30.

21. For a general description of the development of Jewish education in the United States in this period, see Zevi Scharfstein, *Toldot ha-Hinuh be-Yisrael ba-dorot ha-Aharonim* (History of Jewish Education in Recent Generations, New York, 1947), II, 155-72.

22. Aaron Klein, *Toldot Sifre ha-Limud le-Bate ha-Sefer ha-Yehudiim be-Amerikah* (The History of Textbooks for Jewish Schools in America). Unpublished. Jewish Theological Seminary of America (1955), pp. 17-21. Dr. Klein's thesis includes a thorough summary of the objectives of Jewish textbook production and bibliographical appendices in which the textbook publications are arranged chronologically and thematically.

23. Quoted in A. S. W. Rosenbach, "Early American Jewish School Books" in the 89th Annual Report of the Hebrew Sunday School Society of Philadelphia, 1927, pp. 23-4.

24. Klein, *op. cit.*, "Chronological Bibliography," pp. 1b-5b.

25. *Asm*, VII (Jan. 7, 1853), 137.

26. *Occ*, XX (April, 1862), 44-5.

27. Quoted in Salo W. and Jeannette M. Baron, "Palestinian Messengers in America, 1849-79," *Jewish Social Studies*, V (April, 1943), 154.

28. *Occ*, II (April, 1844), 2-3.

29. Leeser's plan, together with a characteristic comment in his postscript, is to be found in Appendix B. See also Solomon Grayzel, "The First American Jewish Publication Society," *Jewish Book Annual*, III (1944-5), 42-5.

30. For the names of the officers, see *Occ*, III (Dec., 1845), 427.

31. *Occ*, VI (Nov., 1848), 411.

32. *Ibid.,* III (July, 1845), 174-6; (Aug.), 222-7. See Appendix B. The full text of the Salomon-Leeser proposal is also reprinted by Joseph Buchler, "The Struggle for Unity," *AJA,* II (June, 1949). See his Appendix I, pp. 39-44.
33. *Occ,* III (Aug., 1845), 225.
34. Bertram W. Korn, "The First American Theological Seminary: Maimonides College, 1867-1873," in *Eventful Years and Experiences* (Cincinnati, 1954), pp. 152-3 and Appendix II, pp. 199-200.
35. *Occ,* I (Sept., 1843), 303-7.
36. Joseph Krauskopf, *loc. cit.,* pp. 65 ff.
37. Isaac Mayer Wise, *Reminiscences,* edited by D. Philipson (Cincinnati, 1901), p. 23.
38. "Education for the Ministry," *Occ,* IV (Feb., 1847), 524. The article begins in the January issue, see especially pp. 471, 475-6.
39. *Ibid.,* VII (May, 1849), 102.
40. The plot was later transferred to the Jewish Theological Seminary of America. *AH,* LXXII (Dec., 1902), 71.
41. For an evaluation of Wise's life and writings, see Philipson, *op. cit.;* Max B. May, *Isaac Mayer Wise* (New York and London, 1916); Adolph S. Oko, *A Tentative Bibliography of Isaac M. Wise* (Cincinnati, 1917); Dena Wilansky, *Sinai to Cincinnati* (New York, 1937); Israel Knox, *Rabbi in America. The Story of Isaac M. Wise* (Boston, Toronto, 1957); Isaac Mayer Wise, "The World of My Books," translated, with an introduction and explanatory notes by Albert H. Friedlander (Cincinnati, 1954).
42. *Asm,* IX (March 10, 1854), 165.
43. *Occ,* XIII (Aug., 1855), 234-8; (Sept.), 302-5. A short biography and selected writings of Dr. Illowy, were published by his son, Henry Illoway, *Sefer Milhamot Elohim* (The Book of Battles of the Lord), *Being the Controversial Letters and the Casuistic Decisions of the Late Rabbi Bernard Illowy Ph. D. with a Short History of His Life and Activities* (Berlin, 1914).
44. May, *op. cit.,* pp. 257-61; Krauskopf, *loc. cit.,* pp. 85-6. An insight into Dr. Wise's energy and outstanding organizational ability can be gained from the resolutions that were adopted at the organizational meeting of the Philadelphia branch of the Zion Collegiate Association.

See *Occ,* XIII (July, 1855), 195. For the development of the project as described in the pages of Wise's periodical, see *AI,* I (Sept. 29, 1854), 94; (Oct. 6), 101; (Oct. 13), 110; (Oct. 20), 116; (Dec. 1), 164; (Jan. 12, 1855), 212; (Mar. 23), 292-3; (May 25), 366; II (Aug. 10), 37-8; III (Aug. 8, 1856), 37; (April 17, 1857), 324.

45. *AI,* IV (Jan. 8, 1857), 212; V (Nov. 26, 1858), 164.
46. *Occ,* XXI (Feb., 1864), 524; XXII (June, 1864), 144.
47. *HL,* IX (Feb. 22, 1867), 4. The discovery of the minute book of the Emanu-El Theological Seminary Society of New York has shed new light on the history of this institution. See Bertram Korn, "The Temple Emanu-El Theological Seminary of New York City," *Essays in American Jewish History* (Cincinnati, 1958), pp. 359-71.
48. *JMes,* XXXIX (May 12, 1867), 2, 4: See also *JT,* VIII (May 12, 1876), 169; (June 2), 213-4; (June 9), 232-4; (June 30), 280.
49. "Proposal to Establish an American-Jewish University," *B'nai B'rith Files,* in Allan Tarshish, *Rise of American Judaism.* Unpublished. Pp. 229-30.
50. For a brief biography of Moses Dropsie, see Appendix A.
51. *Occ,* XXII (Dec., 1864), 425-9. The account of Dropsie's speech reads in part as follows:

Mr. Dropsie on taking chair spoke at considerable length on the necessity of doing something to extend religious education in America. He pointed out, that the increase of means and numbers left us no excuse for continuing as we had hitherto done, in depending on Europe for our religious teachers. He showed how men have rendered themselves immortal by endowing colleges, with which their names are connected, such as Harvard, Yale and others of the kind; . . . He feelingly alluded to the great absence of knowledge respecting our religion among American Israelites, solely owing to the absence of adequate schools, where they can obtain the necessary instruction, and he appealed to the audience, respectable for numbers and intelligence, to remedy the evil now and forever, by enabling the Education Society to make use of that portion of its charter, which authorizes it to establish a high-school in any part of Pennsylvania, in which the higher degrees of arts and divinity can be conferred on its students.

52. For a discussion of the origin of the name "Maimonides College," see Hyman Grinstein, "American Jewry and Maimonides," *PAJHS*, XXXIV (1937), 268-70.

53. *JMes*, XIII (May 29, 1863), 180; XXII (Aug. 16, 1867), 4; (Aug. 23), 4; (Aug. 30), 4; (Oct. 11), 4; (Nov. 1), 4.

54. "Hebrew College," *Occ*, XXIV (Sept., 1866), 283-6. The full text is reprinted in Korn, *op. cit.*, Appendix IV, pp. 202-5.

55. See Appendix B. The document, which has considerable significance in the history of Jewish education in America, is also reprinted in Korn, *op. cit.*, pp. 166-8. See his Appendix V, "The Maimonides College Prospectus," *ibid.*, pp. 206-9.

56. For a brief biography of Aaron Bettelheim, see Appendix A.

57. *Occ*, XXII (Feb., 1865), 513-8. For a short biography of Dr. Bondi, see Appendix A.

58. *HL*, X (June 28, 1867), 4. In another item Bondi compares the number of young Catholics in Philadelphia who wish to be priests and the altogether different situation which prevailed among Jews. *Ibid.*, VIII (May 4, 1866), 28.

59. *JMes*, XXIII (June 26, 1868), 1.

60. *Ibid.*, XXV (May 14, 1869), 2.

61. See Korn, *op. cit.*, pp. 189-94, for his summary of reasons for the failure of the college. Maxwell Whiteman suggests in a letter to the author that "the failure of the Board of Delegates to support the college beyond formal approval was a strong factor in its decline—it seems as if this lack of support was more the result of placating the Reformers than for any other reason."

62. Max J. Kohler, "The Board of Delegates of American Israelites, 1859-1878," *PAJHS*, XXIX (1925), Appendix II, 108. Korn, *op cit.*, gives a brief biographical survey of the careers of the three graduates, Appendix I, pp. 196-8.

63. Cyrus Adler, *I Have Considered the Days* (Philadelphia, 1941-5701), p. 14.

64. *Ibid.*, pp. 16, 38-42.

PART I: CHAPTER THREE

1. Samuel Oppenheim, "The Early History of the Jews in New York, 1654-1664," *PAJHS*, XVIII (1909), 8.
2. Barbara Miller Solomon, *Pioneers in Service:* The History of the Associated Jewish Philanthropies of Boston (Boston, 1956), p. XI. See also Jacob Neusner, "The Impact of Immigration Upon the Boston Jewish Community, 1880-1914," *PAJHS*, XLVI (1956), 71-85.
3. Merle Curti, "The History of American Philanthropy as a Field of Research," *American Historical Review*, LXII (Jan., 1957), 352-363; *Report of the Princeton Conference on the History of Philanthropy in the United States*, Russell Sage Foundation (New York, 1956).
4. David de Sola Pool, *Portraits Etched in Stone* (New York, 1952), p. 362. See also David and Tamar de Sola Pool, *An Old Faith in the New World* (New York, 1955), pp. 171-3; 353. For a description of a pension system unique for that period, see Hyman B. Grinstein, *The Rise of the Jewish Community of New York, 1654-1860*, pp. 134-36.
5. Oscar and Mary F. Handlin, "A Century of Jewish Immigration to the United States," *AJYB*, L (5709, 1948-49), 34-37.
6. Writing about her father's home, Rebekah Kohut describes a typical rabbinic family situation of the day— the invited and the uninvited guests. About the invited guests she says:

   It must not be imagined that we were a closed family circle on Friday evenings and Saturdays. On the contrary. My father, with his big, expansive nature, believed in sociability, and wanted us to broaden our outlook through having many friends. The family's meagre purse did not prevent our entertaining a great many people. My father would have been unhappy had he not been able to act as host. Every year, at the Passover festival, he had us invite our friends and teachers to our home for the first two evenings of celebration, the Seder services, they are called. They were memorable evenings. Usually there were about forty or fifty guests, a great many of whom were Christians. (*My Portion* [New York, 1927], p. 54.)

And as regards the uninvited, she writes elsewhere:

> When he was at home we had a steady stream of visitors, who almost overwhelmed us in our small house. In the 'seventies, one's acquaintances did not stop at hotels when they were visiting a city. If they happened to know anyone, they felt as confident of welcome and bed and board as if they were living in the age of the wandering Jews of Europe. Some rabbis used to visit us for weeks at a time, bringing their families with them. I remember my brother once hurling the visiting rabbi's shoes out of the window every night in hope that he would take the hint and end his visit . . . (*As I Know Them* [New York, 1929], pp. 202-3.)

7. "Jewish Hospitals," *Occ*, XXIII (Oct., 1865), 289-99.

8. *Ibid.*, 300-301. For a biography, selected writings and bibliography of Felsenthal, see Emma Felsenthal, *Bernard Felsenthal, Teacher in Israel* (New York, 1929).

9. *Occ*, XXI (Feb., 1864), 522.

10. This hospital became famous throughout the country under the name adopted in 1866, "Mount Sinai Hospital."

11. Thomas J. Tobias, *The Hebrew Orphan Society of Charleston, S.C.* (An Historical Sketch), 1951, p. 7.

12. Henry Samuel Morais, *The Jews of Philadelphia* (Philadelphia, 1894), p. 121.

13. Nathan Glazer, *American Juduism* (Chicago, 1957), p. 23.

14. Guido Kisch, "German Jewish White Labor Servitude in America," *PAJHS*, XXXIV (1937), 26-7. See also Hanns G. Reissner, " 'Ganstown, U.S.A.'—A German-Jewish Dream," *AJA*, XIV (April, 1962), 23-6.

15. Aug. 12, 1846, p. 300.

16. *Tefilah mi-kol ha-Shanah, Minhah Ketanah le-Holkhe Derekh u-le-Ovre Yamim le-ha-Nosim li-Medinat Amerikah* (Fuerth, 1842).

17. I. J. Benjamin II, in his *Drei Jahre in Amerika*, vol. I, 1859-1862 (Hanover, 1862), pp. 341-84, lists 23 Jewish charitable societies in Philadelphia; 4 in Richmond, Va.; 18 in Cincinnati, Ohio; 4 in New Orleans, La.; and 4 in Louisville, Ky.

Cf. English edition, translated by Charles Reznikoff, Appendix, pp. 302-335.

18. Mikveh Israel Files: Letters to Congregation (26 Elul, 5616–Sept. 9, 1855).

19. *Occ*, XIV (Nov., 1856), 404.

20. Mikveh Israel Files (28 Elul, 5616–Sept. 28, 1856). The text of the letter reads as follows:

> Much of the money [was] employed in procuring [for] our needy brethren the means for subsistence by my purchasing for them either the implements of their trade or merchandise to traffic with. I have also saved many, by it, from remaining without a shelter during last winter. When the severity of the season prevents their earning sufficiently to pay their rent, I have at that period clothed some, whose lightly clad persons were exposed to the intense cold we experienced and relieved others who were lying upon a sick-bed.

See also the letter dated Elul, 5617–Sept. 13, 1857, in which Morais tells the congregation of the assistance given to him in his charitable work by Mr. Lazarus J. Leberman. Leberman's voucher book on which Morais drew warrants for charitable contributions is in the possession of Maxwell Whiteman.

21. Lyons Collection, Library of the AJHS, Scrapbook III, item 129.

22. *Occ*, VI (Jan., 1849), 474-5.

23. *Ibid.*, XIV (Dec., 1856), 413-4.

24. *Ibid.*, I (April, 1843), 28-29.

For a summary of the various efforts in Jewish agricultural settlement, see Leo Shpall, "Jewish Agricultural Colonies in the United States," *Agricultural History*, XXIV (July, 1950), 120-146.

25. *Sefer Masaot Shimon* (The Travels of Simon), (Cracow, 1879), p. 19.

26. *Ibid.*, pp. 18-42. Frank E. Manuel, *The Realities of American-Palestine Relations* (Washington, D.C., 1949), pp. 44-46. For a comprehensive article on Berman and his plans, see E. R. Malachi, "Shimon Berman, Meyassed Hebrat Yishuv ha-Aretz be-Teberyah" (Simon Berman, the founder of the Land Settlement Society in Tiberias), *Israel* (New York, 1950), pp. 102-23.

27. *Occ,* X (Jan., 1853), 468, 475. See also *ibid.,* XI (June, 1853), 180-84; I (July, 1843), 183-7; (March, 1844), 594-9.
28. Touro in his will left $5,000 for the Mission Society. See Leon Huhner, *The Life of Judah Touro* (Phila., 1946), pp. 132, 165, 172.
29. *Occ,* XXIV (Aug., 1866), 229-34. See also X (March, 1853), 577-86; XI (Nov., 1853), 409-13; (Jan., 1854), 510-15.
30. Maxwell Whiteman records that a number of items relating to Palestine are found in the papers of the Philadelphia Land Grants, 1684-1772, Penna. Mss., VII, 39. The oldest reference, dating back to 1763, is a response to an appeal by the Jews of Hebron. "Zionism Comes to Philadelphia," *Early History of Zionism in America,* ed. Isidore S. Meyer (New York, 1958), pp. 191, 207.
31. From the study of Professor and Mrs. Salo W. Baron on messengers sent from Israel to the United States, we can gather a clear picture, based on records and periodicals, of the development of the relationship between the leaders of the communities in Israel and America in that period. See *idem.,* "Palestinian Messengers in America, 1849-79," *Jewish Social Studies,* V (April, 1943), 115-62; (July), 225-92.
32. *Occ,* VII (Oct., 1849), 344.
33. *Ibid.,* 345.
34. The members of the committee were Dr. Lilienthal, Samuel Isaacs, M. M. Noah, Jacob J. M. Falkenau, Simeon Abrahams (who had just returned from Palestine), Henry Moses (president of Anshay Chesed congregation of New York), L. Bomeisler and I. Leeser.
35. Salo and Jeannette Baron, *op. cit.,* 136-37.
36. *Ibid.,* 137-38.
37. Among the participants were Isaacs of Shaaray Tefila; Noah and Abrahams of Shearith Israel; Jacob M. Falkenau and Amsel Leo of B'nai Jeshurun, Henry Moses of Anshe Chesed; Jacob Weinschenck of Rodeph Shalom; Isidore Raphael of Shaarey Zedek; Abraham Schwartz of Shaarey Hashamaim; Max Lilienthal; Isaac Leeser and Abraham Hart of Philadelphia.
38. Salo and Jeannette Baron, *op. cit.,* 241. For a brief description of the first American society in Israel, see

Frank E. Manuel, *op. cit.,* pp. 34-5. For additional material bearing on Benjamin Lilienthal, see Judah Aaron Weiss, *Bi-Shearaikh, Yerushalayim* (In Thy Gates, O Jerusalem: Jerusalem, 1949), pp. 60-1, 71, 265-75.

39. "Palestine and its Prospects," *Occ,* XIII (Feb., 1856), 523. See also G. Kressel's article on Leeser's interest in agricultural settlements in Eretz Yisrael, *Davar* (Jan. 8, 1954).

40. *JMes,* XXIII (May 22, 1868), 4-5. See also Max J. Kohler, "The Board of Delegates of American Israelites, 1859-1878," *PAJHS,* XXIX (1925), 99.

41. W. H. Lynch, *Narrative of the United States Expedition to the River Jordan and the Dead Sea* (Philadelphia, 1849), p. 415.

42. *Occ,* XXII (April, 1864), 13.

43. For references to the statements which follow see: "Religious Equality," *Occ,* V (Jan., 1848), 500-1; Leeser's Countermemorial to the Senate and House of Representatives in *Occ,* XXII (Feb., 1865), 485-91; "North Carolina and the Israelites," quoted from *Philadelphia Evening Journal,* in *Occ,* XVI (Feb., 1859), 531-6; Marcus Jastrow, *Turn Not To Folly Again* (Philadelphia, 1890), pp. 3-5; see also *Occ,* XVII (April 14, 1859), 15-16; (July 13), 92; see *ibid.,* VI (Dec., 1848), 466-467; XVI (Sept., 1858), 269-85.

44. *Ibid.,* VI (Aug., 1848), 217-19, 225. For Isaac M. Wise's position on this matter and his advice to the Jews of Baltimore in opposition to the Sunday Laws, see *AI,* III (June 26, 1857), 404.

45. *JMes,* XXIII (Jan. 24, 1868), 1. In 1877, Jews influenced Senator Gates Jones to introduce a law in Congress for the benefit of Sabbath observers, both Jewish and non-Jewish, but it was not passed.

46. "The Prospect," *Occ,* VI (Nov., 1848), 377-8:

> The churches are open weekly, and presided over by men who have the reputation for eloquence; the Jew is invited by his neighbours to attend, to be entertained and instructed by the fine speeches of these public teachers. He cannot well refuse to go, because, especially in isolated positions, it would look odd to be absent from church when all his neighbours attend,

and perhaps might result in an injurious effect on his business; and in fact we have heard of instances where such persons had seats in churches, and were regular attendants, and contributed the same as the Christians to the expenses of the establishment. Now we do not say that we should not listen once in a while to a sermon from some Christian minister; without determining the admissibility of our so doing on religious grounds, we will admit it, as it has been done of late by men of piety and learning; but this does not say that we should attend church regularly and at stated periods like members of Christian societies, not to mention that it is sinful to be a pew-holder and contributor towards the support of a worship which we must deem erroneous. It is one thing to be charitable to the non-Israelite; . . . we admit that Jews have always contributed towards building of churches for the sake of peace and harmony with their neighbours. Be this as it may, we contend that no Jew has a right to be a pew-holder in a church, though he may have contributed to its erection, or to be a stated attendant, thereby countenancing the idea that he is edified by the religious instructions there imparted . . . you cannot so separate the component portions of a sermon, nor will any honest Christian minister so arrange his discourses as to make the doctrinal subservient to the moral portion.

47. *Occ,* XI (May, 1853), 83-86; (Aug.), 245-8.
48. This society had been granted a charter in 1820 and functioned largely through the efforts of a Jewish convert to Christianity, the "Reverend" Joseph Samuel C. F. Frey. Although it managed to establish missionary branches all over the East Coast of the United States and set up an impressive circulation for its periodical, *Israel's Advocate,* the society did not succeed in making many converts. In 1841, it regained momentary impetus by opening a new fund and by giving its project increased publicity. In 1844, the *Jewish Chronicle* replaced the long defunct *Advocate,* functioning along the same lines as its predecessor. The society lingered on and finally went out of existence altogether in the late 1850s. See

Occ, I (April, 1843), 43-7. For a history and a detailed account of the Society's activities, see "The American Society for Meliorating the Condition of the Jews and Joseph S. C. F. Frey its Missionary," in Lee M. Friedman, *Early American Jews* (Cambridge, 1934), chap. 8.

49. *Occ,* I (April, 1843), 47.
50. *Ibid.* (July, 1843), 210-13. For an illustration of Isaacs' mild reaction to Jewish Christian missionaries as compared with Christian missionaries, see *JMes,* VII (March 30, 1860), 100.
51. *Occ,* VII (Jan., 1850), 487-92. For a critical article by Wise in which he attacks those Christian sects that meddle in Jewish affairs before they succeeded in unifying their own ranks, see *AI,* IV (July 10, 1857), 4. Bondi's reaction is recorded in *HL,* VIII (June 22, 1866), 82. For an incident in which Morais and Jastrow joined forces, see *Occ,* XXV (Nov., 1867), 394.
52. *Ibid.,* VII (Jan., 1850), 525.
53. These two documents can be found in *Occ,* XXVI (Dec., 1868), 425-26.
54. The fact is that before any official requests had reached him, John Forsyth, the American Secretary of State, dispatched a communication to the American representatives in Alexandria and Constantinople to the following effect:

Washington, August 14, 1840

John Gliddon, Esq.,
United States Consul at Alexandria, Egypt
Sir:

In common with all civilized nations, the people of the United States have learned with horror, the atrocious crimes imputed to the Jews of Damascus, and the cruelties of which they have been the victims. The President fully participates in the public feeling, and he cannot refrain from expressing equal surprise and pain, that in this advanced age, such unnatural practices should be ascribed to any portion of the religious world, and such barbarous measures be resorted to, in order to compel the confession of imputed guilt; the offenses with which these unfortunate people are charged, resemble too much those which, in less enlightened times, were made the pretexts of fanatical persecution or mercenary extortion to permit a doubt that they are equally unfounded.

The President has witnessed, with the most lively satisfaction, the effort of several of the Christian Governments of Europe, to suppress or mitigate these horrors, and he learned with no common gratification, their partial success. He is moreover anxious that the active sympathy and generous interposition of the Government of the United States should not be withheld from so benevolent an object, and he has accordingly directed me to instruct you to employ, should the occasion arise, all those good offices and efforts which are compatible with discretion and your official character, to the end that justice and humanity may be extended to these persecuted people, whose cry of distress has reached our shores. I am, sir,

Your obedient servant,

John Forsyth

See Cyrus Adler and Aaron M. Margalith, *With Firmness in the Right* (New York, 1946), p. 4. For the Kursheedt-Seixas letter see Goldstein, *op. cit.,* pp. 64-6, 70-3. The letter is also reprinted in Jacob Ezekiel, "Persecution of Jews in 1840," *PAJHS,* VII (1900), 141-5; Morris U. Schappes, ed., *Documentary History of the Jews in the United States, 1654-1875* (New York, 1950), p. 86.
55. *Occ,* VIII (March, 1851), 613-5. The following excerpt from the *Asmonean* reflects the line of argument (*Asm,* III [Jan. 24, 1851], 110).

Treaty between the United States and the Swiss Confederation.

If this treaty is to extend over Switzerland the all-protecting influence of our flag, she has to treat every American as an American citizen irrespective of his peculiar religious views, and if she cannot eradicate old rotten prejudices towards a long and unjustly persecuted race from her statute book and from the annals of her future history, then is she unworthy of the protection of this country, that owes its greatness and power to wise laws, as well as to its prowess in war, and to the most exalted virtues of tolerance and liberality. We step boldly forward and contend the United States dare not as a general or federal government make sectional treaties, which will deprive a part of her citizens however small in number of their due and guaranteed rights . . .

We expect the American Senate will not lend a helping hand to consummate this treaty unworthy of its greatness and fair fame, incompatible with its sense of justice and duties towards a portion of citizens that have ever sought to distinguish themselves by love of country, obedience to law, and attachment to this cherished Union . . .

See also *ibid.* (March 14), 164.

56. *Occ,* XII (May, 1854), 96-8.
57. *Ibid.,* XXIV (July, 1866), 191-2.
   See Sol M. Stroock, "Switzerland and the American Jews," *PAJHS* (1903), 7-52. See also Adler and Margalith, *op. cit.,* pp. 299-322.
58. The most comprehensive account of the Mortara incident in its historical setting is Bertram Korn's *The American Reaction to the Mortara Case: 1858-1859* (Cincinnati, 1957).
59. *Ibid.,* p. 32.
60. *Occ,* XVI (Jan., 1859), 492-502; (Feb., 1859), 536-42. Charles J. Cohen, "Dr. Morais's Relationship to the Congregation," *Centenary Memorial* (Philadelphia, 1924), pp. 9-10.
61. Bertram Korn, "The Know-Nothing Movement and the Jews," *Eventful Years . . . ,* pp. 74-6.
62. *Occ,* XVI (Feb., 1859), 541-2; *AI,* V (Feb. 11, 1859), 244.
63. Jacob Neusner, "The Role of English Jews in the Development of American Jewish Life, 1775-1850," *YIVO Annual,* XIII (1959), 131-56.
64. Isaacs, "A Board of Representatives," *JMes,* IV (Dec. 17, 1858), 140; V (Feb. 4, 1859), 36; (Feb. 11), 44; (Feb. 25), 60-61.
65. See Goldstein, *op. cit.,* p. 139; see also Grinstein, *op. cit.,* pp. 432-5; Buchler, "The Struggle for Unity," *loc. cit.,* pp. 36-8.
66. The New York congregations present were: Shaaray Tefila, Shaaray Tsedek, Beth El, Shaaray Rachamim,

B'nai Jeshurun, Rodef Sholom, Beth Israel Bikur Cholim, B'nai Israel, Anshe Chessed, Shaaray Shamayim, Shaaray Berocho. From the other parts of the country representatives came from Philadelphia—Beth-El-Emeth and Rodeph Shalom; Richmond—Beth Shalom and Kenesseth Israel; Providence, R. I.—B'nai Israel; New Haven, Conn.—Mishkan Israel; Hartford, Conn.—Oheb Sholom; Wilkes Barre, Pa.—B'nai Brith; Schenectady, N. Y.— Shaaray Shomayim; Charleston, S. C.—Shearith Israel; Boston, Mass.—Ohabei Sholom; New Orleans—Anshay Chesed; Newark, N. J.—Bnai Jeshurun; Washington, D. C.—First Hebrew Congregation. See *Occ*, XVII (Dec. 8, 1859), 219.

67. *JMes*, VI (Dec. 2, 1859), 164-6.
68. *Ibid*.
69. For descriptions of the ideological makeup of the Board, see Allan Tarshish, "The Board of Delegates of American Israelites (1859-1878)," *PAJHS*, XLIX (Sept., 1959), 16-32; and Bertram Korn, *American Jewry and the Civil War*, p. 73.
70. *AI*, VI (Jan. 27, 1860), 236; (Feb. 24), 268; (March 23), 299.
71. *JMes*, VII (March 2, 1860), 68.
72. This parallel was suggested in an address by Edwin Wolf at the 57th Annual Meeting of the AJHS, Feb. 22, 1959 (unpublished).
73. Abraham G. Duker, *The Record*, publication of the American Jewish Conference (July, 1947), p. 5.
74. Max J. Kohler, "The Board of Delegates of American Israelites, 1859-1878," *PAJHS*, XXIX (1925), Appendix II, 102-3.
75. Chap. IV, "A Question of Equality: the Chaplaincy Controversy," *op. cit.*, pp. 56-97.
76. *Occ*, XX (Aug., 1862), 214.
77. *Ibid.*, 214-5.
78. For the incident with General Grant, see *American Jewry and the Civil War*, pp. 122-55; with General Butler, pp. 164-6.
79. Sabato Morais, "Thanksgiving—A Sermon," *Asm*, V. (Dec. 12, 1851), 77. See also Oscar and Mary F. Handlin, *op. cit.*, pp. 64-5.
80. "This country is our Palestine, this city our Jerusalem,

this house of God our temple": David Philipson, *The Reform Movement in Judaism* (New York, 1931), p. 334.

81. "Greene Street Educational Institute," *Asm,* VII (Jan. 7, 1853), 137. See also (Dec. 3, 1852), 78.

82. Translation of Mendelssohn's *Jerusalem,* Introduction, p. XVIII. See also *Occ,* I (Feb., 1844), 522-36.

83. *Ibid.,* II (Dec., 1844), 412.

84. Lee C. Harby, "The Southern Jews in the War between the States," *AH,* LXXVII (Nov. 24, 1905), 769-70.

85. See Walter P. Posey, "The Baptists and Slavery in the Lower Mississippi Valley," in *The Journal of Negro History,* XLI (April, 1956). Prof. Posey writes that "as early as 1823 Richard Furman, a leading Baptist minister of Charleston, made one of the most important pro-slavery statements in behalf of a stand on moral grounds rather than on necessity . . . In this treatise he addressed to the governor of South Carolina an exposition of Baptist views, in which he contended that 'the right of holding slaves is clearly established in the Holy Scriptures, both by precept and example' " (pp. 125-26).

86. *Fast-Day Sermons* (New York, 1861).

87. "The Bible View of Slavery" *loc. cit.* See especially pp. 16-9, 24-31.

88. For further details and an interesting incident concerning Lincoln and Raphall, see Goldstein, *op. cit.,* pp. 125-26.

89. The article, which appeared in the *Jewish Messenger* of April 26, 1861, was reprinted by Bertram Korn in "The Jews of the Union," *AJA,* Civil War Centennial Northern Issue, XIII (Nov., 1961), 136-8.
The letter is presented by Korn together with several other documents pertaining to "The Jews of the Confederacy," *AJA,* Civil War Centennial Southern Issue, XIII (April, 1961), 33-4.

90. For the views of Leeser, Raphall, and Morais, see Korn, *American Jewry . . . op. cit.,* as follows: Leeser, pp. 44-47; Morais, pp. 35-39; Raphall, pp. 16-17.

91. "To the Parnas and members of K. K. Mikveh Israel," 13 Nisan, 5625 (1865). See also, Moshe Davis, "Notes and Documents, The Lincoln-Hart Correspondence," *PAJHS,* XXXVIII, part 2 (Dec., 1948), 139-45.

92. *Centenary Memorial,* pp. 11-12.

93. Sabato Morais: *An Address on the Death of Abraham Lincoln*—delivered before Congregation Mikveh Israel (Philadelphia, April 19, 1865). Even though he was heartbroken, Morais observed the Sabbath and showed no signs of mourning. That day large crowds moved through the Jewish neighborhood and demanded that the American flag be displayed in the windows but even they respected Morais and passed his house in silence. It is recalled by those who knew the Morais family that as soon as the Sabbath was out, Morais mourned "Father Abraham" like a student who mourns his teacher. He even took his children to his grave so that their memory of the emancipating President should never leave them.—Henry S. Morais: "Sabato Morais—A Memoir," in *Proceedings of the 6th Biennial Convention of the Jewish Theological Seminary Association* (New York, 1898), p. 83.

94. "Vaterland und Freiheit," *Abraham Lincoln, The Tribute of the Synagogue,* edited by Emanuel Hertz (New York, 1927), pp. 39-47.

95. "Nationality and the Jews," *The Menorah,* XII (Jan., 1892), 36.

PART I: CHAPTER FOUR

1. Henry Steele Commager, ed., *Living Ideas in America* (New York, 1957), chap. IX.
2. *Ibid.,* p. 447.
3. William Warren Sweet, *The American Churches, an Interpretation* (London, 1947), chap. IV.
4. *Occ,* I (Feb. 1844), 517.
5. *Ibid.,* 520.
6. *Ibid.,* XIV (Jan., 1857), 478; XXIV (Oct., 1866), 299-300.
7. *Ibid.,* I (Jan., 1844), 458.
8. *Ibid.,* 521. The concept of "Catholic Israel" with most of the meanings attached to it by Schechter at the end of the nineteenth century, was emphasized by Leeser at the beginning of his career. See also *Occ,* VI (Oct., 1848), 313-21.
9. See *supra,* chap. II, n. 32.
10. The participants at the decision-making meeting were: Judah L. Hackenburg, Lewis Allen, Isaac Leeser and

Mayer Arnold of the Sephardi group; Simon Elfeld of the German group; Jacob Ulman and Mr. Henry of the Polish synagogue. Tarshish, *op. cit.*, pp. 205-6.

11. Minutes of congregation Beth Elohim of Charleston, South Carolina (Aug. 10, 1841). Quoted in Buchler, *op. cit.*, p. 27.

12. *Occ*, III (May, 1845), 92-3. See also Minute Book of Mikveh Israel. "The communication of I. Leeser on the Committee appointed at the meeting of the congregation held 24th Aug., 1842."

13. *Occ*, II (Aug., 1844), 247-8.

14. Israel Goldstein, *op. cit.*, pp. 82-3.

15. E. Davis, *The History of Rodeph Shalom Congregation*, pp. 83-4.

16. *Occ*, IV (Feb., 1847), 552.

17. *Ibid.*, I (Jan., 1844), 512. The list of those confirmed includes the names of both boys and girls.

18. *Ibid.*, IV (Oct., 1846), 344-9.

19. For an excellent summary of the origin, introduction and spread of the confirmation ceremony, see F. De Sola Mendes, "Confirmation," *AH*, LIII (May 19, 1893), 77-8.

20. On the introduction of the Sermon in English, see *Discourses on the Jewish Religion*, I, p. 2. See also Adolf Kober, "Jewish Preaching and Preachers, A Contribution to the History of the Jewish Sermon in Germany and America," *Historia Judaica*, VII (Oct., 1945), 128-31. On Dr. Jastrow in Rodeph Shalom, see E. Davis, *op. cit.*, p. 85.

21. "The Mission of Israel," *Occ*, II (July, 1844), 171-2.

22. In 1864, Leeser published his revised and corrected version of Hester Rothschild's *Meditations and Prayers* (Philadelphia, 5624–1864). Mrs. Rothschild's book was itself a translation from the volume written by J. Ennery and issued in 1848 at Strasbourg. Part I was divided into supplementary prayers for everyday use, Sabbath, New Moon, New Year, Penitential Days, Day of Atonement, and all festivals, as well as prayers of religious initiation, the marriage service and prayers for use of children. Part II was devoted to prayers and meditations for special occasions and circumstances. Part III introduced prayers for the sick and dying.

23. *Ruhama: Devotional Exercises for the Use of the Daughters of Israel* (New York, 1852), p. XI. In the dedication, the editor and publisher declare the intention of the devotional exercises for the use of the Daughters of Israel "as Maidens, Brides, Wives, Mothers,/And on all other occasions, of joy, or of trial, incidental to their sex,/ For Private or Public Devotion . . ."

24. *Occ,* VI (Dec., 1848), 431-6. Leeser was delighted with Wise's letter, signed his name to the proclamation and called him a "gifted son of Israel." Dr. Max Lilienthal had attempted, in 1846, to establish a *bet din* as a religious advisory council. Wise joined Dr. Lilienthal, Dr. Herman Felsenheld and Rabbi Kohlmeyer. The initial meeting, held in 1847, dealt with the preparation of a catechism, a biblical history for Jewish schools, and Wise's proposal to produce a *Minhag America* under rabbinical sponsorship. Although nothing else came of this one meeting, the decision to produce a new prayer book—which Wise implemented—gave the meeting an enduring significance.

25. *Ibid.* (Feb., 1849), 538.

26. *Ibid.* (March, 1849), 577-8.

27. *Ibid.,* 616. See also 321.

28. For Leeser's remarks see "The Demand of the Times," *ibid.,* I (March, 1844), 571.
   For Wise's letter to Leeser see Maxwell Whiteman in his article "Isaac Leeser and the Jews of Philadelphia," *PAJHS,* XLVIII (June, 1959), 223, n. 83.

29. *Occ,* VII (April, 1849), 41-2; (June, 1849), 178; (Aug., 1849), 267-70. For the criticism directed by Leeser at those who did not answer, see (May, 1849), 61-4.

30. *Ibid.* (June, 1849), 137-9. See also Baron, "The Revolution of 1848 and Jewish Scholarship," in *Proceedings of the American Academy for Jewish Research,* XVIII (1948-49), 26-29. For the opinion of European Jews on whether to emigrate to America or to take a stand in Europe and the views of Leopold Kompert, see Guido Kisch, "The Revolution of 1848 and the Jewish 'On to America' Movement," *PAJHS,* XXXVIII (March, 1949), Part 3, 185-234. For an exhaustive article on the American aspect of this question, see Bertram Korn, "Jewish

48'ers in America," *American Jewish Archives,* II (June, 1949), 3-20.

31. For a description of Wise's relationship to the Society of the Friends of Light, see *Reminiscences,* pp. 84-92; Korn, *Eventful Years . . . ,* pp. 37-8; Buchler, *loc. cit.,* p. 28.

32. *Occ,* VII (June, 1849), 146-8.

33. *Occ,* VI (Oct., 1848), 313-21; (Dec.), 431-5; (Jan., 1849), 508-13; (Feb.), 529-39; (March), 577-83.

34. Leeser lists every congregation individually. The breakdown by states is as follows: New York 33; New England 6; New Jersey 1; Pennsylvania 13; Maryland 7; District of Columbia 2; Virginia 5; North Carolina 1; South Carolina 4; Georgia 2; Alabama 4; Louisiana 6; Texas 2; Mississippi 3; Tennessee 2; Kentucky 1; Ohio 10; Michigan 2; Illinois 2; Indiana 5; Wisconsin 1; Iowa 2; Minnesota 1; Missouri 2; California 5. In addition, there were many Jews in Oregon and Washington territories, as well as in Arkansas, Florida, New Mexico and Kansas, who were not yet organized into communities. See *Occ,* XIV (Dec., 1856), 409-11.

35. *Reminiscences,* pp. 307-8. See also *AI,* I (Feb. 9, 1855), 244; (March 2), 268; (March 9), 276; (April 13), 317; II (Aug. 10), 39.

36. *Occ,* XIII (Nov., 1855), 407-14. The participants were: Isaac M. Wise, Bnai Jeshurun, Cincinnati; J. L. Miller, same; Maximilian Lilienthal, Bnai Israel, Cincinnati; Charles Kahn, Ahabath Achim, Cincinnati; Lipman Adler, Detroit (Michigan) congregation; Benedict H. Gotthelf, Adas Israel, Louisville, Ky.; B. L. Fould, Joseph Levi and Asher Lehman, Anshe Chesed, Cleveland; Isidor Kalisch, F. I. Cohen and Alexander Schwab, Tifereth Israel, Cleveland; Elkan Cohn, Anshe Emeth, Albany, New York; Dr. Rothenheim, Cincinnati and Isaac Leeser, Mikveh Israel, Philadelphia.

37. For Leeser's views on this matter see *ibid.,* p. 412. For Wise's comments on this compromise, see *Reminiscences,* pp. 313-4.

38. See Wise's summary of the resolutions in *Reminiscences,* pp. 313-5.

39. Gratitude to the Shepherds of Israel for the sacred work they accomplished at their gathering in Cleveland:

. . . You did not tarry to follow the Lord and you went to the city of Cleveland where you agreed to unite the Jewish people in the true faith of our fathers, the complete faith that lacks nothing. And I have heard that you probed carefully for all to know that for anyone to be called a Jew it is necessary for him to believe that the whole of the Torah as we have it today is a heritage from Moses and the Prophets as a Divine revelation for those who fear God. It is furthermore incumbent upon us to fulfill all of the Torah as it has been explained by the Sages of the Talmud, not to deviate from it to the right or to the left and whoever does not believe these two principles is not a Jew . . .

Blessed are you my brothers; you have done well. May God increase and multiply your strength. Far be it from me to think that you thought deceitfully in your hearts. Undoubtedly you have acted with an honest and sincere heart and may God act likewise toward you all your days. Who is there fearful of God whose heart and soul do not rejoice in the joy of the Torah? I can therefore not restrain myself from expressing my gratitude and that of many others who have the fear of God in their heart and may He who examines the hearts repay you a thousandfold.

But, my brothers, as much as I love you for your great work, I cannot hide from you that soon some men of high purpose raised objections against you, saying: These people decided for us and not for themselves because many of them did not accept what they themselves said and proclaimed publicly and continue to act as if nothing had happened. They themselves excluded from the ranks of Jewry anyone who denies prophecy and Talmud and yet many of them do exactly that. One of them composed a prayer book in which Prophecy is denied, the Torah rejected and abuse heaped on the Talmud, thereby sinning and causing others to sin. And how can such a man agree to the principles he has agreed to if not with a deceitful heart and mouth . . . ?

And to you, chief shepherd, I say that the eyes of Israel are upon you. Their chief complaint is against you. They say that it is your influence that made them agree to accept all the precepts of the Torah but they did not do so with a pure heart. . . . Now whatever they add or detract from the Law, they do in the name of the Talmud and base their action on the words of the Sages. In the name of the Talmud they dispense with the law of *Yibum* and *Halitzah* for the wife of a deceased brother. In the name of the Talmud they grant permission to shave with razor, to sing and rejoice on fast days, to eat the fowl broiled in butter, to blow shofar on Rosh Hashanah with a metal instrument, to abolish the second day of Yom Tov, to bury Gentiles with Jews, not to separate men from women in the synagogue, to shorten the prayers, believing that whoever shortens prayers is praiseworthy, and finally, to assert that the Redeemer of Israel will not appear. . . . They accepted the Talmud so that their actions would be accepted by the people since they are presented as if sanctioned by the Talmud. My brothers, listen to my voice: far be it from me to judge you without justice. I know your good heart and that you have acted with a pure heart, without deceit. But I advise you to make yourself clear before all. Therefore, chastise those people in public. Tell them that their actions belie their words, and that their spirits are not faithful to Judaism. Let them change their ways and say "We have sinned." Then everyone will believe that you and the men with you are true followers of the God of Israel.

Your humble,

Issakhar Ber Illowy

Translated from the Hebrew, *Occ,* XIII (March, 1856), 585-6; XIV (April, 1856), 38-9. See also *AI,* I (March 9, 1855), 279.

40. *Occ,* XIII (Dec., 1855), 448-9. This conflict had its repercussions in Europe, too. The leaders of Reform in Germany, Ludwig Philippson and Leopold Stein, criticized Wise for his waywardness and praised Einhorn for his faithfulness to Reform principles. See *ibid.,* XIV (May, 1856), 81-3.

41. *Reminiscences,* pp. 321-2.

42. Beryl Harold Levy, *Reform Judaism in America* (New York, 1933), p. 44. Einhorn involved his congregation in

the debate. The target was Wise's stand on the Talmud. The congregation issued a special pamphlet in which the Cleveland platform was attacked. Its main point was that it was incorrect to state that all Jews accepted the Talmud as the only interpretation of the Scriptures. There are many contradictions between the Talmud and Scriptures.

43. See Samuel S. Cohon, "Hebrew Union College Ben Shivim" [The Seventieth Anniversary of the Hebrew Union College], *Hadoar* (Dec. 14, 1945), 131.

44. *Occ*, XIV (Feb., 1857), 508-11. For Wise's views of the conference, see *AI*, II (Sept. 28, 1855), 92; (November 9), 148. For his response to the Reform critics, see *ibid.* (Nov. 30), 173.

45. *Ibid.* (July), 183-4. For Wise's views on this matter, see *AI*, III (Feb. 20, 1857), 260; (March 27), 300. For Wise's complete version of the Cleveland Conference, see *Reminiscences*, pp. 307-23.

46. See Illowy's analysis of the prayer book, *Occ*, XIII (Nov., 1855), 414-7.

47. *Ibid.*, XIV (Feb., 1857), 505-8.

48. *Occ*, XI (Oct., 1853), 355-61. See also XVI (Aug., 1858), 221-31.

49. Tarshish, *op. cit.*, p. 186.

50. *Ibid.*, p. 189.

51. *Occ*, XVII (July, 1859), 86-7.

52. *Occ*, II (Aug. 1844), 224-37.

53. Jacob Rader Marcus, *The Americanization of Isaac Mayer Wise* (Cincinnati, 1931), p. 11.

54. For Wise's views which led to the writing of *Cosmic God*, see his memoir, "The World of My Books" translated by Albert Friedlander, *loc. cit.*, pp. 138-41. An analysis of Wise's theology is given by Beryl Harold Levy, *op. cit.*, pp. 44-9. For a statement of Wise's views in the light of contemporary American thought, see Israel Knox, *Rabbi in America: The Story of Isaac M. Wise* (Boston, 1957), pp. 147-58.

55. *Occ*, XIX (July, 1861), 183, 187. See also XXII (July, 1864), 155-6.

56. See *AI*, VI (March 16, 1860), 292; VII (June 21, 1861), 404; VIII (Aug. 2, 1861), 360; (Oct. 25), 132; IX (Sept. 5, 1862), 76; (May 22, 1863), 364-5.

57. Einhorn was a sharp critic of Szold. He attacked him

violently in an article entitled "Das Schicksal der Oheb Shalom Gemeinde" written immediately after Szold's first sermon. In this article he prophesies the downfall of the congregation under Szold's leadership. Wise, who found Szold congenial to his ideas, supported him. He attacked Einhorn for writing as he did. See *AI*, VI (Dec. 9, 1859), 182; (March 30, 1860), 306-7.

58. Benjamin Szold, *Auch Ein Wort Ueber Jastrow und Hirsch* (Baltimore, 1868). For a bibliography of the writings of Samuel Hirsch, see Adolph S. Oko, "Bibliography of Dr. Samuel Hirsch," (Cincinnati, 1916).

59. Szold, *op. cit.*, p. 7.

60. *AI*, VI (Nov. 25, 1859), 165.

61. Szold's dedication sermon, *Divre Shalom ve-Emet (Gottesdienstlicher Vortrag*, Baltimore, 1859). For Wise's views on this sermon, see *AI*, VI (Nov. 25, 1859), 164.

62. See, for example, the prayerbook of Dr. Leo Merzbacher, rabbi of Temple Emanuel in New York, entitled, *The Order of Prayer for Divine Service* (New York, 1855).

63. For a short biography of Hochheimer, see Appendix A.

64. Szold chose and arranged the prayers and Hochheimer prepared the German translation.

65. H. S. Morais, *The Jews of Philadelphia*, p. 76.

66. E. Davis, *op. cit.*, pp. 86-7.

67. *Ibid.*, pp. 91-2.

68. From notes based on oral interviews with Rebekah Kohut, 1942-45.

PART II: CHAPTER ONE

1. *The War for the Union: The Improvised War 1861-1862* (New York, 1959), p. v.

2. For a list by cities and states, see *Statistics of the Jews of the United States*, compiled under the authority of the Board of Delegates of the Union of American Hebrew Congregations (Philadelphia, 1880). We have no accurate figures for the Jewish population in the United States during the nineteenth century, either in the governmental archives or in surveys by Jewish organizations. The figures used are only general estimates and conjectures based on various statistical compilations. For analyses of immigra-

tion statistics from 1870, see Jacob Lestchinsky, "Di Yidishe Immigratzia in di Fareynikte Shtatn 1870-1900" (Jewish Immigration to the United States 1870-1900), in *Geshikte fun der Yidisher Arbeter-Bavegung in di Fareynikte Shtatn* (History of the Jewish Labor Movement in the United States), ed. E. Tcherikower, I (New York, 1943), 35. See also the summary of Nathan Goldberg, "The Jewish Population in the United States," *The Jewish People. Past and Present,* 2 (New York, 1948), 25-6. A discussion of the East-European immigration during the seventies may be found in the author's "Ha-Zofeh ba-Arez ha-Hadashah" (The Observer in the New Land), *Alexander Marx Jubilee Volume,* ed. Saul Lieberman (New York, 1950), pp. 115-41.

3. See "Friedrich Hassaurek: Cincinnati's Leading Forty-Eighter," *The Ohio Historical Quarterly,* LXVIII (Jan., 1959), 1, 2, 4.

4. Einhorn's position is expressed in the following statement: "Take away from reform Judaism the German spirit, or what is the same thing, the German language, and you have torn away from it the mother soil and it must wither away, the lovely flower. The English sermon can have for its mission nothing else than to utilize the treasures of the German spirit and German literature for our religious life and therewith to enrich it. In a word, where the German sermon is banned, there the reform of Judaism is nothing more than a brilliant gloss, a decorated doll, without heart, without soul, which the proudest temples and the most splendid theories cannot succeed in infusing with life." Cited by David de Sola Pool, "Judaism and the Synagogue," *The American Jew,* ed. Oscar Janowsky (New York, 1942), p. 45.

In 1879 he stated in a sermon: "Germany is my homeland, and after having come from there with thousands of others, I am an *Ibri*—a wanderer—following my brothers to this God-blessed Republic." See Beryl H. Levy, *op. cit.,* p. 44.

Wise, on the other hand, rarely missed an opportunity to speak out against the attempt to "Germanize the American synagogue." With vehemence he declared: "We can not be Germanized, therefore our German preachers could not reach the masses . . ." See Martin B. Ryback, "The East-West Conflict in American Reform Judaism," in *AJA,* IV (Jan., 1952), 17-8. Wise's credo of Americanization versus Germanization is expressed in *Reminiscences,* p. 331.

5. Marshall Sklare, *Conservative Judaism* (New York, 1955), pp. 20-25. See Tarshish, *op. cit.,* pp. 190-4.

6. For an evaluation in retrospect of the founding fathers of the American Reform Movement, see Abraham J. Karp, "The Father of American Reform Judaism," *Judaism,* VII (Fall, 1958), 1-5.

Rebekah Kohut recalls her own fascination for Wise and the admiration which was expressed for him both in her father's household and in that of her husband:

> One could disagree with him on every subject, and still find him irresistibly charming. He was at odds in controversy with my father, Dr. Bettelheim; he was almost ferociously at odds with my husband, Dr. Kohut; yet both men loved him. They trusted his heart, if not his head. He was not a great scholar in the European sense, but he was a great American leader in the organization of congregational life. (*His Father's House* [New Haven, 1938], p. 49).

See also Waxman, *op. cit.,* IV, 1093-4. The author discusses Wise's changes of opinion as reflected in his varying actions. Further examples of Wise's ambivalence, drawn from a study of his German newspaper, *Die Deborah,* from 1870 to 1875, are brought together by Joseph Gutmann, "Watchman on an American Rhine: New Light on Isaac M. Wise," *AJA,* X (Oct., 1958), 135-44.

7. "The World of My Books," translated from the German by Albert H. Friedlander, *AJA,* VI (June, 1954), 128.

8. Quoted in Dena Wilansky, *Sinai to Cincinnati* (New York, 1937), p. 178.

9. I. M. Wise, *History of the Israelitish Nation,* II (Albany, 1854), Preface, p. IV. Bernard J. Bamberger in *Reform Judaism* (Cincinnati, 1949), p. 3.

10. For the above discussion of the mission of Israel, see Wilansky, *op. cit.,* p. 256; also *Occ,* VII (July, 1849), 183-92.

11. Wilansky, *op. cit.,* p. 134.
12. *Ibid.,* p. 165. For an interpretation of Wise's concept of universality and his attitude toward the Tradition, see Israel Knox, *op. cit.,* pp. 124 ff., 137 ff.
13. Wilansky, *op. cit.,* p. 42. One of the reasons for Wise's certainty that Judaism as a universal faith would overcome Christianity was his marked distrust of Christianity, which at times even reached invective, especially against Christian evangelists and missionaries. See Gutmann, *loc. cit.,* pp. 137-9.
14. The full annotated list of these works and Wise's motivations and methods in his struggle against Christian missionizing are described in his memoir "The World of My Books," *loc. cit.,* pp. 136-8.
    See Samuel Sandmel, "Isaac Mayer Wise's 'Jesus Himself,' " *Essays in American Jewish History* (Cincinnati, 1958), pp. 325-58.
15. For a succinct analysis of the theological views of Wise, Einhorn and Samuel Hirsch, see Levy, *op. cit.,* pp. 44-55. See also David Philipson, *The Reform Movement in Judaism* (New York, 1931), pp. 342-53.
16. Joseph Krauskopf, "Fifty years of Judaism in America," *American Jews' Annual,* 4 (Cincinnati, 1888), 79, lists the following participants in the conference: Samuel Adler (New York), Isaac L. Chronik (Chicago), S. Deutsch (Baltimore), David Einhorn (New York), James Gutheim (New York), Bernard Felsenthal (Chicago), Samuel Hirsch (Philadelphia), Kaufmann Kohler (Detroit), L. Mayer (Selma, Alabama). Moses Mielziner (New York), Solomon H. Sonneschein (St. Louis), Isaac M. Wise (Cincinnati). Dr. Hirsch was appointed president. *Loc. cit.,* p. 79. *The Yearbook CCAR,* I (1890-91) also lists M. Schlesinger of Albany, as a participant. See also *JT,* I (June 4, 1869), 8.
17. The seven basic resolutions of this Reform conference are given here in their entirety as recorded in *CCAR Yearbook,* I (1890-91), 117-19:
    1. The Messianic aim of Israel is not the restoration of the old Jewish state under a descendant of David, involving a second separation from the nations of the earth, but the union of all the children of God in the confession of the unity of God, so as to realize

the unity of all rational creatures and their call to moral sanctification.

2. We look upon the destruction of the second Jewish commonwealth not as a punishment for the sinfulness of Israel, but as a result of the divine purpose revealed to Abraham, which, as has become ever clearer in the course of the world's history, consists in the dispersion of the Jews to all parts of the earth, for the realization of their high priestly mission, to lead the nations to the true knowledge and worship of God.

3. The Aaronic priesthood and the Mosaic sacrificial cult were preparatory steps to the real priesthood of the whole people, which began with the dispersion of the Jews, and to the sacrifices of sincere devotion and moral sanctification, which alone are pleasing and acceptable to the Most Holy. These institutions, preparatory to higher religiosity, were consigned to the past, once for all, with the destruction of the second temple, and only in this sense—as educational influences in the past—are they to be mentioned in our prayers.

4. Every distinction between Aaronides and non-Aaronides, as far as religious rites and duties are concerned, is consequently inadmissible, both in the religious cult and in life.

5. The selection of Israel as the people of religion, as the bearers of the highest idea of humanity, is still, as ever, to be strongly emphasized, and for this very reason, whenever this is mentioned it shall be done with full emphasis laid on the world-embracing mission of Israel and the love of God for all His children.

6. The belief in the bodily resurrection has no religious foundation, and the doctrine of immortality refers to the after-existence of the soul only.

7. Urgently as the cultivation of the Hebrew language, in which the treasures of divine revelation are given and the immortal remains of a literature that influences all civilized nations are preserved, must be always desired by us in fulfillment of a sacred duty, yet has it become unintelligible to the vast majority

of our coreligionists; therefore it must make way, and is advisable under existing circumstances, to intelligible language in prayer, which, if not understood, is a soulless form.

18. The background of this conflict within the Reform group is analyzed in detail by Martin B. Ryback, *loc. cit.*, pp. 3-25.

19. Krauskopf, *loc. cit.*, p. 81. Severe criticism of the Cincinnati meeting came from the extreme Reform side and some members of the Historical School. Both opposing bodies attacked Wise for not organizing an all-embracing religious organization. Wise answered that the meeting had proved to meet that very objective. See *AI*, XVIII (Aug. 11, 1871), 8-9; (Aug. 18), 9.
Kaufmann Kohler, *Studies, Addresses and Personal Papers* (New York, 1931), p. 480. For a biography and interpretive essay on Kohler, see Samuel S. Cohon, "Kaufmann Kohler the Reformer," *Mordecai M. Kaplan Jubilee Volume,* ed. Moshe Davis (New York, 1953), pp. 137-55; Kaufmann Kohler, *A Living Faith* (Cincinnati, 1948). Another important personality who joined the Reform movement and became one of the leading lights was Gustav Gottheil. For a biography, see Richard Gottheil, *The Life of Gustav Gottheil* (Williamsport, Pa., 1936).

20. As reported in the *J Mes*, XXIV (Aug. 21, 1868), 2-3, the executive committee was composed of representatives of the following 23 congregations: Adath Jeshurun, Adereth El, Ahavath Chesed, Anshi Chesed, Beth Cholim, Beth El, Beth Hamidrash (Allen St.), Beth Hamidrash Hagadol, Beth Israel Bikur Cholim, Bikur Cholim Ukadisha, B'nai Israel, B'nai Jeshurun, B'nai Sholem, Darech Amuno, Temple Emanuel, Mishkan Israel, Poel Tsedek, Rodoph Sholem, Shaari Berocho, Shaari Rachmim, Shaari Tefila, Shaari Tsedek, Shaari Hashamaim.

21. *Ibid.*

22. The exchange of correspondence between Morais and Isaacs is to be found in the library of Dropsie College and has been summarized by Jacob Pressman (unpublished typescript in possession of the author).

23. *J Mes*, XXXVIII (Nov. 12, 1875), 5; (Nov. 19), 4; (Nov.

26), 5; (Dec. 3), 5; (Dec. 10), 5: See also *HL*, X (June 21, 1867), 4.

24. Samuel Hirsch, one of radical Reform's most fervent adherents, immediately reacted to Morais' proposal by berating his so-called "sacrifice." The letter, in part follows:

635 N. 7th
Phil., December 18th, '75

Rev. Mr. Morais, City.
Dear and reverend sir!

I perused with much attention your articles about the ritual. Allow me to express privately and in my poor English my opinion. Two years ago, when the prayer book accepted in my congregation did only exist in the German tongue, I would not have been astonished about your opinion, because you not reading German were not bound to know what goes on even in your neighborhood. But to day our prayer-book being translated in English I am astonished reading the principles you profess and seeing you seek what exists already.

Yes, Mr. Morais, our prayer-book comes quite to the standard you are asking for . . . :

1. The Hebrew language. We did retain in Hebrew שלש ראשונות, and ברכת שבע and from ברכות י"ח the ושלש אחרונות, the אמצעיות are translated. We did retain in Hebrew שמע and שתים לפניה ואחת לאחריה, in that form that Zunz declared the most ancienne. We have￼ in Hebrew. We read the תורה in Hebrew, certainly translating afterwards the portion read. We have the קדיש in the ancient form. For ראש השנה and יום כפור, there are other passages maintained in Hebrew. That we have not more in that holy language the reason is that we can not hope to teach more Hebrew to our youth. If we could we would accept more but the first principle for us is, prayers must be understood—שמע בכל לשון שאתה שומע, תפלה בלא כונה וכו' [כגוף בלי נשמה].

2. You ask that אתה בחרתנו be retained. Now every page of our prayer-book proclaimes with glowing words the selection of Israel, the holy mission given to our

forefathers, that it is our duty to be a nation of priests, the light of the nations, that our history is a miraculous one and has that signification, etc.

3. But we have Jewish and Christian singers. Certainly, I, too, would prefer Jewish singers if I could have them. I would prefer even singers and readers and rabbis without retribution, but alas, that is not possible . . .

4. But you are opposed to the organ . . . It is quite true, the organ has been only recently introduced in the synagogues. But did the reason thereof never happen to your mind? The reason is quite a simple one. The Jews were here and there in happy times tolerated but not the public Jewish service. Therefore, all ancient synagogues were build (*sic*) facing not the public thoroughfare but a yard. You ask after such a synagogue. In the street you see only a poor building, a private house. Passing it, in the yard of it stands the synagogue. An organ proclaiming loudly a synagogal service would not have been tolerated. But even if a congregation is opposed to an organ, I think, that has nothing to do with the ritual of prayers.

That are the few remarks I feel bound to submit to your judgement hoping you would accept my suggestions in the sense they are given, not for proselyting purposes, but only to serve the holy cause dear to us all.

> Your truly obedient servant,
> Dr. Samuel Hirsch

25. *JMes*, XXX (July 7, 1871), 2.
26. *AH*, LXX (Jan. 17, 1902), 279-82.
27. Tarshish, *op. cit.*, p. 260.
28. The type of congregations established by these East-European immigrants and the resultant opposition of their leaders to Reform can be gleaned from the pages of *Ha-Zofeh ba-Arez ha-Hadashah*. See especially I (July 7, 1871-8 Tammuz, 5631), 19-20; (Aug . 18, 1871–1 Elul, 5631), 59; II (May 17, 1872–8 Iyar, 5632), 82; (July 5, 1872–29 Sivan, 5632), 129–30: (Dec

20, 1872–20 Kislev, 5632), 305-6; (Feb. 21, 1873–24 Shebat, 5633), 353; (March 28, 1873–29 Adar, 5633), 303-4.

See also the author's "*Ha-Zofeh ba-Arez ha-Hadashah,*" *loc. cit.*, pp. 116-8; Bernard D. Weinryb, "East European Immigration to the United States." *The Jewish Quarterly Review,* LV (1955), 505-15; Morris A. Gutstein, *A Priceless Heritage* (New York, 1953), p. 34. The value of the direct help of these congregations to the Historical School can be judged by the extent of their participation in the founding meeting of the Jewish Theological Seminary.

29. See Jacob Kabakoff, "Hebrew Culture and Creativity in America," *Jewish Life in America,* edited by Theodore Friedman and Robert Gordis (New York, 1955), pp. 178-82; J. D. Eisenstein, *op. cit.,* pp. 20-21, 23, 25, 29-30, 34-5.
30. For a personal account of the founding and a history of the *American Hebrew,* see Cowen, *op. cit.,* pp. 41-84.

PART II: CHAPTER TWO

1. *AH,* III (June 11, 1880), 38.
2. The following editorial in the *American Hebrew* illustrates the rationale of the Historical School in its support of the Sunday school (II [May 14, 1880], 146-7):

We may distinctly state that the Sunday School movement among American Jews which commenced by Rebecca Gratz less than half a century ago, is but the legitimate expression of a deep-seated instinct of the Jewish mind. Real nurseries of Judaism, the institution deserves earnest support from the community. No words sufficiently strong can be found to properly express the appreciation of all true lovers of Judaism for those ladies and gentlemen who work heart and soul in a too-often thankless task. Teaching at any time is not the most pleasing profession, especially for amateurs, as many of the Sunday School teachers are . . . We would however like to make a remark about a common mistake in the method of instruction. Of the modes of teaching employed in the metropolitan Jewish Sunday Schools, we prefer

the oral to the use of catechisms of any kind. The results are likely to be far more satisfactory, and the
examination will be a more crucial test of the scholars'
ability.

3. *Ibid.*, XVI (Sept. 28, 1883), 74.

4. *Ibid.*, XXI (Feb. 6, 1885), 202.

5. Eisenstein, *op. cit.*, p. 66.

6. *AH*, III (June 4, 1880), 26.

7. *Ibid.* (May 21), 4.

8. Among these translations are *Humpty Dumpty, Ding
Dong Bell, Old King Cole, Little Bo Peep,* and *There
Dwelt a Man in our Town.* See Cowen, *op. cit.*, p. 52.

9. "Industrial Education," *AH*, XIII (Dec. 1, 1882), 30. See
also Solis-Cohen, *Judaism and Science*, pp. 9-11.

10. *Proceedings of the Union of American Hebrew Congregations*, I-IV (Cincinnati, 1879), I-II.

11. For a short biography of Dembitz, see Appendix A.

12. At the same gathering a letter of commendation was received from Moses Montefiore in which he congratulated
those active in the enterprise of spreading Torah and,
as a sign of his esteem, he sent a copy of the Bible in five
volumes published with the 32 commentaries. The institution had three classes: the preparatory, one for
Hebrew studies, and one for religious studies. A faculty
of five was appointed: the president, two professors and
two instructors.

13. David Philipson describes the early days of this institution in his memoirs. See *My Life as an American Jew*
(Cincinnati, 1941), pp. 1-24. For his advice to candidates
for admission and a selection from his lecture notes, see
AI, XXIII (July 31, 1874), 4.

14. From the Mikveh Israel Files. Cited in Moshe Davis,
"Sabato Morais: A Selected and Annotated Bibliography
of his Writings," *PAJHS*, XXXVII (1947), 84.

15. "Opening Address at the First Commencement of the
HUC," *AI*, XXX (July 20, 1883), 2.

16. *Supra,* Part I, chap. 2.

17. Brochure, in Morais Archives (1876), Dropsie College,
Philadelphia.

18. Mr. Elkin's first name is not given. The reference may
be to Lewis Elkin, for 25 years a member of the Board of

Public Education of the first school district of Pennsylvania (Philadelphia), and chairman of the Committee on Qualifications of Teachers. See Henry Morais, *The Jews of Philadelphia*, p. 406.

19. David Philipson, "The History of Hebrew Union College, 1875–1925" *Hebrew Union College Jubilee Volume 1875–1925* (Cincinnati, 1925).

20. *JMes*, XXXVIII (Nov. 12, 1875), 4-5.

21. *AH*, XXXVII (Nov. 9, 1888), 2.

22. The first Young Men's Hebrew Association was established in Baltimore in 1854. Within the next 20 years, similar groups sprang up in most of the leading cities throughout the East and Middle West, and they existed for varied lengths of time, depending on the community and local leadership. In 1874, a YMHA was founded in New York, and a year later an association was begun in Philadelphia. Both these groups were successful from their inception, and set the tone for the programs of similar organizations across the country. The circulars as well as the constitutions and bylaws of these two leading associations were sent to all the others.

23. A comprehensive account of the rise of the YMHA movement is given by Benjamin Rabinowitz, *The Young Men's Hebrew Associations (1854–1913)* (New York, 1948). See especially pp. 5, 11-18.

24. Cyrus Adler, *op. cit.*, pp. 20-21.

25. *JMes*, XXIX (May 19, 1871), 4. See also *JT*, III (July 28, 1871), 342; (Oct. 27, 1871), 552; IV (May 10, 1872), 206; Solomon Grayzel, "Graetz's *History* in America," *Historia Judaica*, III (Oct., 1941), 53-66.

26. Unpublished letter, November 21, 1873, Morais file, Dropsie College Archives.

27. *AH*, XX (August 29, 1884), 33.

28. Mark Wischnitzer, *Visas to Freedom: The History of HIAS* (Cleveland & New York, 1956), pp. 27-9.

29. Of particular importance is the English edition of George M. Price's "The Russian Jews in America," translated from the Russian by Leo Shpall, *PAJHS*, XLVIII (Sept., 1958), 28-62; (December), 78-133. This primary source material sheds important new light on the period. See also Irving Aaron Mandel, "Attitude

of the American Jewish Community Toward East European Immigration," *AJA* III (June, 1950), 11-36; Zosa Szajkowski, "The Attitude of American Jews to East European Immigration (1881–1893)," *PAJHS,* XL (March, 1951), 221-80, and "The European Attitude to East European Jewish Immigration (1881–1893)," *ibid.,* XLI (Dec., 1951), 127-62; Bernard D. Weinryb, "East European Immigration to the United States," *loc. cit.,* pp. 515-24, and "Jewish Immigration and Accommodation to America: Research, Trends, Problems," in *The Writing of American Jewish History,* edited by Moshe Davis and Isidore S. Meyer (New York, 1957), pp. 366-403.

30. See especially Price, *loc. cit.,* pp. 31 ff., 87 ff., and *passim;* Mandel, *loc. cit.,* pp. 13, 15, 31-2; Szajkowski, "The Attitude of American Jews . . . ," *loc. cit.,* pp. 222-3, 227 ff., 239 ff., 253, 264-71; "The European Attitude . . . ," *loc. cit.,* pp. 127-35.

31. *AH,* VII (Aug. 5, 1881), 135. For Wise's views, see Wilansky, *op. cit.,* pp. 178-9.

32. *AH,* VII (Aug. 5, 1881), 133.

33. Wischnitzer, *op. cit.,* pp. 30-36. See also Gilbert Osofsky, "The Hebrew Emigrant Aid Society of the United States (1881-1883)," *PAJHS,* XLIX (March, 1960), 173-87.

34. *AH,* XX (Sept. 12, 1884), 73.

35. Reported by a member of Morais' congregation in *AH,* VII (June 10, 1881), 39; (Aug. 5), 133; XXII (April 10, 1885), 131-2.

36. Isaac Mayer Wise continued to contend against the Sunday Laws to the end of his career. The following is a selected list of articles dealing with his activity: *AI,* XIV (July 19, 1867), 4; (Feb. 21, 1868), 4; XXVI (April 21, 1876), 4; XXVIII (Jan. 12, 1877), 4; (March 23), 4; (May 25), 4; XXXII (May 20, 1879), 4; XXXIII (Nov. 7, 1879), 4.

37. *JMes,* XXXIII (April 11, 1873), 2.

38. *JRec,* II (June 9, 1876), 3.

39. Letter from S. Morais, Jan. 23, 1881, *ibid.,* XII (Jan. 28, 1881), 4.

40. *AH,* XX (Oct. 17, 1884), 145.

41. (Hamburg, 1868).

42. *Jewish Family Papers; or, Letters of a Missionary*, trans-
    lated from the German of Dr. Wilhelm Herzberg
    ("Gustav Meinhardt"), (New York, 1875).
43. (New York, 1876).
44. Lee M. Friedman, *Jewish Pioneers and Patriots* (Phila-
    delphia, 1942), pp. 267-78. See also Eisenstein, *op. cit.*,
    pp. 42-3. Compare John Higham's interpretation of the
    Hilton-Seligman affair in the light of his structural view
    of discrimination, that "discrimination can arise more
    or less simultaneously at every social level where a crush
    of applicants poses an acute problem of admission." See
    his article "Social Discrimination Against Jews in Amer-
    ica, 1830–1930," *PAJHS*, XLVII (Sept., 1957), especially
    11, n. 29.
45. *JMes*, XXXIX (Jan. 21, 1876), 5.
46. Adler had studied for the rabbinate in the preparatory
    school of Temple Emanu-El and was then sent to Ger-
    many to complete his rabbinical studies at the Seminary
    in Berlin and his secular studies at the Universities of
    Berlin and Heidelberg. In Berlin he was deeply influ-
    enced by the Kantian scholar, Hermann Cohen. He re-
    ceived his doctorate in philosophy in 1873. When he
    returned to New York, Adler began to introduce his
    newly-acquired European views which did not coincide
    with Judaism. The congregation which had sent him
    abroad to prepare him for its ministry rejected him at
    the request of Dr. Gustav Gottheil. Instead, he began
    his new career at Cornell University. This chair was
    made possible by his New York friends who donated the
    necessary funds. In 1876, he came to New York once
    again and organized the Society for Ethical Culture.
    See Richard Gottheil, *The Life of Gustav Gottheil*
    (Pennsylvania, 1936), pp. 40-42.
47. Felix Adler, *An Ethical Philosophy of Life* (New York,
    1920), p. 26.
48. The Society confined its attention to moral problems. It
    gave practical expression to its beliefs by founding a
    workingman's school and a model school for general
    and technical education. Most of its students were not
    Jewish, but for many it became a road out of Judaism.
    The Society also established a system of district nursing

among the poor and a family home for neglected children. Branch societies were formed in Chicago, Philadelphia and St. Louis; and abroad in London, Cambridge and Berlin. Though agnostic at first, the Society acquired a strong influence in Christian circles in some European countries.

49. "Notes from my Tablets," *JRec*, II (March 9, 1877), 4; (March 16), 4; (April 27, 1877), 4; (May 4), 4.

50. Other contemporary modernistic philosophies, far less significant in purpose and achievement, were sweeping America, manifesting themselves through peculiar offshoots of religion. For example, Rabbi Solomon Schindler of Temple Israel in Boston attempted to fuse the moral contents of both Judaism and Christianity into a new, progressive secular faith. Such attempts to give birth to a new faith by blending elements of other religions yielded, for the most part, only aberrations. In the West, one Reform rabbi converted outright to Unitarianism; while in Baltimore, the Har Sinai congregation (formerly the pulpit of Einhorn,), unknowingly appointed a convert to Christianity to its pulpit. See Arthur Mann, ed., *Growth and Achievement: Temple Israel 1854–1954* (Cambridge, 1954), pp. 45-62. See also I. Blum, *Jews of Baltimore*, p. 20. Jastrow was quick to deplore the rampant individualism of the synagogues which so often gave rise to serious outrages: "Here a man qualifies himself, ordains himself; he is his own college, his own professor, his own diploma. He is what he claims to be." See *JMes*, LVIII (Oct. 30, 1885), 5.

51. Unpublished letter, Oct. 19, 1885. Morais file, Dropsie College Archives.

52. Sulzberger, unpublished letter, Jan., 1885, *ibid.*

53. *JMes*, XXXVIII (Nov. 19, 1875), 5.

54. This document is to be found in Appendix B. See also, *JT*, VI (June 5, 12, 19, 26, July 3, 10 1874), 233, 245, 265, 276, 297, 313 respectively.

55. For the full account, see *JMes*, XLI (June 22, 1877), 5.

56. *JRec*, VII (Aug. 9, 1878), 4.

57. The strains, doubts and indecisions of the period were experienced not only on the national scene, but in each individual congregation. An extraordinary example of

the legal and organizational maneuvering within one
congregation is unfolded in the report letter of Isaac
Feinberg to Cyrus Adler concerning the events in
Mikveh Israel at that time. In this case Morais and his
congregation were not carried along by the stream. This
letter was brought to my attention by Maxwell Whiteman. The text is as follows:

THE CONGREGATION MIKVE ISRAEL
IN THE CITY OF PHILADELPHIA
1121 West Danplim Street

February 4, 1917

Dear Dr. Adler:

In compliance with your request of the 28th, I have
looked through the minutes of the Board of Managers
from April 14, 1878 to March 21, 1886 and the
minutes of the Congregation from September 30, 1883
to April 18, 1886 the above books having been in
my possession, in order to determine whether our
Congregation was ever a member of the Union of
American Hebrew Congregations. I have not gone
over the minutes of the Congregation prior to 1883
nor through the financial accounts of the Congregation between 1878 and 1886, these records being in
the safe at the Synagogue. Without keeping you waiting until I shall have the opportunity to take up these
latter books, I have thought it better to let you know
the result of the search.

At a meeting of the Board of Managers held April
14, 1878, a request was presented by the Board of
Delegates of American Israelites, that our Congregation join the Union of American Hebrew Congregations. On motion of Mr. John Samuel, a committee
was appointed to ascertain all the facts and to take
into consideration the financial condition of the Congregation.

At the next meeting of the Board, the committee reported that under its charter obligations, it was in-
expedient for the Congregation to join. The report
of the committee was accepted.

In the minutes of the Board, I find a record that at the Annual meeting of the Congregation held September 2, 1878 a communication was presented that had been sent by Mr. Mayer Sulzberger suggesting a mass meeting of the members and seat-holders of the Congregation for the purpose of considering the question of our Congregation joining the Union. On motion of Mr. Charles J. Cohen, the communication was referred to the Board of Managers to consider the advisability of calling the meeting. The question being brought up in the Board, it was decided that it was inadvisable to call the mass meeting.

At the spring quarterly meeting of the Board, in 1879 a communication dated Cincinnati, February, 1879 from the Union of American Hebrew Congregations was presented, inviting the Congregation to join the Union. On motion the communication was laid on the table for future reference. There is no record of its having been again taken up for consideration.

At a meeting of the Board of February 28, 1886, Dr. S. Solis Cohen and Samuel M. Hyneman were appointed delegates to a meeting to be held in New York, March 7, 1886 to discuss plans for a proposed Jewish Theological Seminary. . . . At a meeting on March 21, following, Mr. Hyneman moved that the question of joining the Seminary be submitted to the next meeting of the Congregation and at its meeting of April 18, 1886 the Congregation voted to join the Jewish Theological Seminary with five delegates at an annual charge of $125. This of course closed any possibility of joining the Union of American Hebrew Congregations. From the above it appears that the Board consistently refused to join the Union whenever the question was brought before it.

Mr. Goodman tells me further that Lazarus Mayer and David Sulzberger were strong opponents of any plan controlled by Dr. Wise and that Mr. Mayer, on the Board always worked against the proposals to join the Union. Mr. Morais, at the time, was in favor of joining the Union and, as you know, accepted the duties of an examiner of the College. He evidently looked upon the College as a means of satisfying what he felt to be a sore need, the diffusion of Jewish education among the growing generation. He was indignant at the objectors to the Union and publicly addressed the Congregation on the subject. It was probably the knowledge of these facts that led the writer in the *American Israelite* to make his erroneous statement. Dr. Morais later thanked Lazarus Mayer for his opposition.

The above seemed to me so conclusive that I thought it well to let you know the facts but if you think it advisable to look up the records not yet consulted for possible further information, let me hear from you and I shall do so at the first opportunity.

Very truly yours,

Isaac Feinberg

Dr. Cyrus Adler
Dropsie College
Broad and York Streets

On page 141 of Henry Morais' *Jews of Philadelphia* there is a statement that Rev. Isaac Lesser was among the founders of the Board of Delegates of American Israelites and the first Vice-President. Abraham Hart was later President. This Board was merged with the Union of American Hebrew Congregations on its formation in 1873. On page 191 he states that the Hebrew Union College was opened in 1875. There is no reference to our Congregation being a member.

I.F.

PART TWO: CHAPTER THREE

1. *AH*, I (Dec. 12, 1879), 38.
2. *Ibid.* A good example of this condition is the autobiographical record of Rabbi Bernhard Louis Levinthal, a leader of Orthodox Judaism until his death in 1952. When he received the invitation from the congregation in Philadelphia to become its rabbi, he sought the advice

of Rabbi S. Zvi-Hirsch Rabinowitz, the son of Rabbi Isaac Elchanan of Kovno, who was then rabbi in Vilna. His answer was: "The difference between European and American congregations must be understood. In Europe the congregation needs the rabbi while in America the rabbi needs the congregation. In Europe there are congregations and Jews who need a rabbi. But in America the congregation as such does not yet exist. It has to be created. And if you feel that you can fulfill such a task, go and may God be with you." Introduction, "Yozer Aman ve-Dabbar shel ha-Kehilah ha-Yehudit be-Philadelphia" (Creative Master and Spokesman of the Jewish Community in Philadelphia) *Jubilee Book "K'Vod Chachomim" in honor of Rabbi B. L. Levinthal on his Seventieth Natal Day Anniversary* (Philadelphia, 1935), p. 67.

3. *AH,* II (March 12, 1880), 38; (March 26, 1880), 62; (April 9), 89; (April 23), 110.
4. *JMes,* XLVIII (Aug. 20, 1880), 4.
5. Henry Morais, *loc. cit.,* pp. 79-80.
6. *JMes,* XLVIII (Aug. 20, 1880), 4.
7. "A Union of American Jews," *AH,* II (May 7, 1880), 134; (April 16), 98. See also (April 23), 210; III (June 4), 26-7; XVIII (April 25, 1884), 162.
8. "A Way of Union," *ibid.,* XVIII (April 25, 1884), 162.
9. *Ibid.* (May 21, 1886), 18-9.
10. *JMes,* LVIII (Oct. 30, 1885), 5.
11. *HL,* X (June 7, 1867), 4. The circular of the Hebrew Sabbath Association is as follows:

New York, June 3, 5627-1867.

Dear Sir:

A number of Jewish young men of this city met on Sunday last and organized a society, "To promote the more effectual observance of the Jewish Sabbath," under the name of The Hebrew Sabbath Association.

In pursuance of a resolution adopted at that meeting, a Committee will wait on you to ask: That you will cause an announcement to be made in Synagogue on Sunday next (the first of Pentacost):

1. That the Society has been organized.

2. That a Committee will be appointed by you to call on the members of your Congregation, and secure their adherence to the Sabbath movement.

3. That a public meeting will soon be held under the auspices of the Society, which your members are cordially invited to attend.

We would further solicit your Minister to direct special attention to this Circular, and the holy object we seek to assist, and in his discourse on Sunday next to allude to it, and request the Congregation to respond favorably when called upon by the Committee.

We believe that it is practicable to secure the general observance of the Sabbath among the Israelites of New York and we are sincerely desirous of doing what can be done towards securing the cooperation of our merchants, and providing for those of our people who seek employment which will not prevent their keeping the Sabbath holy.

The importance of this movement will at once suggest itself to every true Israelite.

Please communicate to either of the undersigned, on or before June 12th, the names of the Committee appointed for your Congregation.

Assured of your co-operation and encouragement, we are

Yours Respectfully,
JACOB P. SOLOMON, Chairman
271 Broadway

JOS. A. LEVY, Secretary
8 & 10 Pine Street

See also *ibid.*, IX (Dec. 14, 1866), 4.

12. *Ibid.*, XXVII (May 13, 1870), 4.

13. *AH*, I (Jan. 9, 1880), 92-3. The following letter (*ibid.*, II [March 26, 1880], 67) describes the situation of most of the young people in New York and elsewhere:

I must confess the fact of my working on Saturday did not worry me much, and I became so little accustomed to Jewish matters that my knowledge of them has become exceedingly limited. I have been reading your paper regularly during the past two months, and have had my interest in Jewish matters somewhat stirred up, and I feel that it does some good to think of such things at times. Now, it has occurred to me that an excellent mode of interesting Jewish young men in Jewish matters would be to have services on Saturday afternoon, with lectures. Saturday afternoons are usually least busy down town, and I think the great majority of young men' could easily manage to get off early on Saturdays, and attend such services. I know that if such services would be instituted that I could manage to attend.

YOUNG HEBREW

14. *Ibid.*, I (Jan. 9, 1880), 92-3.
15. See *AH*, I (Jan. 2, 1880), 73-4; (Jan. 16), 103; II (March 5), 27; (April 23), 109, 117. Two letters are especially interesting. *Ibid.* (March 26), 67; (April 9), 89.
16. *Ibid.*, I (Dec. 26, 1879), 67.
17. *Ibid.*, XIX (Aug. 8, 1884), 193.
18. *Ibid.*, XX (Aug. 29, 1884), 40.
19. *Ibid.* (Sept. 12), p. 65.
20. *Ibid.* (Aug. 29), p. 40.
21. *Ibid.*, XXVIII (Oct. 29, 1886), 178.
22. *Ibid.*, XXIX (Jan. 21, 1887), 161.
23. *Ibid.*, XXX (April 29, 1887), 186.
24. *Ibid.*, XXV (Dec. 18, 1886), 90.
25. *Ibid.*, XXXII (Sept. 30, 1887), 113. In a comment reprinted from the *Spectator* of March 28, 1712, they reminded the general religious community of the bad taste involved in the introduction of secular music into places of worship:

"A great many of our church musicians have introduced in their farewell voluntaries a sort of music quite foreign to the design of church-services, to the great prejudice of well disposed people. Those fingering gentlemen should be informed *that they ought to suit their airs to the place and the business, and that the musician is obliged to keep to the text as much as the preacher . . .*" *Ibid.* XVIII (April 18, 1884), 145.
26. *Ibid.*, XX (Sept. 12, 1884), 65; XXV (Dec. 25, 1886), 100; XXX (March 4, 1887), 49; (May 6), 194; XXXI (June 10), 66.
27. See Cowen, *op. cit.*, pp. 120-2.

28. "Epistle to the Hebrews," *AH*, XIII (Feb. 9, 1883), 149. (See also *ibid.* [Dec. 22, 1882], 64; [Jan. 26, 1883], 125). For the effect of the events of 1881-2 on Emma Lazarus and her work on behalf of the Zionist ideal, see H. E. Jacob, *The World of Emma Lazarus* (New York, 1949), pp. 75-155.

29. *AH*, I (Feb. 6, 1880), 133.

30. *Ibid.*, XIV (Nov. 16, 1883), 51. See also (May 4, 1883), 134.

31. See the author's "Ha-Zofeh ba-Erez ha-Hadashah" (The Observer in the New Land), *loc. cit.*, pp. 136-40.

32. For a discussion of the problem as reflected in the Hebrew press for the years 1886–88, see Joel S. Geffen, *Ha-Yom as a Source of American Jewish History (1886–1888)*, (typescript), pp. 11-4.

33. "Lawrence Oliphant on Palestine," *AH*, XIV (March 16, 1883), 50-51; "Practice vs. Theory," (May 4), 134; Emma Lazarus, "An Epistle to the Hebrews," XIII (Feb. 9), 146-49.

34. "The Restoration," *ibid.*, XIV (Feb. 23, 1883), 18-9.

35. For this letter, see Adolf Kober, "Jewish Religious and Cultural Life in America as Reflected in the Felsenthal Collection," *PAJHS*, XLV (Dec., 1953), 123-6.

36. Philipson, *op. cit.*, pp. 374-5.

37. Wilansky, *op. cit.*, pp. 253-6.

38. *Der Sabbat:* Predigt (Baltimore, 1889); *AH*, XXXVII (Dec. 21, 1888), 137. Henrietta Szold describes her father's feelings and her own about this matter: see Marvin Lowenthal, *Henrietta Szold, Life and Letters* (New York, 1942), p. 29.

39. *AH*, XIX (June 6, 1884), 52. For Jastrow's views, see *ibid.*, I (Feb. 13, 1880), 148.

40. *Ibid.*, XIX (May 16, 1884), 4; XVIII (May 9, 1884), 198.

41. *JMes*, XXXV (May 15, 1874), 4-5.

42. Compare especially the two articles in the *American Hebrew*, one before the occurrence and one after: *AH*, XV (July 27, 1883), 122; (Aug. 10), 146.

43. On the resignation of Beth El Emeth of Philadelphia, see *ibid.*, XVIII (May 9, 1884), 197.

44. F. de Sola Mendes, "Open Answer to Rev. I. M. Wise," *AH*, XIX (May 16, 1884), 4-5.

45. Ismar Elbogen, *A Century of Jewish Life* (Philadelphia, 1944), p. 344.
46. David de Sola Pool, *H. Pereira Mendes* (New York, 1938), p. 38.
47. *AH*, XXXII (Oct. 21, 1887), 162.
48. *Ibid.*, XX (Aug. 15, 1884), 10.
49. *Ibid.*, XVIII (March 14, 1884), 66; (April 18), 146; XIX (June 6), 50-51; (June 13), 72; (June 20), 82-3; (June 27), 99; (July 11), 131-2.
50. Alexander Kohut, *The Ethics of the Fathers* (New York, 1920), pp. 3, 14-7, 48.
51. *Ibid.*, pp. 7, 9.
52. Kohler, *Studies, Addresses and Personal Papers*, pp. 201-35.
53. See *ibid.*, pp. 202-33. See also *AJYB*, XXVIII (1927), 244, 248-50, 254.
54. *AH*, XXXII (Sept. 2, 1887), 51-2. See also the polemic between Wise and Morais, *ibid.*, XXI (Jan. 9, 1885), 130.
55. "The Pittsburgh Convention," *JMes*, LVIII (Nov. 20, 1885), 9.
56. Elbogen, "Alexander Kohut," *AJYB*, XLIV (1942–5703), 77. For a Reform evaluation of the influence of the Pittsburgh Platform on the development of American Judaism, see Julian Morgenstern, "The Achievements of Reform Judaism," *As A Mighty Stream* (Philadelphia, 1949), pp. 147-59 and *Yearbook CCAR*, XLV (1935), pp. 198-206.
57. *Yearbook CCAR*, I (1890-91), 80, 120-23.
58. Elbogen, "Alexander Kohut," *loc. cit.*, 77-8; Rebekah Kohut, *My Portion*, p. 114.
59. For the views of H. Pereira Mendes, Kohut, Jastrow and the others, see *AH*, XXV (Nov. 27, 1885), 35-7.

PART III: CHAPTER ONE

1. *AH*, XXXI (Aug. 5, 1887), 194.
2. *Ibid.*, XIX (June 3, 1884), 65, 70; XX (Aug 15, 1884), 10.
3. *Ibid.*, XXXII (Aug. 26, 1887), 34.
4. *Ibid.*, 37. See also (Sept. 2, 1887), 53-4; (Sept. 9), 69-70.
5. "S. Morais to K. Kohler," *ibid.*, XXXII (Sept. 2, 1887), 53.

6. For Kohler's forceful response, see "Dr. Kohler to Dr. Morais," *ibid.,* (Sept. 9), 68.

7. *Ibid.,* XVII (Jan. 4, 1884), 89; XVIII (May 9, 1884), 193; XIX (June 6, 1884), p. 34; (Aug. 8), 193. For a biography of Mielziner, see Ella McKenna Fried Mielziner, *Moses Mielziner, 1828–1903* (New York, 1931).

8. *AH,* XXV (Jan. 8, 1886), 129, 139.

9. See Solomon Solis-Cohen, "How the Jewish Theological Seminary Was Founded," *Hebrew Standard,* LXXII (July 5, 1918), 4, 5, 10. For Morais' sermon to the Chizuk Emunah congregation in Baltimore, see *AH,* XXVI (Feb. 19, 1886), 19-20.

10. Cyrus Adler, "S. Morais, Founder of the Seminary," *Centenary Memorial,* p. 38.

11. For Kohut's remarks on American Judaism, see *AH,* XXV (Feb. 5, 1886), 194-5. See *ibid.,* XXVI (Feb. 12, 1886), 4. See also *ibid.,* XXV (Jan. 15, 1886), 146.

12. Kohut to Felsenthal, Dec. 25, 1891, quoted by Adolf Kober in "Jewish Religious and Cultural Life in America as Reflected in the Felsenthal Collection," *PAJHS,* XLV (December, 1955), 115.

13. *Ibid.,* XXVI (March 5, 1886), 57; (May 7, 1886), 193.

14. For a biographical note on Blumenthal, see Appendix A.

15. Minute Book of the Shaaray Tefila Congregation (Jan., 1887); E. Davis, *op. cit.,* pp. 97-8, 101.

16. See especially his sharp response to Dr. Gottheil: *AH,* XXXI (Aug. 5, 1887), 195-6, and his later statement "A Stride Forward," *ibid.,* XXVI (Feb. 12, 1886), 4.

17. For a biography of Cyrus Adler, see Abraham A. Neuman, *Cyrus Adler, A Biographical Sketch* (New York, 1942); Adler, *I Have Considered the Days* (Philadelphia, 1943).

18. For a biographical sketch of Drachman, see Appendix A.

19. Cyrus Adler, "Jacob Henry Schiff—A Biographical Sketch", *AJYB,* XXIII (Philadelphia, 1921), 36-8, 44-5. Adler's discussion of Schiff's religious views and practices gives us an idea of the man's spiritual motivations. Schiff had been reared in the rigid school of Frankfort Orthodoxy, of which Sampson Raphael Hirsch was the leader. Upon his arrival in America, he became a member of the Reform Synagogue, and so remained

during all his life. He was attracted to this form of Judaism by a number of circumstances, but the one he mentioned most frequently was that it satisfied the religious cravings of those who could no longer adhere to the ancient rabbinical religion, and thus averted conversion to Christianity. He frequently asserted that had Reform Judaism regularly existed in Germany at the time of Moses Mendelssohn, his family and others like them would not have been lost to Judaism. There were, however, curious lapses in Mr. Schiff's adherence to the Reform Synagogue, and he frequently said that no Jew could be a good Reform Jew unless he had once been an Orthodox Jew. In the discussions connected with the reorganization of the Seminary he expressed his notion of its policy as an adherence to "reasonable" orthodoxy, a phrase which offended some but which nevertheless was not devoid of theological value. He strictly abstained from all secular occupation on the Sabbaths and festivals, and always visited the Synagogue on Saturday mornings. On Friday evening, before dinner, he read the services to his family, and that evening was his family evening. The Seder services at Passover were always a great occasion, never to be forgotten no matter what the circumstances . . .

The Hannukah lights were lit not only in his own house, but he went to the houses of his children and was present at the lighting of them for his children and grandchildren, one of his dearest wishes being the transmission of these traditions to his descendants.

The Day of Atonement was a real day of fasting and prayer to him, and on the very last one of his life, Wednesday, September 22 (he died on the 25th) he fasted the entire day, read the services through with his family (not feeling able to go to the synagogue), and experienced the greatest satisfaction at having been able to get through the day . . .

He was essentially a devout person. Every morning he read his prayers at the stated time. After meals he said grace. He did not eat forbidden food. He

450 Notes [pp. 237-239

stood outside the gate of the cemetery at Dr. Schechter's funeral because of the laws of the priesthood. During his illness he wrote once: "I shall try now to get my sleep, nerve and energy back; with care and with God's help I hope to succeed, but in any event I have so long a stretch of good health and happiness to my credit that I should have naught but gratitude to the Almighty . . ."

He rarely wrote a letter about the Montefiore Home or made a reference to it without speaking of it as his labor of love. In July, 1920, one Sunday morning, when already ill, he came in from the country to make his customary and last inspection and to chat with the older patients. The splendid pavilion which he provided was just approaching completion and he was happy to think that he had been able to create this additional instrument for the alleviation of human suffering. It was always a cause of satisfaction and pride on his part that this institution was conducted strictly according to the Jewish law, and that it contained a dignified and charming synagogue. J. D. Eisenstein writes that Schiff "usually attended Temple Emanuel on Fifth Avenue but on the 'Yahrzeit' of his parents, he would come to the *Beth Hamedrash Hagadol* on Ludlow Street where I saw him praying with talith and tefillin." *Op. cit.*, pp. 24-5.

20. *AH*, XXV (Feb. 5, 1886), 200-1.
21. Jewish Theological Seminary Association, *Constitution and By-Laws*. The Certificate of Incorporation of the Association was issued on February 23, 1887. See Appendix B.
22. *AH*, XXVII (July 16, 1886), 146.
23. *Ibid.*, XXVI (March 12, 1886), 34.
24. *Ibid.*, XXIX (Nov. 26, 1886), 34.
25. *Ibid.* (Dec. 31, 1886), 121; (Jan. 7, 1887), 130.
26. *Ibid.*, 136. See also A. Kohut, *Ethics of the Fathers*, pp. XCIV, CV.
27. *AH*, XXIX (Jan. 7, 1887), 137.
28. See also *PJTSA*, Conventions I-VII (New York, 1888-1900), especially the reports of Morais and Blumenthal in the first volume of 1888.

29. Szold's appointment is discussed by Morais in a letter to Felsenthal (April 30, 1889). G. Lieberman was instructor in Mishna and Gemara from 1886 to 1892. He was succeeded by Joshua A. Joffe, who served in the same capacity until 1902, and as Instructor in Talmud from 1902 to 1917.

30. *Jewish Theological Seminary Association* (New York, 1887), pp. 2 ff.

31. *AH,* XXXVIII (April 19, 1889), 170.

32. Weinberger, M., *Ha-Yehudim ve-ha-Yahadut be-New York* (Jews and Judaism in New York, New York, 1887), p. 21.

Another Hebrew writer, S. B. Shwartzberg, deplored the anarchic state of Jewish education generally. "In the largest Jewish community in the world there does not exist one properly conducted Hebrew school for children." *Tikatev Zot le-Dor Aharon* (Let This Be Recorded for Future Generations, New York, 1893), p. 31.

See also Jeremiah J. Berman, "Jewish Education in New York City," *YIVO Annual,* IX (New York, 1954), 267-75.

33. *AH,* XX (Sept. 5, 1884), 50-51.

34. *Ibid.,* XXXI (May 20, 1887), 18-9.

35. *Ibid.,* 17.

36. "Plans and Methods of Instruction for Sabbath Schools," *ibid.,* XXVIII (Sept. 24, 1886), 99-101.

37. *Ibid.,* (Oct. 8, 1886), 132.

38. The editors of the *American Hebrew* described the confirmation ceremony as it was then practiced in sharp but honest terms: ". . . What is it now in the main? A fine but fleeting show, a gilded but hollow pretence, an exhibition that panders to vanity and spreads a soothing salve over the sore spots of ignorance and irreligiousness." *AH,* XXXI (May 27, 1887), 33. In describing the Jewish educational efforts of the Historical School in that period, we should record the energetic work of H. Pereira Mendes in his Mission school for poor children, and Solomon Solis-Cohen's deep interest in the development of Jewish education in Philadelphia. The editors of the *American Hebrew* were constantly agitating to found additional schools. *Ibid.,* XIX (June

6, 1884), 49. But these efforts were outside the scope of the congregational school system of the Historical School. For De Sola Mendes' essay, see *ibid.,* LIII (May 19, 1893), 77-8.

39. *AH,* LXXI (May 30, 1902), 37-8.

40. *Ibid.,* XXV (Jan. 1, 1886), 117.

41. *JMes,* LVIII (Dec. 25, 1885), 4.

42. "Report by Parnas," Minute Book of Mikveh Israel Congregation (April 15, 1894).

43. The other members were Samuel M. Hyneman, Charles J. Cohen and David Sulzberger, together with the *hazzan,* secretary and president as ex officio members.

44. Letters in Mikveh Israel files dated December, 1893.

45. *Ibid.,* "Letter to Dr. S. Solis-Cohen, Chairman of Gratz Trust Committee" (Feb. 12, 1896).

46. Prior to the formal opening of classes, a special series of lectures was arranged. The first, by Solomon Schechter, who was brought over from Cambridge, on rabbinic theology; the second, a course of lectures by American scholars (among them Paul Haupt and Cyrus Adler); the third, a course on the philosophy of Jewish history by Joseph Jacobs, then of London.
See also J. Greenstone, "Gratz College," *Jubilee Book of the Hebrew Teachers' Union* (Heb.), ed. Zevi Scharfstein (New York, 1944), pp. 276-9.

47. Solomon Solis-Cohen, *Judaism and Science,* pp. 157-8.

48. "A Jewish Publication Society," *Occ,* XXVI (May, 1868), 45-50, 52.

49. Quoted by Solomon Grayzel in "Two Generations of Anglo-Jewish Book-Reading," *YIVO Annual,* IX (1954), 111.

50. The call was issued on April 13, 1888 and it was signed by the committee, consisting of Solomon Solis-Cohen, Rev. Victor Caro, Solomon Blumenthal, Adolph Eichholz, Oscar B. Teller, secretary. The aims of the society are given by Henry S. Morais, *The Jews of Philadelphia,* p. 177.

51. *AH,* XXXV (May 11, 1888), 2.

52. *Ibid.* (May 18, 1888), 24. It was suggested to the author by Professor Jacob Marcus that Morais' sharp opposition had a personal basis. It is true that Morais had no

use for the reforms of Dr. Krauskopf, who, at that time, was considering instituting services on Sunday. But, in addition to his ideological opposition, Morais saw in Krauskopf a young competitor who had great talent for attracting people.

53. *AH*, XXXVII (Dec. 21, 1888), 138.
54. *AJYB* (5664-1903/04), p. VIII.
55. Harry Schneiderman, "Cyrus Adler and the American Jewish Year Book," *AJYB*, XLII (5701-1940/41), 702-6; "American Jewish Year Book, 1899-1948," L (5709-1948/49), 85-104.

Adler's interest in the Society and the *Year Book* was unremitting. Whether in Philadelphia, in Washington, in New York, or on a mission abroad, he was always on Society business. A letter addressed to Judge Sulzberger (in the Sulzberger Papers at Dropsie College), dated August 22, 1894, and with a postmark of Milan, Italy, is characteristic:

Dear Mr. Sulzberger,

It is so cool in England and France that we had to come down here to get even comfortable for summer. I leave for Venice today, then to Trieste, Patras, Athens and Constantinople. You really should have come along.

All of our friends in London with the exception of Jacobs were out of town. He tells me that Macmillan is about to publish a series to be called the Jewish Library of which Jacobs is the editor. I suggested that the Publication Society might care to have the American copyright of some but Macmillan seemed unwilling to enter into such an arrangement.

I hope you will not forget the necessity of arranging the Gratz Trust matters before the Congregation meets at the end of September. I did not see Schechter in London but shall spend a week there before sailing. Waldstein cannot do Philadelphia.

With kindest regards,

Sincerely yours,
Cyrus Adler

56. *AJYB* (5660-1899/1900), IX.
57. *AH*, LVI (Dec. 14, 1894), 181.
58. Bernard Drachman, "Neo-Hebraic Literature in America," *Seventh Biennial Convention of the Jewish Theological Seminary Association*, pp. 53-139.
59. S. B. Shwartzberg, *Tikatev Zot le-Dor Aharon* (New York, 1898), pp. 13-4. See also J. D. Eisenstein, *Ozar Zikronotai* (Autobiography and Memoirs, New York, 1929), p. 100.
60. Moshe Davis, "Parshah be-Hafatsat Daat ha-Ivrit be-Amerikah" (A Chapter in the Propagation of Hebrew Language and Culture in America), *Hadoar 1957 Jubilee Volume*, pp. 206-9. In 1888, Kohut, Drachman and H. P. Mendes joined a committee of Hebraists to try to save Wolf Schur's Hebrew weekly, *Hapisgah* from extinction. See Jacob Kabakoff, "Zev Schur u-Pealo be-Amerikah" (The Work of Zev Schur in America). Unpublished, 1955, p. 3. See also Kabakoff, "The Role of Wolf Schur as Hebraist and Zionist," *Essays in American Jewish History* to commemorate the 10th anniversary of the founding of the American Jewish Archives under the direction of Jacob Rader Marcus (Cincinnati, 1958), p. 427.
61. *Hamelitz*, XXX (March 29, 1890-20 Nisan, 5650), p. 5.
62. Cyrus Adler, "Sources of American Jewish History," *MMo*, V (Sept., 1888), 191-3.
63. *JMes*, LX (Dec. 5, 1886), 3.
64. Cyrus Adler, *op. cit., loc. cit.*, p. 191.
65. For a history of the Society, see Isidore S. Meyer, "The American Jewish Historical Society," *Journal of Jewish Bibliography* (Jan.-April, 1943); Abraham Neuman, *Cyrus Adler*, pp. 50-5. See also Adler's letter to Felsenthal, dated April 15, 1890 (Felsenthal Collection of the American Jewish Historical Society) in which Adler agrees with Felsenthal's views about the organizational form of the new Society. He emphasizes that the Society should be non-denominational and accept into membership Christians and Jews.

See also the interpretive article by John J. Appel, "Hansen's Third-Generation 'Law' and the Origins of the American Jewish Historical Society," *Jewish Social*

Studies, XXIII (Jan., 1961), 3-20. Compare Appel's thesis (that the American Jewish Historical Society was "organized by an elite convinced that historical data could provide the arguments to refute hostile opinion, put down incipient criticism, and help to establish the group's unquestioned loyalty to American principles" [p. 5]) with the account of the origins of the Society by Oscar S. Straus, first president of the Society (*PAJHS,* XXVI [1918], XVII-XVIII).

66. Appel, *loc. cit.,* 14, and note 46. For the support of the Central Conference of American Rabbis, see *Yearbook CCAR,* XI (1901-5661), 58-60.

67. *Hamelitz,* XXXIV (Feb. 7, 1894-13 Adar 5654), 3. The source in Hebrew reads as follows:

‏"...ויהודי אמריקא, האזרחים/, מתערים כארז רענן ועושים חיל גם
‏בגשמיות גם ברוחניות. זה כשנה נוסדה בניויארק חברה ,לחקר קורות
‏ישראל באמריקא', וראש החברה הוא ב"ב אסקאר שטרויס (מי שהיה ציר
‏אמריקא בתורכיא), וזה לא כבר התאספו לאספה שנתית. באספה ההיא
‏נדרשו דרשות נכבדות, ה' מ. קאהלער הודיע כי בראשית המאה השבע
‏עשרה כבר היו באמריקא יהודים יורדי הים באניות מסחר, ובכללם
‏מפורסם היהודי שמשון, כאחד הספנים הגדולים בימים ההם. הפרופיסור
‏גאטטהייל הוכיח, עפ"י כתב יד עתיק, כי היהודים יסדו קולוניות בפערו
‏ובמעקסיקא, עוד בטרם נכבשו המדינות האלה לפני קארטעז ופיזארא.
‏ועוד ענינים כאלה הנכבדים מאד לקורות ישראל".

68. The estimate of the number of 586,537 Jewish immigrants who entered the United States from 1881 to 1900 is found in the article by Bernard D. Weinryb, "East European Immigration to the United States," *Jewish Quarterly Review,* XLV (Tercentenary Issue, April, 1955), p. 520. Weinryb bases his figures on S. Joseph's *Jewish Immigration to the United States from 1881 to 1900* (New York, 1914) and suggests that perhaps more arrived than is indicated by these numbers. The same total is arrived at through compilation from the chart prepared by Wischnitzer, *op. cit.,* p. 33.

69. See, for example, "The Memoir of Doctor George Price," trans. Leo Shpall, *PAJHS,* XLVII (Dec., 1957), 103-8. See also Jacob Neusner, "The Impact of Immigration and Philanthropy upon the Boston Jewish Community (1880-1914)," *ibid.* (Dec., 1956), 71-85.

70. Mandel, *loc. cit.*, pp. 31-32. Szold, after castigating Schindler, added words of hope for the future of these immigrants, assuring them that as time went on, they would benefit fully from the blessings of the United States. He also encouraged Schur not to desist from his efforts. See Kabakoff, "Wolf Schur u-Paalo be-Amerikah," pp. 33-4.

71. Hyman B. Grinstein, "The Efforts of East European Jewry to Organize its Own Community in the United States," *PAJHS*, XLIX (Dec., 1959), 75-6.

72. *The Jews of Russia and Poland* (New York, 1915), pp. 208-9.

73. The translation of the text of Isaiah and the quotation from Morais' sermon are cited in Solomon Solis-Cohen, "S. Morais, Teacher and Leader," *Mikveh Israel-Commemoration of the 100th Anniversary of the Birth of Sabato Morais* (Philadelphia, 1923), p. 26.

74. Quoted in Alexandra Lee Levin, *The Szolds of Lombard Street* (Philadelphia, 1960), p. 262.

75. See the editorial of James Ryder Randall, of the Augusta, Georgia *Constitutionalist,* cited in Levin, *ibid.,* pp. 188-9.

76. H. P. Mendes, "A Young People's Synagogue," *AH,* LXV (Oct. 20, 1899), 736.

77. (Philadelphia, 1889). Martin Douglas' unpublished thesis on "The Jewish Agricultural Communities in South Jersey" (1960) contains extensive new information on these colonies, and some of the following references are from his study with his permission.

78. Klein, *ibid.,* references to the Carmel colony, pp. 55, 63; to the Alliance settlement, pp. 41-3 and *passim.* In Douglas, *op. cit.,* see especially pp. 26-7, 30 ff., 37.

79. See Douglas, *op. cit.,* pp. 33, 35, 43-4.

80. For the full document, see Appendix B. See also *Hamelitz,* XXXI (Oct. 9, 1891), 4-5. In another report which followed (Nov. 12, pp. 1-2) the writer again stresses the theme of Americanization as the chief purpose of the new agency. Describing the plan of the Alliance, he concludes that the thought of the initiative is "to attempt to spread the immigrants over the entire land, in order that they may become in short time complete Americans."

81. George M. Price, "The Russian Jews in America," trans. Leo Shpall, *PAJHS*, XLVIII (Dec., 1958), 111-14.
82. Louis Lipsky, *Thirty Years of American Zionism* (New York, 1927), pp. 8-9.
83. *AH*, XXXVII (Jan. 25, 1889), 216. Excerpts of an address given by Morais at a meeting of the Hovevei Zion in Philadelphia were rendered into Hebrew in *Hamelitz* (March 9, 1890), 1-2. In this address Morais' views on the Palestine situation are forcefully expressed. He affirms the belief that the Jews will return to their Homeland in Palestine, and be an inspiration of peace and truth to the whole world, as told by the prophets and taught by Tradition. Morais urges that settlement in Eretz Yisrael not be postponed but encouraged out of the ranks of the Hovevei Zion in America, who should send "strong and healthy" men to establish new settlements in Palestine. The settlers in Eretz Yisrael should teach their children Hebrew even as they learn to cultivate the land. Thus, the *Yishuv* will assume a vibrant character, for it will be built by individuals who have come to live in Eretz Yisrael, not only to be buried there.
84. *AH*, XLVI (March 13, 1891), 102. Wise published an editorial that week in which he denied that Zionism could help solve the Jewish question. See *AI*, XXXVII (March 19, 1891), 4. See also Adler and Margalith, *op. cit.*, pp. 42-3; 225.

    For a description of the political background in Palestine during this period and the important contributions by representatives of the United States for the improvement of the situation, see Frank E. Manuel, *op. cit.*, pp. 47-87.
85. *AH*, LXIV (Jan. 13, 1899), 391; LXII (March 25, 1898), p. 625.
86. In the report on "Zion as it is," De Sola Mendes makes an interesting suggestion to help fix the topography of Jerusalem in the minds of his listeners:

    . . . In general contour, Jerusalem closely resembles New York City (Manhattan). One can easily place the chief points by remembering then, that such locations as the following coincide: The North River would be the deep valley of Hinnon; the East River, the valley of Kidron; the Battery, Zion; Grand Street Ferry (West), the Jaffa Gate; Grant Street, David Street; Canal Street, the Via Dolorosa or St. Stephen Street; Broadway, Christian Street; the Bowery would mark the Western Wall, the New York Ghetto would be the Temple Area; the Hebrew Institute, the Mosque El Aksa; City Hall, the Offal Gate, etc. . . . (*ibid.,* p. 625.)

87. Selig Adler and Thomas E. Connolly, *From Ararat to Suburbia. The History of the Jewish Community of Buffalo* (Philadelphia, 1960), pp. 217-9.

88. *AH*, LXXIII (Oct. 16, 1903), 696. It seems that Cyrus Adler, too, was attracted to the Federation in his early years. Among Adler's private papers, preserved in the archives, there is an exchange of correspondence between Stephen S. Wise and Adler. Wise asked Adler to be the honorary vice-chairman of the Zionist gathering in 1898, and Adler accepted. Wise wrote a second time to express his gratitude for Adler's help (April 17, May 11, 1898). Similarly, there is preserved an interesting and important letter from Adler to Israel Zangwill (Nov. 1, 1905), in which Adler tells of his correspondence with Herzl through the good offices of Oscar Straus. He concludes his letter with a statement that he could not affiliate with the Zionist movement despite his recognition of the great importance attached to the significant movements on behalf of Eretz Yisrael.

89. See Jacob Kabakoff, "The Role of Wolf Schur . . ." *loc. cit.,* p. 441. Also J. D Eisenstein, *op. cit.,* p. 24.

90. *JMes*, LXXXII (Dec. 24, 1897), 7.

91. Solis-Cohen, *Judaism and Science,* p. 197.

92. *Ruach Hayim (The Spirit of Life), or Jewish Daily Life Ethically Presented* (New York, 1917), pp. 185-88. In his other writings, in the periodical press, Mendes often enlarged upon his belief in the universal significance of Zionism. In the *American Hebrew,* LXII (Dec. 10, 1897), 168, for example, he writes as follows:

> Zion, a state, means a spiritual influence acting for good upon the world through Jewish communities established throughout the world. How else can we perform our priestly duty as the kingdom of priests?

On another occasion he stated (*AH,* LXIV [Jan. 13, 1899], 392):

Should a Jewish state be established? Emphatically yes. It is good to be an American. But it is nobler to be a Jew. An American, as an American has only material aspirations. A Jew stands for what is spiritual. To establish a Jewish state for mere national purposes, such as protection of citizenship rights, is unnecessary . . .

The Jewish State will aim at the spiritual interests of the Jews and of ALL HUMANITY. . . . To hold up a Jewish State as a refuge for oppressed Jews is merely utilizing an accidental . . . The Jewish State must have a higher purpose than merely a refuge . . .

93. *JMes,* LXXXIII (March 11, 1898), 4.
94. Jacob Kabakoff, "Le-toldot Hibbat Ziyyon be-Amerikah" (Toward a History of Hibbat Zion in America), *Hadoar Jubilee Volume 1957,* XXXVII (May 31), 219.
95. Herbert Parzen, "Conservative Judaism and Zionism (1896-1922)," *Jewish Social Studies,* XXIII (Oct., 1961), 236-8. By 1901 the ZBT was converted from its original purpose. It changed formally in 1903, becoming a typical American social fraternity. Later it became a center of anti-Zionism.
96. *AH,* XX (Aug. 15, 1885), 10.
97. *Ibid.,* XXXII (Sept. 2, 1887), 53-4.
98. *PAJHS,* XLII (June, 1953), 371-85.
99. *Ibid.,* 381-2.
100. One of the strangest suggestions came from Judge Mayer Sulzberger, who proposed a second Sabbath day on the principle of the second day of the festivals. Those who were free on the seventh day could worship in accordance with the Tradition; the others would worship on Sunday. This measure, Judge Sulzberger stated, would only be a temporary one. See *AH,* LXIV (Jan. 13, 1899), 372-3.
101. *Ibid.,* XXXVII (Dec. 14, 1888), 106; XXXVIII (March 22, 1889), 98. See also Maurice H. Harris, "An Estimate of Dr. Alexander Kohut's Place in the History of American Judaism," *Ethics of the Fathers,* p. XCI.

102. See *supra,* Part II, chap. 3.
103. *AH,* LXIV (March 24, 1899), 704.
104. *Ibid.,* (Jan. 13, 1899), 372.
105. *Ibid.*
106. Henrietta Szold, "Catholic Israel," *AH,* LXV (May 5, 1899), 9; (May 12), 45-9.

PART III: CHAPTER TWO

1. From the author's lecture notes on "The Meaning of the Jewish Theological Seminary," 1940.
2. See Sidney E. Ahlstrom, "Theology in America: A Historical Survey," James Ward Smith and A. Leland Jamison, *op. cit.,* vol. 1, pp. 232 ff.
3. "Morais to Kohler," *AH,* XXIII (July 10, 1885), 153.
4. *Occ,* II (April, 1844), 4. For an expansion of Leeser's views see "History of Jews and Their Religion," in Rupp, *History of Religious Denominations in the U.S.* (Philadelphia, 1844), pp. 352-65.
5. *AH,* V (Dec. 3, 1880), 27. See also (Dec. 17), 52.
6. "The Jewish Church," *The World's Congress of Religions* (Boston, 1893), p. 129.
7. *JMes,* LXVII (Jan. 17, 1890), 5.
8. *Outlines of the System of Judaism* (Baltimore, 1874), pp. 15-7. See also *The Divine Origin and Rationality of the Decalogue* (Baltimore, 1863); *AH,* III (May 21, 1880), 4.
9. "God-Created or Self-Created?" *AH,* XXX (Feb. 25, 1887), 34.
10. *Ibid.,* (April 1, 1887), 123.
11. *Occ,* I (July, 1843), 161.
12. See also *ibid.,* (Aug. 1843), 222. In the eighth volume of the *Occident* (1850-1851), Leeser wrote seven articles entitled "Judaism and its Principles," in which he derives the idea of the coming of the Messiah and the resurrection of the dead from biblical sources.
13. *Ibid.,* VIII (Aug, 1850), 257.
14. Krauskopf, *loc. cit.,* p. 77.
15. *AH,* VI (March 11, 1881), 39; (May 13), 147. For Kohut's views, see *JMes,* LXVII (Jan. 17, 1890), 5.

16. "Address delivered at the funeral of S. M. Isaacs," May 22, 1878.

17. *Outlines of the System of Judaism*, pp. 27-9.

18. "Ein Neues Gebetbuch," *JT*, III (Dec. 29, 1874), 733-4.

19. See the author's comparative tables in *Yahadut Amerikah be-Hitpathutah*, p. 295.

20. *Outlines of the System of Judaism*, p. 39.

21. "The Jewish Creed," *Occ*, II (Aug., 1844), 219.

22. *AH*, IV (Oct. 8., 1880), 88.

23. "Science and Judaism," *JMes*, LIX (May 7, 1886), 4.

24. *Ibid*.

25. Additional examples can be found in the author's *Yahadut Amerikah be-Hitpathutah*, pp. 307-12, 351, 317.

26. "History of Jews and Their Religion," *loc. cit.*, pp. 362-3.

27. *Occ*, I (April, 1843), 20; (July), 160; XIV (Aug., 1856), 207; XXV (Sept., 1867), 270. Leeser asserted that even though there has been progress in human history and that technical inventions have increased in the course of time, no new truth has been created.

28. *Bible View of Slavery*, p. 22.

29. "The Devil and Evil Spirits," *JMes*, XXVII (April 15, 1870), 4-5.

30. See Joseph Klausner, *Historiah shel ha-Sifrut ha-Ibrit ha-Hadashah* (History of Modern Hebrew Literature, Jerusalem, 1937), II, 80-81.

31. "The Bible," *The Activities of the Rabbi*, pp. 7-15.

32. "Morais to Kohler," *AH*, XXIII (July 10, 1884), 137.

33. "The Bible," *AH*, L (Feb. 26, 1892), 65-6.

34. *Ibid*. See also *JMes*, VII (Jan. 27, 1860), 30; *AH*, IX (Nov. 25, 1881), 14-5; X (Feb. 24, 1882), 17; XXIX (Jan. 7, 1887), 132.

35. *AH*, LI (July 1, 1892), 279-80.

36. *Ibid*.

37. "History of the Jews and Their Religion," *loc. cit.*, p. 355.

38. *Occ*, I (Aug., 1843), 256; (June, 1843), 116. On one occasion Leeser was severely tested. President Zachary Taylor proclaimed a national fast day for August 13, 1849 because of the spread of cholera. Since the date chosen corresponded to the Fifteenth of Ab on the Jewish

calendar, a joyous day in Jewish history, Leeser refused
to fast but did urge the Jews to assemble and pray for
the end of the plague.

39. *Occ,* XIV (Feb., 1857), 543-8; (March, 1857), 577-8.
40. *The Festivals of the Lord* (London, 1840). In 1862 Dr.
Raphall was asked by his congregation whether there
was any specific law forbidding men and women to sit
together in family pews in the synagogue and, "if not
contrary to Mosaic Law, can both occupy the same pew?"
Raphall's answer is not available in the records of the
congregation, but there is no doubt that he did not permit this change, for in his time family pews were not
introduced in congregation B'nai Jeshurun. See Goldstein, *op. cit.,* pp. 128-9.
41. *Ruhama, op. cit.,* p. VIII.
42. *AH,* LXXVI (Jan. 27, 1905), 299.
43. "Morais to Kohler," *ibid.,* XXIII (July 3, 1885), 115.
44. *JMes,* XXXVIII (Dec. 17, 1875), 4.
45. *AH,* XXVII (July 16, 1886), 154; *Ethics of the Fathers,*
p. 87.
46. *Outlines of the System of Judaism,* pp. 54, 60, 71-4.
47. *Ibid.,* pp. 67-8.
48. "Judaism and Proselytism," *Judaism and Science,* pp.
34-5.
49. "History of Jews and Their Religion," *loc. cit.,* pp. 365-
6. See also *Occ,* I (July, 1843), 160; XVI (Oct., 1858),
317-27; (Nov.), 365-75.
50. *AH,* II (May 7, 1880), 135.
51. *Outlines of the System of Judaism,* pp. 79-80.
52. See the author's *Yahadut Amerikah be-Hitpathutah,* pp.
309-12 for other comparative tables.
53. "National and Universal Judaism," *JMes,* LV (Feb. 15,
1884), 7. See also "Israel's Election," *JEx,* IV (Dec.
14, 1888), 5.
   The Messianic days have not yet come, nor is Israel's
   vision fulfilled. The belief in eternity, in a deification
   of man, the remnants of polytheism are still to be
   swept away. Distinctions are still drawn between man
   and man and race and race. Atheism and materialism
   still stare us in the face. Our duty is not yet done.
   Our religious institutions, our Sabbaths and festivals,

our ceremonies and customs, our domestic life, our worship, our sacred language, all that distinguishes us from others, these are the tools, the armaments, wherewith we have yet to work.

See also Szold, *Outlines of the System of Judaism,* pp. 5, 74, 79-80.

54. "Morais to Kohler," *AH,* XXIII (June 26, 1885), 99; (July 10), 137.
55. See the author's *Yahadut Amerikah be-Hitpathutah,* p. 317.
56. *Occ,* I (Sept., 1843), 268-70; II (Aug., 1844), 239; IV (May, 1846), 64-5; (Jan., 1847), 476; V (May, 1847), 87.
57. *JMes.,* XXV (May 21, 1869), 1.
58. *AH,* LVII (Aug. 16, 1895), 357.
59. *An Address Delivered on the Feast of Pentecost* (Philadelphia, 1869), p. 4.
60. "The Synagogue," *AH,* LXII (March 11, 1898), 556.

PART III: CHAPTER THREE

1. Uriah Zvi Engelman, "Jewish Statistics in the U.S. Census of Religious Bodies (1850-1936)," *Jewish Social Studies,* IX (April, 1947), 134-8.
2. For background descriptions of Orthodox Jewry in America in the last decades of the past century, see Judah David Eisenstein, "Between Two Opinions," trans. Robert L. Samuels, *AJA,* XII (Oct., 1960), 123-42; Abraham J. Karp, "New York Chooses a Chief Rabbi," *PAJHS,* XLIV (March, 1955), 129-98;

ח. ר. רבינוביץ, „ציון לדמות שנשתכחה (ר' יעקב יוסף חריף ז"ל)" קובץ שנה בשנה (ירושלים, תש"ב) עמ' 382-398.

3. Circulars dated March-April 1898 (Nisan 5658).
4. *AH,* LXIII (June 10, 1898), 173.
5. *Ibid.,* LXVIII (Jan. 4, 1901), 231-3.
6. *Ibid.,* LXXV (Nov. 25, 1904), 750.
7. See, in order: *ibid.,* 235-7; LXXI (July 11, 1902), 218; LXXV (June 17, 1904), 130; (July 1), 178-9, 180; (July 8), 204.
8. *JMes,* LXXXVII (April 27, 1900), 6. For the angry reaction of Henry Morais, son of Sabato Morais, to this proposal of union, see *ibid.* (May 11, 1900), 4.

9. *AH,* LXIX (May 31, 1901), 40a-b.
10. Adler, *I Have Considered the Days,* pp. 242-4; *The Jewish Theological Seminary Semi-Centennial Volume,* pp. 8-11.
11. *Ibid.,* p. 178.
12. *AH,* LXXI (July 4, 1902), 184.
13. *The Jewish Theological Seminary Semi-Centennial Volume,* p. 155.
14. *The Jewish Theological Seminary of America, Documents, Charter, and By-Laws* (New York, 1903), pp. 12-4. See Appendix B.
15. *Ibid.*
16. *Seminary Addresses and Other Papers.* (Ed. of the Burning Bush Press, New York, 1959), p. 11.

BIBLIOGRAPHY

I. PRIMARY SOURCES

A. *Manuscript Material: Minute Books and Miscellaneous Documents.*

American Jewish Historical Society, New York. Archives.
    Bernard Felsenthal: Correspondence and unpublished materials.
    George Alexander Kohut: Correspondence, lectures, unpublished materials and personal papers.
Congregation Ahavath Chesed, New York.
    Minute Book, 1840–1890.
Congregation Mikveh Israel, Philadelphia.
    Minute Book of the Adjunta, 1840–(1902).
    Minute Book of the Congregation, 1840–(1902).
    Miscellaneous pamphlets and brochures, 1840–(1902).
Congregation Shaaray Tefila, New York (West End Synagogue).
    Minute Book of General Meetings, 1845–(1902).
    Minute Book of Trustees, 1860–(1902).
Dropsie College, Philadelphia. Archives.
    Sabato Morais: Correspondence, lectures, sermons and discourses, addresses, prayers for special occasions and speeches.
    Mayer Sulzberger: Correspondence, unpublished materials and personal papers.
Jewish Theological Seminary, New York. Archives.
    Cyrus Adler: Correspondence, unpublished materials and personal papers.

B. *Periodicals.*

The Occident. Philadelphia, 1843–1868.
The Asmonean. New York, 1849–1858.

The (American) Israelite. Cincinnati, 1854–(1902).
Sinai. Baltimore and Philadelphia, 1856–1862.
The Jewish Messenger. New York, 1857–1902.
The Hebrew Leader. New York, 1865–1882.
The Jewish Times. New York, 1869–1879.
הצופה בארץ החדשה. New York, 1871–(1873).
The Jewish Record. Philadelphia, 1875–1886.
American Hebrew. New York, 1879–(1902).
American Jews' Annual. New York, Cincinnati and Chicago, 1884–1894.
The Menorah Monthly. New York, 1886-(1902).
The Jewish Exponent. Philadelphia and Baltimore, 1887–(1902).
Yearbook of the Central Conference of American Rabbis. Cincinnati, 1889–(1902).

C. Books and Articles.

ADLER, CYRUS, *I Have Considered the Days.* Philadelphia, 1943.
———, and Margalith, Aaron M., *With Firmness in the Right: American Diplomatic Action Affecting Jews, 1840–1945.* New York, 1946.
ADLER, SAMUEL, chairman of Editorial Committee, *Protokolle der Rabbiner Conferenz abgehalten zu Philadelphia vom 3. bis. 6. November 1869.* New York, 1870.
AGUILAR, GRACE, שמע ישראל. *The Spirit of Judaism.* Edited by I. Leeser. Philadelphia, 1842.
The American Jewish Historical Society, Report of Organization. Baltimore, 1892.
American Society for Meliorating the Condition of the Jews, *The First Report.* New York, 1823.
The American Jewish Pulpit. Cincinnati, 1881.

BENJAMIN II, ISRAEL JOSEPH, *Drei Jahre in Amerika, 1859–1862.* Hanover, 1862. *Three Years in America, 1859–1862.* Translated from the German by Charles Reznikoff. Philadelphia, 1956.
BERKOWITZ, HENRY, "A Jewish Summer School and Assembly." *Yearbook CCAR,* vol. V, 1896.
———, "Notes on the History of the Earliest German-Jewish Congregation in America." *PAJHS,* no. 9, 1901.

(BERMAN, SIMON) ‏בערמאן, שמעון, ספר מסעות שמעון. קראקא,‎ 1879.
BERNHEIMER, CHARLES S., "Summary of Jewish Organization in the United States." *AJYB*, 5661, 1900–1901.
CAHAN, ISIDORE, "Mélanges: Le Judaisme Américain." *Archives Israélites*, vol. XVIII. Paris, 1857.
CALISCH, EDWARD N., "Judaism and the Public School System of America." *Yearbook CCAR*, vol. III, 1893.
CARVALHO, SOLOMON NUNES, *Incidents of Travel and Adventure in the Far West*. Edited with an introduction by Bertram W. Korn. Philadelphia, 1954.
COHEN, HENRY, "Settlement of the Jews in Texas." *PAJHS*, no. 2, 1894.
COWEN, PHILIP, *Memories of an American Jew*. New York, 1932.

DEMBITZ, LEWIS N., *A Common Ground for Field and Ingersoll*. Louisville, 1887.
DE SOLA, DAVID AARON, MORRIS J. RAPHALL and S. L. LUDENTHAL, *Genesis*. London, 1841.
——, and MORRIS J. RAPHALL, *Eighteen Treatises from the Mishna*. London, 1843.
DEUTSCH, GOTTHARD, *Modern Orthodoxy*. Chicago, 1898 (reprinted from *The Reform Advocate*).
DRACHMAN, BERNARD, "Jewish Educational Needs and Methods." *The Menorah*, vol. VIII, no. 1, January, 1890.
——, "Neo-Hebraic Literature in America." *PJTSA*. New York, 1900.
——, *The Unfailing Light*. New York, 1948.
DROPSIE, MOSES A., *Discourse on Thanksgiving Day*. Philadelphia, 1864.
——, *Panegyric on Life, Character and Services of the Rev. Isaac Leeser*. Philadelphia, 1868.

EINHORN, DAVID, *War with Amalek*. Philadelphia, 1864.
——, ‏עלת תמיד.‎*Olat Tamid, Gebetbuch für Israelitische Reform-gemeinde* (Vierte Auflage, New York, 1858).
——, *Ausgewählte Predigten und Reden*. Herausgegeben von K. Kohler. New York, 1881.
——, *Inaugural Sermon Delivered before the Har Sinai Verein*. Translated from the German by Rev. C. A. Rubenstein. Baltimore, 1909.

אײנשטײן, י. ד., אוצר זכרונותי. ניו. יורק, (1930). (EISENSTEIN, J. D.)

ELZAS, BARNETT A., *Leaves from My Historical Scrap Book.* Charleston, South Carolina, 1907.

———, *The Reform Society of Israelites. History and Constitution.* New York, 1916.

———, editor, *The Sabbath Service and Miscellaneous Prayers.* Adopted by the Reform Society of Israelites, South Carolina, 1830. Reprinted with introduction by editor. New York, 1916.

פאלק, יהושע, אבני יהושע, ניו־יורק, תר״כ (1860). (FALK, JOSHUA)

FERNANDEZ, BENJAMIN DIAS, *A Series of Letters on the Evidences of Christianity.* Philadelphia, 1858 (reprinted from *The Occident*).

פראנקעל, זכריה, דרכי המשנה. ליפסיא, תרי״ט (FRANKEL ZECHARIAH) (1859).

FREY, JOSEPH SAMUEL, C. F., *The Object of the American Society for Meliorating the Condition of the Jews.* New York, 1827.

FRIEDENWALD, HARRY, *Life, Letters, and Addresses of Aaron Friedenwald, M.D.* Baltimore, 1906.

GOTTHEIL, GUSTAV, "Why I am a Jew." *Why I am What I Am.* Edited by J. S. Ogilvie. New York, 1891.

———, "The Greatness and Influence of Moses," Neely's *History of the Parliament of Religions;* see below.

GRINSTEIN, HYMAN B., "The Minute Book of Lilienthal's Union of German Synagogues in New York." *Hebrew Union College Annual.* Cincinnati, 1943–44.

HACKENBURG, WILLIAM B., "Documents Regarding the Thanksgiving Proclamation of Governor Hoyt of Pennsylvania (1880)." *PAJHS,* no. 20, 1911.

HIRSCH, EMIL G., *Reform Judaism.* Discourse at Dr. Samuel Hirsch's Seventieth Anniversary. Chicago, 1885.

———, "The Philosophy of the Reform Movement in American Judaism." *Yearbook CCAR,* vol. V, 1895.

———, *Twenty Discourses,* New York, s. a. (reprinted from *The Reform Advocate*).

———, *My Religion.* New York, 1925.

HIRSCH, SAMSON RAPHAEL, *Nineteen Letters of Ben Uziel.* Translated by Bernard Drachman. New York, 1899.

————, *Gesammelte Schriften.* Frankfort a. M., 1902–1912.

————, *The Jewish Sabbath.* Translated by Ben Joseph Ussors. Newport, England, 1911.

————, *The Talmud.* Translated by W. Stern, London s. a.

HIRSCH, SAMUEL, Rev. Dr. *David Einhorn, Rabbiner der Beth El Gemeinde, New York. Gedächtnissrede.* Philadelphia, 1879.

HOCHHEIMER, HENRY, *Zwei Reden.* Baltimore, 1861.

————, *Rede, gehalten au 30. April 1889 bei der hundert jahrigen Inaugurationsfeier Washingtons.* Baltimore, 1889.

————, *Zwölf Tischreden an Zwölf Festabenden der Israel* (delivered December 10, 1856—December 17, 1873). Baltimore, s. a.

(HOLZMAN, ELIJAH), האלצמאן, אליהו, עמק רפאים. ניו-יורק, תרכ"ה (1865).

HUEBSCH, ADOLPH, ספר תפלה לשבת, שלש רגלים וחול. *Gebete für den offentlichen Gottesdienst der Templegemeinde Ahawath Chesed.* New York, 1872.

————, מחזור לראש השנה וליום כפור עם תרגום אנגלי. *Prayer for Divine Service of the Cong. Ahavath Chesed.* Arranged by Huebsch; translated by Alexander Kohut. New York, 1889.

ILLOWAY, HENRY, ספר מלחמות אלהים. *Being the Controversial Letters and the Casuistic Decisions of the Late Rabbi Bernard Illowy Ph.D. with a Short History of His Life and Activities.* Berlin, 1914.

ISAACS, MYER S., *The Persecution of the Jews in Russia.* New York, 1882.

————, *The Old Guard and Other Addresses.* New York, 1906.

JASTROW, MARCUS, *Israels Auserwählung.* Berlin, 1860.

————, *Offene Erklärung am Herrn I. M. Wise.* Philadelphia, 1867.

————, *Predigt gehalten am Danksagungs Tage.* Philadelphia, 1868.

————, *A Lecture on Temperance.* New York, 1874.

————, *Der Ganze Mensch.* Philadelphia, 1888.

————, *Turn Not to Folly Again.* Philadelphia, 1890.

————, *A Warning Voice.* Philadelphia, 1892.

————, "The History and the Future of the Text of the Talmud." *Publications of the Gratz College,* vol. I. Philadelphia, 1897.

Jewish Ministers' Association of America, *Conference Papers. Essays and Addresses Delivered at the First Conference of the Jewish Ministers' Association of New York and Adjacent States; Held in New York City, January 19–20, 1885.* New York, 1885.

————, *Jewish Conference Papers; Together With the Reports of the Meetings of the Jewish Ministers' Association of America.* New York, 1887.

Jewish Theological Seminary Association, *Constitution and By-Laws.* New York, 1886.

Jewish Theological Seminary Association, *Proceedings* (of Biennial Conventions). New York, 1888–1902.

Jewish Theological Seminary of America, Preliminary Announcement. New York, 1902.

Jewish Theological Seminary of America, Documents, Charter and By-laws. New York, 1903.

Jewish Theological Seminary Students Annual, vols. I–III. New York, 1914, 1915, 1916.

JOHLSON, J., *Instruction in the Mosaic Religion.* Translated by I. Leeser. Philadelphia, 1830.

KISCH, GUIDO, "Voyage to America Ninety Years Ago: The Diary of a Bohemian Jew on his Voyage from Hamburg to New York, 1847." *PAJHS,* no. 35, 1939.

KOHLER, KAUFMANN, *Grab- und Gedenkrede für Rabbiner David Einhorn.* Milwaukee, 1879.

————, "Old and Modern Judaism." *The Hebrew Review,* vol. I, no. 2, January 1, 1881.

————, *Backward or Forward?* New York, 1885.

————, *Manual of Religious Instruction.* New York, 1887.

————, *Das Volk, und die Religion der Treue.* Predigten. New York, 1891.

————, "The Share of the Moors, Jews and Germans in the Discovery and Civilizing Development of America." *American Jews' Annual,* no. 8. Cincinnati, 1892.

————, "Human Brotherhood as Taught by the Religions

Based on the Bible." Neely's *History of the Parliament of Religions;* see below.

————, "Dr. Alexander Kohut." *The Menorah,* vol. XVII, no. 1, July, 1894.

————, "A United Israel." *Yearbook CCAR,* vol. IX, 1898–99.

————, *Guide for Instruction in Judaism.* New York, 1899.

————, editor, *David Einhorn Memorial Volume.* New York, 1911.

————, *Hebrew Union College and Other Addresses.* Cincinnati, 1916.

————, *Personal Reminiscence of my Early Life.* Cincinnati, 1918 (reprinted from *Hebrew Union College Monthly,* May, 1918).

————, *Studies, Addresses and Personal Papers.* New York, 1931.

KOHUT, ALEXANDER, *Aufrüf zur Gründung eines Talmud-Thoravereins.* Fünfkirchen, 1875.

————, אבני זכרון.. *Erinnerungsdenkmal* (Gedächtnissrede auf Seine Majestät den Hochseligen Ferdinand V, 18, Juli, 1875).

————, זכר זכריה. *Gedächtnissrede auf den Oberrabiner und Seminardirektor Dr. Z. Frankel.* Leipzig, 1875.

————, קוהוט, חנוך יהודה, ספר ערוך השלם. וויען, תרל״ח (1878). הקדמה״, כרך א׳.

————, *Ein Offenes Wort.* Grosswardein, 1882.

————, *Freedom and Enlightenment.* What the Statue of Liberty can teach us. Adapted from the original German by Leon Harrison. New York, 1886.

————, *An Appeal to our Young Men.* New York, 1886.

————, "Immortality." *The Menorah,* vol. VI, no. 4, April, 1889.

————, *Thanksgiving Day: An Appeal to the American People.* New York, 1890.

————, "Secular and Theological Studies." *The Menorah,* vol. XIII, no. 1, July, 1892.

————, "What the Hebrew Scriptures Have Wrought for Mankind." Neely's *History of the Parliament of Religions;* see below.

————, *Ethics of the Fathers.* Translated into English by Max Cohen and edited by B. Elzas. New York, 1920.

KOHUT, REBEKAH, *My Portion,* New York, 1925.

————, *As I Know Them*, New York, 1929.

————, *His Father's House*, New Haven, 1938.

KRAUSKOPF, JOSEPH, "Fifty Years of Judaism in America." *American Jews' Annual*, no. 4. Cincinnati, 1888.

LAZARUS, EMMA, *Songs of a Semite: The Dance of Death and Other Poems*. New York, 1882.

————, *An Epistle to the Hebrews*. New York, 1900.

LEESER, ISAAC, *The Jews and The Mosaic Law*, 2 vols. Philadelphia, 1834.

————, סידור שפתי צדיקים. *The Forms of Prayers According to the Customs of the Spanish and Portuguese Jews*. Philadelphia, 1837.

————, מורה דרך ללמד את נערי בני ישראל דרכי לשון עברית. *Hebrew Reader—Hebrew and English. No. I—Spelling Book*. Philadelphia, 1838.

————, *Catechism for Jewish Children*. Designed as a Religious Manual for House and School. Philadelphia, 1841.

————, *The Claims of the Jews to an Equality of Rights*. Philadelphia, 1841.

————, *Commemoration of the Life and Death of William Henry Harrison*. Philadelphia, 1841.

————, *A Discourse on the Hope of Israel*. Philadelphia, 1842.

————, "The Jews and Their Religion." D. Rupp, *History of Religious Denominations, infra*.

————, *Discourses on the Jewish Religion*, 10 vols. Philadelphia, 1844–1867.

————, *The Law of God*, 5 vols. Philadelphia, 1845.

————, *The Testimony*. Philadelphia, 1851.

————, translator, תורה, נביאים וכתובים. *The Twenty-four Books of the Holy Scriptures*. Philadelphia, 1856.

————, "North Carolina and the Israelites." Quoted from the *Philadelphia Evening Journal* in *The Occident*, vol. XVI, no. 11, February, 1859.

————, *Thoughts Suggested by Bible Texts*. Philadelphia, 1861.

————, and Moses N. Nathan, *Second Annual Examination of the Sunday School for Religious Instruction of Israelites in Philadelphia*. 1840.

A Review of "The Review" of the late controversy between the Rev. Isaac Leeser and the Philadelphia Congregation Mikve Israel by an Israelite. New York, 1850.

The Lyons Collection. PAJHS, no. 27, 1920.

Lyons, Jacques I. and Abraham, De Sola, *A Jewish Calendar for Fifty Years.* Montreal, 1854.

Mayer, M., "Geschichte des religioesen Umschwunges unter den Israeliten Nord-Amerikas." *Sinai,* Band I, no. 4. Baltimore, Mai, 1856.

Mendelssohn, Moses, *Jerusalem.* Translated from the German by I. Leeser. Philadelphia, 1852.

Mendes, A. P., *The Law of Moses, a Catechism of the Jewish Religion.* London, 1870. Reprinted for the West End Synagogue. New York, 1908.

Mendes, Frederick de Sola, *Tyndallism and Judaism.* New York, 1874.

————, *Jewish Family Papers or Letters of a Missionary.* Translated from the German of Dr. Wilhelm Herzberg. New York, 1875.

————, *Defence not Defiance. A Hebrew's Reply to the Missionaries.* New York, 1876.

————, *The Child's First Bible.* New York, 1877.

————, *Synagogue and School: Hymns, Songs, and Religious Memoranda for Jewish Congregations.* New York, 1887.

————, "Leaves from my Tablets." *Jewish Record,* vol. II, nos. 48, 49 (March 9–16, 1877); vol. V, nos. 3, 4 (April 27–May 4, 1877).

Mendes, H. Pereira, *The Sphere of Congregational Work.* New York, 1885.

————, "Why am I a Jew?" *The North American Review,* vol. CXL, no. 367. New York, 1887.

————, *The Lifting of the Veil.* New York, 1888.

————, "Orthodox or Historical Judaism." Neely's *History of the Parliament of Religions;* see below.

————, "The Jewish Church." *World's Congress of Religions.* Boston, 1893.

————, *Jewish History Ethically Presented.* New York, 1896.

————, *An Open Letter to Zionists.* London, 1905.

————, *Responsibilities Not One-Sided.* New York, 1905.

————. *Ruach Hayim (The Spirit of Life), or Jewish Daily Life Ethically Presented*. New York, 1917.

————, "A Habitation for God's Holiness." *The Menorah Journal*, vol. IV, no. 3, June, 1918.

————, "The Sephardic Jews of Newport." *Early Religious Leaders of Newport*. New York, 1918.

————, *And God Spoke*. New York, 1927.

————, *Bar Mitzvah for Boyhood, Youth and Manhood*. New York, 1938.

MERZBACHER, LEO, סדר תפלה. New York, 1855.

MORAIS, SABATO, *An Address on the Death of Abraham Lincoln*. Philadelphia, 1865.

————, *An Address Delivered on the Feast of Pentecost*. Philadelphia, 1869.

————, *Address Delivered at the Funeral of Rev. S. M. Isaacs*. New York, 1878 (reprinted from *The Jewish Messenger*, May 22, 1878).

————, "Ode to the Hebrew Language." Translated by H. Pereira Mendes. *The Menorah*, vol. III, no. 3, September, 1887.

————, "The Hebrew Language." *The Menorah*, vol. III, 4, October, 1887.

————, *Discourse Delivered on Sabbath Bamidbar*. Philadelphia, 1892.

————, "Mickve Israel Congregation of Philadelphia." *PAJHS*, no. 1, 1893.

————, "Italian Jewish Literature." *Publications of Gratz College*, vol. I. Philadelphia, 1897.

————, *Italian Hebrew Literature*. Edited by Julius H. Greenstone. New York, 1926.

Neely's History of the Parliament of Religions and Religious Congresses at the World's Columbian Exposition. Chicago, 1893.

NOAH, MORDECAI MANUEL, *Discourse Delivered at the Consecration of the Synagogue Shearith Israel*. New York, 1818.

————, "Address Delivered at the Laying of the Corner-Stone of the City of Ararat." Reprinted in *PAJHS*, no. 21, 1913.

————, *Discourse on the Restoration of the Jews.* New York, 1845.

Persecution of the Jews in the East. Philadelphia, 1840.
PHILIPSON, DAVID, *Centenary Papers and Others.* Cincinnati, 1919.
————, editor, *Letters of Rebecca Gratz.* Philadelphia, 1929.
————, *My Life as an American Jew.* Cincinnati, 1941.
Prayers for Sabbath, Rosh Hashanah and Kippur. Translated by Isaac Pinto. New York, A. M. 5526, 1766.
PRICE, GEORGE, "The Memoir of Doctor George Price." Translated by Leo Shpall. *PAJHS,* vol. XLVII, 1957.
————, "The Russian Jews in America." Translated by Leo Shpall. *PAJHS,* vol. XLVIII, 1958.

RAPHALL, MORRIS J., editor, גלעד. *The Hebrew Review and Magazine of Rabbinical Literature.* (A Weekly) London, vol. I, October, 1834–March, 1835; vol. II, April–September, 1835; vol. III, January–July, 1836.
————, *Judaism Defended Against the Attacks of T. J. C. of Oxford.* London, 1840.
————, מועדי ה'. *The Festivals of the Lord.* London, 1840.
————, "The Unity of God," *The Distinguishing Feature of the Jewish Faith.* Yarmouth, 1845.
————, compiler-translator, רחמה. *Devotional Exercises for the Use of the Daughters of Israel.* New York, 1852.
————, *Four Seasons in the History of Israel.* New York, 1854.
————, *Post-Biblical History of the Jews,* 2 vols. Philadelphia, 1855.
————, נתיב אל-מות. *Path to Immortality.* New York, 1859.
————, *The Bible View of Slavery.* New York, 1861.
Catalogue of the Private Library of the Late Morris Jacob Raphall. New York, 1868.
Report of the Commissioners of Immigration upon the Causes which Incite Immigration to the United States. Washington, 1892.
ROBINSON, W. D., *Memoir Addressed to Persons of the Jewish Religion in Europe on the Subject of Emigration and Settlement in . . . the United States.* London, 1819.
ROTHSCHILD, HESTER, אמרי-לב. *Meditations and Prayers for*

Every Situation and Occasion in Life. Revised and corrected by I. Leeser. Philadelphia, 1864.

Rules and Regulations of the Polonies Talmud Torah attached to Shearith Israel. 1855. Leaflet, Lyons' Scrapbook, I.

RUPP, DANIEL, *An Original History of the Religious Denominations in the United States.* Philadelphia, 1844.

SCHECHTER, SOLOMON, *Some Aspects of Rabbinic Theology: The "Law".* London, 1895 (reprinted from *The Jewish Quarterly Review,* vol. VIII).

————, Studies in Judaism. First Series. Philadelphia, 1896.

————, Four Epistles to the Jews of England, London, 1901 (reprinted from the *Jewish Chronicle*).

————, *Inaugural Address.* New York, 1903.

SCHWARZ, JOSEPH, *Descriptive Geography and Brief Historical Sketch of Palestine.* Translated by I. Leeser. Philadelphia, 1850.

(SCHWARTZBERG, S.)   שווארצבערג, ש. ב., תכתב זאת לדור אחרון
ניו־יורק, תרנ"ח (1898).

SOLIS-COHEN, SOLOMON, *A Seminary Ideal.* New York, 1919 (reprinted from *PJTSA,* New York, 1894).

————, "Sabato Morais—Teacher and Leader." *The Jewish Exponent,* vol. LXXII, April 20, 1923 (also in *Mikveh Israel—Commemoration of the 100th Anniversary of the Birth of Sabato Morais.* Philadelphia, 1924).

————, *When Love Passed By and Other Verses.* Philadelphia, 1929.

————, *Judaism and Science, with Other Addresses and Papers.* Philadelphia, 1940.

Statistics of the Jews in the United States. Compiled under the authority of the Board of Delegates of American Israelites and the Union of American Hebrew Congregations. Philadelphia, September, 1880.

STILES, EZRA, *The Literary Diary of Ezra Stiles,* 3 vols. Edited by F. B. Dexter. New York, 1901.

SULZBERGER, MAYER, *Address on the 50th Anniversary of the Hebrew School of Philadelphia.* Philadelphia, 1888.

SZOLD, BENJAMIN, דברי שלום ואמת. *Gottesdienstlicher Vortrag.* Baltimore, 1859.

————, *Der Enthüllte Einhorn.* Baltimore, 1860.

————, *The Divine Origin and Rationality of Judaism: The Decalogue.* Baltimore, 1863.

————, *Andachtsbüchlein für Israelitische Kinder für Haus und Schule.* (In hebraeischer, deutscher und englischer Sprache.) 1867.

————, ‏שׂראל‎ *Israelitisches Gebetuch für die Hausliche Andacht.* Baltimore, 1867.

————, *Auch Ein Wort über Jastrow und Hirsch,* Baltimore, 1868.

————, ‏עבודת ישראל‎. *Israelitische Gebetbuch für den Oeffentlichen Gottesdienst im ganzen Jahre.* Zweite Auflage. Baltimore, 1871.

————, ‏אורים ותומים‎. *Outlines of the System of Judaism.* Baltimore, 1874.

————, ‏אמרי בינה‎. *The Proverbs of Solomon.* (In Hebrew, English and German.) Baltimore, 1874.

————, ‏ראשית דעת‎. *Reshith Daath.* Baltimore, 1874.

————, *Moses Mendelssohn.* Baltimore, 1879.

————, *Old Testament Selections.* Baltimore, 1882.

————, *The Hebrew Reader for Schools from the Prayer Book.* Philadelphia, 1884.

———— "The Revised Bible—A Criticism." *The Menorah,* vol. IV, no 4, April, 1888.

————, "The Revised Bible—True Meaning of the Book of Job." *The Menorah,* vol. IV, no. 5, May, 1888; no. 6, June.

————, *The Sabbath.* Baltimore, 1889.

————, "Vaterland und Freiheit." *Tribute of the Synagogue.* Edited by Emanuel Hertz. New York, 1927.

————, and Jastrow, M., ‏שׂראל‎ *Israelitisch Prayer Book for All Public Services of the Year.* Philadelphia 1873.

SZOLD, HENRIETTA, "What Judaism has done for Women." Neely's *History of the Parliament of Religions, supra.*

————, "Knowledge versus Spirituality in the Curriculum of Jewish Religious School." *The Menorah,* vol. XXIII, no. 3, September, 1897; no. 4, October.

VOORSANGER, JACOB, "A Few Chapters from the History of the Jews on the Pacific Coast from 1849 to 1860." *American Jews' Annual,* no. 5. New York, 1889.

————, "The Sabbath Question." *Yearbook CCAR,* vol. XII, 1902.

וויינבערגער, מ., היהודים והיהדות בנויארק. ניו־יורק, (WEINBERGER, M.)
תרמ"ז (1887).

וויס, יצחק הירש, זכרונותי. ווארשא, (WEISS, ISAAC HIRSCH).
תרנ"ד (1894).

————, נצח ישראל. וויען, תרנ"ו (1896).

וויז, אהרן, שלהבת יה. תפילות לראש השנה. (WISE, AARON)
The Temple Service arranged for the Congregation Rodoph Sholem of New York. Vol. II. For the New Year ... Revised by Rudolph Grossman. New York, 1891. Vol. III. For the Day of Atonement, New York, 1891.

WISE, AARON and LEDERER, LEOPOLD, *History of Congregation Rodeph Shalom.* New York, 1892.

WISE, ISAAC MAYER, *History of the Israelitish Nation from Abraham to the Present Time.* Albany, 1854.

————, תפילות בני ישורון לראש השנה כפי מנהג אמעריקא. *The Divine Service of American Israelites for the New Year.* Cincinnati, 1866.

————, *Judaism: Its Doctrines and Duties. Cincinnati,* 1872.

————, *The Cosmic God.* Cincinnati, 1876.

————, *Formula of the Historical Basis of Reform.* (Reprinted from *The Hebrew Review,* October, 1880.)

————, *Judaism and Christianity, their Agreements and Disagreements.* Cincinnati, 1883.

————, "A Sketch of Judaism in America." *American Jews' Annual,* no. 1. Cincinnati, 1884.

————, "American Judaism." *American Jews' Annual,* no. 2. Cincinnati, 1885.

————, "American Judaism—Its Record from New Year 5646 A. M. to December 1887." *American Jews' Annual,* no. 4. Cincinnati, 1888.

————, *A Defence of Judaism versus Proselyting Christianity.* Chicago and Cincinnati, 1889.

————, "The Theology of Judaism." *The World's Congress of Religions.* Boston, 1893.

————, *Selected Writings.* Edited by D. Philipson and L. Grossmann. Cincinnati, 1900.

————, *Reminiscences.* Edited by D. Philipson. Cincinnati, 1901.

————, "The World of My Books." Translated with an introduction and explanatory notes by Albert H. Friedlander. Cincinnati (offprint from *AJA*, Tercentennial Issue, vol. 6, no. 2), 1954.

———— and others, *Hymns, Psalms and Prayers* (English and German). Cincinnati, 1868.

WOLF, SIMON, *The American Jew as Patriot, Soldier and Citizen*. Philadelphia, 1895.

————, *The Presidents I have Known from 1860 to 1918*. Washington, 1918.

Selected Addresses and Papers of Simon Wolf. Cincinnati, 1926.

ZANGWILL, ISRAEL, "On American Judaism." *The Menorah*, vol. XXV, no. 5, November, 1898.

"Zur Geschichte des jüdisch-theologischen Seminars." *Programm zur Eröffnung des jüdisch-theologischen Seminars zu Breslau*. Breslau, 1854.

II. SECONDARY SOURCES

ABELOW, SAMUEL P., "An Index to the Jewish Encyclopedia containing References to Articles that Deal with the History of the Jews in the United States." *PAJHS*, Index to nos. 1–20, 1914, pp. 588-600.

ABRAHAMS, ISRAEL, *By-Paths in Hebraic Bookland*. Philadelphia, 1920.

ADLER, CYRUS, compiler, *Catalogue of the Leeser Library*. Philadelphia, 1883.

————, "American Jewish History." *Yearbook CCAR*, vol. XI, 1901.

————, *Jews in the Diplomatic Correspondence of the United States*. *PAJHS*, no. 15, 1906.

————, "Solomon Schechter, A Biographical Sketch," *AJYB*, vol. 18, 5677, 1916–1917.

————, *Jacob Henry Schiff*. New York, 1921.

————, *Jacob H. Schiff. His Life and Letters*, 2 vols. New York, 1928.

————, *Louis Marshall, A Biographical Sketch*. New York, 1931 (reprinted from *AJYB*, vol. 32).

——, *Lectures, Selected Papers and Addresses.* Philadelphia, 1933.

——, editor, *The Jewish Theological Seminary of America.* Semi-Centennial Volume. New York, 1939.

ADLER, SELIG and CONNOLLY, THOMAS E., *From Ararat to Suburbia.* Philadelphia, 1960.

AGUS, JACOB B., *Modern Philosophies of Judaism.* New York, 1941.

AMRAM, DAVID W., *Address on the Tenth Anniversary of the Death of the Rev. Dr. Marcus Jastrow.* Philadelphia, 1913.

ANTIN, MARY, *The Promised Land.* Boston and New York, 1912.

BARON, SALO W., A Social and Religious History of the Jews, 3 vols. New York, 1937.

——, *Modern Nationalism and Religion.* New York and Philadelphia, 1960.

——, and BARON, JEANETTE, "Palestinian Messengers in America, 1849–1879," *Jewish Social Studies,* vol. V, no. 2, April, 1943; no. 3, July, 1943.

BENTWICH, NORMAN, *Solomon Schechter.* Philadelphia, 1938.

(BERGER, ISAIAH) ברגר, ישעיהו, „חכמת ישראל באמריקה". ספר השנה ליהודי אמריקה, מ. ריבלוב, עורך. ניו־יורק. תרצ״ט (1939).

BERMAN, JEREMIAH J., *Shehitah: A Study in the Cultural and Social Life of the Jewish People.* New York, 1941.

——, "The Trend in Jewish Religious Observance in Mid-Nineteenth-Century America." *PAJHS,* no. 37, 1947.

(BERNFELD, SIMON) ברנפלד, שמעון, דור חכם. וארשא, תרנ״ו (1896).
——, תולדות הריפורמציון הדתית בישראל. קראקא, תר״ס (1900).

BERNHEIMER, CHARLES S., editor, *The Russian Jew in the United States.* Philadelphia, 1905.

"Biographical Sketches of Rabbis and Cantors Officiating in the United States." *AJYB,* vol. 5, 5664, 1903–1904.

BLAU, JOSEPH L., "The Spiritual Life of American Jewry, 1654–1954." *AJYB,* vol. 56, 5715, 1955.

BLOCH, JOSHUA, *Professor Solomon Schechter.* Cincinnati, 1916 (reprinted from *Hebrew Union College Monthly,* vol. 11, nos. 4–5).

——, פרופ׳ שניאור זלמן שכטר. ספר השנה ליהודי אמריקה, מ. ריבלוב וש. ברנשטיין, עורכים. ניו־יורק, תרצ״ה (1935).

————, *Of Making Many Books* (An Annotated List of the Books Issued by the Jewish Publication Society of America, 1890–1952.) Philadelphia. 5714, 1953.

BLUM, ISIDOR, *The History of the Jews of Baltimore*. Baltimore, 1910.

BOGEN, BORIS D., *Jewish Philanthropy*. New York, 1917.

————, "Historical Sketch of the B'nai B'rith," *B'nai B'rith Manual*. Edited by Samuel S. Cohon. Cincinnati, 1926.

BRANN, M., *Heinrich Graetz*. Breslau, 1917 (Sonderabdruck aus der *Monatsschrift für Geschichte und Wissenschaft des Judentums*).

BRAUDE, WILLIAM G., "Liberal Judaism in a Reactionary World." *Yearbook CCAR*, vol. LII, 1942.

BRICKNER, BARNETT R., "The History of Jewish Education in Cincinnati." *Jewish Education*, vol. VIII, no. 3, October-December, 1936.

BRODY, FANNIE M., "The Hebrew Periodical Press in America 1871–1931: A Bibliographical Survey." *PAJHS*, no. 33, 1934.

BUCHLER, JOSEPH. "The Struggle for Unity; Attempts at Union in American Jewish Life, 1654–1868." *American Jewish Archives*, vol. II, no. 1, June, 1949.

(BURGIN, HENRY) ‏בורגין, הערץ, דיא געשיכטע פון דער אידישער‎
‏ארבייטער בעוועגונג אין אמעריקא, רוסלאנד און ענגלאנד. ניו-יורק,‎
‏1915.‎

COBB, S. H., *Rise of Religious Liberty in America*. New York, 1902.

COHEN, BOAZ, *Law and Tradition in Judaism*. New York, 1959.

COHEN, HERMANN. *Graetzes Philosophie der Juedischen Geschichte*. Breslau, 1917. (Sonderabdruck aus der *Monatschrift fuer Geschichte und Wissenschaft des Judentums*.)

COHEN, ISRAEL. *Jewish Life in Modern Times*. New York, 1914.

COHEN, SIMON. *Shaaray Tefila. A History of Its Hundred Years, 1845–1945*. New York, 1945.

COHON, SAMUEL, S., "The Theology of the Union Prayer Book." *Yearbook CCAR*, vol. XXXVIII, 1928.

————, *What We Jews Believe*. Cincinnati, 1931.

————, "The History of the Hebrew Union College."
    PAJHS, no. 40, 1950.

————, "Kaufmann Kohler the Reformer." *Mordecai M.
    Kaplan Jubilee Volume,* vol. I. Edited by Moshe Davis.
    New York, 1954.

COLEMAN, EDWARD D., "A Bibliography of the Writings of
    Max James Kohler." *PAJHS,* no. 34, 1937.

Congregation Adath Israel. *The History of Congregation
    Adath Israel.* Louisville, 1906.

Congregation Bene Yeshurun. *The History of K. K. Bene
    Yeshurun from the Date of Its Organization.* Cincinnati,
    1892.

CURTI, MERLE. *The Growth of American Thought.* New York,
    1944.

DALY, CHARLES P., *The Settlement of the Jews in North
    America.* Edited by M. J. Kohler. New York, 1893.

DAVIDSON, GABRIEL. "The Palestine Colony in Michigan."
    PAJHS, no. 29, 1925.

————, "The Jew in Agriculture in the United States."
    AJYB, vol. 37, 5696, 1935–1936.

————, *Our Jewish Farmers.* New York, 1943.

דייוויס, משה, „ר' יצחק ליסר — מראשוני-הבונים של (DAVIS, MOSHE)
    יהדות אמריקה". הדואר, גליונות ז'-ח', י"ג וכ' כסלו, תש"א
    .(1941)

————,„בנימין סזולד ומרכוס יאסטרוב". ספר השנה ליהודי אמריקה,
    כרך ששי. מ. ריבולוב, עורך. ניו-יורק, תש"ב (1942).

————,„שבתי מוראיס : תולדותיו, דעותיו, ופעולותיו". ספר
    השנה ליהודי אמריקה, כרך שביעי. מ. ריבולוב, עורך. ניו-יורק,
    תש"ה (1944).

————,„ראשית החנוך העברי הגבוה באמריקה". יסודות החנוך היהודי
    באמריקה. צבי שארפשטיין, עורך. ניו-יורק, תש"ז (1946).

————, *Sabato Morais: A Selected and Annotated Bibliogra-
    phy of His Writings.* New York, 1947 (reprinted from
    PAJHS, no. 37).

————, "Religious Life and Institutions in America." *The
    Jews,* L. Finkelstein, editor, vol. 1, *infra.*

————,„הצופה בארץ החדשה", ספר היובל לכבוד אלכסנדר מארכס.
    בעריכת שאול ליברמן. ניו-יורק, תש"י (1950).

DAVIS, MOSHE and MEYER, ISIDORE S., editors, *The Writing of American Jewish History*. New York, 1957.

(DEINARD, E.), דיינארד, אפרים, אור מאיר. ניו־יורק, תרנ"ז (1896).

———, קהלת אמעריקא. סט. לואיס, תרפ"ו (1906).

DEMBITZ, LEWIS N., "Jewish Beginnings in Kentucky." *PAJHS,* no. 1, 1893.

———, *Jewish Services in Synagogue and Home.* Philadelphia, 1898.

DEUTSCH, GOTTHARD, *Heinrich Graetz: A Centenary.* Cincinnati, 1917 (reprinted from *Yearbook CCAR,* vol. XXVII).

DININ, SAMUEL, *Judaism in a Changing Civilization.* New York, 1933.

(DUBNOW, SIMON), דובנוב, שמעון, דברי ימי עולם. כרכים ט'־י'. תל־אביב, תרצ"ו־ת"ש (1936־1940).

DUSHKIN, ALEXANDER M., *Jewish Education in New York City.* New York, 1918.

DYER, MORRIS ALBION, "Points in the First Chapter of New York Jewish History." *PAJHS,* no. 3, 1895.

EISENSTEIN, J. D., "The History of the First Russian-American Jewish Congregation." *PAJHS,* no. 9, 1901.

———, "The Development of Jewish Casuistic Literature in America." *PAJHS,* no. 15, 1904.

ELBOGEN, ISMAR, *Die Wissenschaft des Judentums.* Festrede. Berlin, 1925.

———, "Der Streit um die 'positiv-historische Reform'." Berlin, 1928 (Sonderdruck aus *Festgabe für Claude G. Montefiore ... des Weltverbandes für Religioes-Liberales Judentum in Berlin*).

ELBOGEN, ISMAR, *Heinrich Graetz.* New York, 1941 (reprinted from *AJYB,* vol. 43.).

———, אלבוגן, איתמר (יצחק משה), "אלכסנדר קוהוט", בצרון, כרך 6 חוברת ט'־י' (33), סיון־תמוז, תש"ב (1942).

———, "Alexander Kohut." *AJYB,* vol. 44, 5703, 1942–1943.

———, *American Jewish Scholarship: A Survey.* New York, 1943 (reprinted from *AJYB,* vol. 45).

———, *A Century of Jewish Life.* Translated by Moses Hadas. Philadelphia, 1944.

————, "The Montefiore Testimonial Fund and American Israel." *PAJHS,* no. 37, 1947.

ELIASSOF, HERMAN, "The Jews of Chicago." *PAJHS,* no. 11, 1903.

————, *German-American Jews.* Illinois, 1915 (reprinted from *Deutsch-Amerikanische Geschichtsblaetter Jahrbuch der Deutsch-Amerikanischen Historischen Gesellschaft von Illinois,* vol. XIV, 1914).

ELZAS, BARNETT A., *The Jews of South Carolina: From Earliest Times to the Present Day.* Philadelphia, 1905.

————, "The First Confirmation Ceremony in the American Synagogue." *The Jewish Tribune,* vol. VII, no. 17. Portland, Oregon, May 18, 1906.

————, "New Material on the First Reform Movement in America." Literary Supplement to the *American Hebrew. New York,* December 7, 1906.

ENELOW, H. G., "The Synod in the Past and Its Feasibility in the Present." *Yearbook CCAR,* vol. 1900.

————, "Kaufmann Kohler." *AJYB,* vol. 28, 5687, 1926–1927.

ENGLANDER, HENRY, "Isaac Leeser, 1806–1868." *Yearbook CCAR,* vol. XXVIII, 1918.

ENGELMAN, URIAH Z., "Jewish Statistics in the U. S. Census of Religious Bodies (1850–1936)." *Jewish Social Studies,* vol. IX, no. 2. New York, April, 1947.

Essays in American-Jewish History (To Commemorate the Tenth Anniversary of the Founding of the American Jewish Archives under the direction of Jacob Rader Marcus). Cincinnati, 1958.

EZEKIEL, HERBERT T., *The Jews of Richmond During the Civil War.* Richmond, 1915.

————, and LICHTENSTEIN, GASTON, *The History of the Jews of Richmond, 1769–1917.* Richmond, 1917.

EZEKIEL, JACOB, "Persecution of the Jews in 1840." *PAJHS,* no. 8, 1900.

FELDMAN, ABRAHAM, "Joseph Krauskopf." *AJYB,* vol. 26, 5685, 1924–1925.

FELSENTHAL, BERNARD, "On the History of the Jews of Chicago." *PAJHS,* no. 2, 1894.

————, and ELIASSOF, HERMAN, *History of Kehillath Anshe Maarabh.* Chicago, 1897.

FELSENTHAL, EMMA, *Bernard Felsenthal, Teacher in Israel.* London and New York, 1924.

Fifty Years Work of the Hebrew Education Society. Philadelphia, 1899.

FINK, REUBEN, editor, *America and Palestine.* New York, 1945.

FINKELSTEIN, LOUIS, *The Things that Unite Us.* New York, 1937 (reprinted from *Proceedings of the Twenty-Seventh Annual Conference of the Rabbinical Assembly of America*).

———, *Tradition in the Making.* New York, 1937.

———, editor, *The Jews: Their History, Culture and Religion,* 2 vols. Third Edition. New York, 1960.

FISCHER, JULIUS, *Dr. Alexander Kohut: Ein Lebensbild.* Budapest, 1927 (Sonderabdruck aus *Festschrift zum fünfzigjährigen Bestehen der Franz Josef-Landes-Rabbiner-Schule in Budapest*).

FISH, SIDNEY M., *Aaron Levy, Founder of Aaronsburg.* New York, 1951.

(FRANK, H.)‏ פראנק, ה., „עקאָנאָמישע אָרגאַניזאַציעס פון אידישן‏

‏מיטלשטאנד אין די פאראייניקטע שטאטן‏". ייוואָ בלעטער, באַנד 15,‏

‏נומ' 1‏-2. ניו־יאָרק, 1940.‏

‏———„תנועת ה‏,‏מרכזים' בארצות הברית‏". ספר השנה ליהודי אמריקה,‏

‏כרך חמישי. מ. ריבולוב, עורך. ניו־יורק, תש‏"‏א (1940).‏

Zecharias Frankel: Gedenkblätter su seinem hundertsten Geburtstag. Herausgegeben von Dr. M. Brann. Breslau, 1901.

FREDMAN, J. GEORGE and FALK, LOUIS A., *Jews in American Wars.* New York, 1942.

FREEHOF, SOLOMON B., *Reform Jewish Practice and Its Rabbinic Background.* Cincinnati, 1944.

FREIDUS, A. S., "List of Jewish Periodicals Published in the United States." *AJYB,* vol. 1, 5660, 1899–1900.

FRIEDENBERG, ALBERT M., "The Jews and the American Sunday Laws." *PAJHS,* no. 11, 1902.

———, "Calendar of American Jewish Cases." *PAJHS,* no. 12, 1904. Additions to "Calendar . . ." in no. 13, 1905; no. 25, 1917; no. 29, 1925.

———, "The Jews of New Jersey from the Earliest Times to 1850." *PAJHS,* no. 17, 1909.

———, "Sunday Laws of the United States and Judicial

Decisions Having Reference to the Jews." *AJYB*, vol. 10, 5669, 1908–1909.

———, "An Austro-Hungarian Movement to Encourage the Migration of Jews to America, 1848." *PAJHS*, no. 23, 1915.

———, "American Jewish Journalism to the Close of the Civil War." *PAJHS*, no. 26, 1918.

———, "Thoughts on the Philosophy of American Jewish History." *PAJHS*, no. 28, 1922.

FRIEDLAENDER, ISRAEL, *Past and Present*. New York, 1961.

FRIEDMAN, LEE M., "The New York Synagogue in 1812." *PAJHS*, no. 25, 1917.

———, *The American Society for Meliorating the Condition of the Jews; and Joseph S. C. F. Frey, Its Missionary —A Study in American Jewish History*. Boston, 1925.

———, *Early American Jews*. Cambridge, Massachusetts, 1934.

———, *Rabbi Haim Isaac Carigal. His Newport Sermon and his Yale Portrait*. Boston, 1940.

———, *Jewish Pioneers and Patriots*. Philadephia, 1942.

———, *Pilgrims In A New Land*. Philadelphia, 1948.

FRIEDMAN, THEODORE and GORDIS, ROBERT, *Jewish Life in America*. New York, 1954.

(GAMORAN, EMANUEL)   ‫גמראן, עמנואל, „החינוך הריפורמי בארצות-‬
‫הברית". ספר היובל של אגודת המורים העברים בניו-יורק. צבי‬
‫שארפשטיין עורך. ניו-יורק, תש"ד (1944).‬

GARTNER, LLOYD P., *The Jewish Immigrant in England: 1870–1914*. London, 1960.

GEFFEN, JOEL S., "America in the First Daily Newspaper: Ha-Yom (1886–1888)," *American Jewish Historical Quarterly*, vol. LI, March, 1962.

GINZBERG, LOUIS, "Frankel's Attitude to the Oral Law." *The Menorah*, vol. XXXI, December, 1901.

———, *The United Synagogue of America*. New York, 1918.

———, *Students, Scholars and Saints*. Philadelphia, 1928.

GLANZ, RUDOLF, "Jews in the Early German-American Literature." *Jewish Social Studies*, vol. IV, no. 2, April, 1942.

———, "Jew and Yankee: A Historic Comparison." *Ibid.*, vol. VI, no. 1, January, 1944.

‫גלאנץ, רודאלף, „יידן אין דעם קולטורקריית פון דייטשן אין‬

אמעריקע ביז די 80ער יארן". ייוא בלעטער, באנד 25, נומ' 1,
יאנואר־פעברואר, 1945, נומ' 2, מארץ־אפריל.

——, „יידן אין אמעריקע פאר דער מאסן־איינוואנדערונג". דצ"וו
באנד 4, נומ' 2, יולי־סעפטעמבער, 1946.

——, „יידן אין אמעריקע בעת דער קאלאניאלער תקופה". געדאַנק
און לעבן, באַנד 4, נומ' 1. אפריל־יוני, 1946.

——, „יידן אין אמעריקא אינם 19טן יארהונדערט". דצ"ו. באַנד 4,
נומ' 4, יאנואר־מאַרץ, 1947.

——, *Jews in Relation to the Cultural Milieu of the Germans in America up to the Eighteen Eighties.* New York, 1947.

——, "The Immigration of German Jews up to 1880." *YIVO Annual,* vol. II–III, 1947/1948.

——, "The History of the Jewish Community in New York." *YIVO Annual,* vol. IV, 1949.

——, "Source Materials on the History of Jewish Immigration to the United States, 1800–1880." *YIVO Annual,* vol. VI, 1951.

——, "German Jews in New York City in the 19th Century." *YIVO Annual,* vol. XI, 1956/1957.

——, *The Jews of California From the Discovery of Gold until 1880.* New York, 1960.

(GLATSTEIN, J., NIGER S., and ROGOFF, H.)
גלאָטשטיין, יעקב; ש. ניגער; ה. ראגאָף – רעדאַקציע, פינף און זיבעציק
יאָר יידישע פרעסע אין אַמעריקע (1870–1945). ניו־יורק, תש"ה
.(1945)

GLAZER, NATHAN, *American Judaism,* Chicago, 1957.

GLENN, M. G. (נלן, מנחם ג, „היהודים בעתונות האמריקאית". ספר השנה)
ליהודי אמריקה. ב. ריבולוב, עורך. ניו־יורק, תרצ"ט (1939).

——, „חלוצי היהדות בארצות אמריקה". ספר השנה ליהודי אמריקה,
כרך ששי. מ. ריבולוב, עורך. ניו־יורק, תש"ב (1942).

——, „היהודים בצבא ארצות־הברית". ספר השנה ליהודי אמריקה,
כרך שביעי. מ. ריבולוב, עורך. ניו־יורק, תש"ה (1944).

GOLDBERG, ISAAC, *Major Noah: American-Jewish Pioneer.* Philadelphia, 1936.

GOLDSTEIN, ISRAEL, *A Century of Judaism in New York.* New York, 1930.

GOODMAN, ABRAM VOSSEN, *American Overture.* Philadelphia, 1947.

GOODMAN, PHILIP, compiler, *A Documentary Story of a Century of the Jewish Community Center, 1854–1954.* New York, 1953.

GORDIS, ROBERT, *Conservative Judaism*. New York, 1945.

GOTTHEIL, RICHARD J. H., *Zionism*. Philadelphia, 1914.

————, *The Life of Gustav Gottheil*. Williamsport, Pa., 1936.

GREENSTONE, JULIUS H., *Some Early Catechisms*. Philadelphia, 1909.

————, "Jewish Education in the United States." *AJYB*, vol. 16, 5675, 1914–1915.

————, *The Jewish Religion*. Philadelphia, 1929.

————, גרינסטון, י. ה., "גרץ קוליג׳". ספר היובל של אגודת המורים, כנ״ל.

GRINSTEIN, HYMAN B., The American Synagogue and Laxity of Religious Observance, 1750–1850. (Typescript, December, 1935, at Columbia University Library.)

————, "The Asmonean." *Journal of Jewish Bibliography*, vol. 1, no. 3, April, 1939.

————, "An Early Parochial School." *Jewish Education*, vol. XIII, no. 1, April, 1941.

————, "Studies in the History of Jewish Education in New York City (1728–1860)." *The Jewish Review*, vol. II, no. 1, April, 1944; nos. 2–3, July–October.

————, "Reforms at Temple Emanuel of New York, 1860–1890." *Historia Judaica*, vol. VI, no. 2, October, 1944.

————, *The Rise of the Jewish Community in New York (1654–1860)*. Philadelphia, 1945.

GUP, S. M., "Currents in Jewish Religious Thought and Life in America in the Twentieth Century." *Yearbook CCAR*, vol. XLI, 1931.

GUTSTEIN, MORRIS A., *The Story of the Jews of Newport: 1658–1908*. New York, 1936.

————, *To Bigotry No Sanction*. (A Jewish Shrine in America). New York, 1958.

GUTTMACHER, ADOLPH, *History of the Baltimore Hebrew Congregation, 1830–1905*. Baltimore, 1905.

HACKENBURG, WILLIAM B., "Outline of a Plan to Gather Statistics Concerning the Jews of the United States." *PAJHS*, no. 12, 1904.

HACKER, LOUIS M., *The Shaping of the American Tradition*. 2 vols. New York, 1947.

HALL, THOMAS C., *The Religious Background of American Culture*. Boston, 1930.

HANDLIN, OSCAR, *Adventure in Freedom*. New York, 1954.

———, *The Uprooted*. Boston, 1952.

———, "The Acquisition of Political and Social Rights by the Jews in the United States." *AJYB*, vol. 56, 5715, 1955.

———, "Judaism in the United States." *The Shaping of American Religion*, vol. I of *Religion in American Life*. Edited by James Ward and A. Leland Jamison. Princeton, 1961.

——— and MARY F., "A Century of Jewish Immigration to the United States." *AJYB*, vol. 50, 5709, 1948–49.

HANSEN, MARCUS L., *The Immigrant in American History*. Cambridge, 1940.

HARBY, LEE C., "The Southern Jews in the War Between the States." *American Hebrew*, vol. LXXVII, no. 26, November 24, 1905.

———, "Penina Moise, Woman and Writer." *AJYB*, vol. 7, 5666. 1905–1906.

HARTOGENSIS, BENJAMIN H., "The Sephardic Congregation of Baltimore." *PAJHS*, no. 23, 1915.

———, "The Russian Night School of Baltimore." *PAJHS*, no. 31, 1928.

HARTSTEIN, JACOB I., "The Polonies Talmud Torah of New York." *PAJHS*, no. 34, 1937.

———, "The Yeshiva Looks Back Over Fifty Years." *Jewish Education*, vol. IX, no. 2, April–June 1937.

———, "Yeshiva University (Growth of Rabbi Isaac Elchanan Theological Seminary)." *AJYB*, vol. 48, 5707, 1946–1947.

Hebrew Union College, *Ceremonies at the Installation of Kaufmann Kohler as President of the Hebrew Union College*. Cincinnati, 1903.

Hebrew Union College Alumni, *Reform Judaism. Essays by Hebrew Union College Alumni*. Cincinnati, 1949.

(HEFTERMAN, A.) ספר הפטרמן, א. "הרבנות האורתודוכסית באמריקה". השנה ליהודי אמריקה, כרך ששי. מ. ריבולוב, עורך. ניו-יורק, תש"ב (1942).

HEINEMAN, DAVID E., "Jewish Beginnings in Michigan before 1850." *PAJHS*, no. 13, 1905.

HELLER, JAMES G., *As Yesterday When It is Past*. Cincinnati, 1942.

HELLER, MAX, *Jubilee Souvenir of Temple Sinai (1872–1922)*. New Orleans, 1922.

HERBERG, WILL, *Protestant-Catholic-Jew*. New York, 1955.

HERTZ, EMANUEL, editor, *Abraham Lincoln, The Tribute of the Synagogue*. New York, 1927.

HIGHAM, JOHN, "Social Discrimination Against Jews in America, 1830–1930." *PAJHS*, vol. XLVII, 1957.

HOURWICH, ISAAC, *Immigration and Labor*. New York and London, 1912.

Rev. Dr. Adolph Huebsch, Late Rabbi of the Ahawath Chesed Congregation. A Memorial. New York, 1885.

HÜHNER, LEON, *The Spanish and Portuguese Jewish Cemetery on New Bowery*. New York, 1903.

———, "The Struggle for Religious Liberty in North Carolina." *PAJHS*, no. 16, 1907.

———, *The Life of Judah Touro (1775–1854)*. Philadelphia, 1946.

ISAACS, A. S., "Myer S. Isaacs." *PAJHS*, no. 13, 1905.

———, "Myer S. Isaacs, A Memoir." *AJYB*, vol. 8, 5667, 1906–1907.

———, *What Is Judaism?* New York. 1912.

ISAACS, LEWIS M., "Abram S. Isaacs." *AJYB*, vol. 23, 5682, 1921–1922.

ISAACS, MYER S., "Sampson Simson." *PAJHS*, no. 10, 1902.

———, "A Jewish Army Chaplain." *PAJHS*, no. 12, 1904.

איוונסקי, מ., „המסדרים היהודים באמריקה". ספר השנה (IVANSKY, M.)
ליהודי אמריקה. מ. ריבולוב, עורך. ניו־יורק, תרצ״ט (1939).

JACOB, HEINRICH E., *The World of Emma Lazarus*. New York, 1949.

JACOBS, JOSEPH, "The Damascus Affair of 1840 and the Jews of America." *PAJHS*, no. 10, 1902.

———, revising editor, *The Jewish Encyclopedia—A Guide to Its Contents*. New York and London, 1906.

———, "Federation Movement in American Jewish Philanthropy." *AJYB*, vol. 17, 5676, 1915–1916.

——— and WOLF, LUCIEN, *Bibliotheca Anglo-Judaica*. Publications of the Anglo-Jewish Historical Exhibition, no. 3. London, 1888.

JAMES, EDMUND J. and OTHERS, *The Immigrant Jew in America*. New York, 1906.

Janowsky, Oscar I., editor, *The American Jew*. New York, 1942.

Jastrow, Morris, "Notes on the Jews of Philadelphia from Published Annals." *PAJHS*, no. 1, 1893.

The Jewish People. Past and Present, vol. 4. New York, 1955.

The Jewish Quarterly Review. Tercentenary Issue, vol. XLV, April, 1955.

Jews in American Agriculture. Published on the Occasion of the American Jewish Tercentenary by the Jewish Agricultural Society, Inc. New York, 1954.

Johnson, F. Ernest, editor, *Wellsprings of the American Spirit*. New York, 1948.

Joseph, Morris, *Judaism as Creed and Life*. New York. 1925.

Joseph, Samuel, *Jewish Immigration to the United States from 1881 to 1910*. New York, 1914.

——, *History of the Baron de Hirsch Fund*. Philadelphia, 1935.

(Kabakoff, Jacob). קבקוב.יעקב, מחלוצי הספרות העברית באמריקה. "Pioneers of Hebrew Literature in America," Hebrew ms. in the Jewish Theological Seminary of America, 1958.

Kaplan, Mordecai M., *Judaism as a Civilization*. New York, 1934.

——, *The Jewish Reconstructionist Papers*. New York, 1936.

——, *Judaism in Transition*. New York, 1936.

——, *The Future of the American Jew*. New York, 1948.

——, *The Greater Judaism in the Making*. New York, 1960.

Karp, Abraham J., "New York Chooses a Chief Rabbi." *PAJHS*, vol. XLIV, 1954.

Karpf, Maurice J., *Jewish Community Organization in the United States*. New York, 1939.

Katsh, Abraham I., *Hebrew in American Higher Education*. New York, 1941.

——, כ"ץ, אברהם יצחק. "מקומה של השפה העברית במכללות של ארצות־הברית בעבר ובהווה". ספר היובל של אגודת המורים העברים.

Keneseth Israel 90th Anniversary Booklet. Philadelphia, 1937.

KISCH, GUIDO, "Israels Herold—The First Jewish Weekly in New York." *Historia Judaica,* vol. II, no. 2. New York, October 1940.

———, *In Search of Freedom.* London, 1949.

(KLEIN, AARON)‏קליין, אהרן‏, ‏תולדות ספרי הלימוד לבתי־הספר היהודיים‏ ‏באמריקה.‏

A History of Textbooks for Jewish Schools in America. (Hebrew), *Ms.,* The Jewish Theological Seminary of America, 1955.

KNOX, ISRAEL, *Rabbi in America: The Story of Isaac Mayer Wise.* Boston, 1957.

KOBER, ADOLF, "Jewish Religious and Cultural Life in America as Reflected in the Felsenthal Collection." *PAJHS,* vol. XLV, 1955.

KOHLER, KAUFMANN, "The Origin and Function of Ceremonies in Judaism." *Yearbook CCAR,* vol. XVII, 1907.

———, "David Einhorn, The Uncompromising Champion of Reform Judaism." *Yearbook CCAR,* vol. XIX, 1909.

———, *Jewish Theology.* New York, 1918.

———, *The Mission of Israel and Its Application to Modern Times.* Cincinnati, 1919 (reprinted from *Yearbook CCAR,* vol. XXIX).

———, "A Revaluation of Reform Judaism." *Yearbook CCAR,* vol. XXXIV, 1924.

———, *The Hebrew Union College of Yesterday and a Great Desideratum in its Curriculum Today.* Cincinnati, 1925 (reprinted from *Hebrew Union College Jubilee Volume*).

———, *A Living Faith.* Edited by S. Cohon. Cincinnati, 1948.

KOHLER, MAX J., "Phases of Jewish Life in New York before 1800." *PAJHS,* no. 2, 1894.

———, "The Jews in Newport." *PAJHS,* no. 6, 1897.

———, "The Jews and the American Anti-Slavery Movement." *PAJHS,* no. 5, 1897; no. 9, 1901.

———, "Some Early American Zionist Projects." *PAJHS,* no. 8, 1900.

———, "The German-Jewish Migration to America." *PAJHS,* no. 9, 1901.

————, "Phases in the History of Religious Liberty in America, With Special Reference to the Jews." *PAJHS,* no. 11, 1903; no. 13, 1905.

————, "Judah P. Benjamin, Statesman and Jurist." *PAJHS* no. 12, 1904.

————, "Judah Touro, Merchant and Philanthropist." *PAJHS,* no. 13, 1905.

————, "Some Jewish Factors in the Settlement of the West." *PAJHS,* no. 16, 1907.

————, *Biographical Sketch of Dr. K. Kohler.* Berlin, 1913 (reprinted from *Studies in Jewish Literature*).

————, "An Early American Hebrew-Christian Agricultural Colony." *PAJHS,* no. 22, 1914.

————, "Simon Wolf." *AJYB,* vol. 26, 5685, 1924–1925.

————, "The Board of Delegates of American Israelites, 1859–1878." *PAJHS,* no. 29, 1925.

————, "History of the Board of Delegates on Civil Rights." Reprinted in *Selected Addresses and Papers of Simon Wolf.* Cincinnati, 1926.

———— and others, *The Immigration Question with Particular Reference to the Jews of America.* New York, 1911.

————, and SIMON WOLF, "Jewish Disabilities in the Balkan States—American Contributions toward their Removal, with Particular Reference to the Congress of Berlin." *PAJHS,* no. 24, 1916.

KOHN, EUGENE, *The Future of Judaism in America.* New York, 1934.

KOHN, S. JOSHUA, *The Jewish Community of Utica, New York, 1847–1948.* New York, 1959.

KOHUT, ADOLPH, "Alexander Kohut. Ein Charakterbild." *Semitic Studies in Memory of Rev. Dr. Alexander Kohut.* Edited by G. A. Kohut. Berlin, 1897.

KOHUT, GEORGE ALEXANDER, *A Memoir of Dr. Alexander Kohut's Literary Activity.* New York, 1894 (reprinted from *PJTSA*).

————, editor, *Tributes to the Memory of Rev. Dr. Alexander Kohut.* New York, 1894.

————, *Ezra Stiles and the Jews.* New York, 1902.

————, *Concerning Alexander Kohut, A Tentative Bibliography.* Budapest, 1927.

————, "Jellinek and America." *PAJHS,* no. 33, 1934.

————, "The Contributions of Cyrus Adler to American Jewish History." *PAJHS,* no. 33, 1934.

Kohut, Rebekah, "Jewish Women's Organizations in the United States." *AJYB,* vol. 33, 5692, 1931–1932.

————, *More Yesterdays.* New York, 1950.

(Konowitz, Israel).   קאנוביץ, ישראל. „בראשית החינוך העברי באמריקה". ספר היובל של אגודת המורים העברים. כנ"ל.

Korn, Bertram W., "Isaac Mayer Wise on the Civil War." *Hebrew Union College Annual,* vol. XX. Cincinnati, 1947.

————, "Jewish 'Forty-Eighters' in America." *AJA,* vol. II, no. 1, June, 1949.

————, *American Jewry and the Civil War.* Philadelphia, 1951.

————, *The American Reaction to the Mortara Case: 1858–1859.* Cincinnati, 1957.

————, *Eventful Years and Experiences.* Cincinnati, 1954.

————, *Jews and Negro Slavery in the Old South, 1789–1865.* Philadelphia, 1961.

————, editor, "The Jews of the Confederacy." *AJA,* vol. XIII, April, 1961.

————, "The Jews of the Union." *AJA,* vol. XIII, November, 1961.

Langfeld, William R., *The Young Men's Hebrew Association of Philadelphia.* Philadelphia, 1928.

Learsi, Rufus, *The Jews in America: A History.* Cleveland and New York, 1954.

Lebeson, Anita Libman, *Jewish Pioneers in America, 1492–1848.* New York, 1931.

————, "The American Jewish Chronicle." *The Jews,* L. Finkelstein, editor, vol. I, *supra.*

————, *Pilgrim People.* New York, 1950.

Lebowich, Joseph, *"The Jews in Boston Till 1875." PAJHS,* no. 12, 1904.

————, "General Ulysses S. Grant and the Jews." *PAJHS,* no. 17, 1909.

Lederer, Ephraim, "The Jewish Publication Society Anniversary: The Origin and Growth of the Society." *AJYB,* vol. 15, 5674, 1913–1914.

Leiser, Joseph, *American Judaism.* An Historical Survey. New York, 1925.

לעשטשינסקי, יעקב. "דאָס סאָציאַלע פנים פון (LESTSCHINSKY, JACOB).
אַמעריקאַנער יידנטום". ייוואָ בלעטער, באַנד 17, נומ' 2, מאַרץ־
אפריל, 1941.

——, "יידישע וואָנדערונגען אין די לעצטע הונדערט יאָר". דצ"ו,
באַנד 23, נומ' 1, יאַנואר־פעברואר, 1944.

——, "ההתפתחות הכלכלית של יהדות אמריקה". ספר השנה ליהודי
אמריקה, כרך שביעי. מ. ריבולוב, עורך. ניו־יורק, תש"ה (1944).

LEVENSOHN, LOTTA, "Henrietta Szold: December 21, 1860–
February 13, 1945." *AJYB*, vol. 47, 5706, 1945–1946.

LEVIN, ALEXANDRA LEE, *The Szolds of Lombard Street*.
Philadelphia, 1960.

LEVINE, ALLAN E., *An American Jewish Bibliography*. (A
List of Books and Pamphlets by Jews or Relating to
Them Printed in the United States from 1851 to 1875,
which are in the Possession of the Hebrew Union College—Jewish Institute of Religion Library in Cincinnati). Cincinnati, 1959.

LEVINTHAL, ISRAEL H., *Point of View*. (An Analysis of American Judaism). London, 1958.

LEVINTHAL, LOUIS, *Mayer Sulzberger, P. J.* Philadelphia,
1927.

LINFIELD, H. S. "Statistics of Jews and Jewish Organizations
in the United States." *AJYB*, vol. 40, 5699, 1938–1939.

——, "Jewish Communities of the United States." *AJYB*,
vol. 42, 5701, 1940–1941.

ליפשיץ, י., "ענגלישע און אמעריקאַנער רייזענדער פון (LIPSHITZ, J.).
18טן און ערשטער העלפט 19טן י"ה וועגן יידן אין פוילין און
רוסלאַנד". ייוואָ בלעטער, באַנד 3, נומ' 4־5, אפריל־מאי, 1932.

LIPSKY, LOUIS, *Thirty Years of American Zionism*. Vol. I of
Selected Works. New York, 1927.

LOWENTHAL, MARVIN, *Henrietta Szold, Life and Letters*.
New York, 1942.

מאהלר, רפאל. "יהדות אמריקה ורעיון שיבת ציון (MAHLER, RAPHAEL)
בתקופת המהפכה האמריקנית". ציון, שנה ט"ו תשי"י (1950).

——,דברי ימי ישראל, דורות אחרונים. כרך ראשון. מרחביה, תשי"ב
(1952).

MAKOVER, A. B., *Mordecai M. Noah*. New York, 1917.

מלאכי, א. ר.. "ראשית השירה העברית באמריקה." (MALACHI, E. R.)
ספר השנה ליהודי אמריקה, מ, ריבולוב וש. ברנשטיין, עורכים. ניו־
יורק, תרצ"ה (1935).

MANDEL, IRVING AARON, "Attitude of the American Jewish Community Toward East European Immigration." *AJA*, vol. III, 1950.

MANN, ARTHUR, editor, *Growth and Achievement: Temple Israel, 1854–1954*. Cambridge, 1954.

MANUEL, FRANK E., *The Realities of American-Palestine Relations*. Washington, D.C., 1949.

MARCOVITCH, ANNE, "A History of Temple Beth-El." *Temple Beth-El 80th Anniversary Booklet*. Knoxville, 1947.

MARCUS, JACOB RADER, *The Americanization of Isaac Mayer Wise*. Cincinnati, 1931.

———, *Early American Jewry*, 2 vols. Philadelphia, 1951, 1953.

———, *Memoirs of American Jews*, 3 vols. Philadelphia, 1955, 1956.

———, *American Jewry*. Documents. Eighteenth Century. Cincinnati, 1959.

———, *See also: Essays in American Jewish History*.

MARGOLIS, MAX L., "The Theological Aspect of Reformed Judaism." *Yearbook CCAR*, vol. XIII, 1903.

———, *The Story of the Bible Translations*. Philadelphia, 1917.

MARKENS, ISAAC, *The Hebrews in America*. New York, 1888.

———, *Lincoln and the Jews*. Baltimore, 1909 (reprinted from *PAJHS*, no. 17).

MARSHALL, LOUIS, "The Jew as Elements in the Population, Past and Present." *Notes Relating to the Celebration of the 250th Anniversary of the Settlement of Jews in the United States*. New York, 1905.

MARSHALL, LOUIS, *Leopold Zunz*. Philadelphia, 1905 (reprinted from *The Jewish Exponent*, February, 1905).

Louis Marshall Memorial Addresses. New York, 1931.

MARX, ALEXANDER, "Solomon Schechter." *PAJHS*, no. 25, 1917.

———, "Mayer Sulzberger." *PAJHS*, no. 29, 1925.

———, *Studies in Jewish History and Booklore*. New York, 1944.

———, *Essays in Jewish Biography*. Philadelphia, 1947.

MAY, MAX B., *Isaac Mayer Wise*. New York and London, 1916.

MEITES, HYMAN L., editor, *History of the Jews of Chicago.* Chicago, 1924.

MENDES, H. PEREIRA, "Abraham Pereira Mendes." *PAJHS,* no. 11, 1903.

MEYER, ISIDORE S., *The American Jewish Historical Society.* New York, 1943 (reprinted from *The Journal of Jewish Bibliography,* vol. IV, nos. 1–2.)

————, editor, *Early History of Zionism in America.* New York, 1958.

MIELZINER, ELLA MCKENNA FRIEND, *Moses Mielziner, 1823–1903.* New York, 1931.

MOISE, L. C., *Biography of Isaac Harby.* Sumter, South Carolina, 1931.

MORAIS, HENRY SAMUEL, *Eminent Israelites of the Nineteenth Century.* Philadelphia, 1880.

————, *The Jews of Philadelphia.* Philadelphia, 1894.

————, "S. Morais: A Memoir." *PJTSA,* New York, 1898.

MORGENSTERN, JULIAN, *As A Mighty Stream.* Philadelphia, 1949.

MOSCHIZKER, ROBERT VON, *An Address: Dedication of the Mayer Sulzberger Junior High School.* Philadelphia, 1925.

MOSES, ALFRED G., "A History of the Jews of Mobile." *PAJHS,* no. 12, 1904.

MOSES, ALFRED G., "The History of the Jews of Montgomery." *PAJHS,* no. 13, 1905.

Mount Sinai Hospital, *The Story of the First Fifty Years of Mount Sinai Hospital of the City of New York, 1852–1902.* New York, 1944.

NEUMAN, ABRAHAM A., *Cyrus Adler.* New York, 1942.

————, *Relation of the Hebrew Scriptures to American Institutions.* New York, 1938.

NEUSNER, JACOB, "The Role of English Jews in the Development of American Jewish Life, 1775–1850." *YIVO Annual,* vol. XII, 1958/1959.

"The New English Translation of the Bible." *AJYB,* vol. 19, 5678, 1917–1918.

Ninetieth Anniversary of the Founding of Central Synagogue. New York, 1936.

OKO, ADOLPH S., *Bibliography of Rev. Kaufmann Kohler, 1867–1913*. Berlin, 1913 (Sonderabdruck aus *Studies in Jewish Literature*).

——, *A Tentative Bibliography of Isaac M. Wise*. Cincinnati, 1917.

——, "Kaufmann Kohler." *The Menorah Journal*, vol. XII, no. 5, October-November, 1926.

——, *Solomon Schechter: A Bibliography*. Cambridge, 1938.

——, "Jewish Book Collections in the United States." *AJYB*, vol. 45, 1943.

OPPENHEIMER, SAMUEL, "The Question of the Kosher Meat Supply in New York in 1813: With a Sketch of Earlier Conditions." *PAJHS*, no. 25, 1917.

OSTERWEIS, ROLLIN G., *Rebecca Gratz—A Study in Charm*. New York and London, 1933.

PARZEN, HERBERT, "The History of Conservative Judaism." *Conservative Judaism*. Vol. III, no. 4, July, 1947; vol. IV, no. 2, February, 1948; no. 3, May; no. 4, June; vol. V, nos. 1–2, October–January, 1948–49; no. 3, April; vol. VI, no. 1, October, 1949.

PHILIPSON, DAVID, "Confirmation in the Synagogue." *Yearbook CCAR*, vol. I, 1891.

——, "The Jewish Pioneers of the Ohio Valley." *PAJHS*, no. 8, 1900.

——, "The Principles and Achievements of the Central Conference of American Rabbis." Twenty-fifth Anniversary Address. *Yearbook CCAR*, vol. XXIV, 1914.

——, editor, *Max Lilienthal, American Rabbi: Life and Writings*. New York, 1915.

——, *The Oldest Jewish Congregation in the West—Bene Israel, Cincinnati*. Cincinnati, 1924.

——, "The History of the Hebrew Union College." Cincinnati, 1925 (reprinted from *Hebrew Union College Jubilee Volume*).

——, *The Reform Movement in Judaism*. New York, 1931.

——, "Max Lilienthal in Russia." Cincinnati, 1937–1938 (reprinted from *Hebrew Union College Annual*, vols. XII–XIII).

———, "The Central Conference of American Rabbis: 1889–1939." *AJYB*, vol. 42, 5701, 1940–41.

PHILIPS, N. TAYLOR, "The Levy and Seixas Families of Newport and New York." *PAJHS*, no. 4, 1896.

———, "The Congregation Shearith Israel. An Historical Review." *PAJHS*, no. 6, 1897.

———, "Items Relating to the History of the Jews of New York." *PAJHS*, no. 11, 1903.

———, "Rev. Gershom Mendez Seixas." *AJYB*, vol. 6, 5665, 1904–1905.

PICCIOTTO, JAMES, *Sketches of Anglo-Jewish History*. London, 1875.

PINSON, KOPPEL S., editor, *YIVO Annual of Jewish Social Studies*, vol. IX. New York, 1955.

POLLAK, GUSTAV, *Michael Heilprin And His Sons*. New York, 1912.

POLLAK, J. B., "Forty Years of Reform Jewish Education." *Yearbook CCAR*, vol. XXXIX, 1929.

POOL, DAVID DE SOLA, "Levantine Jews in the United States." *AJYB*, vol. 15, 5674, 1913–1914.

———, *Notes on American Jewish History*. Baltimore, 1914 (reprinted from *PAJHS*, no. 22).

———, "Early Relations Between Palestine and American Jewry." *Brandeis Avukah Annual*. Boston, 1932.

———, *H. Pereira Mendes*. New York, 1938.

———, "Judaism and the Synagogue." O. Janowsky, editor, *The American Jew*, supra.

———, *An Old Faith in the New World*. New York, 1955.

"Proposed American Jewish Historical Exhibition." *AJYB*, vol. 3, 5662, 1901–1902.

Rabbinical Assembly of America, *Convention Proceedings*, vols. I–XXV; 1927–1961.

RABINOWITZ, BENJAMIN, *The Young Men's Hebrew Associations, 1854–1913*. New York, 1948.

(RABINOWITZ, SAUL).   ראבינוביץ, שאול פנחס. ר' זכריה פראנקעל.
ווארשא, תרנ״ח (1898).

(RADIN, ADOLPH M.).   ראדין, אדאלף מ., „מצבת זכרון להרב ר' בנימין
סאלד זצ״ל". ילקוט מערבי, שנה ראשונה, נויארק, תרס״ד (1904).

(RAISIN, MAX Z.).

רייזין, מרדכי זאב. תולדות היהודים באמריקה. ווארשא, תרס״ב (1902).

,ישראל באמריקה. ירושלים ותל־אביב, תרפ״ח (1928).——
,דפים מפנקסו של „ראבי״. ניו־יורק תש״א (1941).——

———, "The Reform Movement as Reflected in the Neo-
Hebraic Literature." *Yearbook CCAR*, vol. XVI, 1906.

———, *A History of the Jews in Modern Times*. New York,
1919.

(REIDER, J.).   רײדר, יוסף, „חכמת ישראל בארצות הברית". בצרון, חוברת
א'. ניו־יורק, תשרי ת״ש (1939).

(REINES, M.).   ריינעס, משה, דור וחכמיו. קראקא, תר״ן (1890).

REZNIKOFF, CHARLES and ENGELMAN, URIAH Z., *The Jews of
Charleston*. Philadelphia, 1950.

(RIBALOW, M.).   ריבולוב, מנחם. עורך. אנתולוגיה של השירה העברית
באמריקה. ניו־יורק, תרצ״ח (1938).

RICHARDS, BERNARD G., "Zionism in the United States."
Cohen, Israel, *The Zionist Movement*. Edited and revised by B. G. Richards. New York, 1946.

RISCHIN, MOSES A., *An Inventory of American Jewish
History*. Cambridge, 1954.

———, *The Promised City* (New York's Jews, 1870–1914).
Cambridge, 1962.

RIVKIND, ISAAC, "Some Remarks about Messengers from
Palestine to America." *PAJHS*, no. 34, 1937.

———, "A Pocket Edition Prayer Book for German Jewish
Emigrants to America, 1842." *PAJHS*, no. 35, 1939.

ROBINSON, L. G., "Agricultural Activities of the Jews in
America." *AJYB*, vol. 14, 5673, 1912–1913.

ROSENAU, WILLIAM, *Benjamin Szold*. Baltimore, 1902.

———, "Sabato Morais, An Appreciation on the Centenary
of His Birth." *Yearbook CCAR*, vol. XXXIII, 1923.

———, "Henry Berkowitz." *AJYB*, vol. 26, 5685, 1924–1925.

———, "Cardinal Gibbons and His Attitude Toward Jewish
Problems." *PAJHS*, no. 31, 1928.

ROSENBACH, A. S. W., *An American Jewish Bibliography*.
PAJHS, no. 30, 1926.

ROSENBERG, STUART E., *The Jewish Community in Rochester,
1843–1925*. New York, 1954.

ROSENBLUM, JOSEPH R., *A Biographical Dictionary of Early
American Jews*. University of Kentucky, 1960.

RUBENSTEIN, CHARLES, *History of the Har Sinai Congregation of the City of Baltimore*. Baltimore, 1918.

SACHAR, HOWARD M., *The Course of Modern Jewish History.* Cleveland and New York, 1958.

SAVETH, EDWARD N., *American Historians and European Immigrants, 1875–1925.* New York, 1948.

SCHAPPES, MORRIS U., editor, *Emma Lazarus: Selections from her Poetry and Prose.* New York, 1944.

————, editor, *The Letters of Emma Lazarus, 1868–1885.* Edited with introduction. New York, 1949 (reprinted with additions and corrections from *Bulletin of New York Public Library,* July–September, 1949).

————, editor, *Documentary History of the Jews in the United States, 1654–1875.* New York, 1950.

שארפשטיין, צבי, „חמשים שנות חנוך יהודי באמרי (SCHARFSTEIN, ZEVI). קה". ספר היובל של אגודת המורים העברים.

————„לתולדות החנוך היהודי בארצות הברית". ספר השנה ליהודי אמריקה, כרך שביעי. מ. ריבולוב, עורך. ניו-יורק, תש"ה (1944).

————,תולדות החנוך בישראל בדורות האחרונים, כרך שני. ניו-יורק, תש"ז (1947).

SCHECHTER, SOLOMON, *Zionism: A Statement.* New York, 1906 (reprinted from *American Hebrew,* December 28, 1906).

————, *Abraham Lincoln Memorial Address.* New York, 1909.

————, *Seminary Addresses and Other Papers.* New York, 1959.

שכטר, ש. ז., אגרות שניאור זלמן שכטר אל שמואל אברהם (————), פוזננסקי. הוציא לאור מגוף כתב-ידו, אברהם יערי. ירושלים, תש"ד (1943).

————, *Selected Writings.* Edited by Norman Bentwich. Oxford, 1946.

SCHNEIDERMAN, HARRY, "Cyrus Adler and the American Jewish Year Book." *AJYB,* vol. 42, 5701, 1940–1941.

שאולמאן, אליהו, „די קאנסערוואטיווע יידישע (SCHULMAN, ELIAS). זשורנאליסטיק אין ניו-יורק". ייווא בלעטער, באנד 10, נומ' 1-2, אווגוסט-סעפטעמבער, 1936.

————,געשיכטע פון דער יידישער ליטעראטור אין אמעריקע 1870- 1900. ניו-יורק, 1943.

שפיראָ ישראל, „הקוהוטים". ספר השנה ליהודי אמריקה. (SHAPIRO, I.). מ. ריבולוב וש. ברנשטיין, עורכים. ניו-יורק, תרצ"ה (1935).

שערמאן, בצלאל, ייִדן און אנדערע עטנישע גרופעס אין (SHERMAN, B.). די פאראייניקטע שטאטן, ניו-יורק, 1948.

שרמן, בצלאל, יהדות ארצות הברית. תל־אביב, תשט״ו
(1955).

SHPALL, LEO, *The Jews in Louisiana.* New Orleans, 1936.

SHWARZ, S. D., "Emil G. Hirsch." *AJYB,* vol. 27, 5686, 1925–1926.

SILVERMAN, JOSEPH, "Samuel Adler." *Yearbook CCAR,* vol. XIX, 1909.

"A Sketch of the History of the Jews in the United States." *AJYB,* vol. 4, 5663, 1902–1903.

SKLARE, MARSHALL, *Conservative Judaism, An American Religious Movement.* Glencoe, Illinois, 1955.

SMITH, JAMES WARD and JAMISON A. LELAND, editors, *Religion in American Life,* 5 volumes, Princeton, 1961.

SNYDER, HERMAN E., *History of Temple Brith Shalom.* Springfield, 1935.

SOLIS-COHEN, SOLOMON, "Sabato Morais: a Necrology." *PAJHS,* no. 8, 1900.

———, "The Sephardic Jews of America." *The Menorah Monthly,* vol. XXXIV. New York, 1903.

———,   סוליס־כהן, ש., מחברת משירי בן יעקב אבן עזרא.
Selected Poems of Moses Ibn Ezra. Philadelphia, 1934.

SOLOMON, ELIAS L., "The Story of Shaarey Zedek." *One Hundredth Anniversary of Congregation Shaarey Zedek.* New York, 1937.

SOLTES, MORDECAI, *The Yiddish Press.* New York, 1925.

SONNESCHEIN, S. H., "Judaism and Its Religious Development in the Nineteenth Century." *Yearbook CCAR,* vol. XI, 1901.

(STARKMAN, M.).‏ שטארקמאן, משה, „צו דער געשיכטע פון דער יידישער
סאציאליסטישער פרעסע אין די פאראייניקטע שטאטן". ייווא
בלעטער, באַנד 4, נומ׳ 5-4. דעצעמבער, 1932.

"Statistical Summary by States of Jewish Organizations in the United States." *AJYB,* vol. 3, 5662, 1901–1902.

(STEINBERG, B.).‏ שטיינבערג, בנימין, „צו דער געשיכטע פון יידיש אין
אמעריקע". יארבוך פון אמאפטייל, צווייטער באַנד. ניו־יורק, 1939.

STERN, MYER, *The Rise and Progress of Reform Judaism from the Records of Temple Emanu-El.* New York, 1895.

STERN, NATHAN, "Historical Review of Congregation Shaarey Tefilah." *Celebration of the Ninetieth Anniversary of* the Founding of Congregation Shaarey Tefilah. New York, 1935.

STRAUS, OSCAR S., *The Origin of the Republican Form of Government in the United States.* New York, 1901.

STROOCK, SOL M., "Switzerland and American Jews." *PAJHS,* no. 11, 1903.

————, *Louis Marshall.* New York, 1936.

Studies in Jewish Literature. In honor of Kaufmann Kohler. Berlin, 1913.

SULZBERGER, DAVID, "The Growth of Jewish Population in the United States." *PAJHS,* no. 6, 1897.

————, "Moses Aaron Dropsie." *PAJHS,* no. 16, 1907.

————, "The Beginnings of the Russo-Jewish Immigration in Philadelphia." *PAJHS,* no. 19, 1910.

SULZBERGER, MAYER, *The Am Ha-Aretz, The Ancient Hebrew Parliament.* Philadelphia, 1909.

————, *Termination of the Treaty Between the United States and Russia.* 1911.

————, *The Ancient Hebrew Law of Homicide.* Philadelphia, 1915.

————, "Joseph Jacobs." *AJYB,* vol. 18, 5677, 1916–1917.

Addresses Delivered in the Memory of Mayer Sulzberger. Philadelphia, 1924.

SWEET, WILLIAM W., *The Story of Religions in America.* New York, 1930.

————, *The American Churches.* New York, 1948.

SZAJKOWSKI, ZOSA, "How the Mass Migration to America Began." *Jewish Social Studies,* vol. IV, no. 4, October, 1942.

————, "The Attitude of American Jews to East European Immigration (1881–1893)." *PAJHS,* vol. XL, 1951.

————, "The European Attitude to East European Jewish Immigration (1881–1893)." *PAJHS,* vol. XL, 1951.

SZOLD, HENRIETTA, "Marcus Jastrow." *PAJHS,* no. 12, 1904.

TARSHISH, ALLAN, *Rise of American Judaism.* (Typescript.)

————, "The Board of Delegates of American Israelites (1859–1878)." *PAJHS,* vol. XLIX, 1959.

(TARTAKOWER, A.). טרטקובר, אריה, »מפרשת ,בראשית' של אמריקה

היהודית". בצרון חוברת ט'-י'. סיון-תמוז, ת"ש (1940)

Temple Rodeph Sholom, *History of Congregation Rodeph Sholom, 1842–1892*. New York, 1892.

TRACHTENBERG, JOSHUA, *Consider the Years*. Easton, Pennsylvania, 1944.

(TSCHERIKOWER, E.).   טשעריקאָװער, א., געשיכטע פון דער ייִדישער
ארבעטער־ באַװעגונג אין די פאַראײניקטע שטאַטן. ערשטער באַנד,
ניו־יורק, 1943; צװייטער באַנד, ניו־יורק, 1945.

The Two Hunded and Fiftieth Anniversary of the Settlement of the Jews in the United States. PAJHS, no. 14, 1906.

United Charities of New York, *Fifty Years of Social Service*. New York, 1926.

(VILNAI, Z.).   ‏וילנאי, זאב, „חלקה של אמריקה בחקירתה של ארץ־ישראל".
ספר השנה ליהודי אמריקה, מ. ריבולוב, עורך. ניו־יורק, תרצ"ט
(1939).

(VORNBERG, K.).‏פאַרנבערג, ק., „ייִדן אין די פאַראײניקטע שטאַטן צוריק.
מיט 40 יאָר". ייװאָ בלעטער באַנד 4, נומ' 4־5, דעצעמבער, 1932.

WALDMAN, MORRIS D., "Cyrus Sulzberger." *AJYB*, vol. 35, 5694, 1933–1934.

WAX, JAMES A., "Isidor Bush, American Patriot and Abolitionist." *Historia Judaica*, vol. V, no. 2, October, 1943.

WAXMAN, MEYER S., *A History of Jewish Literature*, vol. IV. Second edition: New York, 1947.

WAXMAN, MORDECAI (editor), *Tradition and Change: The Development of Conservative Judaism*. New York, 1958.

WEINRYB, BERNARD D., "East European Immigration to the United States." *Jewish Quarterly Review*, vol. XIV, Tercentenary Issue, 1955.

————,   ‏וויינריב, דוב, „מאה שנה של הגירה יהודית לאמריקה".
ספר השנה ליהודי אמריקה, כרך חמישי. מ. ריבולוב, עורך. ניו־
יורק, תש"א (1940).

WHITEMAN, MAXWELL, "Isaac Leeser and the Jews of Philadelphia." *PAJHS*, vol. XLVIII, 1959.

WIEMAN, HENRY NELSON and BERNARD E. MELAND, *American Philosophies of Religion*. Chicago and New York, 1936.

WIERNIK, PETER, *History of the Jews in America*. New York, 1914.

WILANSKY, DENA, *Sinai to Cincinnati*. New York, 1937.

WISCHNITZER, MARK, *To Dwell in Safety*. Philadelphia, 1948.

————, *Visas to Freedom: The History of HIAS*. Cleveland and New York, 1956.

WISCHNITZER, RACHEL, *Synagogue Architecture in the United States*. Philadelphia, 1955.

(WISE, STEPHEN). וייז, סטיפן, „לזכרונו של ד״ר אלכסנדר קוהוט ז״ל"
בצרון, חוברת ט׳-י׳. סיון-תמוז, ניו-יורק, תש״ב (1942).

WITTKE, CARL, "Religious Influences in American History." *University of California Chronicle*, October, 1924.

————, *We Who Built America*. New York, 1946.

WOLF, EDWIN, and WHITEMAN, MAXWELL, *The History of the Jews of Philadelphia from Colonial Times to the Age of Jackson*. Philadelphia, 1957.

WOLF, SIMON, *Mordecai Manual Noah*. Philadelphia, 1897.

(YIDDISH SCIENTIFIC INSTITUTE). יארבוך פון אמאפטייל, ערשטער
באנד. ניו-יארק, 1938.

(ZUKUNFT, DI). די צוקונפט, 300 יאר יידיש לעבן אין אמעריקע.
דעצעמבער, 1954.

INDEX

Aaron, Joseph, 48
Abne Yehoshua, 168
Abodat Israel, 142, 143, 288, 291, 339, 361
Abolitionist preachers, 109, 342
Abrabanel, 216
Adath Israel, congregation in Louisville, 136
Adler, Cyrus, 265, 313, 315, 338, 355; and American Jewish Historical Society, 259, 260; and *American Jewish Yearbook,* 256, 257; on Jewish education, 243, 250; and Jewish Publication Society, 254; and Jewish Theological Seminary, 235, 236, 237, 322-5, 394-5; and Maimonides College, 63, 64; on Sunday Sabbath, 276, 277; and Y.M.H.A., 183
Adler, Felix, 193, 194
Adler, Henry, 176
Adler, Liebman, 176
Adler, Samuel, 57, 156, 180, 193
Adler, Selig, 271
Adult education, Jewish, 48-53, 181-183, 241, 251-3, 256, *see also* Jewish Publication Society; YMHA
Agricultural settlements of Jews, in America, 76-8, 187, 188, 264-5, 351, 364; in Eretz Yisrael, 85, 86
Ahavath Chesed, congregation in New York, 222, 225, 301
A Key to the Hebrew Language and the Science of Hebrew Grammar Explained, 48

Albany, N.Y., 27, 125, 138, 287
Albo, Joseph, 285, 286
Alexander III, 186-7
All-day schools, 26-7, 37, 38, 39, 40, 133, 247
Allgemeine Zeitung des Judentums, 340
Alliance, colony in New Jersey, 265
Alliance Israélite Universelle, 101, 188, 265, 338, 343
Alliance Land Trust, 265
Altmayer, A.R., 395
America, religious tradition in, 4-9, 66-7, 88-9, 89-96, 105, 115-6, 151, 155, 188-90, 193
American Hebrew, 169-70, 173-4, 184, 190, 197, 200, 225, 231-2, 242-4, 254, 267, 269, 312, 332, 334, 350, 352, 359; advocates synod, 200-3, 205-7, 278; and Jewish ritual, 209-13, 220-221
American Hebrew College of New York, *see* Emanu-El Theological Seminary
American influences on Jewish community, *see* American Jewry
American Israelite, 133, 138, 145, 153, 156, 170, 225
American Jewish community, attempts to unify, *see* Central Religious Council; Leeser, Isaac; Synod; Wise, Isaac Mayer
American Jewish Historical Society, 260, 353, 364

507

57-8, 182, 243-4; and Eretz Yisrael, 212, 213, 226-7, 269-70, 271, 272; groups in, 133, 145, 156, 217; growth, 149-59, 175-6, 198-9, 205, 207, 234, 311, 312, 352; and Historical School, 18-19, 135-46, 159-160, 217-28, 272, 297, 301, 308-9; influenced by German Reform Judaism, 7, 46; interprets Mission of Israel, 154-6, 227, 303; and Jewish hospitals, 69; and Jewish Publication Society, 253, 255; and Jewish Theological Seminary, 237, 321-3; platform and practices, 11-12, 69, 103-4, 108, 119, 128, 139-40, 153-6, 159, 211-12, 217-18, 222, 225-8, 287, 338; prayer books, 134, 141, 142, 220, 308-9; rabbinate, 121-123, 131-3, 156-9, 217, 228, 234, 338; innovations of, 121-3, 217-8, 222, 244; seminaries and training, 57-8; relations with Historical School, 125-34, 171-99, 200, 206, 216-7, 231-4, 275-9, 301, 313, 346, 349; and Sabbath Associations, 209, 217-8; *see also* Hebrew Union College; Wise, Isaac Mayer

Reformed Society of Israelites, 31

Reformer and Jewish Times, 169

Rehiné, Zalma, 347

Religion in American Life, 9

Religious equality, *see* Church and State, separation of; Civil Rights, defense of

Religious tradition, American, *see* America, religious tradition in

Reminiscences, of I.M. Wise, 55

Republican party, 334, 338, 363

Resurrection of the dead, doctrine of, 128, 141, 227, 287, 288, 291

Revelation, doctrine of, 285-7, 289, 292, 293, 316

Revolutions of 1848, 339, 360-1, 363

Reward and punishment, doctrine of, 227, 287, 288, 292

Rhode Island, 39

Rice, Abraham, 43, 55, 131, 314, 339

Richmond, Va., 30, 41, 51, 52, 97, 99, 150, 152, 330, 347

Ritual, Jewish, *see* Ashkenazi *minhag;* Historical School, theology; Mitzvot; Sephardi *minhag;* Services, in the synagogue

Rochester, N.Y., 99, 276, 338

Rodeph Shalom, congregation in N.Y., 166, 365, 366

Rodeph Shalom, congregation in Philadelphia, 53, 107, 119, 121, 123, 143, 144, 343

Roeder, Simon M., 395

Roman Law of Testaments, Codicils, and Gifts in the Event of Death, 338

Rosenau, William A., 64

Rosenbach, A.S.W., 46, 47

Rosenberg, Stuart, 276

Rosenhayn, colony in New Jersey, 265

Rosenthal, Isaac, 386, 387

Rosenzweig, Franz, 168

Rosh Hashanah, 136, 154, 162

Rothschild, Edward L., 395

Rubenstein, Raymond, 239

Ruhama, Devotional Exercises for the Use of the Daughters of Israel, 124, 357-8

Rumanian Jews, 214

Rush Hospital for Consumptives, 359

Russian Jews, 25, 78, 79, 84, 134, 167, 168, 185-7, 213, 215, 261-8, 319, 321, 338, 343, 351, 356, 362, 388-392; *see also* Immigration from Russia

Russian Jew in America, 267

Saadia Gaon, 216

Sabbath (*also Shabbat*), 45, 76, 177, 314; attempts to strengthen, 318; desecration, 104, 127, 131, 208; in Historical School, 145, 160, 161, 201, 216, 222, 301, 308-9, 326; prayers, 100, 142, 143, 144, 165, 211; sermons, 112, 123, 348, 361; and Sunday laws, 91, 92; and Sunday services, 218

Sabbath Associations, 208-9, 217, 277, 336

Sabbath School Union, 158

Sachs, Moses, 86

Sachs, Michael, 139, 342, 343